Couture Culture

The MIT Press   Cambridge, Massachusetts   London, England

Couture Culture

A Study in Modern Art and Fashion

Nancy J. Troy

This book was set in Adobe Garamond by Achorn Graphic Services, Inc.
Printed and bound in the United States of America.

Library of Congress Cataloging-in-Publication Data

Troy, Nancy J.
    Couture culture : a study in modern art and fashion / Nancy J. Troy.
        p. cm.
    Includes bibliographical references and index.
    ISBN 0-262-20140-2 (hc : alk. paper)
    1. Costume design. 2. Fashion and art. 3. Fashion—France—History—20th century.
4. Clothing trade—France—History—20th century. 5. Fashion designers—France—
History—20th century. 6. Fashion merchandising—France—History—20th century.
7. Theater and society—France—History—20th century. 8. Poiret, Paul. I. Title.

TT507 .T845 2002
746.9′2′0904—dc21

                                         2002023338

Illustration credits are found on page 415.

10 9 8 7 6 5 4 3 2 1

For Wim, Daniel, and Elias de Wit

Contents

Acknowledgments

My interest in the relationship between modern art and fashion emerged while I was a Scholar at the Getty Research Institute in 1989–90, finishing a book on the decorative arts in France in which couturier Paul Poiret played a small, but important, role. Over the course of the ensuing twelve years, I have pursued that interest with the financial support of many institutions and with intellectual and practical help from a large number of individuals. It is a pleasure to be able to thank them here.

The research for this book has been generously supported by fellowships from the American Council of Learned Societies, the Getty Research Institute, the John Simon Guggenheim Memorial Foundation, the AT&T Research Fellowship at Northwestern University, the Zumberge Faculty Research and Innovation Fund at the University of Southern California, and the Raubenheimer Award for Excellence in Teaching, Research, and Service, also at the University of Southern California.

It would be impossible to mention individually all the library and archive personnel who have assisted me over the years, but I would like to acknowledge the principal institutions where I received invaluable assistance with my research: in Bath, England, the Fashion Research Centre; in Berkeley, the Bancroft Library at the University of California–Berkeley; in Los Angeles, the Architecture and Fine Arts Library, the Doheny Memorial Library and the Law Library at the University of Southern California, the Getty Research Institute, the Los Angeles County Museum of Art, the Department of Special Collections in the Young Memorial Library at University of California–Los Angeles; in New York, the Brooklyn Museum of Art, the Costume Institute at the Metropolitan Museum of Art, the Fashion Institute of Technology, and the New York Public Library; in Paris, the Bibliothèque de l'Arsenal,

Bibliothèque Doucet, Bibliothèque Forney, Bibliothèque Nationale de France, Institut Français d'Architecture, Musée de la Mode de la Ville de Paris, Musée de la Mode et du Textile; in San Francisco, the San Francisco Public Library.

Two individuals have been particularly generous in sharing reminiscences of members of their families as well as documents and photographs. Madame Perrine Poiret-de Wilde welcomed me into her home on several occasions, as did Admiral Albert Joire-Noulens. I am grateful for their invaluable encouragement and help.

I have been extraordinarily fortunate that many good friends and knowledgable colleagues have contributed their expertise and assistance in diverse ways. Without their help, no doubt this book would have languished or never been completed. I would like to thank Alina Payne for inviting me to give the Teezel Lectures at the University of Toronto, where my research first assumed a shape similar to the form it takes here; Victoria Kahn, who has always been my most astute reader and supportive friend; David Román, who brought his keen editorial eye to bear on a related essay he solicited for *Theatre Journal;* and Rick Richman, who asked the staff of his law firm library to locate on my behalf a crucial legal decision from 1915. Roger Conover at the MIT Press has sustained a long-term interest in my work while challenging me to broaden its scope through his intellectual engagement with the topic and incisive comments on my manuscript. Deborah Cantor-Adams did a superb job in the production editing of this volume, with its sensitive design by Emily Gutheinz, and Terry Lamoureux skillfully coordinated the production process. I am particularly indebted to Andrew Perchuk, not simply for research and editorial assistance over several years but, more importantly, for the lasting intellectual exchange we developed in innumerable conversations about the material explored in this book. Leila Kinney, Molly Nesbit, Alexandra Palmer, and Lisa Tickner were especially generous in sharing their extensive knowledge and deep understanding of the issues that inform this study. Other colleagues who have also shared knowledge, insights, and resources with me include Annie Barbera, Yve-Alain Bois, Michael Bonnet, Leo Braudy, Frédéric Chèvre, Hollis Clayson, Jean-Louis Cohen, Jo Cooper, Pierre Curie, Elizabeth Easton, Monique Eleb, Carol Eliel, Leonard Fox, Pamela Golbin, James Herbert, Robert Herbert, Stéphane Houy-Towner, Eunice Howe, Amelia Jones, David Joselit, Betty Kirke, Juliet Koss, Alexandra Kowalski, Karen Lang, Mitzi Maras, Steve Maras, the late Richard Martin, Margot McBath, Elizabeth Anne McCauley, Richard Meyer, Patricia Miers, Laurie Monahan, David Peyceré, Marie-Hélène Poix, Christopher Reed, Thomas Reese, Sandra Rosenbaum, Steven Ross, Angelica Rudenstine, Debora Silverman, David Solkin, Valerie Steele, Sally Stein, the late Alan Suddon, Françoise Tétart-Vittu, Ruth Wallach, Martha Ward, Eugen Weber, and William Zulker.

In gaining access to the disparate resources that form the basis for this book, I have been able to rely on the excellent research skills of several graduate assistants: Karen Roswell, Rebecca Cramer Steiner, Sarah Stifler, Stacey Uradomo, Sarah Warren, and Andrea Zaharia-Roth. I have also had the pleasure of developing some of the ideas explored here together with the students in several graduate seminars I taught at the University of Southern California. An earlier version of parts of chapter 2 was published as "The Theatre of Fashion: Staging Haute Couture in Early 20th-Century France" in *Theatre Journal* 53 (2001), and parts of chapter 3 appeared as "Paul Poiret's Minaret Style: Originality, Reproduction, and Art in Fashion" in *Fashion Theory* 6 (June 2002). I thank the publishers of those journals for permitting me to develop those materials further in this book.

The life of this project is just about coextensive with that of my younger son, Elias, whose older brother, Daniel, scarcely remembers a time when I was not working on this book. They have patiently—and sometimes not-so-patiently—accompanied me to museums or waited outside while I consulted a library or archival collection, and I am enormously grateful not only for their support of my work, but especially for the grace with which they learned to share my time and attentions with an undertaking that often seemed alien to their own interests. Who was looking after Daniel and Elias while I was in all those libraries and archives? Occasionally, it was my sisters, Jill Werner and Susan Troy, for whose encouragement, support, and endurance I will always be grateful; more often it was my parents, Joanne J. Troy and William B. Troy, who have always been proud of my work and thrilled when it gave them an opportunity to be with their grandchildren. But most of the time it was my husband, Wim de Wit, who spent innumerable vacations, weekends, and evenings devoting his attention either to caring for our children so that I would be free to work, or to reading, analyzing, and discussing seemingly endless drafts of my evolving book manuscript. As Curator of Architecture and Head of Special Collections at the Getty Research Institute, Wim has introduced me to innumerable resources, accompanied me on myriad research trips, and encouraged my work in every possible way. I am happy to dedicate this book to him and to our children, with my thanks and my love.

Couture Culture

Introduction   ⌒

It is safe to say that dominant accounts of early twentieth-century art have failed to see the relevance of fashion for their object of study. Typically, fashion has been regarded as superficial, fleeting, and feminized. If historians of modern art and architecture acknowledged the issue of fashion, their considerations of the topic were largely confined to discussions of clothing designed by artists from Henry van de Velde and Josef Hoffmann to the Italian Futurists and Russian Constructivists, all of whose work is understood as an effort at rationalization or reform, a rejection of commercial dress design as practiced in France by the most successful professional designers of women's clothing of the period, including Jacques Doucet, Jeanne Paquin, and Paul Poiret.[1] On the other hand, the work of these professionals, with few exceptions regarded as marginal if not irrelevant to the history of modern art, has been pursued by costume historians, but their insights have rarely been integrated into the mainstream art historical narrative.[2] Recently, however, as contemporary artists and scholars have become increasingly interested in the potential of sartorial display to articulate problems of identity construction and to explore issues surrounding race, gender, and sexuality, art museums have joined in the effort to excavate the historical background for current artistic practice. Several have focused exhibitions on the relationship between art and fashion across the twentieth century, including the 1996 Florence Biennale, a related show at the Solomon R. Guggenheim Museum, and a show mounted at the Hayward Gallery in 1998.[3]

Given the art-institutional framework in which these large surveys were conceived and carried out, it is hardly surprising that their catalogues generally failed to deliver an intellectually convincing presentation of their subject, since they vastly underestimated the historical significance of the French clothing industry and largely ignored the impact of its commercial interests. Settling for a narrow definition of the relationship between art and fashion in terms of garments designed by artists or clothing that qualifies as art, their approach privileged formal similarities that are often visually powerful but, nevertheless, generally lack substance when it comes to the exploration of deeper, structural relations which, in turn, do not necessarily result in any stylistic or formal resemblances between particular items of clothing and specific works of art.[4]

The present book is not a survey. Neither does it compare works of art with clothing or seek sources for the visual effects of one medium in the creations of the other, as might be expected from a more conventional approach to costume history or art historical inquiry. And although fashion's role in the discursive construction of gender is broached—in my discussion of Orientalist cross-dressing, for example—I do not pursue what might be described as a feminist, psychoanalytic approach to the female subject nor do I explore fashion as a cultural expression of the performance of the female body, either in works of art or in the actual wearing of clothes. These strategies have borne fruit in work by scholars ranging from Judith Butler and Kaja Silverman to Ewa Lajer-Burcharth, to name a few examples of significant interventions in this vein, but my interests and my objects of study differ from theirs.[5] My aim is to provide an alternative conceptual model of how the domains of art and fashion were linked in the early twentieth century. In pursuing that goal, I ignore visual parallels, including instances in which couturiers responded to the work of artists or artists incorporated references to clothing in their work (the mutual influence of surrealist painter Salvador Dali and couturière Elsa Schiaparelli would be a case in point). Instead, I explore the commercial practices of one of the leaders of the French fashion industry, Paul Poiret, to unveil a logic of fashion based on the tension between originality and reproduction that bears directly on the framing of art historical issues of the period. One of my principal strategies involves a sustained examination of the discursive role that fine art played in the realm of clothing and fashion. By this I do not mean the ways in which dressmakers looked to works of art as a source of inspiration or historical recreation. Nor do I want to rehearse Anne Hollander's more intriguing suggestion, in *Seeing through Clothes,* that art has determined, rather than reflected, both past and present concepts of beauty and fashion.[6] To the limited extent that I deal with actual clothing and women's fashions, my attention is focused on the production of professional dress designers, rather than that of vanguard artists and architects who occasionally experimented with costume design. I explore the sector of the fashion industry known as *haute couture,* which produced the most luxurious and expensive women's clothing of the period. Couture clothes were not purchased exclusively by the wealthy. Instead, couturiers created seasonal models that were intended to be copied or adapted either for individual, wealthy clients or for the developing made-to-order and ready-to-wear trade in department stores and other clothing outlets catering to a broader consumer market.[7] My interest in haute couture lies in the contradictions engendered by its production of supposedly unique garments for elite clients and multiple copies for mass consumption, rather than in what might be called the "art quotient" of the dresses themselves.[8] One of my goals in bringing fashion and art history into contact with one another in this way is to expose the uses to which the visual and performing arts were put in constructing the cultural position of haute couture and those engaged in its production during the early years of the twentieth century. From this heretofore largely unexplored perspective, the familiar tropes of avant-garde modernism—not only the unstable connection between originality and reproduction, but also the relationship between elite and popular culture, the unique art object and the mass-produced commodity, even the presumed polarity of Orientalist and classicizing sensibilities—assume new and sometimes surprising significance.

The shifting, often ambiguous relationships between elite and popular culture, between the original artwork and the mass-produced commodity, are now acknowledged to be an essential feature of modernist art, but the particular strategies that artists and others employed to negotiate the dissolving boundaries between elite and popular culture and to respond to pressures that commerce exerted on the visual arts and elite culture in general have still not received the attention they deserve. On the other hand, the subject of clothing, and of women's dress in particular, has been broached in numerous studies of modern art and visual culture, particularly during the late nineteenth-century. The rise of the ready-to-wear industry at that time coincided with the consolidation of the department store, and both institutions contributed directly to the development of a culture of consumption that has been the focus of cultural studies and feminist scholarship. However, art historical interest in women's dress, whether that of our own day or of earlier periods, has generally focused on questions of gender construction and the performance of sexual identity, and, even in the specialized field of costume history, little sustained attention has been paid to the mechanisms of fashion marketing in the early twentieth century. Only recently has that subject been brought into contact with the theater, for which all the couturiers of the pre–World War I period worked, or with institutional studies of the French art market, another area of inquiry that has recently begun to receive serious attention from scholars.[9] In placing these typically distinct cultural spheres in proximity to one another, my aim is to expose issues and strategies common to all of them in the early twentieth century: when the claims to art status on the part of haute couture were challenged by the implications of industrial production and mass-marketing techniques, when professional theater appeared to many observers to be increasingly undermined by ever-franker allusions to commerce, and when the market for modern art was being transformed by private dealers operating outside the traditional system of public salon exhibitions.

I maintain that during this period, Paul Poiret and other early twentieth-century French dress designers patronized the arts and often constructed themselves as artists in an effort to employ high culture and its discourses, not only to sell their dresses to wealthy and aristocratic clients, but also and at the same time to follow the seemingly opposed course of promoting the popular appeal and potential for mass production of their work. In their hands, the visual and performing arts functioned as potent rhetorical tools enabling them to secure their positions as transgressive modernists even as they appealed to audiences who customarily disdained the avant-garde: on the one hand they cultivated a wealthy and elite, even aristocratic, clientele, while on the other hand they reached out to a broader, middle-class market. Negotiating a similarly hybrid terrain, modern artists, for example the cubist painters, also needed to promote their work, either in the discrete privacy of the gallery owned by the dealer, Daniel-Henry Kahnweiler (in the case of Pablo Picasso and Georges Braque), or in the public sphere of large, officially sanctioned salon exhibitions and publications such as Albert Gleizes and Jean Metzinger's 1912 book, *Du "cubisme."* I show that these two domains were not only not entirely divorced from one another, they were, in fact, interdependent; Kahnweiler was a master at manipulating the public sphere for the benefit of the artists who showed in Paris only in his private gallery and, moreover, recognition of his artists, particularly Picasso and Braque, was due in part to the attention that Gleizes, Metzinger, and others identified with cubism garnered in the public arena. I compare the strategies French cubist painters and couturiers developed to make themselves visible, and I suggest that each group sought validation in the context of a readily identifiable movement, the critical recognition of which functioned to inscribe an authentic style as fashion. However, success in defining and circulating a distinctive style, whether in art or in clothing, assured its vulnerability to copying and pastiche. The contradictions that structure this predicament, which I see as the central problem of the logic of fashion, suggest a rationale for the desire of many modernist artists (and, to be sure, their contemporaries in the high-end clothing industry) to explore, control, and channel (though not necessarily to stave off) the supposedly corrupting influence of commerce and commodity culture.

The tension between originality and reproduction, between the unique work of art and the mass-produced commodity, has long been regarded as a crucial problem in the history of modernism. In an influential essay of 1981, Rosalind Krauss described originality as one of the founding tropes of avant-garde modernism.[10] "More than a rejection or dissolution of the past, avant-garde originality is conceived as a literal origin, a beginning from ground zero, a birth," she writes. "The self as origin is the way an absolute distinction can be made between a present experienced *de novo* and a tradition-laden past. The claims of the avant-garde are precisely these claims to originality." Krauss goes on to assert that the original has no ontological status on its own but is, instead, a function of the copy, which is "necess[ary] to the concept of the original, the spontaneous, the new." Her purpose is to establish terms for understanding the relationship between the original and the copy, not just in turn-of-the-century avant-garde modernism (where her argument begins, with Rodin), but especially in recent postmodern practice. Her argument, based on close analysis of Rodin's work, is largely formal and theoretical, and it completely avoids the universe of commodity culture in which the inextricably interrelated discourses of originality and the copy have played a crucial role. This is peculiar because, as Krauss is surely aware, the emergence of avant-garde modernism with its problems of originality and reproduction occurred at precisely the moment when banal objects of consumer culture began to appear in the rarefied context of the so-called fine arts, for example in Picasso's *papier collé, Au Bon Marché* of 1913, and in Marcel Duchamp's readymades of the middle and late teens. This encounter between the unique work of art and the industrially produced commodity was a function of—just as it helped to bring about—the crisis of originality within the avant-garde that Krauss so eloquently describes.

In fact, the crisis of originality, which I identify as well in the ways in which fashions were generated, celebrated, exploited, and compromised, is a problem that preoccupied not only fine artists but also those engaged in the production of haute couture. At stake in both domains were the originality, authenticity, and aesthetic aura of the individual object, which are essential to the establishment of any fashion, whether in dresses or in vanguard art production. The problem is readily apparent in the confrontation of the authentic object of fashion, the couture dress, for example—which, as mentioned above, is already reproduced from a generic model and adapted to the size and shape of an individual client— with its pirated copy, an industrially produced commodity masquerading as an original couture creation. Cubist painting has also been understood in these terms, for example by Douglas Cooper and Gary Tinterow (1983) who insisted that the work of Picasso and Braque constituted "original" or "true" cubism, whereas that of Gleizes and Metzinger, among others, was no more than a poor adaptation, a "pastiche" of the genuine article.[11] This hierarchical distinction was not the invention of scholars devoted to promoting a particular strand of modernist formalism; it has historical roots in the commercial practices of Daniel-Henry Kahnweiler. As his biographer, Pierre Assouline, has pointed out, Kahnweiler saw a potential threat to the artists he was promoting in "the increasingly important place granted by the art world to those artists Kahnweiler would call 'the false cubists,' the imitators he so thoroughly disliked."[12] Thus couturiers and the cubist painters represented by Kahnweiler faced a similar situation, I argue, insofar as they sought to maintain their elite status as creators of unique and original objects while at the same time they capitalized on the potential of copies or, in the case of Picasso and Braque, what Kahnweiler and they considered to be pastiches of their work, to reach a larger audience, generate recognition, and arouse widespread appeal.

The juxtaposition of haute couture and other products of the fashion industry with the manufactured objects that Marcel Duchamp singled out as "readymades" in the 1910s and early 1920s will, I believe, provide insights that are equally revealing of the fundamental tensions that industrialization and mass consumption provoked in early twentieth-century culture. On the simplest level, both couture dresses and such readymades as *In Advance of the Broken Arm* and *Fountain* (discussed in chapter 4; see figures 4.4 and 4.6) depend in each case for their efficacy as singular, auratic objects on the addition of their creator's signature—the couturier's authentic label or the name of the artist—to an object of serial if not mass production. The fact that couturiers often gave their dresses distinctive titles also finds a parallel in Duchamp's rhetorical practice of naming as he played upon the ironic contradictions inherent in the creation of objects that occupied (if they did not exactly bridge) the gap between mass-produced commodities and unique works of art. Moreover, the fact that Duchamp developed the concept of the readymade, an English-language term that is central to the industrialization and commercialization of clothing, while living in the United States during the First World War, has important parallels with the contemporaneous activities of Poiret and other French couturiers. Their interest in the American market intensified during the First World War, when differences between French and American copyright laws emerged as major obstacles to international commerce, and at the same time couturiers began to explore ways of overcoming or undermining the traditional distinction between couture "originals" and mass-produced dresses. In 1916–1917, when Poiret designed a line of dresses intended to appeal in particular to American women, he introduced a special label that identified these garments as "authorized reproductions." In effect, he created a new category of objects. Like Duchamp's readymades of the same period, these dresses were at once authentic objects signed by their creator and mass-produced commodities. Duchamp's own engagement with women's clothing and perfume through the figure of his alter ego, Rose Sélavy, whose name along with a claim to copyright protection are inscribed on *Fresh Widow* (a variation on the readymade, produced in New York in 1920), reveal that his exploration of the more general problem of the relationship between originality and reproduction was linked to the world of fashion, where not only gender and sexuality but also copyright, intellectual property, and the status of the creator as artist were crucial concerns.

If scholarly work on twentieth-century art history, focused on the revolutionary potential of a left-oriented historical avant-garde, has been blind to the commonality of these issues, traditional scholarship in costume history, focused until recently on the production of luxury clothes for a wealthy elite, has proved equally ill-equipped to explore such parallels. Costume history has been shaped in large measure by connoisseurs whose familiarity with individual objects enables them to attend to costume materials and the details of facture, as well as to formal and stylistic developments; but, in this model, structural issues and discursive analysis are too often ignored.[13] Historians of labor, on the other hand, have begun to draw attention to the ways in which mechanization of clothing production during the late nineteenth and early twentieth centuries placed enormous pressure on the relationship between art and industry that, as

Nancy L. Green has pointed out, is "an issue fundamental to all cultural production in industrial societies."[14] Green offers a historically grounded study of how industrialization and divided labor practices affected haute couture, and, most significant for my purposes, she exposes discursive strategies privileging art and national identity that were developed at both the high and the low ends of the clothing industry in response to the increasing availability and competitive marketing of readymade clothing.

This kind of study, which attends not just to the historical specificity of clothing in terms of modes of production and distribution but also to the discursive construction of fashion, has become more common as the fields of costume and design history are increasingly informed by one another and by the interdisciplinary study of visual culture more generally. Yet, despite its basis in historically specific research, recent scholarly literature on fashion continues to be indebted in part to Roland Barthes's analysis of what he called "the fashion system."[15] According to Barthes, whose book was first published in French in 1967, clothing is not, or not simply, a functional necessity but, more importantly, the material ground of fashion. Fashion, in turn, is a semiotic language through which cultural meanings are constructed. As a structuralist, Barthes's concern was to create a rhetorical model for understanding the operations of what he called "written clothing" (le vêtement écrit) as a linguistic code; in fact, the code itself, the system, was his principal interest: fashion was a pretext for his exploration of how linguistic signs are made and how they function systematically in the production of social discourse. Thus, although Barthes attended to the details of particular costumes in constructing his semiotic model, he ignored the historical and material specificity of clothing and its manufacture. Nevertheless, his theoretical work has had a profound impact on subsequent examinations of actual clothing and the operations of fashion, especially in France during the nineteenth century, and many scholars have sought to apply his theoretical insights to particular historical situations. Philippe Perrot, for example, clearly echoes Barthes when he notes that clothing oneself "is essentially an act of signification. It manifests through symbols or convention, together or separately, essence, seniority, tradition, prerogative, heritage, caste, lineage, ethnic group, generation, religion, geographical origin, marital status, social position, economic role, political belief, and ideological affiliation. Sign or symbol, clothing affirms and reveals cleavages, hierarchies, and solidarities according to a code guaranteed and perpetuated by society and its institutions."[16] Leila Kinney investigates the same historical and geographical terrain in her work on the relationship between modern art and fashion in France during the second half of the nineteenth century. But unlike Perrot, in articulating the character of that relationship she is concerned to preserve the fundamental theoretical distinction Barthes made between fashion as a specifically linguistic system of signification and the separate (though related) "vestimentary" system constituted through the signifying operations of actual clothing in the real world.[17] Indeed, what makes Kinney's contribution to the understanding of these issues especially valuable is the fact that she treats the separation of the discourse of fashion from that of real clothing not only as an abstract, theoretical premise, but as a circumstance that can be located historically. In an essay that explores fashion as a means of understanding salient aspects of modern-life painting in France during the second half of the nineteenth century, Kinney describes Charles Baudelaire's essay, "The Painter of Modern Life" (probably begun in 1859 but not published until 1863), as "the place in aesthetic discourse where fashion is isolated from a history of costume, clothing, or dress itself." In that essay, Baudelaire recognized the potential of fashion plates to function as models for a modern theory of beauty in which fashion, contemporaneity, and that which is circumstantial formed the necessary complement to the eternal and invariable aspect of beauty. According to Kinney, by suggesting that fashion occupied an important position in artistic theory, Baudelaire effectively distinguished "fashion as a principle or a system" from the operations of clothing, to which he reserved the function, "increasingly unworkable in the late nineteenth century, of social denomination."[18]

If from the 1860s onward in France, fashion would operate as a linguistic or discursive system and a sign of contemporaneity, clothing, it was assumed, would continue to perform its customary work of delineating status, class, and rank. However, in the wake of the French Revolution, sumptuary laws no longer guaranteed the regulation of vestimentary practices, which had already been subject to increasing challenge by a rising bourgeoisie during the course of the eighteenth century. When, in 1793, the Convention overturned the hierarchical and legally constituted symbolic system of social differentiation, it initiated a hundred-year period during which clothing became increasingly uniform—not only for men frockcoated in black, but for women, as well. As garments began to be produced industrially and production was increasingly rationalized after the mid-nineteenth-century introduction of the sewing machine, images of clothing circulated more widely and actual garments were marketed in new and more democratic ways.[19] Indeed, the availability of readymade, industrially produced garments for women as well as men in the late nineteenth and early twentieth centuries coincided with the consolidation of the department store, and that institution as well as the garment industry contributed directly to the development of a culture of consumption that tended to ignore traditional class boundaries. So, as mass production, mass-circulation publications, and department-store merchandising of readymade articles of clothing made fashionable garments available to an ever-broader population, by the late nineteenth century clothing was losing its ability to provide a readily available guide to rank or social standing; therefore, it became correspondingly difficult for urban dwellers to secure their respectability in the public sphere. In the words of Honoré de Balzac, ". . . in our society, differences have disappeared: only nuances remain."[20] Richard Sennett has described how this crisis in sartorial representation affected the self-consciousness and outward behavior of women in particular: "There arose out of this dilemma a need to pay great attention to details of appearance and to hold oneself in, for fear of being read wrongly or maliciously; indeed, who knew, perhaps, if one gave off miniature signals of being loose, one really was. . . . One's only defense against such a culture was in fact to cover up, and from this came the stony feminine fear of being seen in public."[21] This is precisely the dilemma that motivates Hollis Clayson's study of the role played by clothing within the complex structure of Impressionist paintings of women, where the discourses of fashion operated in tandem with the depiction of other social phenomena and with the formal features of these paintings to underline the ambiguous moral position of the female figures portrayed, many of whom were, therefore, interpreted as prostitutes by contemporary audiences. Ambiguity of appearance, Clayson argues, became a tool of male sexual politics, offering Manet, Degas, and others a means of mastering and containing their own and their society's anxieties about women, their sexual availability, and their increasing visibility in the public sphere.[22]

The democratization of fashion not only destroyed clothing's ability to signify social distinction, Kinney suggests, it also played a part in producing the uniformity and regularity that are the hallmarks of paintings such as Georges Seurat's *A Sunday Afternoon on the Island of the Grande Jatte* of 1884–1886. Kinney notes that the stiffness and sobriety of the figures "encased in their rigid armature are consistent as well with the uniformity of mass-produced manufactured goods."[23] Seurat's emphasis on the readymade pervades the painting, its fashion of conformity providing a thematic parallel to the regularity of the surface treatment, as well as to the picture's relatively rigid formal structure in general.

If it is true that in the second half of the nineteenth century mass production and uniformity across traditional class boundaries produced anxieties about clothing and individual identity that are figured in numerous French Impressionist and Post-Impressionist paintings, these anxieties are also present in the counter-discourses of individuality and uniqueness that circulated throughout the culture. Indeed, the tensions between individuality and group identity, elite and popular culture, are central to the cultural construction of both art and fashion during the period that is the focus of the present book. In examining the relationship between art and fashion during the early twentieth century, unlike Kinney, Clayson, and other art historians, I do not base my study on the image of fashion conveyed in works of art but on the discourse of art as it was appropriated and manipulated by principal players in the world of fashion. I treat Paul Poiret in particular as a symptom of the contradictory forces that shaped cultural production, distribution, and consumption across the visual and performing arts at a time when anonymous production was placing enormous pressures on the creative individual. Poiret's preoccupation with securing his identity as an artist while developing a mass market for his clothes finds a parallel in the fetishization of the trademark and brand name that enabled consumers to distinguish virtually identical commodities from one another in the marketplace for mass-produced goods. Similarly, Poiret's engagement with both Orientalism and classicism in couture fashion and costumes for the theater reveals that these tropes did not belong to antithetical discourses, the one understood as transgressive and the other as sustaining traditional culture and class interests. Poiret deployed both Orientalism and classicism in a variety of theatrical contexts, including lavish private parties and performances, as well as on the professional stage, to position and promote his fashion statements as expressions of luxury and sumptuousness steeped in the cultural politics of a wealthy and aristocratic French elite. He also directed these same fashion statements to the middle-class consumers who flocked to American department stores to see and to purchase adaptations of his most outrageous designs.

The contradictory circumstances that Poiret grappled with at the beginning of the twentieth century need to be studied in all their historical specificity, but they nevertheless resonate with the experience of contemporary clothing designers. Many successful purveyors of fashionable clothing and so-called lifestyle accessories continue to explore the theatrical tropes that Poiret pioneered, using them much as he did both to under-mine and to exploit the apparent contradictions between aristocratic elit-ism and populist appeal. The best example may be Ralph Lauren, whose company posted worldwide wholesale sales of $4.5 billion in 1999.[24] Described as no mere fashion designer but "the ultimate producer of a completely packaged, perfect life," according to Paul Goldberger, Lauren "has come to symbolize in this culture . . . something we might call the artifice business."[25] Like Poiret's artfully decorated couture house in Paris (discussed in chapter 1), Lauren's flagship retail outlet in New York, the former Gertrude Waldo Rhinelander mansion at 888 Madison Avenue, was transformed during the mid-1980s into a carefully staged fantasy envi-ronment designed to market a clubby style of Edwardian upper-class gen-tility that finds its perfect complement in Lauren's other signature image: the down-home ranch-cowboy appropriated from American Western movies of the 1950s. Drawing attention to the ways in which Lauren's enterprise exemplifies a late twentieth-century collapse of the designed environment into the values and systems of fashion, Goldberger further notes, "Mr. Lauren's designs are at once elitist and popular, at once mass and class, positioned carefully and knowingly right between the mass mar-ket and something more exclusive."[26] Lauren's extraordinary success in overcoming these categorical distinctions eluded Poiret some eighty years earlier, when the French couturier attempted to align the exclusivity of his Parisian couture operation with the American paradigm of mass marketing.

It was in the public arena of the American department store, as dis-tinct from the private sphere of his artfully designed Parisian *hôtel de cou-ture,* that Poiret confronted the conditions governing the merchandising of fashion in the mass market. There the multiple tangents of his trajec-tory through the world of fashion converged to expose the predicament of the individual artist in the face of mass production. In America he not only understood the danger that industrial production posed for haute couture, he also began to come to grips with the fact that no aesthetic discourse, not even his self-construction as an artist, could protect him from the consequences of his own success as a purveyor of fashion. The very strategies that he had employed to position his clothes as unique creations in the realm of elite culture—the exploitation of art, architecture, photography, interior and graphic design, as well as his work in the theater—had elicited the production of a profusion of pirated examples destined for mass consumption, thereby effecting a popularization that simultaneously validated and destroyed his aspirations to elite culture. When Poiret sought to protect his designs as intellectual property, the law, instead of shoring up his status as an artist, forced him to acknowledge his identity as a businessman. After the First World War, when financial and commercial considerations gradually overwhelmed his artistic persona, Poiret surrendered his place at the crossroads of fashion and art. He then lost control of his name when a corporation took over his business and forced him out of his *maison de couture*. It is difficult to imagine a more potent image of the dissolution of the romantic ideal of the individual artist as genius under the pressures of commodity capitalism. That Poiret himself contributed to his own demise by continuing to spend vast sums of money to express his personal aesthetic vision and regain his stature as a dominant figure in the post-war fashion world makes his defeat all the more emblematic of the fate of the modern artist committed to the values of individuality, originality, and authenticity. That the woman who took over his preeminent position, Coco Chanel, secured her success on the basis of couture fashions that projected an image of standardization—clothes that were favorably compared to mass-produced commodities—suggests not so much the ways in which her "little black dress" differed from Poiret's colorful, eye-catching clothes, but rather that, like Poiret before her, but now in a fashion redolent with the values of conformity and reproduction, she found a means of representing the contradictory forces at work in modern culture.

One
Fashion, Art, and the Marketing of Modernism

The birth of haute couture, which has been described as one of the modern period's most important innovations in the production and social meaning of clothing, is generally credited to Charles Frederick Worth.[1] Although vast changes in social or cultural practices are rarely due to the actions of a single individual, the story of Worth's dramatic rise to prominence as an innovator in the world of fashionable women's clothing bears retelling because it establishes a framework for understanding how the discourses of art were deployed in the business of elite fashion during the late nineteenth and early twentieth centuries. Worth was an Englishman who moved to Paris in 1845, and began working at an exclusive shop for silks and other fine fabrics on the rue de Richelieu, in a neighborhood where the most accomplished French dressmakers were located and where prominent members of the European aristocracy, as well as the best-kept *demi-mondaines,* had their clothes made. During the ensuing decade Worth developed a small dressmaking department into a lucrative business and a winner of international prizes for his employers. By 1858, he was looking for opportunities to strike out on his own. He entered a partnership that provided sufficient financial resources to establish a dressmaking company, Worth et Bobergh (which lasted until the Franco-Prussian War of 1870–71; thereafter, the company was known as the Maison Worth), located at 7, rue de la Paix. Worth's subsequent progress has become a familiar tale: how he managed to convince the wife of the Austrian ambassador, Princess Pauline von Metternich, to wear one of his designs at the court of Napoléon III, where the Empress Eugénie soon became his greatest patron, which in turn ensured the establishment of Worth at the pinnacle of French and, therefore, of world fashion beginning in the early 1860s.[2]

What set Worth apart from previous dressmakers to the international aristocracy and wealthy bourgeoisie was not simply that he was male rather than female (although this did constitute a potentially scandalous departure from the prevailing norm, it also effectively raised the stature of the heretofore predominantly female dressmaking profession[3]), but rather that, for the first time, fashionable women's wear was the creation of a single designer who not only selected the fabrics and ornaments that made up any given outfit but who developed the design and produced the final product (figure 1.1). Worth's success in consolidating these previously distinct operations enabled him to exercise extraordinary influence over the direction of France's luxury textiles industry and to gain control of all aspects of the dressmaking process. He was, therefore, in a position to dictate the character of each dress he designed down to its smallest details and, more importantly, to position haute couture as a powerful force for regularization in the increasingly rapid pace of fashionable innovation through the semi-annual rhythm of its presentations of new models. (This can be compared to the rhythm of annual spring and autumn art exhibitions where, after the 1903 addition of the Salon

Figure 1.1

Charles F. Worth, princess afternoon dress,
c. 1879.

d'Automne to the more established salons held in the spring, the majority
of French artists would present their latest work to the Parisian public.)

As Elizabeth Ann Coleman has pointed out, Worth's significance for
the history of dressmaking was due less to the uniqueness of his designs
than to his unprecedented business strategy: "The essential innovation
attributed to Worth does not reside in the cut of his designs; it is, rather,
the creative aspect of producing 'models,' which then could be distributed
commercially throughout the world."[4] The distinction between *haute couture* and *couture à façon,* Coleman suggests, is precisely the difference

between Worth's practice as a dressmaker and that of his predecessors: "During the 1860s haute couture—the presentation of a collection of models, from which could be selected a complete gown or appropriate parts—came to replace *couture à façon,* or dressmaking for the individual. In *couture à façon* the dressmaker had generally been a technician executing an outfit in the fabric and design of the client's preselection. In haute couture, however, the house supplied both the design ideas and the fabric selections, sometimes even having fabrics executed after their own designs."[5] According to Palmer White, "Haute couture commercialized de luxe made-to-order garments by repeating models and selling to buyers for French and foreign dress shops as well as to private customers."[6] Thus Worth's business, and haute couture generally, were forged out of seemingly incommensurate elements: on the one hand, extremely expensive items destined for elite patronage and, on the other, widespread commercial distribution at reduced prices; in other words, models described as unique creations that were nevertheless subject to endless adaptation and repetition: the original and the reproduction at one and the same time.

Having taken command of the design, production, and distribution processes for the gowns he created, Worth was able to set the tone for high fashion during the last third of the nineteenth century, and to charge his clients accordingly. Costume historian Diana de Marly notes that "it did not suffice to be merely wealthy to go to Worth, a client had to be in the millionaire or rich aristocratic class."[7] Worth gowns, particularly those intended to be worn at formal court appearances and masquerade balls, typically incorporated extremely expensive materials such as silk, brocade, or handmade lace. The labor-intensive nature of hand embroidery and the other specialized sewing techniques required in their production also contributed to the high price of his dresses. It may have been the case that Worth, like other top dressmaking firms, charged his clients differentially, establishing one price for wealthy Americans "and one for Christians of every other denomination."[8] Worth's staff grew exponentially in the 1860s to accommodate a rapidly expanding client base; yet, despite the fact that needleworkers constituted a notoriously underpaid labor force, Worth was apparently unable to earn a very substantial income from his business. According to his son, Jean-Philippe, "the wealth he acquired did not come from the shop in the rue de la Paix. Had he not made investments in other than his own business, our inheritance would have been very little. For it must not be thought that fortunes are made in a single business, particularly in that of making dresses."[9]

When the house of Worth et Bobergh opened in 1858, its staff numbered fewer than twenty,[10] but a dozen years later, by 1870–1871 (when the partnership dissolved and Worth took over the business on his own), there were as many as 1,200 employees, a number said to have been maintained until Worth died and his sons took over the business in 1895.[11] Despite this army of workers, the enormous reach of his operations required Worth to rely on machinery and divided labor practices.[12] According to Zuzanna Shonfield, "By the late [eighteen] seventies . . . , C. F. Worth was in fact beginning to run his *salon de couture* on an almost industrial scale," resulting in "blatant duplication of models."[13] Sewing machines speeded the assembly of gowns from standardized patterns with interchangeable parts; only the cutting, finishing, and embroidery had to be done by hand. The use of different fabrics or colors in individual versions of a given model helped to ensure that such industrial practices went unnoticed. It was also necessary for Worth's business to maintain a large and efficient filing system to account for what gowns were sold to whom for which occasion, so that wealthy clients would not be embarrassed by face-to-face encounters with other women clothed in the same designs.

In addition to in-house adaptations or modifications of his own designs—for example, with a lowcut bodice suitable for evening wear (figure 1.2) in place of the high neck and long sleeves of the more versatile version of the same basic dress (figure 1.3)—Worth also sold models designed to be copied by others, especially American dry goods and department

Figure 1.2 ℛ

Charles F. Worth, multifunctional ensemble composed of day and evening bodices, skirt, and sash, c. 1869. Shown here with the low bodice for evenings. See figure 1.3 for daytime version.

Figure 1.3 ℑ

Charles F. Worth, basque and full-trained
trimmed skirt, 1874.

stores. (The dress shown in figure 1.3 was exported for the purpose of
copying by Lord & Taylor.) In such establishments, by the late nineteenth
century bespoke garments could be ordered but readymade garments for
both men and women were also becoming available alongside fabrics for
made-to-order clothes. According to Coleman, "The leading *modistes* of
Europe and America bought garments from Worth to use as models;
many of the house's cloaks and gowns were produced with slight modifications many times over."[14] It was this proliferation of virtually identical
garments that presumably necessitated the introduction of the house label
in the early 1860s in order to identify genuine Worth products (figure 1.4).

 *Figure 1.4* ↻

Worth label, stamped gold on white and black
and woven gold on white petersham,
c. 1870–1985.

Eventually, however, the label itself was subject to copying; the earliest fake Worth label has been dated to the late 1880s, indicating the existence by then of a robust trade in counterfeit dresses intended to exploit the success of Worth's legitimate couture business (figure 1.5).[15]

It is surely no accident that the development of the couture label in the second half of the nineteenth century coincided with a growing commercial emphasis on brand names, especially in the burgeoning field of

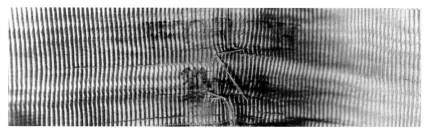

Figure 1.5 ↻

Fake Worth label, stamped gold on white,
c. 1870s.

advertising, where it was widely recognized that profits could be made by linking a desirable commodity with a particular brand name. Alan Trachtenberg has noted the relationship that the nascent advertising industry forged between naming and selling around the turn of the nineteenth century: "Commercial trademarks and brand names came into their own in the Gilded Age, proliferating especially as the consumer-goods industries so rapidly expanded their productive powers and corporate structures in these years. The mark or name is a particular kind of expression, originating not as a spontaneous act of naming on the part of people discovering a new object in their midst but an act from above, the manufacturer's act, sanctioned and protected by the law of copyright: a fiction underwritten by laws protecting what came to be known as property, the brand name."[16] But if the couture label had a frankly commercial function that could be rationalized and protected by law, at the same time it introduced an entirely different, more elusive dimension due to the fact that it signified a creative individual as well as a corporate entity, the identity of the former becoming inextricably linked to the latter, since the name of the person and that of the brand were one and the same. Pierre Bourdieu and Yvette Delsaut have described how this dual character of the couture label functions to effect a symbolic transubstantiation of a manufactured garment into a couture creation, a process that corresponds closely, they argue, to the "magical" effects produced when the artist's signature is applied to an object, which the signature transforms into a work of art. "The couturier does nothing different from the painter who constitutes a given object as a work of art by the act of affixing his signature to it," Bourdieu and Delsaut write. "If there is an instance where one makes things with words, as in magic . . . it is certainly in the universe of fashion."[17] But although the label functions as the couturier's signature, its role in signifying an authorial source is complicated by the fact that, as Jacques Derrida has observed, a signature testifies not only to the (past) presence but also to "the actual or empirical nonpresence of the signer."

Moreover, Derrida explains, a signature is anything but singular or original: "In order to function, that is, to be readable, a signature must have a repeatable, iterable, imitable form; it must be able to be detached from the present and singular intention of its production. It is its sameness which, by corrupting its identity and its singularity, divides its seal [*sceau*]." As signature, then, the label functions both to imply presence yet reveal absence, to communicate what Derrida calls "the absolute singularity of a signature-event" while its form is necessarily reproducible insofar as any particular instance of the signature must look like every other.[18] Seen in this light, the label itself becomes a manifestation of the contradictory tensions between originality and reproduction that structure fashion in general and the development of early twentieth-century haute couture in particular.

Hillel Schwartz has noted that "signatures acquired their full authority only with the Romantic celebration of genius,"[19] but when Bourdieu and Delsaut state that "[t]he 'signature label' [*la griffe*] . . . is without doubt, along with the signature of the consecrated painter, one of the most economically and symbolically powerful words among [all] those in circulation today,"[20] the point they seek to emphasize is economic as well as cultural and theoretical. For them the signature label is ultimately a signifier of value which, in fashion as in art, is a function of rarity: "It is the rarity of the producer (that is to say the rarity of the position that he occupies in a field) that establishes the rarity of the product. How else, if not by one's faith in the magic of the signature, can we explain the ontological difference—which reveals itself economically—between the replica, signed by the master himself (this multiple *avant la lettre*) and the copy or the fake?"[21] If it is indeed a question of the "rarity of the producer," rather than of the object produced (which in the case of haute couture was by its nature a replica or multiple rather than a unique creation, as the example of Worth's production demonstrates), the couturier is compelled to construct a singular and charismatic identity for himself, which the label, in turn, confers upon the garment it identifies as his or her design.[22] These circumstances not only help to explain the urgency with which couturiers, beginning with Worth, repeatedly expressed their artistic aspirations, they also underscore the profound relationship of those aspirations to the couturiers' business practices.

It was, then, not only ironic but strategically significant that, just as Worth's couture house was perfecting methods and procedures common to industrial production, Worth was increasingly distancing himself from the model of the modern manufacturer and entrepreneur that he in fact was becoming. Photographs of the couturier as a younger man show him in a conventional frock-coated business suit (figure 1.6), but by 1892, when he was photographed by Nadar, he had adopted the persona of the great artist. Wearing a velvet beret and a fur-trimmed coat opened at the neck to reveal a floppy tie, he struck a pose reminiscent of several self-portraits by Rembrandt (figure 1.7).[23] However, even if Worth managed to decouple the professional identity of the dressmaker from that of the lowly craftsman by appealing to a visual discourse elevated by its association with fine art,[24] his middle-class origins and intimate knowledge of his client's bodies as well as their social activities would have prevented him from circulating in aristocratic society as an equal. Nevertheless, by the late 1860s his financial success did enable Worth to construct a princely lifestyle for himself and his family in a luxurious, richly appointed country house west of Paris at Suresnes.

According to de Marly, Worth's villa "was reputed to be so splendid that the nobility vied for invitations to it, in much the same way that they craved invitations to the imperial châteaux at Compiègne and Fontainebleau. Here was wealth on a scale that other dressmakers had not dreamed of."[25] Worth spent lavishly on the decoration of his home, gradually transforming what had been acquired as a relatively small villa into a virtual dream castle. According to Princess von Metternich, who visited regularly, "Whilst Worth had taste in everything which concerns the toi-

Figure 1.6

Photo of Charles F. Worth, 1858.

lette, he lacked it, in my opinion, for everything else. The villa at Suresnes which he enlarged and expanded adding a wing here, a wing there, and pavilions and chalets, gave the effect of a confusion of buildings on a site which was much too restricted, all clashing with each other."[26] The interiors, of which no photographs survive, presented a comparable overcrowding of heterogeneous elements in an eclectic decorating scheme. To quote another contemporary account, "There was a perplexing mixture of patriarchal simplicity and of the assertiveness of modern money, of thoroughly natural unaffectedness and of showy surroundings, of total carelessness in some things and of infinite white satin in others, which was so

Figure 1.7 ☉

Félix Nadar, Charles F. Worth, 1892. Centre
des monuments nationaux.

new to me that, at first, I felt a little bewildered, and wondered whether I
was dining with Haroun el Raschid in one of the disguises he so often
wore."[27] When Edmond de Goncourt paid a visit to Suresnes in 1882, the
esthete connoisseur of eighteenth-century arts and decoration was thoroughly put off by the spectacle of new-found wealth that Worth seemed
so eager to display: "Everywhere on the walls there are plates of every
period, and of every country. Mme Worth says there are 25,000 of them,
and everywhere, even on the backs of chairs, drops of crystal. It is a delirium of bits of porcelain and carafe stoppers . . . resembling the interior of

a kaleidoscope."[28] Although Worth's voracious collecting and eclectic display practices might perhaps be appreciated as characteristic manifestations of contemporary taste, however hyperbolized, there can be little doubt that his crowded and sumptuous interiors expressed his class aspirations while providing a setting designed as a stage for his self-presentation as an artist and a patron of the arts.

Worth's penchant for obvious material excess dated his interactions with the arts and were not imitated by subsequent generations of couturier collectors, who greatly refined Worth's characteristically Victorian approach to art and interior decoration. The most prominent amongst them, including Jacques Doucet, Jeanne Paquin, and Paul Poiret, all heeded the lesson of restraint preached by the generation of esthetes inspired by the Goncourt brothers. Rather than hoarding vast numbers of miscellaneous decorative objects, Doucet and Poiret, in particular, formed significant personal collections containing carefully chosen examples of modern art and design, and Poiret was even engaged indirectly in promoting works of art. In addition to its investment potential, these couturiers recognized and exploited the value of advanced art as a cultural sign of social distinction. Indeed, like Worth, they too sought to use the arts as a means of deflecting attention from their engagement with the industrialized aspects of dressmaking and from the increasing necessity of publicizing and building a market for their wares within an evolving consumer culture. Also like Worth, these early twentieth-century couturiers associated with, and often took pains to represent themselves as, fine artists. For their part, modern artists, architects, decorators, and graphic designers stood to gain visibility as well as financial stability from their collaboration with fashionable dress designers, particularly those with well-publicized interests in the arts. Such associations may have seemed especially attractive to artists because, in the early twentieth century, the officially sanctioned salons and other traditional exhibition venues were losing their effectiveness as marketing tools in favor of private, contractual arrangements between individual artists and independent dealers.

Figure 1.8 ↄ

Man Ray, photo of Jacques Doucet, c. 1925.

Of all the couturier collectors, Jacques Doucet (figure 1.8) was undoubtedly the most important patron of the arts, and the only one to realize a spectacular rise in the value of his art and interior design collections.[29] Born into a family of shirtmakers and lingerie and lace producers who had been in the business of making clothes for men and women since about 1820, Doucet entered the well-established family firm, located just down the street from Worth's *maison de couture* on the rue de la Paix, around 1870. Thereafter, the growth and increasing visibility of both firms contributed substantially to the consolidation in the second half of the nineteenth century of the rue de la Paix as the center of the most fashionable and expensive shopping district in Paris. The dresses produced by the Maison Doucet have been associated with the fluidity, relative informality, and surface decoration of the Art Nouveau style, but costume historians have found it difficult to identify precisely to what degree and how Jacques Doucet was responsible for the designs that emanated from his firm. Indeed, it appears that he disdained the dressmaking profession and, according to Coleman, "came to regard any association with fashion as frivolous and demeaning."[30] Instead, Doucet devoted his attention—and the funds he was able to draw from the family business as well as lucrative outside investments—to the extraordinarily impressive art collections he began to assemble in earnest in the mid-1890s. (He bought his first work of art, a painting by Raphaelli, in 1875, when he was 21 years old.[31]) The first of these collections was composed exclusively of eighteenth-century art and artifacts, including major paintings by Boucher, Fragonard, Hubert Robert, Saint-Aubin, Vigée-Lebrun, and Watteau; genre pictures by Chardin; sculptures by Clodion and Houdon; and furniture by the great decorators of the Louis XV and Louis XVI eras. Beginning in 1907, these objects were housed in an appropriately rococo environment created for them in Doucet's villa at 19, rue Spontini (figure 1.9). Legend has it that it was in response to a disappointing love affair that, in 1912, Doucet suddenly decided to sell this collection at public auction, but there may also have been significant financial incentives that Doucet, who closely guarded his privacy, did not choose to acknowledge. In any event, the four-part sale of his eighteenth-century holdings realized the enormous total of more than 13.75 million gold francs, or about 4 million old francs. Doucet's professional associates clearly believed that the collection had been assembled less for the love of art than for investment purposes that were realized by the sale. According to Jean-Philippe Worth, for example, by the time Doucet retired in the 1920s, he had amassed "an enormous fortune." Worth quickly dispelled the notion that Doucet's wealth came from his dressmaking establishment, declaring that instead it came

Figure 1.9

Interior of Jacques Doucet hôtel, 19, rue
Spontini, Paris, before 1912, from *L'Oeil,* 1961.

"chiefly from his shrewd investments in pictures and works of art! When
he sold his art gallery [by which Worth must have meant Doucet's first art
collection] about ten years ago, it created almost as great a sensation in the
world as the latest international scandal and brought him about fourteen
million francs, whereas it had probably cost him approximately two millions [*sic*]." And, Worth continued, "In addition to his pictures he
[Doucet] had bought shares in the Suez Canal at the right moment, acted
upon other tips on the market and had the good fortune to have a father
who bought land in the suburbs of Paris at four or five francs a meter,

which to-day is worth four or five hundred francs. Naturally the original capital with which he had speculated came from his dressmaking business, but it can readily be seen that nine tenths of his fortune did not come from that business."[32]

Doucet was careful to keep his collecting practices entirely separate from his affairs as a couturier.[33] As his biographer, François Chapon, has noted, "It is certain that Doucet never proclaimed himself a couturier. No one was ever absent as Doucet was from all the professional situations where one would have expected to find him."[34] He was neither a member of the Chambre Syndicale de la Couture nor an exhibitor in the world's fairs in which Worth, Paquin, Poiret, and other prominent French firms took part. Chapon suggests that couture simply did not interest Doucet and "[a]lthough he knew how to draw—his status as painter *manqué* betrays at least some ability in this domain—he does not seem to have made even an initial attempt [at drawing a model dress design]."[35] Instead of acknowledging the role he played in directing a large and complex business, Doucet projected an air of disinterest in such mundane activities, casting himself as a great Maecenas and making a major show of his dedication to the world of art and literature. Having disposed of his initial collection of eighteenth-century works of art, in 1913 he moved to new quarters at 46, avenue du Bois and began to collect Impressionist and Post-Impressionist paintings; soon he was buying contemporary works by Braque, Derain, Laurencin, Matisse, Picasso, and Dunoyer de Segonzac, among many others.[36]

Although Doucet has been described as an unusually passionate and discriminating collector, at least one of his closest associates has suggested that Doucet himself was rarely responsible for selecting the works he acquired. According to André Breton, whom Doucet hired in 1919 for 500 francs per month to build his collection of contemporary art, "Doucet was not really a connoisseur of painting. He had 'taste,' the taste of a couturier. As for the paintings he bought, it was never he who chose them." As a result, Breton concluded, ". . . I find it strange that today a myth of finesse is attached to the name of Doucet."[37] Jean-François Revel suggests that what really excited Doucet was the creation of ensembles of objects; "once the goal was attained, he became disinterested." This was apparently true of the extraordinarily rich library and archive of art history that Doucet assembled, at first as a means of documenting the works of art he owned and later as a collection of great significance in its own right. "Antique and new editions, in-folios and revues, he bought everything, subscribed to everything. Each day, crates would arrive by the dozen at the rue Spontini, for this library of 100,000 volumes, 500 manuscripts, 150,000 photographs, 10,000 prints, 2,000 albums of engravings was formed in scarcely three or four years." It seems obvious that this was never meant to be a personal library, and Doucet could not have read or even looked at many of the items that were in it or in the other literary collections he assembled after he donated his art history library to the University of Paris in 1918. "As was the case with his collections of works of art," Revel contends, "he largely assigned to his advisors the choice of purchases, contenting himself with stimulating them and pursuing by dint of a great deal of money the goal that was dear to him: constituting the best 18th-century collection, the largest library, the most complete collection of contemporary books, or of modern painting."[38]

Worth and Doucet thus pioneered the accumulation and display of fine and decorative art not simply (or even primarily) in the interests of aesthetic contemplation but, also and perhaps most importantly, for the purpose of reconstructing their individual personas as artists rather than dressmakers, connoisseurs rather than businessmen. It was Paul Poiret (figure 1.10) who proved to be by far the most sophisticated of all these couturiers in terms of his ability to exploit what was by all accounts a genuine, life-long interest in modern art for the purposes of self-promotion and the benefit of his multifarious commercial enterprises. Having emerged from a middle-class Parisian background (his father owned a

Figure 1.10

Paul Poiret.

fabric shop near the Bourse), Poiret worked first for Doucet, beginning in 1898, and then for the house of Worth before establishing his own couture business on the rue Auber, near the Opéra, in 1903. Poiret learned important lessons from his mentors, especially Doucet, about how to gain the greatest possible benefit from his immersion in the world of art and artists. Soon after his marriage to Denise Boulet in October 1905, Poiret later recalled in his memoirs, ". . . I began to receive artists, and to create around me a movement."[39] Among the many contemporary artists with whom Poiret associated and whose work he purchased before his collection was sold at auction in 1925 were Jean-Louis Boussingault, Constantin Brancusi, Robert Delaunay, André Derain, Kees van Dongen, Raoul Dufy, André Dunoyer de Segonzac, Roger de la Fresnaye, Paul Iribe, Marie Laurencin, Georges Lepape, Henri Matisse, Jean Metzinger, Amedeo Modigliani, Luc-Albert Moreau, Bernard Naudin, Francis Picabia, and Pablo Picasso. Today this might appear to be an eclectic assemblage and mixed in value, but before World War I, when Poiret presumably purchased the majority of works in his collection, these were recognized as being among the most advanced painters, sculptors, and graphic artists of the period.[40]

Poiret got his start in the couture business when he was still a teenager by selling sketches of dress designs to established couturiers including Madame Cheruit and Jacques Doucet, and he was from the beginning a reasonably accomplished artist. As a young man he dabbled in painting, a pastime he pursued with varying intensity throughout his life, and early on he seems to have sought out the company of artists. According to Poiret's biographer, Palmer White, Francis Picabia was a childhood friend, and Poiret met the fauve painters André Derain and Maurice de Vlaminck while he was still a bachelor, thus before the autumn of 1905.[41] The following year Poiret was attracted to the work of the illustrator Bernard Naudin, whose drawings he saw published in

Le Cri de Paris. Naudin was responsible for the stationery and related graphic materials for Poiret's couture house when it relocated from the rue Auber to the rue Pasquier in 1906, and thereafter he drew programs for several intimate private concerts held at the Poiret home between 1910 and 1912.[42] Poiret evidently made a point of scanning the illustrated and satirical press for sympathetic material, because this is how he came into contact with the work of Paul Iribe, a graphic artist and designer of jewelry and furniture whom Poiret invited to create the first of his deluxe albums of couture designs in 1908. It was probably then or in the following year, when Poiret moved his business to the avenue d'Antin, that Iribe also designed the couture house label that Poiret would use for the next twenty years (figure 1.11).[43] In 1909, Poiret asked the painter and printmaker Raoul Dufy to design vignettes for his new couture house stationery (a different image for each day of the week, including Sunday showing a model at the racetrack, figure 1.12), and later for that of his interior design outlet as well as the invitations and decorations for one of Poiret's most famous parties. After seeing the black and white woodcuts inspired by popular *images d'Épinal* that Dufy produced between 1909 and 1911 to illustrate a book of poems by Guillaume Apollinaire, Poiret launched Dufy's career as a textile designer by commissioning him to make woodcut designs for

Figure 1.11

Paul Iribe, couture label designed for Paul Poiret.

Figure 1.12

Raoul Dufy, stationery header designed for
Poiret couture house: Dimanche.

fabrics in a similarly archaic but powerful graphic style that exploited the
stark contrast between black and white, or light and dark colors (figure
1.13).[44] While Poiret's contacts with these and other artists resulted in commissions for works by them related to his professional activities, the couturier was also building his personal art collection during these years,
and the two spheres constantly overlapped and enriched one another.
Examination of an exhibition catalogue and of an auction catalogue
devoted to Poiret's art collection dating from 1923 and 1925, respectively,
reveals that virtually all of the graphic artists who produced designs for his
businesses were also included in his collection, as was the case with Boutet
de Monvel, Dufy, Iribe, Lepape, and Naudin.[45] But the connections
between his professional work and his art patronage were more complex

than this paradigm would suggest. For example, in 1909, after painter and printmaker Jean-Louis Boussingault was introduced to Poiret as the artist chosen to illustrate an article he was writing for *La Grande Revue,* Poiret became Boussingault's most supportive patron by inviting the artist to create a large decorative painting for his new *maison de couture.*[46] Boussingault, in turn, was closely associated with two other young painters, Luc-Albert Moreau and André Dunoyer de Segonzac, whom Poiret also supported, not only by purchasing works of art,[47] but, more importantly, by arranging for all three to exhibit their work together in

Figure 1.13

Paul Poiret, "La Perse" coat, 1911.

1910 at the Galerie Barbazanges, a commercial art gallery on the premises of his couture house that Poiret rented to an art dealer while retaining the right to organize one or two shows each year. In March 1911, the gallery held an exhibition of work by graphic designers in Poiret's orbit: Bernard Boutet de Monvel (who had made several color prints advertising Poiret's couture business in 1907, when it was still located on the rue Pasquier), Jacques and Pierre Brissaud, and Georges Lepape, who created the second deluxe album of Poiret couture designs in 1911.[48] Then, in late February and early March 1912, Poiret invited Robert Delaunay and Marie Laurencin to share the gallery in a two-person exhibition that provided the occasion for the first large-scale showing of each artist's work. By this time Poiret could legitimately claim to be an important patron and promoter of advanced tendencies in contemporary art. The above-mentioned catalogues of his collection show that he owned an early landscape, *View of Collioure,* by Matisse as well as five works by Picasso, at least two of which can be dated before 1912 (a still life in tempera on wood from autumn 1908, and a harlequin figure in gouache on paper from spring 1909[49]). In 1912, not only did Poiret purchase Brancusi's *Maiastra* (the polished bronze sculpture, which he acquired directly from the artist, is visible in figure 1.14), he also bought de la Fresnaye's *The Card Players* and four smaller decorative paintings by Laurencin from the Maison Cubiste, a controversial decorative arts ensemble that was prominently displayed at the Salon d'Automne that year.[50] Indeed, many of the artists whose work he collected were associated in one way or another with cubism as that movement was presented to Parisian audiences, not only in Kahnweiler's gallery where Picasso's work was shown, but also in large, officially sanctioned salons and smaller group exhibitions in 1911 and 1912. This is a point to which we will return.

In addition to his principal business as a dress designer, Poiret was involved, though intermittently and tangentially, in the Galerie Barbazanges from 1910 on, as we have seen. Beginning in 1911, he manufac-

Figure 1.14

Delphi, photo of Madame Paul Poiret in
Poiret's "Mythe," posed next to Brancusi's
1912 *Maiastra,* 1919.

tured a luxuriously packaged line of perfumes named after his eldest
daughter, Rosine (figure 1.15), and he ran a loosely organized decorative
arts school that furnished designs for his decorative arts atelier and marketing outlets, named after his second daughter, Martine (figure 1.16). The
interlocking and mutually reinforcing character of his collecting and
other artistic pursuits on one hand and his various entrepreneurial activities on the other differed markedly from Doucet's practice of separating
these, and this integration struck contemporary observers as a brilliant

Figure 1.15

Le Minaret perfume, from *Les Parfums de Rosine*.

marketing strategy that would benefit all his products. In an article of 1912 describing the interior of the newly inaugurated Martine boutique, a correspondent for the American women's magazine *Vogue* remarked that, while it was common practice to combine the sale of hats, caps, bags, belts, and other apparel accessories, "certainly couturiers have never before insisted that chairs, curtains, rugs and wall-coverings should be considered in the choosing of a dress, or rather that the style of a dress should influence the interior decorations of a home."[51] *Vogue*'s correspondent failed to note that turn-of-the-century architects and interior decorators including

Peter Behrens, Henry van de Velde, and Frank Lloyd Wright (among others) had already established compelling precedents for conceiving of dress and interior design as mutually reinforcing arenas for aesthetic expression. However, the garments designed by these architects were unique objects made for specific settings in response to particular formal concerns; none of the three tried to market dress designs on a broader scale. In this they differed from their Austrian counterparts in the Wiener Werkstätte, whose dresses were available for retail sale. Poiret was deeply impressed by his first-hand experience of Wiener Werkstätte design when he visited Vienna in the fall of 1910 and again the following year, during trips that

Figure 1.16

Raoul Dufy, stationery designed for Martine.

also took him to Berlin and other European cities. He sent home large quantities of Wiener Werkstätte textiles for use in his dresses, and the work of the Austrian group, especially the totally coordinated environment of the Palais Stoclet in Brussels (which Poiret went specifically to see), was a major inspiration for founding his own design studio, Martine, in 1911. Like Hoffmann and other members of the Wiener Werkstätte, as well as Behrens, van de Velde, and Wright, Poiret embraced a *Gesamtkunstwerk* ideal that positioned his clothing within a larger (interior) design context. But while those architects saw the *Gesamtkunstwerk,* or comprehensive, approach to design as a means of social engineering and tended to impose their own aesthetic preferences on their clients, Poiret took a more liberal view, explaining, "This substitution of the taste of the architect for the personality of the proprietors has always seemed to me a sort of slavery—a subjection that makes me smile."[52] For him, the *Gesamtkunstwerk,* or total work of art, was less a utopian design ideal than the physical expression of a personal business empire applied to the feminine spheres of haute couture, perfumes, and the decorative arts ranging from textiles to furniture. Poiret's mutually reinforcing spheres of activity also included his art collecting, which functioned as part and parcel of an over-arching entrepreneurial strategy directed at obfuscating its own commercial nature.

In order to sell clothes, perfume, and furnishings to the aristocratic and wealthy bourgeois clients for whom his products were designed, Poiret had to eschew practices associated with establishments appealing to lower- and middle-class markets. If early European and American dry goods and department stores initially created their mass audiences by extensive advertising of cut-rate merchandise on billboards and in cheap newspapers and magazines, and by displaying their wares in enormous quantities,[53] the couturier maintained the distinctive allure of his products by not advertising (at least not to large audiences) and by appropriating the fine arts to promote the originality, uniqueness, and aesthetic quality of his designs. This posture was maintained even in the brochure published to advertise Rosine perfumes, which were described in the "Preface" commissioned from the writer Nozière as "the knowing, meticulous, refined creations of an artist."[54] "I am not commercial," Poiret told reporters in 1913. "Ladies come to me for a gown as they go to a distinguished painter to get their portraits put on canvas. I am an artist, not a dressmaker."[55]

Poiret's pejorative view of advertising went hand in hand with his public disavowal of commerce. In both postures he aligned himself not simply with a modernist art discourse of aesthetic purity but also with widely accepted notions of bourgeois gentility that regarded mass production with disdain because of its proletarian associations and advertising with suspicion because of its potential for charlatanism and misrepresentation. As the French advertising industry was consolidated in France toward the end of the nineteenth century, as Aaron Segal has shown, advertisements gradually ceased to address existing needs in rational terms and instead developed suggestive, indirect, yet psychologically potent means of creating desires and, thereby, encouraging consumption on the part of their audiences.[56] Poiret actively participated in this trend, all the while proclaiming his distance from undignified commercial practices and stressing instead his manifold associations with artists, architects, and graphic designers whose work for him was, to borrow a phrase from Ellen Garvey's *The Adman in the Parlor,* "artfully constructed not to seem like advertisements."[57]

Avoiding conventional publicity, Poiret used his own tailored image to call attention to himself not only in the streets of Paris but also while traveling abroad (figure 1.17). During a tour through Germany, Eastern Europe, and Russia in October and November 1911, he and his wife wore beige coats to ride in their beige Renault Torpedo driven by a chauffeur in beige livery (his mannequins, or live female models, and trunks of dresses traveled ahead of him, by train).[58] On the streets of the Faubourg

Figure 1.17

Photo of Paul Poiret, 1909.

St.-Honoré in Paris, Poiret was seen sporting a coloristically up-to-date version of artistic costume that combined Worth's ostentation with Doucet's exquisitely tasteful waistcoat and highly polished boots, as reported in the American trade journal *Women's Wear* in 1912: "The cause [of the excitement] was a Havana brown suit he was wearing, a red vest of the most brilliant hue imaginable, and a brilliant purple tie. This suit, set off with a slouch hat and an attractive cane, made quite a picture. The dashing color was quite in keeping with his originality."[59] Such thematics of originality surface frequently in descriptions of Poiret the man, as well as in reports devoted to his activities in decorative design and couture production. The following quotation from a report published in the *New York Times* in 1913 exemplifies the way in which writers put the concept of originality to work in somewhat contradictory ways, not only to characterize Poiret's production as a couturier but also to downplay his identity as a dressmaker in order to situate him more convincingly in the realm of creative art: "If he had not turned out a dressmaker," the *Times* correspondent remarked, "he would have been an artist, or a musician, or an interior decorator, or a writer of ballads, or an actor. And the amazing truth is that he is all of these things now. . . . Oh, he is original, this many-sided artist. He travels like a comet, in an orbit all his own."[60]

In working to create circumstances that would bring attention to himself and his businesses while nevertheless disdaining obvious and direct forms of publicity, Poiret was, perhaps unconsciously, following the advice offered by contemporary advertising manuals such as Jules Arren's *Comment il faut faire de la publicité* of 1912. As Arren pointed out, publicity was unavoidable. "You hear talk about houses 'that make no publicity': examine any one of them and you will see that it makes it and *cannot avoid doing so*. The merchant most hostile to advertising generally has a shop sporting its name, a *sign*. This is Publicity. . . . He has letterhead paper and envelopes with an indication of prizes won at expositions, perhaps a view of his factories or warehouses: Publicity."[61] There was no sign on the exterior of the Poiret couture house, a stately eighteenth-century *hôtel* renovated for him in 1909 by the young architect, Louis Süe, but after 1910, when Poiret began using an image of the facade drawn by Georges Lepape as a vignette on all his packages (figure 1.18), the building became well known through its representation and circulation in this artistic form of advertising. Poiret's establishment was not located on the rue de la Paix, where the well-established and comparatively traditional couture houses of Worth, Doucet, and Paquin each occupied its own building (figure 1.19), nor was it nearby in the vicinity of the Opéra, but further west, on the avenue d'Antin in the Faubourg St.-Honoré.

Figure 1.18

Georges Lepape, vignette designed for Paul
Poiret packing boxes, 1910. Cliché Bibliothèque
Nationale de France, Paris. © 2002 Artists
Rights Society (ARS), New York/ADAGP,
Paris.

Figure 1.19

G. Agié, photo of the rue de la Paix.

Approached through a formal garden supposedly modeled after those at Versailles, Poiret's distinguished looking, neo-classical building, which once belonged to the Marquise de Thorigny and later housed the pages of Louis XV, was adjoined by two other structures to form a complex that served not only as his home (entered from the rue du Colisée), but also as the headquarters of all his businesses, in which well over 300 people were employed.[62] Nevertheless, Poiret took pains to assure his clients that upon entering his couture house, "[Y]ou will not feel that you are in a shop, but in the studio of an artist, who intends to make of your dresses a portrait and a likeness of yourself."[63] Visitors appreciated not only the interior but the spacious garden setting with its fountains, foliage, and flowers, which distinguished Poiret's palatial couture house from the conventional urban structures of his rivals situated on the more centrally located rue de la Paix.[64] A contemporary observer described the facade of the house, noting the contrast between its calm and noble *ordonnance* and its actual function as a "commercial establishment, and a very prosperous one at that. Yet there is no name in gold letters, large or small, no marble plaque engraved with a name that is famous among *mondaines;* and this is already the first original act of this couturier artist: not to have followed the example of so many others by defiling a superb architecture."[65]

Obviously going to great lengths, and substantial expense, to create publicity that would share the discretion and aesthetic quality characteristic of the *hôtel* that housed his business, Poiret made every effort to present that publicity in a form that would be construed as art. In connection with his move to the avenue d'Antin in 1909, he commissioned graphic artist Paul Iribe to design a change-of-address announcement and Raoul Dufy to make the series of seven colored woodcuts, depicting scenes associated with the activities that took place on the new premises, to adorn his business stationery, with a different page and hence a different scene designated for each day of the week (figure 1.12).[66] Having early on invited artist friends including Bernard Naudin and Bernard Boutet de Monvel to produce several attractive fashion plates for discrete advertisements and tasteful catalogues of his dress designs, in 1908 he approached Iribe with an idea for a truly deluxe publication: a limited-edition album of dress designs (unaccompanied by text) that Poiret intended to present to his best clients.[67] For this project, of which only 250 signed and numbered examples were published, Iribe produced ten plates depicting seventeen gowns, three coats, and seven hairstyles (figure 1.20). Each gown is presented as worn by a standing figure and these, in turn, are informally posed singly or in groups, generally beside pieces of furniture, a painting, or other interior decorations in most cases inspired, like the garments, by the style of the Directoire period. In contrast to the decors rendered exclusively in black and white in a technique evocative of etching and aquatint,

Figure 1.20

Paul Iribe, *Les Robes de Paul Poiret racontées par
Paul Iribe,* plate 3, 1908.

the women and, especially, their garments stand out by virtue of their intense, sometimes brilliant colors, applied in a complex and labor-intensive pochoir process involving the printing of between four and thirteen color templates for each plate. The resulting album, entitled *Les Robes de Paul Poiret racontées par Paul Iribe,* appeared in October 1908 and Poiret proudly announced its impending arrival by writing to his clients, on cards printed to reproduce his own handwriting, "Madame, I have the pleasure of sending you tomorrow an example of an album in which I have gathered some very charming drawings of my dresses by Paul Iribe. The care that I have bestowed upon this publication leads me to hope that it is worthy of your liking and that you will fix your interest upon it."[68] As if to drive home the notion that the album constituted a work of art rather than a mere piece of advertising, Poiret managed to have it exhibited in the Salon d'Automne in 1909.[69] In February 1911, Georges Lepape produced a second deluxe album of pochoirs, *Les Choses de Paul Poiret vues par Georges Lepape* (figure 1.21); 1,000 were printed by the firm of Maciet, located on the rue de la Paix, of which 300 were signed and numbered. Once again, Poiret scarcely treated them as promotional vehicles but, instead, like works of art he offered them for sale at 50 francs each, and he arranged for the original drawings to be exhibited the following month at the Galerie Barbazanges.[70]

In subsequent years Poiret made a point of asking these and other artists and graphic designers to create hand-colored invitations to his parties, decorated programs for those occasions, and advertisements for Martine and Rosine. Professional writers were also enlisted to contribute to other, more conventional promotional materials to which they lent comparable cachet. For the Rosine brochure mentioned above, for example, Roger Boutet de Monvel wrote evocative texts to accompany color photographs of each of the bottled perfumes, which were themselves presented in carefully crafted boxes designed by Martine to hold the hand-painted bottles described in the brochure as individual works of art

Figure 1.21

Georges Lepape, *Les Choses de Paul Poiret vues par Georges Lepape,* plate 6, 1911.

Figure 1.22 ↺

Le Fruit défendu perfume, from *Les Parfums de Rosine.*

especially created to harmonize with the scents they contained (figure 1.22). Excerpts from poems by Baudelaire and Verlaine as well as endorsements by famous actresses reinforced the message that Rosine perfumes were unusual, aestheticized, and glamorous commodities, "the most expensive because [they are] THE BEST," as the text proclaimed of Rosine's "True Eau de Cologne."[71] Many of the contributions to the Rosine brochure also appeared in another of Poiret's promotional vehicles, this one packaged as a 252-page volume entitled *Almanach des lettres et des arts* that was published by Martine—despite the deprivations of war—in 1916.[72] Lacking the sumptuousness of laid papers and pochoir colors that characterized Poiret's prewar publications, the *Almanach* did nevertheless appear in six numbered examples on China paper and twenty-five copies on laid paper, in addition to the commercial edition. Prepared under the direction of André Mary, the text included prose and verse pieces by such well-known figures of the period as Guillaume Apollinaire, Max Jacob, and André Salmon. Raoul Dufy was responsible for the art, which included a dozen original woodcuts of his own (one for each month of the calendar that furnished the *raison d'être* of the publication) and thirty-two illustrations *hors texte* by other artists. The *Almanach* opened with sixteen pages of written and drawn advertisements for Rosine perfumes and closed with fourteen more by artists including Boussingault, Iribe, Laboureur, and Naudin, as well as Dufy, plus two ads for carpets by Martine. A bookmark in the shape of a bottle of Nuit de Chine perfume and two color photographs of other Rosine products were inserted between the pages of the volume, whose back cover included boldly written Chinese characters and the translation, "Nuit de Chine, pleasant perfume." By these means, the advertising function of the project was effectively integrated with its artistic and literary content.

Although Poiret's marketing strategy, designed to attract a wealthy and elite clientele, was distinctive for its luxury and expense, in its disdain for conventional paid publicity, and refusal to appeal directly to the crowd, it paralleled the commercial practices of the most innovative Parisian dealer in advanced art at the time, Daniel-Henry Kahnweiler (figure 1.23). Five years younger than Poiret, Kahnweiler was born in Mannheim in 1884 into a family of wealthy German Jews who trained him for a career in international trade and finance. Although eventually Kahnweiler decided not to remain in the family business, which controlled gold and diamond mines in South Africa, the knowledge he acquired during several years of apprenticeship about the workings of monopoly capitalism and the trade in precious commodities appears to have stood him in good stead after 1907, when financial backing from his uncles enabled him to become an art dealer in Paris. Adapting the practices of the commodity speculators from whom he chose to distance

Figure 1.23 ◯

Photo of Daniel-Henry Kahnweiler in Picasso's
studio, at 11 boulevard de Clichy, 1910. Musée
Picasso, Paris. Photo Réunion des Musées
Nationaux.

himself, as a dealer Kahnweiler exercised strict discipline in building up a
large stock of a particular artist's work at a low price and holding on to it
over the long term, until it would accrue sufficient value to be sold at a
substantial profit. Like Doucet, however, he also appreciated the benefits
to be gained from disguising his business acumen behind a mask of disinterest and disdain. But even more like Poiret, who also chose to distance
himself both physically and spiritually from the established couture houses

on the rue de la Paix, in setting up his gallery Kahnweiler avoided the rue Lafitte and the rue Le Pelletier in the belief that they were "already too old-fashioned and associated with the styles and tastes of the nineteenth century."[73] Instead, he rented a small shop in the neighborhood of the Madeleine, on the rue Vignon. Among his first purchases were works by Kees van Dongen, Henri Matisse, and André Derain, artists with whom Poiret was also associated during the same period. Within five years, however, Kahnweiler signed contracts with Georges Braque and Pablo Picasso to become their exclusive representative; Juan Gris and Fernand Léger signed on a year later, in 1913, making Kahnweiler the commercial representative of artists whom he would succeed in positioning as the canonical figures of cubist art.[74]

Kahnweiler secured the vanguard status of the artists he represented by protecting them from the increasingly obvious commercialism of crowded exhibitions in large public spaces, as Malcolm Gee has pointed out. "D.-H. Kahnweiler actively discouraged his artists from sending to the *salons*," Gee writes. "In an interview in 1927 he denied that he *prohibited* them from doing so—he claimed that they abstained from their own accord, in order to maintain 'une certaine attitude discrète et aristocratique.'"[75] By Kahnweiler's account, the fact that his artists never participated in public exhibitions in Paris—instead of mounting shows, after 1908 he simply hung their pictures at random when the works arrived in the gallery—"shows you the absolute contempt in which we held not only the critics but also the general public."[76] But if the paintings of Braque and Picasso were largely absent from public view in Paris, where the market for cubist paintings was extremely small, works by these artists were easily available to the public abroad. Kahnweiler shipped them out for exhibition in virtually every major city in the West: Amsterdam, Berlin, Bremen, Budapest, Cologne, Düsseldorf, Edinburgh, Frankfurt, London, Liverpool, Moscow, Munich, New York, Prague, St. Petersburg, Stockholm, and Zürich in 1912 and 1913 alone.[77] In addition to working with dealers and critics to show works by his artists abroad, including Alfred Flechtheim in Germany and Roger Fry and Clive Bell in England, Kahnweiler made a point of providing foreign journals and other publishers of all sorts with photographs of paintings by the artists he represented, reminding editors to credit his gallery as the source of the images.[78] He also employed a professional photographer to record his artists' work systematically, making it even easier to disseminate abroad—in reproduction as well as in its original form.

The dichotomous nature of Kahnweiler's practice, characterized by resistance to the crowd at home while embracing it abroad, suggests that Kahnweiler, like Poiret, was caught in the web of contradictions that united elite and popular culture, the private and the public spheres. To become recognizable as a movement, and therefore marketable as a style, cubism, like fashion, required not only adherents, but audiences and avenues of dissemination. It might be argued that Kahnweiler's success as a dealer and his ability to establish an elite position for Picasso and Braque depended in part not only on an active foreign market for their work, but also on the broader appeal and ready visibility at home of those whom David Cottington has called the salon cubists: Henri Le Fauconnier, Albert Gleizes, Jean Metzinger, and their circle. These artists regularly exhibited in Paris at the Salon d'Automne, the Salon des Indépendants, and other public venues. Moreover, in contrast to the steadfast silence of Kahnweiler's artists—the so-called gallery cubists—the salon cubists published numerous books and articles in an effort to explain cubism to the diverse audiences that frequented those public exhibition sites.[79]

Lacking contractual arrangements with a private dealer like Kahnweiler, who supported Braque and Picasso even though there were scarcely any buyers for their work on the Paris art market, Le Fauconnier, Gleizes, Metzinger, Robert Delaunay, and, until 1913, Léger were compelled to create an audience for themselves in the public domain of the officially sanctioned salons and in smaller exhibitions of their own devising. The annual exhibitions of the traditionally oriented Salon des Artistes Français and the Société Nationale des Beaux-Arts, as well as those of the more progressive Salon des Indépendants, had grown steadily over the course of the late nineteenth century to the point where the Indépendants routinely displayed several thousand paintings and sculptures.[80] By the early twentieth century, when the increasing incoherence of the jury-free Salon des Indépendants led to the creation of the juried Salon d'Automne, it had become almost impossible for young or emerging artists to assure that their works would be seen to any advantage by discerning critics, not to mention the others who visited such huge exhibitions. Occasionally, however, the committee of artists responsible for installing the works might recognize a relationship between the submissions of artists with shared interests and consequently show their work in proximity to one another, as happened at the Salon d'Automne of 1910 to paintings by Gleizes, Metzinger, and Le Fauconnier, enabling the artists themselves as well as a few discerning critics to appreciate certain features the painters had in common. It was at this same exhibition, according to Gleizes, that these artists, as well as Delaunay and Léger, discovered one another in a meaningful way, and also "understood what affinities brought us together. The benefit of spending time together, to exchange ideas, to unite [*de faire bloc*] seemed crucial."[81] A desire to assure that such group solidarity would be repeated and even enhanced at the Salon des Indépendants the following spring helps to explain the rationale for the successful attempt by Gleizes, Metzinger, Le Fauconnier, Delaunay, and Léger to influence the rules as well as the selection of the hanging committee in the days leading up to the opening of the salon. Gleizes later recalled how their thinking developed: "Metzinger, Le Fauconnier, Delaunay, Léger and I had decided to enter the next Salon des Indépendants. But how would we be placed? In all likelihood we would be dispersed to the four corners of the salon and the effect produced on the public by a harmonious movement would be lost." Accordingly, the five young painters took it upon themselves to submit an alternate roster of candidates for the hanging committee, artists whom they could count on to be sympathetic to their cause (many of them represented in Poiret's collection): "We had a list of candidates among which we were of course included, but drawn up with care and a sense of fairness. On this list were André Lhote, [André Dunoyer de] Segonzac, [Roger de] La Fresnaye, Berthold Mahn, Jean Marchand and other painters whom we knew more or less but who seemed to us capable of representing if not a tendency then at least a value." After a tumultuous general meeting and a vote with many irregularities, the group of younger painters had their way. This enabled Gleizes, Metzinger, Le Fauconnier, and Léger to place their work together with that of Marie Laurencin in Salle 41, and in an adjacent room hang works by their associates, André Dunoyer de Segonzac, André Lhote, Roger de La Fresnaye, and Luc-Albert Moreau (again, artists whose work Poiret bought around this time; he was on particularly close terms with Dunoyer de Segonzac, Lhote, and Moreau). The impact on critics and guests invited to the opening was immediate and explosive, as Gleizes described: "We were, in sum, violently attacked by the old guard of the critics, while the young critics, those of our generation, accepted us in principle." [82] Thus, by ensuring the cohesion of their presentation, the salon cubists managed to establish their group identity as a movement in the public eye. Indeed, Gleizes claimed not only that the appellation "cubism" dated from the opening of the 1911 Salon des Indépendants but that, at the time, "Braque and Picasso were never called cubists"; instead the epithet was at first reserved for the painters of Salle 41. Only later was it applied more broadly, to "those who appeared more or less to come close to them, in form if not in spirit."[83] The point to be emphasized is not the efficacy or possible accuracy of Gleizes's claim, but the fact that he felt justified in making it. As far as he was concerned, cubism was first established as a movement in the public domain; the gallery cubism of Braque and Picasso was another matter.

It appears, in fact, that Gleizes had a point: the salon cubists did have an impact on the perception of gallery cubism when that began to take on a profile of its own in the popular domain. As Pierre Assouline has noted of the salon cubists' exhibition at the Salon des Indépendants the following year, "The brouhaha raised by the cubists at the salon in April 1912 had the happy result that for the first time ever a popular newspaper sent a reporter to investigate [Kahnweiler's] notorious gallery on the rue Vignon where such strange experiments were being conducted." The resulting article, which appeared in *Je Sais Tout* on April 15, 1912, was, Assouline asserts, "enormously important to the history of the gallery, its artists, and the promotion of their works."[84] Clearly, the public response to the work of Gleizes, Metzinger, and their circle in 1911 and 1912 (see, for example, figure 1.24) drew crucially important critical attention to Kahnweiler's alternative model of cubism (exemplified by figure 1.25). Ultimately, Kahnweiler established his cubism as the original, true or essential version—*haut cubisme,* one might call it—in contrast to the works that were shown in the salons and other public exhibition venues in prewar Paris: works that not only Kahnweiler but Picasso and Braque apparently regarded as pastiches or copies of the genuine article, as paintings made for public consumption rather than private contemplation.

Where Gleizes and Metzinger courted critical attention, Kahnweiler tried to shield his artists from it. Where they proudly, even jealously, laid claim to the cubist label, defending it as if it were not simply a stylistic epithet but a commercial trademark, Kahnweiler rejected the term on behalf of his artists. Kahnweiler professed himself to be so concerned about how cubism was represented in the local press that he discouraged journalists working for French publications from writing about his artists because, he said, ill-informed articles would only compound public misunderstanding and ridicule of the works. When, in response to the public's scandalized reaction to the cubist paintings shown at the Salon des Indépendants in

Figure 1.24 ☉

Albert Gleizes, *Man on a Balcony (Portrait of
Dr. Morinand),* 1912.

1912, the correspondent from *Je Sais Tout* appeared at his gallery and
inquired about the other cubists exhibiting there, Kahnweiler responded
by distancing his artists from the cubist label, which he considered to have
been debased by its association with artists interested primarily in publicity. "Sir," he said to the reporter, "I know that there exist 'cubists' or
rather people who for love of publicity pretend to be so named. My
painters are not cubists." When the correspondent reminded Kahnweiler
that his purpose in seeking information was simply to enlighten readers of

Je Sais Tout, the dealer continued to resist. "I would prefer that your magazine not speak of my painters. I don't want anyone to try to ridicule them. My painters, who are also my friends, are sincere people, earnest searchers, in a word, artists. They are not these showmen who pass their time stirring up the crowd."[85]

Kahnweiler clearly drew a distinction between those whom he considered to be mere showmen, who consciously addressed themselves to an audience, and sincere artists, who refused to engage with anything that might smack of theatrical or promotional techniques. But it seems at least

Figure 1.25

Pablo Picasso, *Daniel-Henry Kahnweiler,* 1910.

plausible to suppose that Kahnweiler himself was posturing as he articulated this position, given the fact that he assiduously wooed audiences and publicity for his artists abroad. Moreover, one notices a peculiarly self-satisfied, elitist tone in his description of the opening of his gallery in 1907, for which, Kahnweiler recalled, he avoided both advertising and the courting of publicity: "There was nothing—no publicity campaigns, no cocktail parties, nothing at all. And I'll tell you something even stranger: I didn't spend a cent on publicity before 1914, not one cent. I didn't even put announcements in the papers; I didn't do anything."[86] Martha Ward has shown that the practice of shunning the public salons in favor of private exhibition venues was pioneered by the Impressionists and other private exhibiting societies, as well as certain dealers active in the second half of the nineteenth century.[87] Kahnweiler adopted their strategic use of the private sphere, but where the Impressionists' exhibition spaces, according to Ward, had been decorated as harmonious ensembles and designed to evoke the intimacy of the feminized, domestic interior, Kahnweiler's gallery was installed in a manner that marked it as a masculine space. Purposely distinguishing his gallery from the overcrowded venues of the officially sanctioned salons, as well as from the ornately furnished, palm-bedecked interiors of other art dealers, Kahnweiler used plain sackcloth on the walls and otherwise made no special effort to call attention to the interior decoration of his gallery. The space must nevertheless have been striking for its simplicity and for its conspicuous departure from customary practice.

Kahnweiler's marketing strategy clearly emanated from the dealer's desire to ensure that works by his stable of artists would be available only to a small, well-informed and self-selected circle of critics and collectors in a private atmosphere visibly divorced from the domestic environment of the middle-class home.[88] His gallery thus staked out a terrain distinctly different not only from traditional salon displays, but also from Poiret's couture house, a quasi-domestic commercial environment in which the couturier and his family lived; there, art and interior design functioned both to mask and to promote the business purpose of Poiret's principal enterprise: selling clothes. Unlike the anti-decorative, anonymous, and male-oriented environment of Kahnweiler's gallery, or the apparent informality and eclecticism of the dealer's private apartment where period photographs show that in rooms decorated with striped wallpaper and sturdy wood furniture, African sculptures were displayed alongside French cubist and other vanguard paintings,[89] in Poiret's couture house the carefully composed and harmoniously orchestrated salons and fitting rooms embraced the feminine sphere of up-to-date bourgeois domesticity so that his dresses could be marketed as products of an all-embracing aesthetic attitude, part of what we might call a totally designed "life style," rather than as a miscellaneous collection of mere commodities. Despite the fact that this was a place of business, Poiret's couture house was so private that a visit to the dressmaker could even be described in metaphorical terms as a pilgrimage to a mysterious, sacred space: "After having passed through a vestibule decorated in an appealing stone, we came to an initial reception room, but not without having satisfied administrative formalities that already drove home the seriousness of our course, the importance of the favor that admission to so closed and well guarded a sanctuary confers on the profane."[90] The neo-classical interiors, inspired by the recently revived Directoire style, that Louis Süe designed for Poiret were intended to evoke French design traditions, although their intense colors and relatively sparse furnishings imparted distinctly modern overtones, as suggested by one of Georges Lepape's plates from his album, *Les Choses de Paul Poiret vues par Georges Lepape* (figure 1.26), and by a description of the couture house dating from 1912:

> The walls [of one of the salons on the ground floor], decorated with panels of Nile green, are enriched by frames threaded with dark green and antiqued gold. On the floor, a raspberry-colored carpet,

Figure 1.26

Georges Lepape, *Les Choses de Paul Poiret vues par Georges Lepape,* plate 2, 1911.

on the windows, taffeta curtains in the same tone. The very clear opposition of these two colors, the one neutral and the other hot, produced a bizarre atmosphere, at once soft and vibrant, and which must harmonize happily with the fresh and buoyant colors from which Poiret likes to take his effects.

The furniture belongs to that delicious Directoire period that recalls the scarcely vanished graces of the Louis XVI era, and does not yet do more than presage the severe correction of the Empire. The chairs, covered in strawberry and green striped velvet, correspond to the general tonality, while here and there oriental embroideries and marquetries play and change lustre.[91]

Thus the public rooms of the couture house were clearly created with contemporary design principles in mind. These were set pieces that would allow Poiret's controversial fashions to look reasonable, not disjunctive, outrageous, or threatening, as they reportedly did when seen on the street, and presumably also in interiors not specifically crafted to enhance the allure of women wearing his garments. According to an account of Poiret's dresses and the supporting interior decoration of the couture house written in 1911, "One sees these gowns in a modern setting whose furniture design and coloring reflect the same aesthetic tendencies. The paintings offer the same vivaciousness of color, the drawings the same rather delicate simplicity of outline."[92]

This last comment was made by Paul Cornu, a writer and friend of Poiret (both were founders of a gastronomic club, La Compagnie du Verre de Vin, in 1913), who was librarian of the Union Centrale des Arts Décoratifs in Paris. His lengthy article devoted to Poiret's dresses appeared not in a women's magazine devoted to fashion, but in *Art et Décoration,* a respected journal devoted to fine art and high-end decorative arts. Appropriately for that venue, Cornu's essay focused attention on the art quotient of Poiret's dresses, as even the title ("L'Art de la robe") made clear. Not only did Cornu draw parallels between Poiret's designs and the work of contemporary painters and designers, his text was illustrated throughout with numerous ink drawings made for the purpose by Georges Lepape (figure 1.27), and with several images lifted from Lepape's recently published album, *Les Robes de Paul Poiret vues par Georges Lepape.* In addition, the article featured thirteen photographs (two of them in color) of Poiret's mannequins posed in his couture house, the first fashion

L'ART DE LA ROBE

Figure 1.27

Georges Lepape, illustration for Paul Cornu,
"L'Art de la robe," from *Art et Décoration,* 1911.

photographs taken by Edward Steichen, who went on to become one of the most prominent fashion photographers of the twentieth century (figures 1.28 and 1.29). Like Lepape's images and like Paul Iribe's earlier album for Poiret, Steichen's photographs functioned to confound art and commerce. His pictorialist-inspired, soft-focus style endowed the images with an aura of aestheticism and undermined the fashion photograph's potential for conveying detailed information about the clothes they represented. We may never know if the selection of Steichen as photographer was motivated by a desire to secure images that would defy the pirating of new dress designs, which at the time was often associated with the circulation of fashion photographs of mannequins wearing the latest styles to the races at the beginning of each season. On the other hand, Steichen himself may have sought deliberately to distance even his fashion-related work from the businesslike, sharply focused photographs of the front and back of new models that eventually came into widespread use as records for the purposes of registration and design protection. What is clear in any case is that the blurred images Steichen produced of Poiret's models directed attention away from any strictly commercial purpose and, instead, aligned these fashion photographs with the art discourses that characterized Poiret's approach to the commercial dimensions of his activities.

Throughout the teens, Poiret pursued a complex, seemingly contradictory strategy of embracing fashion while simultaneously attempting to hold it at bay. An article published in *Harper's Bazar* in 1913 described him as a creator of clothing, interior decorations, and perfumes who was "ahead of his time," but immediately qualified that characterization in terms that reveal a great deal about how Poiret negotiated the conflicting demands of fashion for both avant-garde innovation and a degree of adherence to accepted conventions sufficient to make his designs attractive to a wide range of clients. Thus, the *Harper's Bazar* article continued, Poiret "is never so far ahead as to be out of reach. His ideas, new, fearless,

Figure 1.28 ☙

Edward Steichen, "Battick" and "Négus,"
costumes by Paul Poiret, from *Art et
Décoration,* 1911.

Figure 1.29 ↺

Edward Steichen, "Bakou" and "Pâtre,"
costumes by Paul Poiret, from *Art et
Décoration,* 1911.

and individual, nevertheless always contain an element which makes them valuable to the woman of to-day [*sic*], no matter where she be or how she be situated."[93] Indeed, Poiret recognized that from a certain perspective fashion itself could become a problem, not only for the couturier who alienates potential clients by identifying his or her work too closely with risqué designs or transgressive new styles, but also for the woman who sacrifices taste and restraint in an effort to make a distinctive fashion statement. For example, he repeatedly expressed disdain for women who followed fashion slavishly rather than dressing in a manner appropriate to their individual needs. He also argued that dresses should be characterized by simple lines and architectural construction rather than "all sorts of draperies and furbelows" in the belief that "the woman should be the dominant note, and not the gown." To bring these points home, he told a story about the actor Coquelin who modestly appeared in public with a small boutonniere in his lapel: "Someone asked him why he did not wear a larger one and he replied: 'Were I to wear a large ribbon everyone would see it. As it is now, some will notice it.' "[94] Thus, while Poiret repeatedly sought to create circumstances that would call attention to himself and to his gowns, the very novelty of which would attract attention in any case, he also understood that anything smacking of garishness or ostentation might signal an absence of taste that could compromise his ambition to establish himself and his designs at the pinnacle of elite culture. His attitude thus seems perfectly to capture the dialectical workings of the logic of fashion, which requires a carefully calibrated oscillation not only between novelty and tradition, but between distinction and conformity, the quest for visibility and the determination not to be seen. A striking similarity can be drawn with his practice as an art collector, for, as Poiret recalled in 1934, although he had purchased works by avant-garde artists, "The rest [of my collection] was composed of sure values, because I was always a prudent pioneer."[95]

Many of Poiret's rivals at the high end of the couture business also recognized the dangers inherent in unqualified and continual embrace of the new. They too were committed to a rhetoric that construed fashion not as superficial, decorative, and fleeting, but as something deeper, more meaningful, and enduring. This was the sense that Henry Bidou imparted to the notion of *bon ton* in the opening essay of the *Gazette du Bon Ton,* a deluxe monthly journal sponsored by seven of the most important French couturiers of the pre-World War I period, including Doucet, Paquin, and Worth, as well as Poiret. Devoted—according to its subtitle—to "*arts, modes et frivolités,*" and initiated in 1912, the same year as several other high-end fashion journals inspired by luxurious late eighteenth- and early nineteenth-century fashion publications,[96] the *Gazette du Bon Ton* took off where Poiret's two deluxe albums left off. Instead of the photographs (primarily in black and white but occasionally in color) that were increasingly used to present new couture clothes in the pages of more popularly oriented journals and women's magazines, the *Gazette du Bon Ton* was illustrated with pochoir plates of women's clothing and accessories by artists in Poiret's orbit, including not only the creators of his albums, Paul Iribe and Georges Lepape, but also Bernard Boutet de Monvel, Georges Barbier, and André Marty, among others (figure 1.30).[97] Setting the tone of the publication in its inaugural issue, Bidou wrote, "In order to be of *bon ton,* it is not enough to be elegant. One can be elegant in a hundred ways and even scandalously: *le bon ton* is the same for everyone. Elegance changes; *le bon ton* does not vary; the former follows fashion, the latter follows taste."[98] Reserved, discrete, simple, and refined, a person of *bon ton,* Bidou suggested, avoids ostentation and, while prizing beauty, does not wish to be noticed. Above all, *le bon ton* was a signifier of social distinction, an almost ineffable quality that could be recognized but was difficult to describe; constructed in discourse but impossible to define or contain in any particular object, it was a matter of style and taste rather

LE CONSEILLER DES DAMES

Robe et Manteau pour le Théâtre

Figure 1.30 ◌

Georges Barbier, "Le Conseiller des Dames,"
from *Gazette du Bon Ton*, plate 5, 1913.

than a particular object of manufacture or possession. Like a refined product of aristocratic breeding, *le bon ton* could be acquired by inheritance
but it could not be bought.

The journal itself, embodying the collaboration of couturiers and
graphic artists under the direction of Lucien Vogel (former art director of
Femina and editor-in-chief of *Art et Décoration*), was conceived and produced as a work of art, printed in a custom-designed typeface on handmade vellum paper; every issue included seven plates *hors texte,* each
presenting a new fashion creation by one of the sponsoring couturiers, as

well as original designs by three of the graphic artists associated with the journal. Thus, every element of the journal was designed to please the eye. The pochoir illustrations in particular were presented not simply as renditions of existing or imagined garments but as "veritable portraits of dresses, painted and drawn by the most subtle artists of our time."[99] The *Gazette du Bon Ton* thus embodied Poiret's strategic and rhetorical alignment of contemporary fashion and art under the sign of late eighteenth- and early nineteenth-century French design traditions. His identification with the publication was reinforced when, during the summer of 1914, he hosted a dinner party in the garden of his couture house to celebrate the first eighteen months of its existence, an event recorded in another article by Henry Bidou accompanied by drawings by André Marty. Here again Bidou stressed the enduring nature of transitory fashion, whose memory survives even when tumultuous historical events have been forgotten: "It is no small thing to have given shape to one's century," he wrote. "The whole world has forgotten the war of the Austrian succession, the upsetting of alliances, the diplomacy of Louis XV and the minister Choiseul. But everyone remembers hoop dresses. There must have been some profound reason for this choice of events made by public memory. Fashion which changes each month is the only thing that will endure."[100]

These ideas linking fashion's ephemerality (reinforced and institutionalized, it is worth noting, by the regular, seasonal presentation of new couture models) to the timelessness of art clearly recall the terms in which Charles Baudelaire had written of fashion more than fifty years earlier in "The Painter of Modern Life."[101] Ostensibly devoted to the work of Constantin Guys, the essay might best be described as a paean to contemporary experience in which Baudelaire sings the praises of an artist who rejects academic history painting in favor of "that indefinable something we may be allowed to call 'modernity', for want of a better term to express the idea in question."[102] But while embracing the fleeting moment of modernity, the artist is compelled simultaneously and in the same sources to seek what only appears to be its opposite, that which endures through time: "The aim for him is to extract from fashion the poetry that resides in its historical envelope, to distill the eternal from the transitory."[103] For Baudelaire, Guys' work exemplifies and embodies a theory of art in which fashion, contemporaneity, and that which is circumstantial form a necessary and essential complement to the eternal and unchanging aspect of beauty: "Beauty is made up, on the one hand, of an element that is eternal and invariable, though to determine how much of it there is is extremely difficult, and, on the other, of a relative circumstantial element, which we may like to call, successively or at one and the same time, contemporaneity, fashion, morality, passion. Without this second element, which is like the amusing, teasing, appetite-whetting coating of the divine cake, the first element would be indigestible, tasteless, unadapted and inappropriate to human nature."[104] Although Baudelaire does not use *le bon ton* to characterize the posture of Guys' subjects to the world described in his drawings and watercolors sketched from contemporary life, there is an unmistakable affinity between what Baudelaire writes of Guys, "a man of the world" who "loves mixing with the crowds, loves being incognito, and carries his originality to the point of modesty,"[105] and the qualities of *le bon ton* adumbrated by Bidou: "*Le bon ton* is not at all stiff, and yet it loves reserve. It is never dull, but still it is discrete. It is never flashy, and yet it is free. An innate grace serves as its talisman: guided by it, everything is permissible, and it would never cease to be charming without ceasing to be itself. It has an air of being very simple, and this simplicity is refined. It takes centuries to create it. . . . Ingenious in its inventions, it does not want to be noticed; it has a sense of that which is graceful and beautiful, but a horror of ostentation; it is witty: witty in its drawing, as in the lively arrangement of colors; and it is because it is witty that it seems at ease."[106] This description of *le bon ton* comes remarkably close to what Baudelaire wrote, not so much about Guys as about the related figure of the dandy, for whom, he noted, "perfection in dress consists in absolute simplicity, which is, indeed, the best way of being distinguished."[107] And although the dandy described by Baudelaire—wealthy and blasé, discerning and original, yet always self-effacing—is a man, not a woman, he nevertheless conjures the type of person whom the *Gazette du Bon Ton* might claim as its ideal audience: "These beings have no other status but that of cultivating the idea of beauty in their own persons, of satisfying their passions, of feeling and thinking. Thus they possess, to their hearts' content, and to a vast degree, both time and money, without which fantasy, reduced to the state of ephemeral reverie, can scarcely be translated into action."[108] Wealthy enough to afford a journal costing 10 francs per issue (but only available by subscription at 100 francs per year for ten issues) readers of the *Gazette du Bon Ton* and similar expensive, deluxe publications of the pre–World War I period were in a position to obtain their clothes from the most expensive couture houses in Paris. In both contexts—the high-end fashion journal and the elite *maison de couture*—they were encouraged to appreciate the discursive construction of fashion as fine art in terms comparable to those laid out by Baudelaire fifty years before: "Fashion must therefore be thought of as a symptom of the taste for the ideal that floats on the surface of the human brain, above all the coarse, earthy and disgusting things that life according to nature accumulates, as a sublime distortion of nature, or rather as a permanent and constantly renewed effort to reform nature. For this reason, it has been judiciously observed (though without discovering the cause) that all fashions are charming, or rather relatively charming, each one being a new striving, more or less well conceived, after beauty, an approximate statement of an ideal, the desire for which constantly teases the unsatisfied human mind."[109]

Two

Theater and the Spectacle of Fashion

If it was Paul Poiret's goal in his multifarious enterprises to collapse the distinction between fashion and fine art, he set about doing so not only by assiduously collecting contemporary art and repeatedly presenting himself as an artist, but also by operating in an artfully conceived environment where the clothes he designed were displayed in proximity to the works of art exhibited on-site in the Galerie Barbazanges, and all the components of his business empire—from the couture house stationery and publicity photographs to the luxurious and imaginative perfume packaging—worked together to mask the commercial character of his interlocking activities. In this sense, as in many others explored in this chapter, Poiret self-consciously staged his performance as a couturier, designer, art collector, party-giver, and entrepreneur. Poiret himself has been described as a highly theatrical figure and the theater, in turn, was a prominent feature of all his activities. After the First World War, when he briefly ran a small theater called L'Oasis in the garden of his couture house, Poiret admitted to a reporter that he had always nurtured an interest in the theater: "When I was young I dreamed of becoming an actor, of having the crowd in front of me."[1] Toward the end of his life when his career as a couturier had already been eclipsed, Poiret did attempt a few theatrical and film roles, although these were minor efforts that paled in comparison to the performative and theatrical dimensions of his activities as a businessman. The theater was, in fact, a driving force of the commercial imperative that Poiret as well as his colleagues in the couture industry all pursued; this is an important—if sometimes overlooked—aspect of their commitment to the integration of art and fashion, and to the union of these spheres of activity with the theater in the early years of the twentieth century.

Historians of modern art have typically focused on the avant-garde theater, ballet, or film as principal sites of artistic intervention and modernist collaboration in the performing arts. The work of well-known painters on costume and set designs for the Ballets Russes and Ballets Suédois has been studied in some detail, and the same is true of avant-garde artists' contributions to modernist films and Dada theatrical performances. Remaining relatively unexplored, however, are the more popular productions, such as those in which Poiret and his couturier colleagues participated as costume designers before the First World War, as well as the theatrical tropes that permeated haute couture and fashion in general at that time. These emerge here as equally valuable cultural tools for understanding period discourses such as Orientalism, and for exposing the deeper, structural relations between art and fashion that this study aims to explore.

In the modern period the connections between fashion and theater are multiple, encompassing not simply the design of costumes for the stage, or the dramatic potential of fashion shows, or even the performative aspect of wearing clothes, but also the exploitation of the "star" system for the purpose of launching new clothing styles.[2] The familiar commodity tie-ins that during the 1930s repeatedly enlisted Hollywood movie stars in the promotion of consumer products to female audiences of films were already operational, although in somewhat less sophisticated form, in the early twentieth-century French theater. Indeed, a parallel exists between the advertising purpose behind the Hollywood movie industry's strategic positioning of domestic furnishings, kitchen items, clothing, and cosmetics on the screen in visual or narrative proximity to a star actress and the ubiquitous presence in early twentieth-century French theater and fashion magazines of famous stage actresses featured in full-length portrait photographs. These photographs were accompanied in each case by a prominent caption identifying not only the actress and the title of the dramatic production in which she starred, but the designer of the dress she wore and, in some instances, that couturier's business address (figure 2.1). Without clearcut evidence that these latter images were to be understood either as advertising on the one hand or as visual support for editorial copy on the other, they functioned ambiguously, and perhaps for that reason especially effectively, to convey the impression that the stars were "endorsing their favourite couturiers' clothes and encouraging readers to follow suit."[3] If in such circumstances the actress appeared to be making an independent decision about which clothes she chose to wear on stage, there were others in which her role was merely that of a mannequin, a living fashion model, in a dramatic production that amounted to little more than a convenient vehicle for promoting a couturier's commercial interests.

Charles Eckert has described how the star system functioned like a well-oiled machine in 1930s Hollywood, where commodity tie-ins were often formative influences on the development of a movie script.[4] Something very close to this was already becoming commonplace in Paris theaters in the 1910s, when couturiers collaborated in the presentation of plays about couture houses, mannequins, and dresses, recognizing these as ideal opportunities to parade their latest styles before audiences made up

Mlle Vermeil, du « Théâtre des Bouffes-Parisiens »
Création de la Maison Paquin

Figure 2.1

Photo of Mademoiselle Vermeil of the Théâtre
des Bouffes-Parisiens in a costume by Jeanne
Paquin, from *Comoedia Illustré,* 1910.

in large part of wealthy bourgeois women who were said to patronize the theater simply because it satisfied their desire to see the latest styles modeled in a spectacular and, therefore, compelling context. According to Marie Monceau, reporting on French couture in the *Philadelphia Inquirer* in 1912, ". . . the theatres which have anything new to offer are well patronized, regardles [*sic*] of whether the play is a success or not. It is the dresses that are of vital interest."[5] Robert Forrest Wilson remarked some years later that providing the costumes for what he described as "Parisian society plays" was an expensive undertaking that required couturiers to offer special designs and discounted prices to the theaters, but the costs could be assigned to the advertising account, "for the *couturier's* name appears on the program, and it is regarded as good business."[6] Sometimes the couturier extended his or her promotional practices beyond the stage and into the audience, as Poiret clearly did when he allowed his mannequins to wear his latest creations to the theater. The graphic artist and designer Erté described one particularly scandalous event that occurred shortly after he began working for Poiret as a dress designer in January 1913: Through one of Poiret's mannequins whom he was accompanying to a particularly fashionable dress rehearsal (of Henry Bataille's *Le Phalène,* with stage sets by Paul Iribe, at the Théâtre de la Renaissance), Erté "managed to get hold of the most extravagant dress in the whole collection, together with a fantastic ermine-and-red-velvet coat, which I believe was called 'Eminence'. I wore the dress and coat, with a red velvet turban (no wig), long red gloves, and huge earrings."[7] Far from annoyance or embarrassment at this potentially outrageous act of crossdressing, Poiret was apparently pleased by Erté's ostentation, presumably because it garnered quite a lot of attention for his couture creations in Parisian newspapers.

Like every other couturier of the period, Poiret appears to have been anxious to have his designs circulate in elite venues under the most advantageous conditions and, therefore, as Charles Castle has pointed out, he and his colleagues often dressed actresses and other well-known women "for no payment whatsoever, and in return [those women] were seen wearing the clothes at Longchamps, the Opéra, or on stage."[8] Thus the theater and the disparate spaces related to it were sites of considerable commercial and promotional significance for couturiers, who assiduously cultivated their connections with female stars by providing the clothes they wore in public or by occasionally employing them to promote the couturiers' perfume lines. Poiret drew on the thematics of his perfume, *Le Fruit défendu,* as the inspiration for part of the decorative ensemble that, through Atelier Martine, he provided for the interior of the Paris home of the actress Spinelly. As suggested by a photograph of Spinelly playing the role of Eve and seemingly biting the forbidden fruit from a tree painted on the wall of her salon, the private, domestic interior became a theatrical space in which she, a star dressed provocatively in a halter top and skirt designed by Poiret, enacted the erotic deployment of his fruit-scented perfume (figure 2.2).[9] If Poiret could be described as having here used his interlocking business enterprises to transform Spinelly from an actress and client who consumed his products into a mannequin who promoted them, the reverse was also possible: mannequins could be described as actresses insofar as they had to adopt a different demeanor—play a new role—with each new dress they modeled. According to the author and critic Arsène Alexandre, "Everything about them and their profession recalls the theater." Most telling, in his estimation, was the acting required of a mannequin to effect the sale of a garment: the mannequin had not only to adopt behavior appropriate to each gown she modeled, she also had to convince the buyer that the buyer, in turn, would look and act the same way if she were to wear the same clothing. "Just as in the theater we think, when one of the characters pronounces a beautiful speech or accomplishes a sublime action, simply: 'That's how I would do it in her place;' so, fascinated by the ease of the young woman who turns and twirls around before the client, playing the role of her dress of the moment, the client says to herself all of a sudden: 'That suits my kind of beauty exactly.'"[10]

Many contemporaries realized that the parallels between the operations of a couture house and those of the theater revealed a great deal about the nature of the couture enterprise, but it was Alexandre who, in his 1902 study of the needle trades, took the analogy the farthest. Like the couture house, where relatively small showrooms belied the presence behind the scenes of vast premises where hundreds of women worked, in the theater, Alexandre pointed out, the stage and the seating areas often

Figure 2.2 ↻

Delphi, "Mademoiselle Spinelly préfère le 'Fruit
Défendu,'" from *Les Parfums de Rosine.*

added up to no more than a quarter of the space given over to the back-stage preparation of the spectacle. Alexandre also compared the rhythm of the fashion seasons with those of the theater, drawing an analogy between the cycle of winter and summer fashion presentations on one hand and the repetitions of a two-act play on the other; he also noted that, like each theater, each couture house had its own repertoire, its own signature style.[11]

Writing in 1927 about the rue de la Paix, which by then had become virtually synonymous with the couture houses that lined the street and were the source of its cachet, Paul Reboux described the evolution of the mannequin who in the nineteenth century had been an ordinary couture-house employee and modeled dresses simply to help buyers decide whether to acquire them. "Since then," Reboux observed, "presentations by mannequins have acquired a kind of theatrical pageantry. The people to whom one shows a collection are seated as they would be for a theater performance [*spectacle*]. Sometimes at the rear there is a small stage to which stairs give access. The curtain rises. The fashion show begins."[12] As costume historian James Laver has remarked, the theatricalization process accelerated in the early twentieth century, when "mannequin parades of the fashionable dressmakers became themselves fashionable occasions, which had certainly never happened before in the whole history of dress. People went to a fashion parade as their fathers had gone to a play or to a private view of pictures. They expected a luxurious *décor,* soft lights, music, a procession of beautiful mannequins, and, what is even more important, they expected something startlingly new and original in the clothes presented before their eyes."[13] Laver's comments echo those of a *New York Times* correspondent who remarked in 1911 that putting a display of fashions on stage "is surely the most dramatic way of showing off splendid gowns that has ever been invented. . . . [Such a spectacle] is something well worth going to see, even if one does not buy the gown."[14]

Given the importance of the theatrical spectacle in the rituals atten-
dant upon the sale of women's clothing, it is not surprising that Paul
Poiret required his architect, Louis Süe, to include a stage for the presentation of fashion shows in the artful environment Süe created for the interior of Poiret's couture house when he renovated the building in 1909.
Several preliminary drawings survive to provide a sense of how Süe initially conceived the project, presumably influenced by the work of the
Viennese architect and designer, Josef Hoffmann, whose most impressive
design, the Palais Stoclet, was nearing completion in Brussels, where Süe
finished a villa project of his own in 1911. Not only does the Palais Stoclet
include a rectangular theater or music room with an elevated stage at one
end, making it similar in certain fundamental respects to one of the interiors Süe designed for Poiret, but the geometric motifs and graphic style
that Süe used in his preliminary drawings were clearly indebted to
Hoffmann's formal vocabulary and distinctive draughtsmanship. Thus
the decorative roundels that Süe envisioned for the ceiling of the so-called
salle fraîche, a light-filled rectangular interior with floor-to-ceiling windows on the two longer walls and a small stage at the far end (figure 2.3),
bear a striking resemblance in terms of both their circular form and the
manner in which they were rendered to Hoffmann's treatment of the
theater/music room ceiling in his preliminary drawing of that space (figure 2.4). Similarly, Susan Day has pointed out the correspondences of
style and decorative motif between Hoffmann's design for the vestibule of
the Palais Stoclet and Süe's project for a salon in which a full proscenium
stage is visible at the rear (figure 2.5).[15] There are no photographs indicating that either of these particular designs for Poiret were eventually realized by Süe, but a little theater does appear to have been created in the
couture house. A drawing by Pierre Brissaud, published in *Femina* in
February 1911 of the theater of an unidentified *grand couturier* (figure 2.6),
shows an elegant interior in a simplified neo-classical style that can be
identified as Poiret's ground floor salon (its rectangular shape and the

Figure 2.3

Louis Süe, sketch for the "Salle fraîche" in the
couture house of Paul Poiret, 1909.

location of windows are comparable to the elements represented in Süe's
two drawings). The striped chairs in which clients are shown to be seated
correspond to period descriptions of the furnishings in Poiret's couture
house, and the mannequins visible in the foreground as well as on the
stage in the distance wear high-waisted columnar-style gowns constructed
from multilayered sheaths like those Poiret was showing at the time. The
caption accompanying this image in *Femina* indicates that such settings—
introducing a theatrical stage into the heart of the couture house—were
being widely adopted by important French couturiers: "In imitation of

Figure 2.4

Josef Hoffmann, design for the music and
theater room, Palais Stoclet.

their American colleagues, most of the great Parisian couturiers have now
installed in their *hôtels* a real theater stage, on which mannequins, dressed
in the latest modish creations, can turn at their ease to show to best advantage the thousand and one little details of the gown being introduced. . . .
Streams of light, artistically calculated, inundate the scene and play off
one another in the mirrors that decorate the room; seated at an appropriate distance and in a propitious daylight, the clients can proceed . . . with
the choice of what attracts them. Clients, couturiers and mannequins all
praise this innovation . . ."[16]

Although this text suggests that the couture house stage originated
in North America, it was more likely pioneered in London, where, apparently around the turn of the century, the couturière Lucile, also known as

Lady Duff Gordon, made an effort to develop "the social side of choosing clothes, of serving tea and imitating the setting of a drawing-room."[17] Like Poiret, Lucile was anxious to avoid the crassness associated with obvious merchandise promotions and recalled in her memoirs that she decided not only to treat her presentations like a private tea party in a domestic setting but to combine that concept with "the idea of a mannequin parade, which would be as entertaining to watch as a play." Accordingly, she built a miniature stage hung with chiffon curtains at one end of the showroom in her shop on Hanover Square, and hired an orchestra to play music while her mannequins paraded in gowns listed in a printed program. "Then I

Figure 2.5

Louis Süe, sketch for a "salon de présentation,"
couture house of Paul Poiret, 1909.

Figure 2.6

Pierre Brissaud, "The Theater of the Great
Couturier," from *Femina,* 1911.

sent out the invitations on dainty little cards, keeping the illusion that I was inviting my friends to some afternoon party rather than to a place of business." The strategy of imitating polite culture proved to be an instant entrepreneurial success: Lucile's showroom was crowded with customers and orders "flowed in by the dozen, so that the saleswomen could hardly cope with them."

Drawing upon Lady Duff Gordon's memoirs published in 1932, Joel Kaplan and Sheila Stowell have recently called attention to the ways in which, as Lucile, she used the trappings of the stage "to establish a voyeuristic bond between mannequin and spectator." They point out that her mannequin parades were intended for both male and female audiences:

> The complex eroticism of her spectacles—working-class women dressed as society ladies promenading silently before audiences of middle- and upper-class men—was further augmented by Lucile's decision to replace the numbers by which gowns had hitherto been identified with suggestive titles like "Passion's Thrall," "Do You Love Me?," and "A Frenzied Song of Amorous Things." Beginning with a series of simple walk-abouts called collectively "Gowns of Emotion," such displays soon took the form of thematic pageants. The most elaborate had texts prepared by Lucile's sister, society novelist Elinor Glyn. The series culminated in 1909 . . . with the ambitious *Seven Ages of Woman,* a stage piece in seven acts tracing from birth to death the dress-cycle of a society dame.[18]

Just as the couture house, whether in London or Paris, began at this time to mimic the theater, so the theater put the couture house on stage.[19] Titles of plays such as *My Lady's Dress, Les Midinettes* (the French term for a young dressmaker or milliner), *Le Mannequin,* and *Rue de la Paix* provide only the most readily identifiable examples of an interest in women's clothing that pervaded both dramatic and popular theater. Although many traditionally staged plays, including those mentioned above, used couture or millinery houses as a narrative frame, couture and couturiers were even more prevalent in the context of the popular revue, which, Jeffrey Weiss has pointed out, was composed of a sequence of numerous, often unrelated, short satirical scenes that generated humor by commenting on current events or contemporary culture.[20] As Robert Dreyfus noted in 1909 in his history of this theatrical genre, the nature of the revue had changed a great deal since the 1860s: "The text had a constantly diminishing importance in comparison with the magnificence of the '*mise en scène.*' And, gradually, the revue distanced itself from the satirical intent of the old vaudeville theater in order to come close to pure fantasy, or to lose itself in what Parisian nomenclature calls the 'women's theatrical play [*la 'pièce à femmes*'].'"[21] *Kill That Fly!,* which played in January 1913 at the Alhambra Theatre in London, was one of many revues that took on the subject of contemporary fashion in order to appeal especially to females in the audience. It featured a scene with a French title, "Robes et modes," in which the principal character was named Lucille, the supporting character was a mannequin, and these two were accompanied by a corps of eight additional mannequins. Nine months later, in October 1913, the Alhambra staged another revue, *Keep Smiling,* in which a scene entitled "Fashions" contrasted a character identified as "Early Victorian" with eight "Ultra Moderns" clothed in designs that were clearly inspired by the latest couture dresses. Also showing in London in October 1913 was an English version of a farce that originally premiered in France, called *This Way, Madam!,* about a handsome and attractive dressmaker in the rue de la Paix whose clients patronized his couture house "only for the satisfaction of having [their dresses] fitted by this incomparable Adonis, who . . . rules over the establishment and its customers like a very autocrat. . . ." A critic for *The Bystander* noted that in *This Way, Madam!,* "ladies have the opportunity of studying all the very latest things in Parisian gowns. There is also a practical demonstration included in the programme of how at least one of these gowns should be put on—but we haven't got a photograph of that part of the performance."[22] Another commentator pointed out that the mannequin displays might help draw audiences for the play—but on the other hand, they might not: "The ladies will certainly want to go and see those frocks; but their husbands may try to dissuade them from visiting the theatre for fear they should come home with over-exalted ideas as to what they really must have in the way of morning and evening gowns. Some of the figures quoted to the customers as the price of the lovely goods exhibited made me gasp."[23] Here is ready evidence that the presentation of contemporary fashions in the context of a theatrical spectacle could have a direct impact on the sale of expensive couture dresses; the clothes were not only offered for visual delectation but their prices might be advertised in the course of the dramatic performance.

As in England, so in France popular theaters were engaged with fashion, an issue presented through both drama and satire. In a play of 1912 entitled *La Petite Jasmin* by Willy and Georges Docquois, two of the three acts took place in a couture house that was also a *salon de thé*. The modernism of the establishment, run by Madame Jasmin, was conveyed by the sets, which were said to have been inspired by Max Reinhardt's staging of a play at the Théâtre du Vaudeville the previous year. Striking in their simplicity, the sets for *La Petite Jasmin* were described by one commentator as neither realist nor photographic but "synthetic" in the sense that "a small desk suggests an office; a wooden mannequin and some fabric the couturier's salon."[24] Reviewing the play, a columnist for *Comoedia Illustré* imagined a not-too-distant future when a couture house showing dresses and furs would add to those functions a tea salon as well as an art gallery (as Poiret had already done) and, in the evening, a show accompanied by supper: "In the evening, during the intermissions, do you think our beautiful women would recoil from the temptation of a fur exhibited in the foyer, or of jewelry artistically presented in a vitrine designed for art? At the end of a cheerful supper, purchases would be made over champagne. It would be charming and new."[25] By calling such a possibility "very Parisian" but also "very Yankee," this reviewer implied that a marketing strategy operating on so many levels simultaneously would almost automatically be associated with American entrepreneurial practices; in fact, however, the reviewer's description of such a multifaceted couture business evokes the many intersecting enterprises Poiret pursued at his headquarters in Paris. (It also comes remarkably close to Poiret's vision for reviving his dress business after World War I, when he opened a nightclub called L'Oasis—he later transformed it into the theater of the same name—on the grounds of his *maison de couture*.) Indeed, Poiret was such a pervasive presence on the stage that, in 1911, a theater critic complained about a revue scene set in Poiret's couture house (entitled "Chez le grand couturier," see figure 2.7): Jean Dulac, bored with what he described as a stale subject, observed that it had already been "served up to the public a thousand times in all the revues."[26] Several

Figure 2.7 ↻

"Chez le grand couturier," in "Vlan! Revue en
2 actes et 7 tableaux de MM Rip et Bousquet,"
from *Comoedia Illustré*, 1911.

LA SUPPLIANTE   LE MAITRE

Figure 2.8

Jean Dulac, "The Suppliant [and] the Master,"
from *Comoedia Illustré,* 1911.

months earlier, in response to another revue, *Avec le sourire,* Dulac had caricatured Poiret as "Le Maître" before whom three women dressed in what were clearly examples of his most recent designs bowed down in supplication (figure 2.8).[27] No doubt Poiret profited from his notoriety, as Lucile must have done, too, for as Marcel Serano wrote in 1913 of those who were satirized, "it is always publicity for the victims."[28]

It should be obvious that the theatricalization of Poiret's fashion house presentations around 1910 was related to his engagement with actual theater productions, whether as a member of the audience, as a designer of theatrical costumes, or as the humorous subject of satirical revues. It is also very likely that Poiret was responding to the challenge presented by Lucile, who must have been an increasingly visible competitor after 1911, the year in which she opened a branch of her business nearby on the rue de Penthièvre in Paris. Not only did Poiret apparently follow her lead in exploiting a number of scenic props and theatrical practices, he too adopted evocative titles for his dresses, as he did for example in Spring 1911, when among the names he selected were "Bakou," "Caucase," "Magyar," and "Byzance," all references to Eastern Europe and Russia, areas he would tour with his mannequins in October–November of the same year.[29] Although Poiret must have been aware of the heightened political tensions in the region that would lead to the First and Second Balkan Wars in 1912 and 1913, it is difficult to imagine that his clients would have wanted to signal complex international politics in the clothing they wore. But given the rising prominence of Eastern Europe in current affairs, it does seem plausible that some of the associations suggested by Poiret's titles would have resonated with the contemporaneity of his designs to underscore the Orientalist references that characterized his clothes throughout the pre–World War I period. By the same token, the titles as well as the Orientalist outfits he introduced in 1911 must have conjured up associations with historical traditions in French painting, for example with the work of Ingres, Delacroix, and the host of other artists identified with Orientalist subjects and aesthetics during the nineteenth and early twentieth centuries.[30]

The practice of naming his models imparted a symbolic, potentially dramatic dimension to Poiret's fashion presentations and was presumably intended in part to suggest that each gown was a unique and highly aestheticized creation, an evocative work of art; nevertheless, assigning such titles may also have had a straightforward commercial dimension for him and other couturiers who shared this practice. Unlike the numbers that were ordinarily used to identify individual dresses, these names could presumably have been registered, perhaps even copyrighted, a formality that might have made them useful tools in protecting against the pirating of styles that plagued couturiers and dressmakers in Europe and the United States.[31] That a desire to protect his designs as valuable intellectual property might account in part for Poiret's assignment of evocative names to his garments is suggested by an article, entitled "They Steal Styles and Numbers," published in the *New York Times* in 1914. Lamenting the piracy of designs for sale at prices substantially below those attached to authentic versions emanating from the couture houses, the *Times* columnist noted that the problem went beyond the stealing of styles; copyists also used the same numbers on their pirated garments as those used by the originators of the stolen styles: "This has led at least one well-known manufacturer to use names for his important models instead of numbers. These names are copyrighted."[32] Thus, if Poiret responded to Lucile's theatricality in general, and to her use of evocative titles with narrative connotations in particular, his own mobilization of these practices was, like hers, probably motivated by artistic aspirations that cannot be fully understood if they are isolated from the couturier's economic interests.

Having apparently learned a lesson or two about the theatricalization of fashion presentation from Lucile, Poiret quickly outstripped his English source of inspiration. For example, both he and Lucile used the gardens of their couture houses as well as the theaters in their salons as backdrops for their fashion shows (figures 2.9, 2.10, and 2.11); however, only Poiret seized upon the outdoor setting as an opportunity to film his mannequins in motion. The resulting film (now lost) made it possible for Poiret to take his fashion show on the road, even when he could not afford to have all the mannequins travel with him. But the garden functioned not only as a film set, it was also a backdrop for at least one of the highly theatrical and wildly extravagant costume parties Poiret staged, and in which he performed the starring role. These *fêtes,* modern versions of ancien régime masquerade balls, were widely reported in the Parisian press and enthusiastically copied in high social circles. As such, they provided yet another, extremely effective, if unconventional, form of publicity for Poiret's diverse business operations. Poiret's vociferous denials that advertising or self-promotion had anything to do with his parties seem only to

Figure 2.9 ᴐ

Henri Manuel, promenade of mannequins in
the garden of Paul Poiret's couture house, from
L'Illustration, 1910.

prove this point: "Naturally there have been people who have said that I
gave these fêtes as an item of advertisement, but I want to destroy this
insinuation, which can only have originated in stupidity."[33] Whatever
their creator's intention, these affairs contributed significantly to Poiret's
widespread renown and, upon closer scrutiny, their many strong links to
his commercial interests, as well as to his engagement with the theater,
become readily apparent. Here, entertainment became the pretext for

exploring the overlapping territories not only of fashion and theater, but also of Orientalism, gender identities, and the character of French national traditions.

The most famous of Poiret's extravagant parties, to which he gave the title "The Thousand and Second Night," was a fantasy based on the tales of *The Arabian Nights* that came to life on the evening of 24 June 1911. For that occasion, Poiret and his wife required their 300 guests (mostly artists and patrons of the arts) to dress up in "Oriental" costumes

Figure 2.10

Henri Manuel, mannequins modeling outfits in
the garden of Paul Poiret's couture house, Paris,
from *L'Illustration,* 1910.

Figure 2.11　⊃

Henri Manuel, half-turn of mannequins in
front of a trellis portico, from *L'Illustration,* 1910.

(figures 2.12 and 2.13). Those who failed to do so were refused entry, unless
they were willing to outfit themselves on the spot in Persian-style clothes
that Poiret had designed "according to authentic documents."[34] Thus,
Poiret used the occasion of an extraordinarily sumptuous party to demand
that everyone in his circle accept the controversial features of his latest
couture creations, including the so-called *jupe-culotte* and harem trousers
(figure 2.14) which dominated his spring 1911 collection of women's
clothes introduced early that year, probably in response to the impact of
Léon Bakst's designs for the Ballets Russes production of *Schéhérazade,*
which Poiret, who regularly attended the theater and other prominent cultural venues in Paris, had seen when it premiered there on 4 June 1910
(figure 2.15).

Although Poiret always resisted any suggestion that he was indebted to the Ballets Russes for his introduction to "Oriental" styles of dress,[35] and there is evidence to support the contention that he arrived independently at an interest in the tales of *The Arabian Nights,* particularly Schéhérazade (the female character who plays a central role in the tales, especially in the opening sequence),[36] Bakst's costumes and stage designs had indeed been hugely influential.[37] Bakst himself noted in a letter to his wife written after the public dress rehearsal of *Schéhérazade* that "the

Figure 2.12

Thousand and Second Night Party at the couture house of Paul Poiret, 24 June 1911.

103

Figure 2.13

Thousand and Second Night Party at the
couture house of Paul Poiret, 24 June 1911.

whole of Paris now dresses in 'Oriental' clothes."[38] As Alexander Schouvaloff has pointed out, "At the time, everything east of Suez was called
'Oriental,' but *Schéhérazade* was not the real Orient. It was a Russian idea
of an Orient as seen by the French, and they were taken in by it because
they had not seen anything like it on stage before. There was, after all,
nothing new about the Orient as such—it had been more or less in
fashion since the time of Delacroix—but everything was new about
Schéhérazade."[39] Schouvaloff makes an important distinction between the
familiar, if malleable, French construction of the Oriental "Other" and

Figure 2.14 ☉

Paul Poiret, sultana skirts for the interior, from
L'Illustration, 1911.

Figure 2.15

Léon Bakst, "La Sultane," costume for
Shéhérazade, from *L'Illustration,* 1927.

the highly original conception of every aspect of the Ballets Russes production of *Schéhérazade,* including the inspiration of Rimsky-Korsakov's
music in Russian folk traditions, the primitivist choreography by Folkine,
and the dazzling colors of Bakst's sets and costumes. These innovations
helped to revitalize what was, in fact, a long tradition of French interest in
the Orient, not only the particular geographical locale of Napoleon's con-
quest in 1792, but also the fantasy image of a more generalized exotic East
that French writers and artists developed from the eighteenth century forward. According to Ian Richard Netton, the European Enlightenment

idea of the Orient had initially been shaped by fear of the Ottoman Empire's potential threat and an aversion to its alien nature as much as by a fascination with its exotic cultural manifestations.[40] Gradually, however, as Peter Wollen has noted, drawing upon the work of Edward Said and Perry Anderson, the Orient became "the site of scientific and political fantasy, displaced from the body politic of the west itself, a field of free play for shamelessly paranoid constructions, dreamlike elaborations of western traumas. In the nineteenth century, the Orient became more and more the site for erotic as well as political projection. Rather than fear, it was fearful desire that was now projected on to the screen."[41]

Far from a static formulation, the French idea of the Oriental "Other" was open to constant change and reinterpretation, a fact that is clearly supported by even a brief examination of the very different versions of Schéhérazade's stories made available in two French translations of *The Arabian Nights,* the first by Antoine Galland, published in twelve volumes between 1704 and 1717, and the second by Dr. Joseph Charles Mardrus in his sixteen-volume *Livre des milles nuits et une nuit,* which appeared two centuries later, between 1899 and 1904.

The stories of *The Arabian Nights* have been traced at least as far back as the tenth century but, according to Robert Irwin, some version of them existed even earlier than that and, although they began to be codified in a fifteenth-century manuscript, other stories were added to the original corpus during the next 400 years.[42] The tales, which feed directly into Western fantasies of Oriental violence and eroticism, begin with a King Shahariyar's discovery that his wife had been unfaithful and his subsequent decision to punish her with nothing less than execution. Thereafter, to prevent further marital infidelity, Shahariyar took a new wife to bed each evening and had her executed the following morning. This horrific scenario repeated itself until the vizier's daughter, Schéhérazade, volunteered to become the king's wife. After she was deflowered by Shahariyar, Schéhérazade found a way to tell a long story which she left unfinished in the morning so that, in order to hear its completion the next evening, the king had to postpone her execution until the following day. On each ensuing night Schéhérazade rehearsed the same strategy, telling one story after another, breaking each one off before it was finished, until, after 1,001 nights, she had borne two children and the king decided to remove the threat of her execution.

When Antoine Galland created the first European translation of the story of Shahariyar, Schéhérazade, and the 1,001 nights it took to tell her tales, he apparently relied on numerous sources, only some of which have been identified, and, as was customary at the time, he took many liberties with the principal manuscript upon which he probably based his version. Aiming to make the stories and their Oriental setting not only comprehensible but acceptable to his French audience, Galland often substituted familiar images for ones that might be strange or foreign, and he exercised modesty and a sense of good taste where he determined that the original text might have shocked a French reader. For example, he suggested the splendor of princely Arabian palaces through descriptions of columned facades that, as Sylvette Larzul has pointed out, "evoke French classical architecture more than that of medieval Islam,"[43] and the original manuscript's profusely detailed descriptions of the beautiful garden of paradise are replaced in Galland's translation by what amounts to a park *à la française*, comparable to those at Sceaux or Versailles.[44] Careful not to refer directly to the harem, which would eventually become a widespread and profusely embellished Western image of Oriental sexual availability, Galland avoided any mention of polygamy and in the first several volumes of his translation he systematically replaced the term for "concubine" with that for "slave."[45] According to Irwin, "Galland's decorous aim in translating the *Nights* was not so much to transcribe accurately the real texture of medieval Arab prose, as to rescue from it items which he judged would please the salons of eighteenth-century France. Therefore, the barbarous and the overly exotic were toned down or edited out. The gallant and the pleasing were stressed or inserted."[46] Nearly two centuries later, when Mardrus offered another translation of *The Arabian Nights,* the Ottoman Empire was no longer perceived as a serious threat to European power and references to Oriental sexual practices had lost their original political import. Claiming to have corrected Galland's liberties, Mardrus suggested that his was a literal translation of the tales but, in fact, he too made significant adaptations: "Mardrus embroidered the original Arabic and inserted whole new stories. Many of Mardrus's interpolations were erotic ones, for he shared [English translator Sir Richard] Burton's unspoken conviction that the *Nights* was not dirty enough and he seems to have thought that the stories would be improved if the erotic element in them could be heightened."[47] Working in the context of a continuously evolving Western colonialist fascination with Oriental sensuality, sexuality, and brute force, and responding as well to the Symbolist literary environment in which he circulated in late nineteenth-century Paris, Mardrus produced a translation that was in many respects at the other end of the Orientalist spectrum from Galland's rendition; it was, according to Irwin, "a belated product of *fin-de-siècle* taste, a portrait of a fantasy Orient, compounded of opium reveries, jewelled dissipation, lost paradises, melancholy opulence and odalisques pining in gilded cages."[48] It was precisely such a hot-house vision of the East on which the Ballets Russes relied and on which Mardrus' friend Poiret drew in creating the scenario for his "Thousand and Second Night."[49]

Poiret later recalled that the idea of staging the *fête* had first occurred to him after "returning from a Bal des Quat' Z'Arts, in the month of May 1911, I think." The Bal des Quat' Z'Arts was a massive affair organized each year on a different theme by the students of the École des Beaux-Arts; although it was attended primarily by students, professors, other artists, and their guests, at least some of the 4,000 tickets reportedly available were sold to the public; in any case, Poiret was apparently a regular attendee. For the 1911 ball, which took Babylon as its theme, Poiret outfitted himself in the theatrical costume he had originally designed for the famous tragedian, Edouard de Max, to wear in *Nabuchodonosor,* a one-act play about the Chaldean king written by Maurice de Faramond that premiered in Paris at the Théâtre des Arts on 30 January 1911, with costumes by Poiret and sets by the painter, André Dunoyer de Segonzac (figure 2.16).[50] At the time, the Théâtre des Arts was run by Jacques Rouché, formerly publisher of *La Grande Revue,* a literary journal for which, in May 1909, Poiret (using the pseudonym Al. Terego, a pun—on the term "alter ego"—of the sort that Duchamp would later exploit in signing his ready-

Figure 2.16

Nabuchodonosor, Act I, from *Le Théâtre,* 1911.

mades) wrote a short piece entitled, "Les Opinions de Monsieur Pétrone." This story, told in the first person, involves Al. Terego in an interview with a fictional couturier, Jean Pétrone, who ardently argues for principles of fashion etiquette that coincided with Poiret's views on the subject. These were characterized by disdain for the conventional approach to fashion that encouraged ostentatious displays of jewelry or clothing and induced women to copy new styles worn by others, regardless of their appropriateness, rather than wear simple, elegant clothes that expressed a respect for the enduring values of taste and decorum.[51] That these ideas about fashion would have been of interest to Rouché becomes comprehensible in light of the theater director's comparable approach to the integration of modern art and stage design, which stressed "simplification of decor by choosing the plastic elements necessary to each scene and disposing them in a manner most appropriate for creating the desired atmosphere; stylization and complete harmony between decor and costume; the rejection of *trompe l'oeil* [realism] and the desire to leave to the frame only the charm of the composition and of the color."[52] To achieve these goals, Rouché made a point of hiring contemporary painters and designers to create the sets and costumes for his plays, as Dunoyer de Segonzac and Poiret did for *Nabuchodonosor*.

Press accounts of *Nabuchodonosor*'s premiere describe impressive scenery that seems, in the extant photographs, to have been somewhat at odds with Rouché's commitment to stylization and simplification. It takes a leap of faith for today's audiences to appreciate the novel design features of what appears to be a clichéd and ultimately racist representation of Oriental splendor in the tradition that included, for example, colonial villages constructed both to educate and to entertain western visitors to the universal expositions mounted in Paris and other European cities in the second half of the nineteenth century.[53] Like the evocation of a timeless past in those theatricalized models, Dunoyer de Segonzac's set evoked an immense columned hall of Nabuchodonosor's Babylonian palace decorated with a frieze of leopards and griffins, gold and silver sculptures including a colossal statue of Baal-Hammon, god of the sun, as well as sumptuous tapestries and tripods containing burning incense and myrrh. In the midst of this splendor, Nabuchodonosor (wearing what might be described as a feminized costume with a long, flowing robe superimposed by multiple strands of beaded jewelry) and his favorite, Uamma, were surrounded by concubines, black slaves, and eunuchs, and joined by a young dancer, played by Natacha Trouhanova (figure 2.17). Maurice de Faramond's stage instructions offer stock imagery familiar from generations of formulaic French Orientalist paintings (Delacroix's *Death of Sardanapalus*, 1827, is an example of the genre at its best) of disempowered men and sexually available women in their call for creating "the impression of an orgy. Half nude slaves serve drinks. Most of the gen-

Figure 2.17   ↻

Natacha Trouhanova in *Nabuchodonosor,* from *Femina,* 1911.

erals and ministers are drunk. Several of them recline on carpets. The women there are asleep."[54] According to the artist and theater critic, A.-E. Marty, the staging was "one of the most magnificent things ever seen. In a décor of sober and grandiose lines, of powerful colors that reveal A[ndré Dunoyer] de Segonzac to be a great colorist, the couturier Paul Poiret realized an ensemble of costumes of unimaginable sumptuosity and tonal beauty. When, in the midst of the greens, yellows and oranges, de Max entered, covered in a coat of somber purple, all the artists [in the audience] trembled in admiration."[55] Later that year, the designs for sets and costumes received another, more official stamp of aesthetic and cultural approval: they were exhibited at the Salon d'Automne, where, in effect, they assumed the status of works of art.[56]

In his memoirs, Poiret recalled that in *Nabuchodonosor* de Max wore the first theatrical costume the couturier had ever made. "It was an immense cloak that I had specially dyed to a tint which must have been that of the Tyrian purple. It was heightened with great strips of gold braid and on the head of the king . . . there was a monumental tiara, weighing thirteen pounds. . . . This tiara was conceived like a piece of goldsmith's work; it seemed as if sculpted in virgin gold, and was crowned with belfries, turrets and minarets [figure 2.18]. It was this costume I had borrowed to go to the Quat' Z'Arts Ball."[57] For that occasion, Poiret himself played the role of Nabuchodonosor, "his chariot pulled by slaves costumed in green and blue . . . his head covered by a magnificent tiara of gold, stones and jewels, and behind him came gamboling his entire cavalry of soldiers armed with lances, chariots of war and of triumph."[58] Such descriptions of the Bal des Quat' Z'Arts, when read alongside the reviews of *Nabuchodonosor,* make clear the degree to which both spectacles participated in the Orientalizing theatrics that received new impetus from the Ballets Russes,[59] and also functioned as dress rehearsals for Poiret's next performance, "The Thousand and Second Night," where he once again recreated himself as a sexually charged Oriental potentate.

Figure 2.18 ↻

Edouard de Max in costume for
Nabuchodonosor, from *Comoedia Illustré,* 1911.

Indeed, "The Thousand and Second Night" enabled not just Poiret
but also his art-world guests—male and female—to act out another fantastic evocation of the Orient, this time staged like an extravagant fashion
show, a theatrical performance on the grounds of his *maison de couture.* As
Poiret later wrote, "My house was closed [off] by tapestries, in such [a way]
that glances from the street could not penetrate. The guests were received
as in a theatre by a squad of old gentlemen in evening dress . . . [who] most
carefully screened the arrivals," to ensure that no one would "disfigure the
ensemble of the fête."[60] Georges Lepape's recollections highlight the overlapping racial and sexual dimensions of the clothes on display when "six
Negroes, black as ebony, nude to the waist and wearing bouffant culottes
in Veronese green, lemon yellow, orange, and vermilion chiffon"[61] sum-
moned guests to follow them through the house, past salons strewn with
multicolored pillows, until they came upon a professional actor, "the great

tragedian De Max . . . [who] told stories taken from the *Thousand and One Nights.*"[62] In the garden, where Persian carpets were spread on the lawn, Poiret was seated under a canopy painted by Raoul Dufy, who had also created the hand-printed, delicately colored program made for the occasion, which was inspired by Persian miniatures and included a short but evocative text by Dr. Mardrus, translator of the tales that functioned as the pretext for the evening's entertainments (figure 2.19).[63]

Figure 2.19

Raoul Dufy, program design for Thousand and Second Night Party, 24 June 1911.

Easily dominating this extravagant scene and commanding the attention of his supporting cast, Poiret played the role not necessarily of Nabuchodonosor but at least of a similarly despotic sultan, holding an ivory-handled whip in one hand and a scimitar in the other, while his concubines presumably cowered at his feet (figure 2.20). Guests were brought to him in order, he said, to "make their obeisance according to the tradition of Islam."[64] After his favorite, played by his wife Denise, and her maids of honor were released from their golden cage and while drinks of all sorts were being served, a series of spectacles was performed by acrobats, a pythoness, a monkey merchant, and several exotic dancers, including Natacha Trouhanova, who presumably performed a version of her *Nabuchodonosor* role (figure 2.21). As Peter Wollen has noted, the event "firmly established Poiret's reputation as *Le Magnifique,* after Suleiman the Magnificent. From then on, alongside the all-pervasive influence of the Russian Ballet, the Oriental look dominated the fashion world and the decorative arts."[65] In fact, Poiret's "Thousand and Second Night" soon became the model for parties thrown by some of the most prominent figures of the wealthy elite: during the summer of 1912, the magazine *Femina* filled several pages as well as one of its covers with photographs of the *fête Orientale* hosted by Countess Blanche de Clermont-Tonnerre (figures 2.22 and 2.23), and of the guests who attended Countess Aynard de Chabrillan's *Bal des mille et une nuits* (figures 2.24 and 2.25) in Orientalist outfits that featured the feathered turbans and lampshade dresses worn by Poiret's wife and ordered by the guests at his fête the year before (figure 2.26).[66]

Even as it was becoming the pinnacle of fashion, however, the Oriental mode, particularly the harem dress, or *jupe-culotte,* pioneered by Poiret in early 1911 and from then on closely associated with his couture signature, proved to be extremely controversial on two related accounts. First, it threatened to confuse traditional sexual roles by putting women in trousers;[67] and second, its racially marked exoticism was regarded by many as literally foreign to traditional French sartorial taste. The billow-

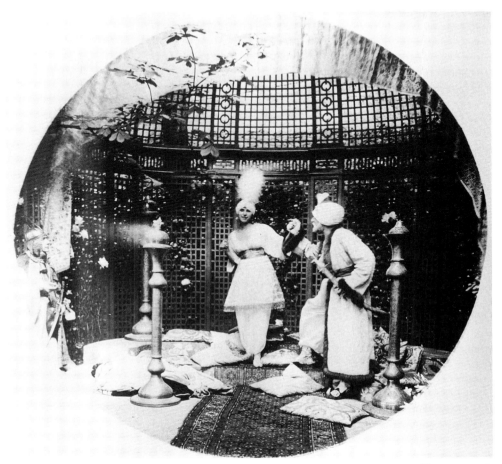

Figure 2.20

Henri Manuel, photo of Paul and Denise
Poiret at the Thousand and Second Night
Party, 24 June 1911.

Figure 2.21

"A Persian fête at the home of a great
couturier," from *Femina,* 1911.

ing form of such garments—ballooning trousers tied tightly at the ankles
and often partially concealed by an overdress or smock of variable length
(see figure 2.14)—was not only identified with a racial "Other," it had also
been associated since the mid-nineteenth century with dress reforms proposed in the context of feminist movements that sought to expand bourgeois women's roles beyond the domestic sphere circumscribed by
marriage and childcare. After 1880, French women gained access to state-
sponsored secondary education and subsequently began to enter the job
market in areas that had traditionally been restricted to men. Their potential mobility and independence, whether they wore culottes or not, were
increasingly perceived as a threat to the traditional social structure based
upon the sexual division of labor and a conventional role for women
within the confines of the family rather than out in the public domain.

Around the turn of the century, the image of a culotte- or trouser-clad woman on a bicycle circulated widely on posters and in cartoons where this *femme nouvelle* was often represented as a muscular, cigarette-smoking androgyne. Comparable suggestions of sexual inversion were at work in the Oriental costumes that Bakst designed for the Ballets Russes, and not only because women wore trousers; men's clothing could also challenge conventional gender categories. For example, in *Schéhérazade*, Nijinsky wore billowing trousers and a brassiere-like top supported at the

Figure 2.22

An Oriental fête at the home of the Comtesse
de Clermont-Tonnerre, from *Femina*, 1912.

Figure 2.23

An Oriental fête at the home of the Comtesse
de Clermont-Tonnerre, from *Femina*, 1912.

shoulders and decorated at the midriff by strands of pearls; as represented
in a gouache by Georges Lepape, the jewel bedecked dancer—apparently
meant to be leaping, though his pose initially suggests that he is reclining
on the bed of pillows behind him—might easily be mistaken for a
woman, an Oriental odalisque.[68]

The *jupe-culotte*'s distinct but certainly not unrelated threats of sexual inversion on one hand and racialized, foreign exoticism on the other
converged in the views of many Parisian commentators; in an article cast
as an interview with a man named Boissonnot, Aline Raymonde, publisher of *La Mode Illustrée,* repeated the clichés used to condemn what she

Figure 2.24

The Thousand and One Nights Ball at the
home of Madame A. de Chabrillan, from
Femina, 1912.

LES INVITÉS DE MME AYNARD DE CHABRILLAN

Figure 2.25

The Guests of Madame Aynard de Chabrillan,
in *Femina*, 1912.

Figure 2.26

Henri Manuel, photo of Madame Poiret
dressed to attend the Thousand and Second
Night Party, 24 June 1911.

described as this "bizarre silhouette." Raymonde quoted Boissonnot's opinion that the *jupe-pantalon* (a version of *jupe-culotte* in which there was an attempt to reconcile billowing trousers with a more conventional women's garment silhouette[69]) "marked a terrible development for traditional morality by attacking a kind of personal propriety, respected until now [even] by the most audacious. . . . The adepts of the *jupe-pantalon* envision something other than to charm or surprise. They represent the desire to break with the traditions of their sex, of their race, of their country. They want to break the last chains holding back their complete emancipation. They claim from men parity of costume, as well as all other equalities. . . . So much for feminism. Now, in their bouffant trousers, a vague reminiscence of the odalisque, of the Persian woman, of the Jewess. . . . So much for showy foreign adventurism [*rastaquouerisme*]."[70] The anxieties provoked by sartorial challenges to traditional gender roles, racial and national identities that characterize this statement, which smacks of racism and anti-Semitism as well as anti-feminism, have a history that can be traced to the beginnings of widespread Western European trade with, and travel in, Turkey in the early eighteenth century, as Marjorie Garber has observed in her discussion of Orientalist cross-dressing.[71] She suggests, moreover, that "questions of gender and of nationalism . . . [have often been] addressed, if not resolved, through a recourse to cultural 'otherness' as represented by the intervening figure of the phantom 'Oriental,' the woman in Turkish trousers."[72] In Paris in 1911, the Oriental mode that Poiret chose to champion was the subject of just such an ideologically charged debate in the pages of widely circulating journals such as *L'Illustration* where, on February 18, Poiret's luxurious *jupes-sultanes* (as his culottes and billowing trousers were called on this occasion, presumably to reinforce their Oriental associations) were contrasted with a distinctly western version of the style designed by the house of Bechoff-David (figure 2.27). Poiret's models, in satin or other light fabrics in tender colors, were defended as "outfits for the interior, for dining, for

Models wearing *jupes-sultanes* designed by Paul
Poiret (top and left) and *jupes-culottes* adapted
for the street by Bechoff-David (right and bottom
right and left), from *L'Illustration*, 1911.

the evening [*toilettes d'intérieur, de dîner, de soirée*]," intended to be worn in the private sphere of the elegant domestic interior, not out in public. In contrast, Bechoff-David's designs were photographed on women who were shown crossing the street and promenading down a sidewalk in broad daylight. Furthermore, it was noted, virtually all the top couturiers, including Drecoll, Redfern, even Doucet, were prepared to sell bouffant or straight pantalons to those clients who wished to wear them.[73] Where Poiret's *jupes-culottes* or *jupes-sultanes* made explicit references to the fabled Orient with their supple silk fabrics, embroidered ribbons, and associated turban headgear, the *jupes-culottes* and pantalons by other couturiers were adaptations of manifestly western dress designs, conventional in fabric and cut except at the legs. Bechoff-David's models were accompanied by broad-brimmed, low-slung hats that could have been designed to accessorize any conventional dress or outfit of the period. These latter costumes clearly offended traditional values because, unlike Poiret's *jupes-culottes* designed as evening wear for private occasions, they were meant to allow women in something like trousers to move freely and participate actively in everyday life on the street. So current was the controversy these clothes aroused that a week later *L'Illustration* published a caricature of such fashions on its cover in which two young women were shown at the Auteil racecourse wearing a version of *jupes-culottes* which gave them so much freedom of movement that they made fools of themselves by racing, like the horses they had come to see, past a crowd of more reasonably dressed spectators in the background (figure 2.28). Poiret deliberately avoided the liberal political implications, particularly the suffragist associations, of such clothing: "In our democratic times," he told the *Miroir des Modes,* "when everything is measured according to the banality of the masses, women who understand the *jupe-pantalon* would not dare put it on out of fear for what people might say. However, we wouldn't dream of adapting it to ordinary usage. Our outfits for the street, suits and dresses, are of such sobriety, such perfect correctness, that they pass by entirely unnoticed. My personal pleasure leads me to dress only women who have

Figure 2.28 ↻

L. Sabattier, *The Races at Auteil,* from
L'Illustration, 1911.

attained a degree of erudition and grace sufficient to wear my outfits in the
context of their aristocratic homes [*leur sied*]. There are residences of such
an artistic cachet, so individual, so far above the crowd, that my clothes
seem to complete the harmony in them. Because these milieux represent
the elite of the art, it is to them that one should orient oneself."[74]
Elsewhere, too, Poiret defended the *jupe-culotte* primarily in class terms,
arguing that it "will not be popularized, that it will remain a possession of

the 'chic' woman with delicate joints, small feet, rich enough to encircle her ankles with precious bracelets incrusted with rare stones. Instead of 'masculinizing' the woman, this severely criticized costume is intended to show her in all the harmony of her form and all the freedom of her native suppleness."[75] Having unleashed what Garber has characterized as the potential of the Orientalist costume to disrupt racial, gender, and class categories, and thereby to destabilize the larger social codes by which those categories were policed and maintained,[76] Poiret sought to control the potentially damaging results by constructing rhetorical boundaries around his work that would confine it to the private homes of wealthy and aristocratic clients, thereby avoiding the defiant signals that the *jupe-culotte* or *jupe-pantalon* could convey in other, more public circumstances.

While Poiret staked his commercial success on the promotion of Orientalizing styles as aesthetically pleasing and appropriate to his elite clientele, his principal rival in the French couture business, Jeanne Paquin (figure 2.29), was quick to seize an opportunity to claim a more conventional and, therefore, presumably a more broadly acceptable position, one pointedly opposed to that of Poiret. In a statement prepared for the press in early 1911, Paquin declared her rejection of the *jupe-culotte* and "informed her clientele that she would in no way accede to this style."[77] Initially, at least, this proved to be an astute move, allowing Paquin to protect herself from the kind of scornful criticism that dogged Poiret throughout much of 1911, when his "eccentricities" were repeatedly described as a distinct liability leading to reduced sales and threats from his financial backers to withdraw their support.[78] Paquin seems to have experienced few such problems; maintaining thriving couture houses in both London and Paris, she opened a shop to sell furs in New York in 1912, and is reported to have had as many as 2,700 employees during this period. When in autumn 1911 she did appear to have been influenced by Poiret—although she never adopted the culotte—her collection was criticized for assimilating "barbaric color effects that were not her style."[79]

Figure 2.29 ◌

Photo of Jeanne Paquin, c. 1913.

Jeanne Paquin was born in 1869 near Paris on the Île Saint Denis to a French mother and a German father (they were not married, but Guillaume Beckers acknowledged his daughter before he disappeared from her life, perhaps during the Franco-Prussian War).[80] Raised by her Catholic mother, Jeanne entered the couture business as an apprentice during the 1880s; in 1891, soon after she began working for Paquin Lalanne et Cie, she married one of the partners, Isidore Jacob dit Paquin (his use of the surname Paquin—presumably to mask his Jewish heritage—was not legalized until 1899) and together they took over the firm. While her husband dealt primarily with administrative and financial issues, Jeanne

Paquin became the house's principal dress designer and in less than a decade she was well established and a highly successful figure in the Parisian couture industry. In 1900, she was selected to preside over the Fashion Section of the Exposition Universelle in Paris, where the enormous statue of *La Parisienne* that towered over the exhibition from atop the Porte Binet entrance was represented in a costume specially designed by Paquin (figure 2.30). Seven years later, when her husband died, Jeanne Paquin took over direction of the firm, whose commercial success she

Figure 2.30

La Parisienne atop the Porte Binet, Exposition Universelle, Paris, 1900.

managed not only to maintain but even to enhance in the years leading up to the First World War. One of the most important reasons for this achievement seems to have been Paquin's ability to gauge the degree of innovation that her clientele would be willing to accept before it would begin to sense that elegance and good taste might be threatened. As a *New York Times* correspondent put it in October 1911, "She has introduced more lasting fashions than probably any other woman in Paris, for she has had the good sense never to be extreme, and her artistic husband never allowed her to wear anything that was bizarre or that would cause unpleasant comment. So the fashions she has created are lasting because they were simple and dignified."[81] In 1914, *Harper's Bazar* noted that Paquin was a fashion leader despite (or, one might argue, because of) the fact that she was less daring than other couturiers and she preferred styles inspired by French traditions to those based on an imaginary Orient.[82] Thus, Paquin positioned herself carefully with respect to debates about Orientalizing fashions, which she embraced—but only to a point: harem trousers always remained unacceptable to her. Although she was not alone in condemning the *jupe-culotte,* she held to that position more tenaciously than any of her colleagues. "Of all the houses which have declared themselves against the jupe culotte," a *New York Times* correspondent reported in April 1911, when controversy over the style was at its height, "Paquin is the only one that has really remained true to its colors. Mme Paquin, having declared her enmity, has stuck to her guns. . . . Being a very feminine woman, Mme Paquin loves feminine lines." Indeed, the correspondent pointed out, Paquin could be credited with inventing what was described as the appropriately feminine tight skirt, which revealed the "feminine outline" of the woman wearing it, as opposed to the "mannishness of the new garment."[83]

For all its interest as a locus of gender construction and racial stereotyping based on the standard cliché of the sensually alluring and sexually active Oriental woman, the French controversy over Oriental styles in dress during the pre–World War I period opened onto issues other than,

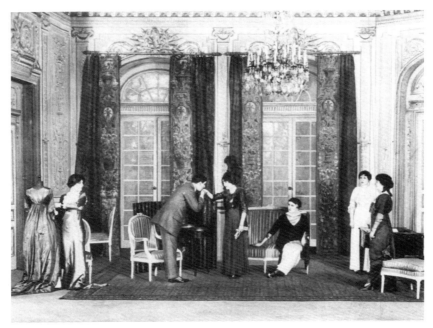

Figure 2.31

Rue de la Paix, Act II, from *Le Théâtre,* 1912.

although nevertheless related to, the immediately identifiable ones of masculinization and racial exoticism. The debate also exposed the infiltration of the visual and performing arts by commerce, as well as the breakdown of the barriers between elite and popular culture that both Poiret and Paquin participated in, profited from—and yet, paradoxically, they were concerned to resist. Paquin was directly involved but Poiret was also implicated when in 1912 the discursive construction of Orientalism and the business interests of haute couture collided on the Parisian stage. Just how much was at stake, for the couture industry as well as French theater, in the issue of exotic clothing emerged quite clearly with the January premiere of a satirical comedy by Abel Hermant and Marc de Toledo entitled *Rue de la Paix.*

Rue de la Paix, as has already been noted, was the name of the Paris street on which were located many of the most fashionable French couture houses, including those of Worth, Doucet, and Paquin, but—especially noteworthy for this analysis of the significance of the eponymous play—not that of Poiret, who in 1909 had chosen an admittedly impressive building but one with a less obviously prestigious address, situated further west in the eighth rather than the second arrondissement. The tensions between established traditions and upshot modernity that were implicit in these urban markers were the subject of *Rue de la Paix,* whose plot (a love triangle with an Orientalist twist: an affair between a couturière and an Egyptian prince) revolved around the rivalry between a highly successful couture business, "a classic house where the traditions are respected," located on the rue de la Paix (figure 2.31), and a stridently modern one, in the Faubourg Saint-Honoré, decorated as an Egyptian-style salon in which "'sensational' outfits are presented" (figure 2.32).[84] As Joseph Galtier noted in his review of the play, only one of the acts was situated in the couture house on the rue de la Paix: "The other two take us to the Faubourg Saint-Honoré. . . . Sign of the times! . . . [F]ashion, by changing neighborhoods, exiles itself and undergoes influences that are foreign to good French taste. It goes through troublesome, dangerous experiences and dresses ridiculously in tawdry finery of a flashy exoticism. It disguises itself *à l'Orientale* and the rooms for trying on clothes— thanks to esthetes run riot—adopt the decors of the harem."[85] There can be little doubt that the firms portrayed in the play were, on one hand, any one of the highly respected couture houses located on the rue de la Paix, and, on the other hand, Poiret's more daring *maison de couture,* which posed itself as a challenge to the better established businesses—including

Figure 2.32

Rue de la Paix, Act III, from *Le Théâtre,* 1912.

those of Worth and Doucet (figure 2.33), for whom Poiret had once worked, and that of Paquin (figure 2.34), for whom Poiret had emerged as a principal competitor.[86] Although Poiret's own interiors, unlike the modern couture house portrayed in the play, made no direct references to anything Egyptian, they did contain Orientalist references (for example, pillows piled on canapés and occasionally strewn across the floor [see the couture house interior rendered in figure 1.26 and the decoration of Poiret's domestic environment, visible in figure 2.35]) that complemented the styles of the gowns Poiret was designing and showing in those spaces.

Figure 2.33 ↻

Photo of a salon in the Doucet couture house,

1910, from *L'Illustration,* 1910.

Figure 2.34 ↻

G. Agié, photo of a salon in the Maison

Paquin, Paris.

These interior design features became especially prominent, and might well have provoked Orientalist fantasies of a harem for his guests, when he organized a fête such as "The Thousand and Second Night" to draw special attention to them. Indeed, the discursive and symbolic differences between the actual houses on the rue de la Paix and Poiret's, located at the convergence of the avenue d'Antin (now avenue Franklin Roosevelt) and the rue du Faubourg Saint-Honoré, emerge rather strikingly from what is known of their furnishings. These were traditional Louis XVI-style repro-

Figure 2.35

Henri Manuel, photo of Madame Poiret looking in a mirror in the Maison Poiret.

duction antiques upholstered in pastel colors in the case of the Maisons Doucet, Paquin, and Worth, as distinct from Poiret's headquarters, which contained the most up-to-the-minute Directoire or Directoire-inspired furniture and decorations, with strident colors—green and raspberry stripes in one case—and plenty of imported cushions prominently displayed, as is evident from visual images and textual descriptions of those spaces.[87]

As *Rue de la Paix* opened to the public, the play was treated to intense interest on the part of the press, where designer Paul Iribe's approximately fifty costumes, all realized by the couture house of Jeanne Paquin, were greeted by uncommon curiosity and elicited a mixed response (figures 2.36 and 2.37). A correspondent for London's *Daily Mail* noted, "The extraordinary display of bizarre frocks seen on the stage of the Vaudeville Theatre, Paris . . . has provoked lively indignation in the real rue de la Paix."[88] Much of the commentary was critical of the dresses, which were described as a "biting satire of our infatuation with certain exotic styles that do a terrible disservice to French and Parisian taste."[89] One account even compared them unfavorably to designs by Poiret: ". . . M. Paul Iribe's creations are of a poor taste and a tone that smacks of Scandinavia, not to mention Germany. These cuts which begin at the breasts [*tétons*] might perhaps be pleasing to Teutons, but they lack the grace of models by Poiret, rejuvenated by the Oriental mode, and a house as Parisian as that of Mme. Paquin will face a lot of problems getting them accepted by French women who care about an aesthetic line."[90] According to her biographer, Paquin was simply "amused by the controversy" the costumes aroused, but she was sufficiently concerned about its impact on her business to make clear, in a personal appearance to introduce the costumes at a rehearsal for the press, that her role was confined simply to producing the dresses; Iribe alone was responsible for their design.[91] Anxious to distance herself from any outrage associated with Orientalism and declaring that the dresses seen in the play would not become her models for the next fashion season, Paquin explained that *Rue de la Paix* was intended to promote a tasteful and recognizably French—rather than

Figure 2.36 ↺

Paul Iribe, costume designs for *Rue de la Paix,*
from *Excelsior,* 1912.

foreign—version of contemporary fashion: "The idea of the playwright
was to protest against the influences of exoticism and foreign taste that so
often infiltrate the milieux of creators of elegance and denature the essentially Parisian and French inspiration that always remains the one guiding
the world of flirtation and good taste."[92] Paul Iribe also found it necessary
to defend himself publicly against accusations of aesthetic heresy such as
the following comment from the critic for the *Daily Mail:* "One of the

principal female characters wears a black satin dress with a white linen jacket, such as Paris waiters wear, trimmed with a little flounce and a great green bar across the front, 'like a gate,' as a lady correspondent declares. The appearance of this creation provoked a gasp of astonishment in the audience."[93] In an interview published in *Comoedia Illustré* Iribe declared, "It appears that I am being reproached—on account of the drawings that I submitted to that great artist of the rue de la Paix, Mme Paquin, for

Figure 2.37

Dresses from *Rue de la Paix*, from *Comoedia Illustré*, 1912.

whom I profess great admiration—for having 'committed' unacceptable eccentricities. However, in my conception [of these costumes] I inflicted on our modern Parisian women neither the hobble-skirt nor the *jupe-culotte,* nor the hooped skirt over bouffant trousers [all of which were hallmarks of Poiret's recent styles]!"[94]

From the vantage of almost 100 years of hindsight, it may at first be difficult to discern what it was about the costumes seen in the play that could have elicited such intense reaction, particularly because, as Iribe noted, none of them involved harem trousers or any of the other most controversial stylistic features of current fashion. It is, therefore, particularly puzzling that the dresses were described in terms redolent of Orientalist exoticism. What many critics seem to have found offensive was the way the dresses drew attention to the bodies they clothed, "emphasiz[ing] curves of the female form divine that have not hitherto been indicated in dress modeling"[95] (figure 2.38). Calling the designs "truly astounding," and implying they were improperly suggestive, one critic remarked, "I cannot say that I would very much like to go out with a young woman dressed in models such as these."[96] The uncharacteristically bright colors and bold stripes of some of the fabrics used for the dresses also posed a problem (figure 2.39). These differed markedly from the muted tones that were the hallmark of Doucet's couture house and to which Paquin's customers were presumably also accustomed, if we accept the slightly out of date yet possibly telling evidence of the whites, light beiges, soft pinks, and faded greens of the garments visible in an oil painting of 1906 by Henri Gervex depicting a showroom in Paquin's couture house crowded with her clients.[97] Over the next five or six years, color photographs of models wearing her typically graceful, flowing garments (reproduced in upscale women's magazines such as *Les Modes,* for example) continued to exhibit this same range of muted colors, from which the much more strident colors and dramatic cuts of the designs by Iribe could understandably have been seen as an abrupt and unfortunate departure.[98] Critics regarded such bold colors and their striking combinations as

Figure 2.38

Jeanne Iribe (star of the play and Paul Iribe's
wife) in *Rue de la Paix,* from *Le Théâtre,* 1912.

evidence of foreign influence, not simply from an exotic Orient via the
Ballets Russes, but from the north—from Scandinavia or, more threatening
to that traditional French taste with which Paquin worked hard to align her
name, from Germany. This is an issue to which we will return.

For all the ink spilled over the manifest content of *Rue de la Paix*—
brightly colored and provocatively cut fashions betraying foreign influences versus more conventional modern clothing in a recognizably French
tradition—this was only one of several problems it exposed. Critics also
noted that the play revealed the essentially commercial nature of the link

Figure 2.39 ☉

Paul Iribe, costume design for *Rue de la Paix,*
from *Comoedia Illustré,* 1912.

between couture and theater; looking beyond the subject of the play to the
form it took as a fashion show on the professional stage, several objected
to its commercial implications and failure to project any deep, philosoph-
ical idea.[99] Many regarded the way it presented fashion as theater as
unabashed commercialization of the stage. As a critic writing under the
name Furet put it in the journal *Dramatica,* "*Rue de la Paix* at the
Vaudeville is more of a chronicle of fashion written and sketched by
Paquin than a real theatrical play. The public very much enjoyed the mannequins who filed past before them throughout the evening, and if the

eyes of these women were satiated, by contrast their brains settled down to a soft quietude."[100] André Gilliard was in substantial agreement with this view, though his complaint was aimed at the director of the Vaudeville Theater rather than at Paquin; for him the play exposed the debasement of the theater in thrall to publicity and the commercial success that fashion guaranteed: "The play that M. Porel presents at the moment on the stage that he directs was doubtless, for him, no more than an excellent pretext for exhibiting several women and a certain number of models by a great couturier. He said to himself that the principal ingredient for success of fashionable plays is dress and that his play, in which there are nothing but dresses rather than roles, and only mannequins where there should be actresses, would go much further than 365 degrees. And it was presumably thus that he came to welcome *Rue de la Paix* into his theater."[101] According to the journalist Gaston de Pawlowski, who declared himself to be more intrigued than bothered by the issues these developments raised for the drama critic, the problem with *Rue de la Paix* was not so much that it attempted to make serious theater out of what amounted to no more than a commercial battle between the relatively conservative fashions of the rue de la Paix and the risqué Oriental modes newly launched by Poiret; he was persuaded that "today the great commercial conflicts are capable of replacing, in literature, the great moral conflicts of earlier times."[102] Instead, de Pawlowski lamented the fact that in this "frankly commercial study of the world . . . of fashion," the couturiers themselves were too intimately involved; the theater was being used for their own publicity purposes: "Over the past several years in France advertising [*la publicité*] has made remarkable progress. Industrialists and merchants finally understood that they had to offer something to the public in return for the attention they demanded. This explains why we have seen our best artists and our best writers collaborate in the production of catalogues or posters that are, very often, veritable works of art. The theater . . . [with few exceptions] had always remained untouched by this development. The new play at the Vaudeville presages some changes on this point." Virtually all the critics recognized the commercial core of plays such as *Rue de la Paix,* "amusements in which all the roles are replaced by dresses," and which therefore amounted to "no more than a pretext for the display of dresses, coats and hats." In them the customary relationship between high and low culture was inverted; serious drama gave way to lightweight fashion, and commerce rather than culture was in the dominant position: "The fashionable author works for the hat-makers. From him the great couturier commissions three acts made to measure. He is the shop-clerk that one assigns to do the puff show, while the mannequins promenade. . . . Who could have conceived this excellent idea if not a publicity agent?"[103] Gilliard, writing for *Bravo,* expressed a similar range of concerns: "*Rue de la Paix* functions, in the annals of the theater, only to accentuate the decadence of certain drama writers who subject their talent to a work by those who court publicity, rivals of those who are established in the arcade theaters, go-betweens or procurators." The result, he declared, was that a great theater like the Vaudeville "had necessarily transformed itself into an advertising agency."[104]

Joel Kaplan and Sheila Stowell have shown that a similar configuration of interrelationships between theater, fashion, and society was operative in London at this same time. "Its starting-point," they write, "is the convergence in the early 1890s of an aggressive fashion press, innovative merchandising by a new breed of independent dressmakers, and the transformation of a select group of West End theatres into an essential part of the London Season. Upon stages like the Haymarket, the Criterion, and the St. James's, . . . leading ladies not only served as living mannequins, displaying for their more affluent patrons a selection of couture house goods, but in so doing completed within the playhouses themselves a voyeuristic triangle between stage, stalls, and gallery that echoed the arrangements of semi-public society events like Ascot, Henley, and Derby."[105] Many of the French critics pointed to a similar dynamic at work in the

Vaudeville presentation of *Rue de la Paix,* which proved to be especially attractive to female viewers who, by getting their husbands to pay for them to see this display of the latest fashions (similar to those presented for free, but only to a committed clientele, at the couture houses), sealed the bond between female spectatorship, fashion, and consumer culture.

In France, however, the so-called "fashion-play" was not focused exclusively around questions of gender and spectatorship. Nor was condemning the transformation of dramatic theater into a fashion show or the infiltration of advertising into the domain of the theater simply a matter of protecting elite culture from what was widely regarded as crass commercialism. In addition, these propositions coincided with pervasive racist and nationalist discourses that were exacerbated by international politics in the years leading up to World War I. In the disturbing words of one reviewer of *Rue de la Paix,* "What to us appears most amusing about the play, is that in it the Maison Paquin puts itself forward to defend French taste against the corrupting exoticism of various rival houses. When one recalls that the Paquins are Jewish butchers who, after having bled kosher meat in the Judenstrasse of Frankfurt, came to France to set the tone for Parisian fashion, aren't their nationalist pretentions just an impudent joke?"[106] This remark attests to the development in France of an increasingly conservative and chauvinist political climate after 1905, when the coalition of leftist groupings in the Bloc des Gauches collapsed and the French government faced down the German Kaiser in a dispute over France's annexation of Morocco as part of its pursuit of larger colonial ambitions. In the following years, as the French became increasingly aware of the possibility of war with Germany, nationalist ideology was nurtured, particularly by the right-wing Action Française, and vitriolic rhetoric such as that directed at Paquin was not particularly unusual.[107] In this context, participating in the production of *Rue de la Paix* turned out to be a risky business venture for Jeanne Paquin, whose long-established position as one of the preeminent representatives of the French couture industry was threatened by anti-Semitic stereotypes of Jewish mercantilism mixed with nationalist antipathy to anything that could be associated with German culture. Never mind that Paquin had been born in France and raised as a Catholic; linked to Germany through her father and to Judaism through her husband, she was vulnerable to the conservative and nationalist condemnation of modernism as foreign both to French taste and to French traditions. Exploring a comparable situation faced by Poiret in 1915, Kenneth Silver has shown how, during the First World War, the ideologically charged connections popularly drawn between modernism, cubism, and Orientalism on one hand, and France's enemies, Germany and Turkey, on the other, worked to position Poiret as a German sympathizer and a traitor to the French cause—despite the fact that he was at the time in uniform, serving as a soldier in the French army.[108]

Like Poiret, and in certain instances actually following his example, Paquin became adept in using the arts to negotiate these overlapping and potentially dangerous terrains. She, too, was a collector and patron of the arts, as portrait photographs taken in her home, where she was shown surrounded by works of fine and decorative art, were presumably intended to attest (figure 2.40). Although she associated herself with the arts in publicly visible ways, her patronage and collecting steered clear of the contemporary, modernist sensibilities that Poiret's collection embodied. In 1910, she made a donation to the City of Paris that included almost 500 bronze and pewter medallions, numerous antique and modern medallion casts, as well as plaster, terracotta, and wax models, in addition to one painting, a large, academically inspired nude entitled *Dido* by Paul-Albert Laurens. The painting is close in style to the work of the artist's father, history painter Jean-Paul Laurens, who had been the teacher at the Académie Julien of many of the artists with whom Poiret was most closely associated during these years: André Dunoyer de Segonzac, Jean-Louis Boussingault, and Luc-Albert Moreau; Guy-Pierre Fauconnet, who worked as a furniture and interior designer for Martine, had also been a

Figure 2.40

Photo of Jeanne Paquin posing with works of
art in her home, c. 1913.

student there.[109] In comparison to their experimentation during the prewar period with more modernist tendencies, Paquin's aesthetic inclinations, signaled in the works she donated to the Petit Palais, appear to have
been relatively conservative. Another manifestation of her tastes surfaced
in 1911 at the International Exposition celebrating the fiftieth anniversary
of the establishment of the Kingdom of Italy in Turin, where she constructed an elegant pavilion in a modified classical style—it was described
in the press as a "little Greek temple"—for the display of her own

Figure 2.41

The Paquin Pavilion, International Exposition,
Turin, from *Catalogue officiel de la Section
Française, Turin,* 1911.

clothing designs (figure 2.41). A larger pavilion dedicated to "La Mode"
housed the combined exhibition of all the French contributors in that category, including additional models by Paquin (Poiret was not represented),
but hers was the only couture house to build a freestanding pavilion at the
Turin exposition, and Paquin thereby positioned herself as the most
prominent representative of French haute couture on this highly visible
international platform. According to the official catalogue of the French
displays, "Mme Paquin managed to mount a second exhibition, in a pavil-

ion strategically situated next to the pavilion of the City of Paris, seeming to want thereby to affirm the bond that ties feminine fashion to that great city."[110] The classicizing message of the architecture, underscored by André Marty's painted frieze of classically garbed women (figure 2.42; presumably inspired by the highly simplified draperies of costumes Paquin had designed for the play, *Xantho chez les Courtisanes,* at the Théâtre des Bouffes-Parisiens in spring 1910, figure 2.43), was clearly intended to

Figure 2.42

Images from the Paquin Pavilion, International Exposition, Turin, 1911, from *Comoedia Illustré,* 1911.

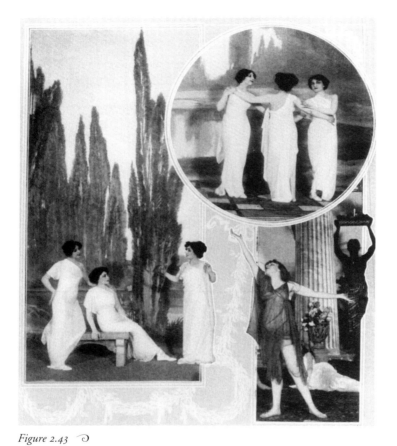

Figure 2.43 ◌

Jeanne Paquin, costumes from *Xantho chez les Courtisanes,* from *Comoedia Illustré,* 1910.

construct Paquin as an up-to-date representative of traditional Mediterranean style. The point was further reinforced by the display inside the building of a diorama with wax mannequins posed as dancers in even flimsier draperies.[111] That arrangements were made for the pavilion to be inaugurated by the Grand Duchess of Aosta, Princesse Laetitia Napoléon (figure 2.44), was clearly a means of indicating Paquin's acceptance in artistocratic and officially sanctioned circles. When photographs of the pavilion and the opening ceremony were published in *Comoedia Illustré*, Madame Paquin was congratulated not only for her pavilion—a "marvel of the purest Parisian taste"—but for once again assuring that "French taste would occupy the most advantageous position abroad."[112]

Figure 2.44

The Grand Duchess of Aosta accompanied by
Madame Paquin leaving the Paquin Pavilion,
International Exposition, Turin, 1911.

No wonder Paquin was dismayed to see her assiduously cultivated reputation as a bastion of Frenchness and good taste compromised by the critical response to *Rue de la Paix* only six months later.

On the other hand, perhaps it was this successful public relations campaign to link her own name with the essence of French and Parisian classicizing taste that emboldened Paquin to collaborate with Iribe on the costumes for *Rue de la Paix* in the first place. She must have realized that to maintain her position on the crest of the French fashion wave, she had to take risks, balance her reputation for acceptable fashions in the French and Mediterranean tradition with some element of more daring, even if arguably foreign, sensibility—nothing as controversial and racially implicated as the *jupe-culotte,* but at least the intense colors that, problematically for Paquin, Parisians associated with alien (read: German) taste. If Paquin thereby risked being vilified as a foreigner and a Jew, her efforts to control the negative response to the costumes for *Rue de la Paix,* to remind her clients that Iribe and not she was really their author, were obviously successful. Less than a year after the play opened, on 1 January 1913, Paquin became the first woman in the couture industry to be decorated as a Chevalier of the Legion of Honor.

Given these testimonials to Paquin's success in positioning herself as the officially sanctioned representative of French haute couture, it is notable that she continued to flirt with what would presumably have been considered a more transgressive conception of modern dress. According to an article in *Harper's Bazar,* it was her idea to approach that fountainhead of Russian Orientalism, Léon Bakst, "just for the love of art, to persuade this famous artist to sketch a dress pattern."[113] None of the designs they collaborated to produce in spring 1913 were unequivocally Orientalizing in style; instead, they conjured both ancient Egypt and classical Greece, as their names—including Atalante, Alcyone, Aglaé, Isis, Niké, and Hébé—must have been intended to suggest (figures 2.45 and 2.46).[114] Although their intense colors received some criticism and the collaborators were chastised

Figure 2.45

Léon Bakst, designs for dresses made by Jeanne
Paquin, from *Comoedia Illustré,* 1913.

for pursuing the new, or "*jamais vu,*" the general reaction was extremely
positive, if we are to believe Gabriel Mourey, writing in the *Gazette du Bon
Ton:* "In salons and artists' ateliers, in tearooms and theaters, in the halls of
great hotels and steamships, in the cars of deluxe trains, everywhere, at this
moment everywhere one speaks only of the dresses designed by Bakst, and
realized by Mme. Paquin and M. Joire [her half-brother, whom she had
recently taken on as a business partner, together with his wife, Suzanne
Joire]."[115] Not surprisingly, then, more gowns designed by Bakst specifically
for Paquin followed in short order, and the two also collaborated on costumes for the Ballets Russes production of *Jeux,* which opened in May 1913
at the recently inaugurated Théâtre des Champs-Élysées.

Figure 2.46 ↻

Léon Bakst, "Philomèle" dress, made by Jeanne
Paquin, from *Gazette du Bon Ton,* 1913.

The combination in Paquin's professional profile—of her well-publicized rejection of the *jupe-culotte,* the classicizing garments she showed in
the temple-inspired pavilion in Turin, and her entrance into the Legion
of Honor, on the one hand, with her collaborations first with Iribe and
then with Bakst and the Ballets Russes on the other—indicates something
of the complexity of the couturière's self-construction, the way in which
she negotiated the conflicting dictates of fashion. In her case, like that of
Poiret, this involved adherence to prevailing notions of French and
Mediterranean traditions at the same time that her traditionalist reputa-

tion had to be mitigated so as to be seen as daring, advanced and, to a carefully calibrated degree, willing to collaborate with designers who were associated at the time with foreign tendencies. Bakst may have represented the ideal collaborator for her purposes, since he was best known in Paris for the bright colors and exotic decorative features of his Orientalist costume designs for *Schéhérazade,* but he also made striking and effective costume designs for ballets with classical subjects, as was the case with *L'Après midi d'un faune,* first performed in Paris in May 1912. Alexander Schouvaloff's description of the costumes for the nymphs in that production could, with few changes, be applied to some of the couture dresses Bakst and Paquin collaborated to produce the following year: ". . . modeled on the Greek peplum, [these] were armless diaphanous dresses of finely pleated gauze bordered at the hem with tiny squares or wavy lines of blue or dull red, the white overskirt being decorated also with wavy lines, bands of ivy leaves, or dots of the same color as the squares."[116] Indeed, Bakst was no mere Orientalist; he also possessed excellent credentials as far as the discursive construction of modernist classicism was concerned. Already in the early 1900s in St. Petersburg Bakst had designed productions of classical Greek dramas and his writings of the pre-war period indicate he considered himself to be working in the classical tradition.[117] That Paquin carefully considered the advantages of working with Bakst must have been sensed by a reporter for the *New York Times* who in October 1913 wrote of a suspicion that their collaboration "was arranged for purposes of advertising the house, although no French dressmaker would admit for a fleeting second that she could bring herself down to anything so inartistic as advertisement. She maintains the attitude of an artist, but we know she is the most commercial artist alive."[118]

If Iribe and Bakst were often linked to Orientalism—Bakst was perhaps its most prominent exponent in prewar France, and Iribe was associated through his design of the journal *Schéhérazade* and also (though indirectly) through his work for Poiret—overt Orientalist references were carefully downplayed in their collaborations with Paquin, thereby allowing her (not without protests to the contrary in the case of *Rue de la Paix*) to maintain her reputation for restraint, good taste, elegance, and typically Parisian grace. These were the qualities she was said to have displayed, for example, in her contribution to the French section at the Brussels exposition of 1910, where Paquin recreated with wax mannequins what was described in the press as "the solemn ceremony that is the *lever* of the Parisienne."[119] The Parisienne, symbol of French femininity, was in fact closely associated with Paquin, who, it will be recalled, had designed the dress in which the statue of the Parisienne that crowned the main entrance to the Exposition Universelle of 1900 had been clothed (figure 2.30). In the Brussels diorama, the Parisienne received "the '*demoiselle de chez Paquin*' who brings for her difficult choice all the splendors of modern lingerie imagined with taste and fantasy by that veritable artist, Madame Paquin."[120] It was a display that, according to the correspondent for *Le Figaro,* went beyond anything the imagination could dream of to become "the most sumptuous, the most gracious, the most elegant, in a word, the most Parisian."[121] Despite the potential hazards of working with Iribe and with Bakst, Paquin succeeded in maintaining her reputation for these qualities, and for an affinity with the classical tradition which she in fact shared with the Russian artist, who was described in 1913 by the correspondent for *Comoedia Illustré* as "so Athenian, [having] become the most refined of Parisians." At the same time, Paquin reaped the benefit from their collaboration of Bakst's reputation for greater daring: Bakst's designs were described as "ultra modern" ensembles, and the Maison Paquin was said to have been "honored by such an artistic effort."[122] Thus Paquin found a way to sustain her reputation for tasteful designs that upheld traditional French qualities of elegance and grace while associating her label with names that signaled transgressive modernism and might, in certain circumstances, have been thought to introduce potentially dangerous foreign influences. The strategy worked especially well with Bakst, whose assimilation into French cultural discourse reinforced Paquin's position as the preeminent exemplar of good taste in prewar French fashion.

During this period, Poiret was struggling with the same discursive constraints as Paquin: trying to construct himself as an artist—a man of culture, not commerce—while simultaneously incorporating virtually everything he touched into one merchandizing scheme or another. And he, too, shifted regularly between the Orientalizing thematics of "Otherness" and the classicizing modes that were commonly identified with French national traditions. For example, less than a year after he created "The Thousand and Second Night," and while he was trying to resolve the financial problems he faced as a result of his widely acclaimed but nevertheless controversial and commercially problematic Orientalism of the 1911 fashion seasons, on 6 January 1912 Poiret staged another extravagant and theatrical fête, this time on a thoroughly traditional and thoroughly French theme: the *lever* not of the Parisienne (which had been Paquin's theme at the Brussels exposition a year and a half earlier) but of the Sun King. Calling it the *Fête des Rois,* he conceived the extravaganza from start to finish in theatrical terms, according to which each guest was assigned a particular role: Louis XIV was played by a friend named Decroix, Kees van Dongen played the architect Le Nôtre, André Dunoyer de Segonzac was an old manservant, Jean-Louis Boussingault was dressed in violet watered silk to play a father confessor; Poiret, fittingly enough, assumed the role of Tailor to the King.[123] Taking this royalist theme still further, six months later Poiret mounted yet another classically inspired party, *Les Festes de Bacchus.* This time the fête was held at an appropriately ancien régime site: an eighteenth-century *folie* called the Pavillon du Butard that had been built as a small hunting lodge for Louis XV in the woods of Fosses-Reposes, near St. Cloud, by the architect Ange-Marie Gabriel. Poiret had rented the abandoned property and spent a small fortune renovating it with the help of his friend Raoul Dufy. The party he gave there on 20 June 1912, was apparently conceived as a revival of the festivals of Bacchus that Louis XIV had offered at Versailles.[124] Guy-Pierre Fauconnet designed the program, consisting of a pair of elegant scrolls with delicate cursive lettering and decorative drawings inspired by Greek vase paintings (figure 2.47). The evening's *divertissements* featured Poiret himself in the role of Jupiter, made up to look like an animated classical sculpture with kohl shadowing his eyes, a gold-painted wig of matted curls, sandals, and a short tunic of white fabric edged with gold; his wife Denise played Juno, also in sandals and a short tunic, this one made from a printed fabric by Fortuny (figure 2.48). The two received their guests—

Figure 2.47

Guy-Pierre Fauconnet, program for *Les Festes de Bacchus* (detail), 1912.

Figure 2.48

Photo of Paul and Denise Poiret dressed for
Les Festes de Bacchus, 1912.

"fifty musicians and actors; a hundred spectators [Poiret said he invited 300 guests]"[125]—on the steps of the pavilion, its facade flood-lit so it could serve as the backdrop for the evening's outdoor entertainments. These included the presentation of a newly discovered and freshly restored seventeenth-century Italian ballet by G. di Caravaggio, cantatas by Rameau and Boisfleury, two pieces by Handel, and Lully's pantomime ballet, "Les Festes de Bacchus." According to the program, "Dances and *jeux* in period taste" were performed by five female dancers, including Natacha Trouhanova (appearing in a classicizing role, rather than as the Orientalist she had played in *Nabuchodonosor* and at Poiret's "Thousand and Second Night" fête), but costume historian and Poiret scholar Guillaume Garnier claims that the principal attraction of the evening was Poiret's client and friend, Isadora Duncan, who danced "in a very simple costume of Greek inspiration."[126]

Described at the time as having been "executed by artists and for artists, directed by a magician of decorative art," the *Festes de Bacchus* "set the standard for a manifestation of this type in 1912."[127] Thoroughly classical in character, predominantly French or at least Mediterranean in its geographical associations, and decidedly aristocratic in the connections it drew with the ancien régime, the event offered Poiret a means of mitigating the wild, Orientalist reputation he had acquired for his dress designs and the related party he had thrown the previous year. Isadora Duncan was, perhaps, the perfect performative vehicle to achieve this goal, given her self-construction as an "artiste," a fervent exponent of naturalist dance as an expression of the spirituality, morality, and nobility of classical Greek culture. Like Poiret, whose loosely fitted, corsetless dresses she started wearing around 1909 (he named one for her in 1910–11),[128] Duncan surrounded herself with artists, including Louis Süe, André Dunoyer de Segonzac, and Antoine Bourdelle, as well as Auguste Rodin, for whom her dances were an inspiration. As Ann Daly has pointed out, "Duncan reimagined the form and content of dance as an aesthetic object and convinced an audience of its legitimacy as a 'high' art. She created a 'taste' for dance, and, furthermore, made it a matter of 'good taste' . . . an emblem of Cultural refinement."[129] Thus Duncan's strategic alignment of a classically inspired modern dance with upper-class, white, European cultural elites corresponded closely with Poiret's own performative practices, in particular his attempts to stage his fashionable, often risqué costumes (including those that were classical in their stylistic derivation) in his couture house and at the theater, to embrace high culture (while calling attention to his wealth and success) through his art collecting, and to capture the cachet of the classical as well as the exotic through his parties. Both the well-known promiscuity of Duncan's lifestyle and the way in which she put her scantily clad body on public display in her performances (figure 2.49) suggest that Duncan, like Poiret (and Natacha Trouhanova, as well), personified an often-neglected yet crucially important link between the

Figure 2.49   ↄ

Arnold Genthe, photo of Isadora Duncan, 1916.

discourses of classicism on the one hand and those of Orientalist sexual abandon on the other. It was precisely by bringing these discourses into dialogue with one another that Poiret successfully cultivated a wealthy and culturally elite clientele (including Isadora Duncan) for his clothing, perfume, furniture, and decorative arts businesses.

We can shed more light on the balancing act both Poiret and Paquin were attempting in the overlapping realms of fashion, art, and visual culture if we consider Paquin's collaboration with Paul Iribe on the costumes for *Rue de la Paix* in a context that extends beyond the bounds of the theater and related performance media to encompass other cultural arenas in which Paquin and Poiret competed. For *Rue de la Paix* was only one of many efforts on Paquin's part to lay claim to artistic territory already staked out by Poiret beginning in 1908, when he commissioned Iribe to make the drawings for his first limited edition album of couture designs (figure 1.20) (as well as stationery for Madame Poiret), and followed this in 1909 by asking Iribe to design the house label sewn into each of his couture creations (figure 1.11). The album provided the images and the label provided the trademark that established Poiret's distinctive commercial identity and both were characteristic expressions of Iribe's graphic style. In choosing to work with Iribe, Paquin must have been aware—indeed, she must have desired—that her name would share the aura, participate in the same confluence of associations, that Iribe's designs helped to create around Poiret. Three years after the appearance of his album for Poiret, in November 1911 Paquin again employed Iribe among several other graphic artists to produce a deluxe album for her own couture house, entitled *L'Eventail et la fourrure chez Paquin,* in a limited edition of 300 that was published little more than a month before the premiere of *Rue de la Paix.* The two images Iribe created on this occasion illustrated actual fans of his own design, also created for Paquin, showing, in the first instance, an *Occidental Woman* (figure 2.50) and, in the second, an *Oriental Woman* (figure 2.51). These provide another indication of Paquin's desire—at least

Figure 2.50

Paul Iribe, *The Occidental Woman,* from
L'Eventail et la fourrure chez Paquin, plate 2,
1911.

Figure 2.51 ↻

Paul Iribe, *The Oriental Woman,* from *L'Eventail
et la fourrure chez Paquin,* plate 7, 1911.

before *Rue de la Paix* opened and the costumes designed by Iribe were crit-icized—to associate her work on some level with both of these cultural constructions. On the one hand, the first fan displays an attractive yet innocent *Occidental Woman,* wearing a simple, demure azure dress, shown in a sun-drenched scene as she closes her eyes and throws back her head while inhaling the scent of a single rose plucked from a bouquet displayed in a light blue pot with white decorations in relief reminiscent of Wedgewood ware (in its style and in the classical allusions of its imagery). The other fan, in contrast, displays a highly made-up and sexually allur-ing *Oriental Woman,* shown with breasts exposed, her head and body draped in strings of pearls, gold bracelets on her arms and wrists, and emerald rings on her fingers as she kneels on a large tasseled cushion to look out over the sea at a mottled, fiery red sky.[130] Iribe thus established an ideological framework between the oscillating poles of classicism and Orientalism within which Paquin's message to her clients was inscribed. But the binary opposition thus far suggested seems upon further exami-nation not to hold. If we look again at the *Classical Woman,* we can dis-cern hints of her sexual availability as well: young and lithe, she appears almost to faint from physical pleasure as she experiences the scent of the flower, her clothed body and averted gaze offset by the naked body on the vase, which is shown presenting itself forthrightly to the viewer. Here Iribe's work, like the dances of Isadora Duncan (figure 2.49), serves as a reminder that the tropes of classicism and Orientalism often find common ground in the sensuality and allure of the nude, or partially clothed, female body.

Paul Iribe was not the only graphic artist whom Paquin plucked from Poiret's orbit to contribute to *L'Eventail et la fourrure chez Paquin;* she also invited Georges Lepape, who in 1910 had created the engraving of Poiret's couture house used on all his packages (figure 1.18). The image that Lepape created for Paquin's album—a circular bouquet of flowers—

was far less freighted with meaning in its own right than the two images by Iribe, but, I would argue, it is noteworthy that this first plate in *L'Eventail et la fourrure chez Paquin* was by an artist who, perhaps even more than Iribe, had played an important role in constructing Poiret's public image. Not only had Lepape created Poiret's packing label, but only eight months before contributing to *L'Eventail et la fourrure chez Paquin,* he had produced his own deluxe album for Poiret, *Les Choses de Paul Poiret vues par Georges Lepape,* in an edition four times larger than that of Iribe. Several of the eleven pochoir plates in Lepape's album showed mannequins posed in and around Poiret's couture house, for example in one of the salons (figure 1.26), or in front of a window over-looking his formal garden (figure 2.52). Poiret adapted several of these images for use on stationery and business invoices (figure 2.53), in which format they became closely linked not only to his name and couture designs, but to his distinctive style as an entrepreneur. Poiret arranged to have all Lepape's plates for *Les Choses de Paul Poiret vues par Georges Lepape* exhibited in the Galerie Barbazanges (together with works by three other graphic artists in his circle, Bernard Boutet de Monvel and the latter's cousins, Pierre and Jacques Brissaud) just as the album was being made available for purchase by the public at a cost of fifty francs each. As a result of its high visibility, there can be little doubt that Paquin knew of *Les Choses de Paul Poiret vues par Georges Lepape.* Although she hired several artists who figured significantly in Poiret's public relations gambits, she was not in a position to mimic his merchandizing coup by having the plates for *L'Eventail et la fourrure chez Paquin* publicly exhibited, since she lacked both access to an art gallery and the kind of close relations with a dealer that Poiret cultivated with Barbazanges.

During these years, Paquin and Poiret frequently employed not only the same young graphic artists, but also the architect, furniture designer and interior decorator, Louis Süe. Once again, Poiret was the first to work

Figure 2.52

Georges Lepape, *Les Choses de Paul Poiret vues par Georges Lepape,* plate 11, 1911.

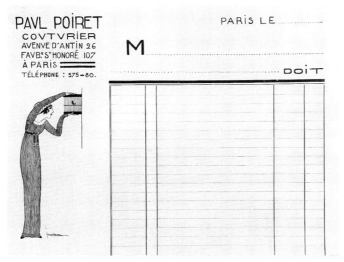

Figure 2.53

Georges Lepape, invoice designed for Paul
Poiret.

with Süe, whom he had hired in 1909 to renovate his maison de couture.
Three years later, Paquin commissioned Süe to enlarge and remodel her
villa, Les Treillages, in Saint-Cloud (figure 2.54), and in 1914 she put
him in charge of adding space to the building in which her couture house
was located, at 3, rue de la Paix. In the meantime, she employed another
young architect, Robert Mallet-Stevens, whose Directoire-inspired work
was comparable in style to Süe's, for projects including the interior decoration of the fur shop she opened on Fifth Avenue in New York in 1912
(figure 2.55) and an exhibition stand of similar style installed at the
Exposition Universelle in Ghent in 1913.[131] The two widely noticed interiors Mallet-Stevens exhibited at the 1913 Salon d'Automne in Paris were
also for Paquin, in this case projects for another villa, Les Roses Rouges, in

Deauville (figures 2.56 and 2.57), which remained unrealized due to the outbreak of war the following summer. Paquin also expected to gain status from another project that the war forced Mallet-Stevens to abandon. In spring 1914 Mallet-Stevens was making plans to publish an international journal, entitled *Nouvelle Manière,* that would focus on the fine and decorative arts, including architecture, furniture, interior design, theater decor, gardens, and notably, clothing and personal adornment. An honorary board was to be composed of prominent cultural figures from France and Belgium, including sculptor Antoine Bourdelle, composer Claude Debussy, painter Maurice Denis, architect Frantz Jourdain, playwright Maurice Maeterlinck, writer and art critic Alexandre Mercereau, and theater director Jacques Rouché (with whom Poiret had

Figure 2.54

Louis Süe, elevation of "Les Treillages," villa for
Madame Paquin, 1912.

Figure 2.55 ⊙

Robert Mallet-Stevens, interior design of Paquin
shop in New York City, 1912, from *Vogue,* 1914.

earlier collaborated on several projects). Paquin was also represented
amongst this elite group, thereby sharing the cultural cachet of the artists
and intellectuals whose names appeared alongside hers on the masthead of
Mallet-Stevens's aborted journal project.[132]

Like Poiret's architect of the prewar years, Louis Süe, in his architectural work Mallet-Stevens was strongly influenced by Josef Hoffmann
and the Wiener Werkstätte, which Mallet-Stevens knew at least as well as

Süe did. Mallet-Stevens was the nephew of Suzanne Stoclet, whose husband, Adolphe Stoclet, had commissioned Hoffmann to design and decorate the strikingly modern and exceptionally luxurious Palais Stoclet that was constructed on the outskirts of Brussels between 1905 and 1911. During that period, Mallet-Stevens was completing his architectural training in Paris (he graduated at the top of his class from the reformist École Spéciale d'Architecture in 1906), and in frequent visits to the Belgian branch of his family he was able to witness the emergence of the Stoclet structure itself as well as the development of the interiors, which were decorated in their totality as a harmonious ensemble by Hoffmann and the Wiener Werkstätte. The forceful impact of this experience can be

Figure 2.56

Robert Mallet-Stevens, hall for a villa in
Deauville, 1913, from *Art et Décoration,* 1914.

Figure 2.57

Robert Mallet-Stevens, music room for a villa
in Deauville, 1913, from *Art et Décoration,* 1914.

discerned in virtually all Mallet-Stevens's subsequent work, particularly in
his early architectural drawings and his pre–World War I efforts at interior design. The geometric simplicity and juxtaposition of black and white
that characterize the two interiors for Paquin's Deauville villa, for example, are frequently cited examples of Mallet-Stevens's debt to Viennese
design. Curiously, when the same elements were combined with brilliant yellow and blue decorative details in the fur shop Mallet-Stevens designed for Paquin in New York, the result was characterized as a "Persian
Salon."[133] The individual elements of the design that contributed to this
effect included "a black Persian table decorated with bright red, yellow,
blue and white figures" placed at the center of the room on a circular rug
of "Oriental yellow bordered with purple"; the lighting was said to have

been achieved "by the generous use of silver Oriental lanterns placed on the walls."

This account of Paquin's New York shop is noteworthy for two reasons; first, the commentator pointed out that "[r]ugs, chairs, lights and everything used in the quaint rooms were designed to order in France," and second, the only surviving photograph of the interior (figure 2.55) betrays no sign amidst its rectilinear severity of anything that might today elicit the adjectives "Persian" or "Oriental." How then might one account for this apparent mismatch between visual and textual evidence? If none of the objects came from an exotic source, and none of them seem to have borne any discernible stylistic relationship to Persian or other Middle Eastern designs, why was this association made by contemporary viewers? The answer to these questions appears to be that various period discourses converged on this interior to make the geometric forms and bright, contrasting colors characteristic of certain contemporary European decorators signify an Orientalist sensibility. Such a collapse of difference between West and East was the hallmark of Poiret's identity as a couturier, and we have already seen that it was an important factor in the theater, for example in conditioning the reception of the dresses designed by Iribe and produced by Paquin for *Rue de la Paix*. When observers criticized the bright colors and unusually revealing shapes of Iribe and Paquin's dresses, they described them as exotic and foreign, conjuring both Oriental and German influences—never mind that today these are commonly regarded as obviously distinct formal alternatives. Because they came together in the highly visible work of Poiret—both his dresses and Martine's decorative arts designs were shot through with Orientalist references as well as Wiener Werkstätte (and thus Austrian, not German) influences—the two became discursively intertwined. This confusion of the Oriental and the Germanic began to build on the perception of a foreign cultural invasion beginning in 1910, on the one hand with the Ballets Russes production of

Schéhérazade, and on the other with a major exhibition of German decorative arts at the Salon d'Automne that year.[134]

During this same pre–World War I period, Paquin apparently realized that such a palimpsest of complex, sometimes contradictory, associations could serve her interests, as they did Poiret's, and this might explain why she sought out many of the artists, decorators, and architects whom Poiret had initially employed to help him construct a public image for himself and his *maison de couture.* And the strategy worked well; despite her disavowal of the *jupe-culotte* and the distance she put between herself and any "foreign" influences when she responded to criticism of the costumes she collaborated with Iribe to make for *Rue de la Paix,* Paquin could be just as important a player on the Orientalist scene as Poiret or Iribe. This point is driven home by the fact that in the summer of 1912, when the Comtesse Blanche de Clermont-Tonnerre threw her "Thousand and One Nights Ball," described as "the great society event of the season," the focus of attention in the weeks leading up to the event was the "epic" competition that developed between two of her guests, the Princesse Murat and the Duchesse de Guiche, "the one being supported by the couturier Poiret, and the other by Mme Paquin, whose ardent rivalry is well known. It has been learned that the princess will make her entry at the ball perched on an elephant and escorted by semi-nude black slaves; but the duchess has sworn to do better still!"[135]

The intense competition between Paquin and Poiret was thus enacted on the public stage in productions such as *Rue de la Paix* and also underwritten and reinforced by their aristocratic clients, as illustrated by the rivalry for "most Orientalist" honors at the fête thrown by the Comtesse Blanche de Clermont-Tonnerre. The constant jockeying for position by these two couturiers in the unstable world of fashion, their oscillation between emulation and opposition, were played out in the theater and at spectacular parties thrown by wealthy aristocrats, as well as in the popular press. It even functioned as the structuring principle in a satire of the Parisian couture industry published on the eve of the First World War by Sem, a widely acclaimed French caricaturist. Far from a popular send-up, however, this large-format deluxe album, entitled *Le Vrai et le faux chic,* was printed in only 300 signed and numbered examples on Japan paper, and sold for 60 francs; a version with a deluxe binding was available for 125 francs.[136] Predictably, perhaps, the text praised the couturiers of the rue de la Paix, including Worth, Paquin, Callot Soeurs, Cheruit, and Doeuillet (the latter two were actually located on the adjacent Place Vendôme, at the south end of rue de la Paix; Callot Soeurs was headquartered close by on the rue Taitbout, near the Opéra). These were described as the creators of "'refreshing' toilettes of a healthy and traditional inspiration, deserving of being put forth as models of 'vrai chic' français."[137] According to Sem, one of the finest examples of this true fashion was a creation by Madame Paquin (figure 2.58): "This gown of a youthful, ingenuous grace . . . inspired by pure French tradition, is clearly the work of Mme Paquin, queen of the rue de la Paix, whose face, animated *à la Fragonard* . . . evokes the charm of the eighteenth century." Although Sem did not identify Poiret by name, Poiret is evidently the villain of the piece. This is only suggested in the text, but made clear in numerous accompanying images, described as a *Musée d'Erreurs,* many of which are caricatures of Poiret's most famous dress designs, including several cruelly hilarious parodies of the lampshade tunic (figure 2.59).

In his diatribe against contemporary fashion run amok, Sem condemned Poiret and the other unnamed couturiers of the *faux chic* for their vulgar theatricality, to which they were said to have been driven by a dearth of clients. Sem, at least, clearly saw the spectacle of fashion as a merchandising strategy designed to lure patrons at any cost (figure 2.60). He further vilified purveyors of *faux chic* for the sexually suggestive appeal of their clothes, which the caricaturist lampooned in harsh terms for their popular theatrical appeal and for being entirely foreign to French taste. The acrimonious tone of Sem's critique was similar to, though seemingly

Figure 2.58   ↄ

Sem, dress by Jeanne Paquin, from *Le Vrai et le faux chic,* 1914.

Le cierge entouré de papier frisé.

Le cocher fou qui a mis son carrick
autour des reins.

QUELQUES FANTAISIES SUR LES ROBES A VOLANTS

La carcasse de robe en feu
rongée par des chenilles.

Le mât de cocagne avec son cerceau.

Figure 2.59

Sem, images from *Le Vrai et le faux chic,*
reproduced in *L'Illustration,* 1914.

even more intense than, the attitude informing his *Tangoville sur Mer,* an
album published in August 1913 that satirized the contemporary craze for
the tango (figure 2.61). Imported from Argentina, this was, according to
Sem, a sexually suggestive dance in which "closely coupled men and
women undulate, snake, their bodies entwined, entangled, chest to chest
and stomach to stomach, caressing one another, fitting together with
mutually supporting movements, regular and knowing, slowly turning,
almost convulsing on the spot."[138] In *Tangoville sur Mer,* Sem offered an
indulgent as well as humorously critical view of the tango. He recognized
that the dance had a sportive as well as a seductive allure, and when he

Figure 2.60 ☽

Sem, fashion show, from *Le Vrai et le faux chic,*
1914.

Figure 2.61 ☽

Sem, tango scene, from *Tangoville sur mer,* 1913.

wrote about it he suggested that, beyond the moral vice for which it was condemned by the Archbishop of Paris, this foreign import had evolved to the point where it became "the tango of Paris, perfumed, wavy, adorably chiffonned, a product of the rue de la Paix."

Sem's alignment in *Tangoville sur Mer* of the *vrai chic* of the rue de la Paix with a domesticated version of the tango would presumably have been considerably complicated later in 1913, when Poiret (an exemplar for Sem of *faux chic*) became closely associated with the popular dance phenomenon through his costumes—and Martine's contributions to the set designs—for *Le Tango,* a play in four acts by Jean Richepin and his wife that premiered at the Théâtre de l'Athénée on 29 December 1913.[139] In that production, the tango figures as the means by which a modern young woman, Marie-Thérèse (played by Spinelly), and her equally young husband, Zigi de Lusignan (played in drag by Eve Lavallière), discover their love for one another. Having been made to marry early, initially the two see their union simply as a means to freedom from adult supervision; although they are friends, there is no ardor in their relationship and they remain untouched by the morally dubious places they begin to frequent, including the studio of a cubist painter and a fashionable nightspot where the clientele dances the tango. Even when they are taken to Algeria to experience a passionate atmosphere redolent of Orientalist sensuality where "the air is tepid, the nights voluptuous," they continue to be unaffected by carnal desire. The denouement comes in the last act when, back in Paris, the couple themselves dance the tango, and this "dance of complex lasciviousness" finally sparks their ardor for one another. The tango, more than any other marker of a potentially dangerous, sexually charged modernity with which that dance might be associated—whether French cubist painting or Orientalist North Africa—thus prompts the lead characters' discovery of amorous desire. At the same time, the dubious moral status of the dance is redeemed by its role in bringing the lovers together: "[T]he Tango, this discredited Tango, which is accused of corrupting youth, has served it in precisely the opposite way, by providing for the revelation of an indomitable and very sweet power . . ." Significantly, the costumes and elements of the sets that Poiret and his decorative arts outlet, Martine, contributed to the play were seen by at least one critic as crucial to its success: "They form part of the action. They contribute, as much as the spoken lines, to articulating the modernism of the characters, their snobism, their inclinations, their audacity, their cleverness, their weaknesses. . . . In truth, the name of M. Paul Poiret very much deserves to be hailed by applause when, at the end of the play, the [names of the] authors are proclaimed." As Lise-Léon Blum remarked in the *Gazette du Bon Ton,* it was Poiret who possessed the "ingenuity, barbarity and refinement to clothe the characters in this exotic and Parisian drama," and Martine was the appropriate choice "to furnish the ateliers, the villas, the *salles de sport* and even the gardens" where the play's two lovers meet.[140]

Thus on the basis of a play that thematized the tango, Blum, for one, saw Poiret as a model of both the exotic and the familiar French qualities that the dance in the play was said to combine. For Sem, on the other hand, Poiret seems to have exemplified the purveyors of *faux chic* who were beholden to foreign influences, spectacular extravaganzas, and dangerous seductive techniques. As far as Sem was concerned Poiret and his ilk therefore posed a pressing cultural and social problem: "These shameless charlatans, who have become veritable impresarios, mount all kinds of galas at each new season and, under the pretext of launching new fashions, organize the presentation of their models like a music-hall drama. Between a tango by Mistinguett and a song by Fursy, they parade to music from a stage surrounded by paper flowers and Chinese lanterns into the middle of the audience . . . a strange corps de ballet more or less Russian, Persian or Romanian, a whole procession of disjointed mannequins, women-serpents smeared with venomous toilettes who undulate, slowly convulsing, their stomachs pushed forward and a foot trailing (figure 2.62), miming a sort of empty tango under the gaze of

Figure 2.62 ↺

Sem, image from *Le Vrai et le faux chic,* 1914.

the female spectators—unhappy little snobs whom these unscrupulous managers enervate with adulterated tea and mysterious dopings, waiting for the approaching day when they extend their cynicism to the point of drugging these women with cocaine and ether, the better to prepare them, to reduce them to poor unconscious women ready to submit to the most extravagant exploitation." This condemnation of women's supposedly irrational, drug-induced submission to the seductiveness of theatricalized fashion was accompanied in *Le Vrai et le faux chic* by a racist commentary embedded in the narrative of a fictional man who disappears to deepest Africa where he is cut off from the modern world for ten years. Upon his return to western civilization represented by the city of Paris, he is able to find only a few of the well-dressed Parisiennes he used to know and love; the rest of the female population has been transformed as in a dream into "bizarre creatures with paradoxical silhouettes" whom

Sem likens to bugs "bristling with prickles, legs, and antennas" (figure
2.63); or "others, poisonous green with busts too flat for their heavy
abdomens exposed for sale, showing the terrible obscenity of demented
praying mantises ready to devour their mates"; or still others, "sluggish,"
"slimy," "convulsing." Traumatized by this bewildering vision, the man
sees not fashionable women but savages everywhere, whether a "redskin
with green hair" (figure 2.64) or, running toward him, a "frizzy-haired

Figure 2.63

Sem, two-page spread from *Le Vrai et le faux
chic*, 1914.

Figure 2.64

Sem, image from *Le Vrai et le faux chic,* 1914.

cannibal . . . her body strangled, almost cut in two by a yoke, her nose run through by a ring, her bloody mouth cloven to her ears" (figure 2.65). The language of these descriptions seems even more venomous than the degrading and distorted figures that Sem drew to illustrate them. The point is forcefully yet succinctly made in a single sentence at the end of the story: "Finally driven crazy, overcome with panic, [the man] closes his suitcase and takes the first camel bound for Timbuktu." Paris fashions, Sem thus tells us, have become more savage, more dangerous, more threatening than anything one might encounter in deepest Africa, which, paradoxically, becomes a refuge for a sophisticated world traveler seeking to escape the irrational horrors of contemporary women's fashions in Paris. Turning from this nightmare narrative to his

de manitou, canaques aux tignasses colorées, troglodytes chargées de peaux de bêtes pendantes, Peaux-Rouges à cheveux verts, hérissés de plumes écarlates. Et voilà que, suprême horreur, il aperçoit, courant vers lui, une cannibale crépue — une vraie, celle-là — le corps étranglé, presque coupé en deux par un carcan, le nez traversé d'un anneau, la bouche sanglante fendue jusqu'aux oreilles...

Définitivement affolé, pris de panique, il boucle sa valise et prend le premier chameau pour Tombouctou.

Sans doute cette parabole est-elle excessive, et point n'est besoin de revenir de Huronie et d'avoir la fièvre tropicale pour être frappé de la crise de mauvais goût qui sévit à Paris en ce moment. Mais nous l'avons vu naître et se développer peu à peu, et nos yeux déjà gâtés, vaccinés, si je puis dire, ont eu le temps de s'y habituer progressivement. Nous sommes moins impressionnés que notre Huron africain, sevré de Paris pendant dix ans et placé brutalement devant ces invraisemblables réalités.

Bien plus, il arrive ce fait inouï que les pires

Figure 2.65 ◌

Sem, detail of page from *Le Vrai et le faux chic,* 1914.

treatment of the details of those fashions, Sem allows for no ambiguity in his comparison between *faux chic* caricatured in the form of self-satisfied, aging, and corpulent women, for whom the latest fashions were surely inappropriate (figures 2.66 and 2.67), and *vrai chic,* exemplified by a slim, young, attractive figure, elegant in her bearing, as well as the restraint of her clothing (figure 2.68)—"such a masterpiece of harmonious and discrete simplicity!"

Figure 2.66

Sem, page from *Le Vrai et le faux chic,* 1914.

Figure 2.67

Sem, page from *Le Vrai et le faux chic,* 1914.

discrètement dissimulées au milieu de ce défilé de mi-carême, non pas quelques-unes, mais des milliers de Parisiennes exquises, habillées avec un goût sûr par une élite de couturiers et de modistes qui savent encore soutenir le bon renom et la suprématie de Paris.

Voyez cette petite robe d'un bleu cendré, comme pastellisé par la lumière modérée de Paris. C'est un rien : une tunique retenue par une ceinture sur une jupe droite. Mais quel petit chef-d'œuvre de simplicité harmonieuse et discrète ! Le buste fragile de cette jeune femme se meut aisément dans ce souple velours adouci d'un col et d'une bande de fourrure, tandis que la jupe claque allégrement entre les pieds alertes, à la cadence de la démarche réglée sur l'amble du lévrier. Il faudrait avoir des yeux bien peu exercés, de bien mauvais " callots ", dirait une arpette indignée, pour ne pas deviner à première vue que cette charmante promeneuse s'est échappée des mains divines des deux sœurs fées que l'univers nous envie.

Figure 2.68

Sem, page from *Le Vrai et le faux chic,* 1914.

Sem's album may not have reached a wide audience directly, but it was reviewed and its argument was summarized in *L'Illustration* where, in addition, quite a few of the illustrations were reproduced (figure 2.69).[141] Moreover, Sem's critique of contemporary fashions elicited a response from Paul Iribe, whose defense of *la mode* was published in *Le Miroir* on July 26, 1914.[142] There, Iribe drew attention to the internal contradictions that underlie so many aspects of the discursive construction of fashion: "People who say they have taste, criticize fashion, scorn it, and follow it," he declared. "This means that it is easy to criticize fashion (any fashion), but also that, on pain of being ridiculous, and I would say even badly brought up, it is strictly necessary to follow it, because the truly elegant person being the one who does not call attention to herself, it is obvious that she could not be out of fashion [*démodée*] since, in that case, she would be noticeable." In fact, Iribe wrote, the only valid criticism of any particular fashion would be that it lasted too long, since the purpose of fashion in general is endless variation. He therefore drew a sharp distinction between rapidly changing fashion and enduring Art (with a capital A), arguing that it would be inappropriate to judge fashion according to aesthetic criteria. "Fashion is less or more than that, and it is also something else indefinable: the expression of feminine fantasy which it appears that men are condemned never to understand. Our role, and I find it a delicious one, is therefore to admire its manifestations, occasionally to smile at them, and always to be surprised by them. But we have the right, in exchange, to demand variety and change; let us demand it, first of all because the dresses that troubled M. Sem will disappear, and then because fashion has to be ephemeral; the most beautiful fashion, as soon as it is born, has to die: it would not be good if it were immortal." Here Iribe embraced the qualities of ephemerality and instability that Baudelaire had so admired in modern fashion but which others, notably Sem, more often condemned as evidence of the feminized character of fashion. Indeed, the

Figure 2.69

Sem, images from *Le Vrai et le faux chic*,
reproduced in *L'Illustration*, 1914.

link between fashion's variability and female inconstancy was made at several points in Sem's *Le Vrai et le faux chic* diatribe, as he sought to lambaste the current interest in fashion as "a new case of pathology . . . a modern hysteria," and to condemn women who followed fashion for their "unbridled fantasy, their feverish changeability and their disorder. This approaches vice. One finds in this furor the same symptoms that characterized the hysteria for the tango. It is the delirium of chiffon, '*Modomanie*,' if I may say so." These were the qualities that, according to Sem, unscrupulous couturiers of the *faux chic* took advantage of when they mounted their "repugnant and grotesque spectacles that compromise the good reputation of Paris." Now, as if its debased theatricality were not sufficient grounds for condemning contemporary fashion, "to crown this delirium, the department stores, enticed by these bad examples, join the movement, bringing to it their monstrous business and getting involved with intensive fashion." These emporia, often described as taking advantage of women's uncontrollable desire for fashion consumption, raised the problem of women's submission to the theatrical and primitive character of contemporary fashion to a new level of hysteria and frenzy. But the commercially motivated intervention of the department store was only one of several recent developments lamented by Sem. "Alas!" he concluded, "it is no longer a French revolution that today submits to fashion. The movement comes to us from abroad, where the words *Droits de la Femme* are applied to every extravagance. It is the triumph of the goddess of Unreason." It thus becomes apparent that, in contrast to the argument running throughout the album regarding fashion's tendency to disempower and subjugate its adherents, the ultimate threat it posed, according to Sem, lay in its potential to liberate modern women rather than enslave them.

In Sem's diatribe against the theatricality and dangerously seductive appeal of fashion, published on the eve of the First World War, we encounter yet another articulation of the tensions surrounding a number of overlapping and interpenetrating period discourses, the complexity of which is inadequately if conveniently characterized as a series of oppositions between modernity and tradition, domestic and foreign, classicism and Orientalism, dramatic theater and commercial spectacle, art and industry. French couturiers attempted to negotiate these conflicting—although as we have seen also increasingly conflated—constructs by deploying the discourses of high art and individual style to position themselves simultaneously on both sides of the divide conjured up by these overly simplified oppositions. Ultimately, their success would be measured in the marketplace, where the efficacy of any particular design or line of dresses was subject to commercial considerations from which the discursive implications of style (e.g., classicism, Orientalism, etc.) cannot be entirely disentangled. In fact, the couture industry of the early twentieth century depended upon a subtle, elusive, and perennially unstable balance between the modernist art imperatives of individualism, originality, and uniqueness on one hand, and the modern commercial imperatives of repetition, appropriation, and mass appeal on the other. This aspect of fashion's complex and contradictory logic—specifically, the integration of art and theater with mass production, advertising, and related strategies developed for the purposes of mass marketing—is the subject addressed in the following chapter.

Three
Fashioning Commodity Culture

Haute couture was developed and promoted in the late nineteenth and early twentieth centuries by dress designers who regarded the commercial world with disdain. These men and women carefully constructed their personas as great artists or discerning patrons of the arts for whom the banal and potentially degrading aspects of business were beneath the elite status to which they aspired. While Jacques Doucet was careful to segregate his business operations from his art-related activities, Paul Poiret presents a strikingly different paradigm of the couturier insofar as he openly incorporated the visual arts, as well as diverse approaches to theatrical display, in his efforts to sell expensive dresses and other products in the discrete and aestheticized environment of his couture house. Unlike Doucet's home, Poiret's *hôtel* was a business setting that doubled as a domestic space in which his wife circulated like a mannequin and his friends tried out his latest styles at extravagant costume parties, thus ensuring that the difference between commercial and private activities would always be ambiguous. The precarious balance that Poiret strove to maintain after 1909 between an allegedly disinterested commitment to high culture and the demands of an increasingly complex, sophisticated, and diversified commercial enterprise was constantly being challenged, not only by rival couturiers, but also by changes in the couture industry and even by the success of his own fashions. This chapter examines a number of conflicting forces that influenced the marketing of haute couture in the early twentieth century, and it explores in particular the ways in which Poiret's self-construction as an artist (the focus of chapter 1) and his theatrical strategies of display (discussed in chapter 2) were affected by the circumstances he encountered when, in the early teens, he began seriously to cultivate the American market for high-end women's clothing by going to the United States to present his models to women there, rather than waiting for them to seek him out in Paris. Poiret's discovery that his work (like that of Jeanne Paquin and many other French couturiers) was being copied and his label counterfeited, evidently on a vast scale, exposed a serious challenge to the elite business of haute couture, as well as to its discursive construction of originality, in ways that bear comparison with contemporaneous developments in the realm of high art.

Imitation has always been central to art in the western classical tradition, and copying was for centuries institutionalized in the education of the artist. During the course of the nineteenth century, however, romantic notions of artistic genius, changing social conditions, and art market forces converged to create circumstances in which originality came to be privileged in the discursive construction of modernism. While artists struggled to confront—or, at the turn of the century, more often to escape—the implications of industrialization and mass production, the ubiquity of reproductive printing processes encouraged a resurgence of interest in fine art prints even as photography came to be recognized as an art form.

Both photography and traditional printmaking draw in their serial nature from a singular template—a negative in the case of photography, and, typically, a woodblock, metal plate, or stone in that of printmaking. This template functions as the basis for the production of (nearly) identical images, much as the couturier's model provides the foundation for the production of nearly identical clothes. Although the number of high quality "original" prints that can be produced from a woodblock or metal plate are limited by the progressive degeneration of the materials under the pressure of the printing press, re-engraving of the plate was already a common practice in the Renaissance and re-impressions of famous prints by Rembrandt, for example, repeatedly pulled from surviving copperplates during the centuries after his death (even as late as 1906), resulted in what have been described as "crude travesties of his etchings—Rembrandt 'originals' that were less faithful than even the feeblest reproductions."[1] Thus, well before the invention of lithography at the end of the eighteenth century and subsequently of steel engraving, photography, photogravure, and a range of other mechanical processes, the potential for unlimited reproduceability of the image had already complicated the always ambiguous distinction in the print media between the original and the reproduction. Michel Melot has written about this aspect of the print media in terms that correspond closely to what I have been calling the logic of fashion and, in particular, to the contradictory pressures for art status on the one hand and industrial production on the other which haute couture found itself facing in the early twentieth century: "Recognition of the print as a work of art in its own right came with the founding in Paris, in 1889, of the Société des Peintres-Graveurs," Melot observes. "One of its aims was to see that prints, drawings, and paintings were exhibited side by side on an equal footing; the point being, obviously, to raise the print to the same status as the other two. . . . The print could only consolidate its position in the world of art so long as it remained carefully barricaded against any intrusion by industry. Such a position was tenable so long as the demand from art lovers remained low. But as the number of collectors grew, intent on hunting out prints known to be scarce, the possibility of reproducing these in series, to which the print readily lent itself, was soon being exploited—and exploited now in the very heart of the art market, creating an insuperable contradiction."[2] Some of these same conditions apply to the medium of sculpture, where casting in bronze, for example, results in original works that, like prints and photographs (as well as couture dresses), are by their nature reproductions.[3] Moreover, artists working in all these media typically collaborate with craftsmen in the realization of their work. Bronze casting is of course an expensive and therefore self-limiting process but even sculptors, like printmakers and photographers, found it advantageous to develop procedures that would protect the rarity and, hence, the value of their output by setting limits on editions of their work. Although the solutions to these problems were markedly diverse, there are parallels to be found in the early twentieth century between the visual arts and the world of haute couture, where the number of high-quality dresses produced from a single model was limited because couturiers charged extremely high prices in order to secure the rarity of the design in circulation, and to cover their costs associated with experienced labor, fine materials, high real estate overhead, and heavy investment in a diverse array of promotional activities. Illegal but largely uncontrolled piracy and counterfeiting practices allowed unscrupulous manufacturers to avoid the majority of these expenses and, therefore, fostered the development of a reproductive economy of copies that posed a significant threat to haute couture. Under these circumstances, it became increasingly difficult for couturiers to charge high prices based on the rarity of the original, because copies with convincing (though counterfeit) labels were widely available at prices far below those charged for couture "originals."

In the fine arts—even in printmaking where reproduction was practiced on an almost industrial scale—neither piracy nor counterfeiting were endemic or systematic, as they were in haute couture; illicit practices did not create the pressure for originality that is such a prominent feature of modernist discourse. But copying was nevertheless at issue in the marketing of modern art, as we have seen in the case of Daniel-Henry Kahnweiler, who regarded imitation and pastiche in the form of salon cubism as a distinct threat to the authenticity and marketability of the cubist works on offer in his gallery. It was precisely his fear that the public might accept Gleizes, Metzinger, and their colleagues as legitimate representatives of cubism (no matter how much Kahnweiler disliked the label) that led the dealer to describe Braque and Picasso as "sincere," "earnest" artists—the genuine, authentic cubists, in contrast to the imitators and "showmen" who entertained the crowd by displaying their work in public exhibitions.[4]

If the discourse of the copy was imbedded within the very construct of the original work of art, as Rosalind Krauss has argued,[5] the same could be said of the couture dress. Yet for all the similarities between them and between the discourses that surround them, dresses and works of art generally differ in fundamental respects. Poiret always strove to collapse such differences, but he was eventually forced to acknowledge the incompatibility of art and couture when he sought protection for his designs—and, not incidentally, for his status as an artist—under the provisions of American copyright law. American law privileged function and use, and it therefore failed to recognize in dresses the intellectual property rights developed for works of art as products of the mind. Instead of reinforcing Poiret's claim to authorship as an artist, the law recognized only his right to commercial trademark protection of his couture label, and as we shall see it compelled him to acknowledge that his name signified his status as a businessman, not a fine artist.

The narrative of this chapter culminates in a discussion of the discursive construction of authorship according to French and American law, but its larger focus is on issues of originality and reproduction—the professionally mounted theatrical production and its offshoot in the commercially staged fashion show, the authentic couture dress and its pirated copy. Although the chapter begins and ends in pre–World War I Paris, much of it centers on America in an effort to expose precisely how the theater of fashion examined in the previous chapter functioned for Poiret and other couturiers as a particularly effective marketing tool there as well as in France. An exemplary case in point is Poiret's work for *Le Minaret,* a three-act play by Jacques Richepin that was originally produced in a Paris theater and shortly thereafter was reinvented as a fashion show and commercial vehicle in numerous department stores in New York.

Le Minaret opened on March 19, 1913 at the Théâtre de la Renaissance, which was managed by Richepin's wife, the actress Cora Laparcerie. Poiret produced several hundred costumes for the play— most, if not all, actually designed by his employees, Erté and José de Zamora—according to a color scheme Poiret established in conjunction with the highly stylized sets, designed by Ronsin.[6] As its title suggests, *Le Minaret* was a typical Orientalist fantasy along the lines of *Nabuchodonosor,* involving "slaves, musicians, [and] eunuchs," that was set, according to the published text, "in the Orient of the Thousand and One Nights"[7] (figure 3.1). The play's convoluted yet conventional story of romance and implied eroticism was launched by the decision of an old sultan that upon his death his harem should not be dispersed but instead his eight wives should be kept together, and they themselves should determine who would become their new master. A competition amongst the pretenders, initiated by the Grand Eunuch a month after the sultan's death, quickly eliminated all but three rivals. The narrative heated up in the second act (figure 3.2) when, on the night before the wives were to make their decision, one of them was disguised as the muezzin in the minaret overlooking the walled garden, while the suitors appeared one after another to try to gain the favor of the inhabitants of the harem. The last act (figure 3.3) took place inside the sumptuous hall of the seraglio,

Figure 3.1 ☉

Le Minaret, Act I, from *Le Théâtre,*1913.

where, after several complications and plot reversals, the various wives were united with their chosen lovers and a great celebration ensued.

Given the clichéd nature of the Orient represented in the play, which one critic characterized as "whimsical and rather conventional," it was understood that Richepin had no desire to present a work of theatrical realism but had opted instead for "pleasing and harmonious *tableaux.*"[8] Rather than displaying a commitment to research or attention to any factual basis in local detail, the author of *Le Minaret* envisioned "a voyage to a dream land, according to our dreams."[9] The sets and costumes accordingly created what was described in the press as "a spectacle of the most delicious refinement. It is a feast for the eyes, a symphony of colors, a veritable dream of a Thousand and One Nights, inspired by Persian miniatures, a little *munichois* decorative art, but with more taste, and also a little of the Englishman Aubrey Beardsley."[10] As one critic noted, "The symbolism of the title is very general. *Le Minaret* embodies the Orient as a whole, with its fashions, its costumes and its beliefs; the action is situated in Persia, and the author has tried to make an expressive and lively image of this kingdom. . . . It was not about presenting the traditional Orient, with its multicolored tones; it was necessary to offer nuances that are very simple in themselves. Each act would have its own colors, and the costume designer and decorator have, it appears, arrived at the most pleasing effects."[11] Ronsin and Poiret indeed worked together to ensure

Figure 3.2 ☾

Le Minaret, Act II, from *Le Théâtre,* 1913.

Figure 3.3 ◯

Le Minaret, Act III, from *Le Théâtre,* 1913.

the harmonious effect of every scenographic element. Green, black, and silver were the dominant colors used for both the sets and the costumes in the first act; red, black, and gold signified the fiery emotions and sensuality that characterized the garden scene in act 2; and in the final act, white, black, and silver established a sumptuous yet festive mood for the harem interior.[12] Several theater critics compared these striking color schemes favorably to the design practices that were by this time familiar features of the Ballets Russes, pointing out the "very French gaiety" of *Le Minaret*,[13] its nuanced use of colors in contrast to what were said (with self-serving exaggeration) to be the heavy-handed audacities of its sources. These were said to have included the work of Léon Bakst, Wladimir Egoroff's designs for *L'Oiseau bleu,* and especially the "synthetic decors" that Ernst Stern designed for Max Reinhardt's *Sumurun,* an Orientalist pantomime based on *The Tales of the Arabian Nights* that premiered in Berlin in 1910 and thereafter toured several European cities before its presentation at the Théâtre du Vaudeville in Paris in 1913.[14] Instead of the clumsy awkwardness for which the French defensively criticized German scenography and decorative art, the impression made by *Le Minaret* was described as "sumptuous and entirely joyful, like the play itself."[15] The successful effort to harmonize the costumes with the sets and the lighting in terms of their colors as well as their design was interpreted as an "indication of a new kind of art, very superior in its distinction and its tact to that of the much heralded Ballet Russes,"[16] from which such efforts at coordination undoubtedly had in fact derived a good deal of inspiration.

Despite the timeless quality of its story, evidenced, for example, by the fact that *Le Minaret* shared with virtually every other *Arabian Nights* scenario of the period its focus on the seductive charms of the inhabitants of an attractive Oriental harem, at least one critic noted the topicality of this drama set in Persia that premiered while the Balkan Wars were at their height.[17] But if Orientalism in the visual arts could be perceived as a potential danger, this was not the result of any direct or immediate association with current events in the Balkans. Rather, the contemporary political problem that coalesced around Orientalism in the cultural realm was rooted in long-term French and German economic competition that encompassed issues as diverse as the nations' colonial rivalries and their efforts to dominate international marketing of the decorative arts. For decades, even centuries, Orientalist discourse had embraced images of North Africa and the Middle East that maintained and reinforced distinctions between, on one hand, the alien cultures of those regions and, on the other, a familiar French culture. But when contemporary French women donned harem trousers or attended parties set in imaginary Persian seraglios, such distinctions broke down (as did the strict differentiation between male and female sartorial signifiers). However, such practices cannot have been regarded unconditionally as threatening to traditional French values, given the fact that these social occasions were hosted by prominent French aristocrats who competed with one another for the distinction of wearing the most fashionable Orientalist costume. Clearly, class difference worked to secure the acceptability of an otherwise transgressive Orientalist theatricality among the wealthy elite. As was pointed out in chapter 2, Poiret's own rhetoric about the appropriateness of his Orientalist costumes for an exclusive, upper-class, and aristocratic clientele helped to establish this very effect.

A different but not unrelated set of circumstances worked to make the sphere of the decorative arts an equally charged field of conflicting associations, as German modernists made significant headway in competing with French decorators for markets that the French had traditionally controlled. When a group of decorators from Munich exhibited their work in a series of thirteen coloristically coordinated and harmoniously integrated interiors displayed at the Salon d'Automne in Paris in 1910, the often intense or sharply contrasting color schemes they favored marked their contributions as foreign, alien to French taste. This in turn made it possible for French critics to align these *munichois* designs with works by other outsiders such as Léon Bakst and Ernst Stern. At the same time, however, many critics associated the designers from Munich with the French cubist painters, including Gleizes and Metzinger, who showed their work publicly in the Salon d'Automne and in other exhibitions together with their decorator friends, all of whom also used intense colors in their work.[18] Moreover, those French decorators' stylistic predilections for the Directoire and especially the Louis-Philippe styles appeared to many observers to be equally antagonistic to entrenched French aesthetic traditions exemplified by the ancien régime styles of Louis XV and Louis

XVI, which were carried forward in the delicate forms of Art Nouveau. In this palimpsest of significations, and against the backdrop of increasing hostility between France and Germany during the several years prior to the outbreak of World War I in August 1914, the work of cosmopolitan modern artists, decorators, and designers was often viewed as an undifferentiated phenomenon such that French as well as German expressions of Orientalism were frequently associated with *munichois* interior decoration, which in turn was thought to be affiliated with French cubism. All became suspect for their links to foreign tendencies or commercial interests that were believed to undermine French hegemony in the visual and decorative arts.[19] Thus Poiret found himself in the paradoxical situation where his cosmopolitan ideology in the decorative arts, his interest in the Wiener Werkstätte—manifested in his dresses and even more obviously in the products of his design atelier, Martine—and especially the Orientalizing features of his clothing designs and perfumes not only assured his position as a fashionable and successful French couturier to the wealthy elite, these aspects of his design practice also made him appear to be a threat to traditional French taste. He was, therefore, perceived at one and the same time as an innovative creator of modern French fashions and as an insidious promoter of all sorts of decorative arts and costumes alien to the national identity. (This is precisely what happened in 1915 when, even while he was serving in the French army, Poiret was accused of representing German taste, of introducing "*boche, munichois, berlinois* fashions" and imposing them on unsuspecting French women.[20])

Although Poiret's fashions enjoyed increasingly widespread appeal before and even during the war, critics like Sem, playing to conservative and nationalist sentiments, began to condemn his work as alien, "Other," German. At least as early as 1912, Poiret's designs were commonly identified with those presented in the productions of the Ballets Russes, for example, and *Le Minaret,* in particular, was frequently compared with the recent Paris production of Reinhardt's *Sumurun*. While French artists and audiences absorbed these Russian and German influences, their rhetoric stressed a desire to distance themselves from any such sources, and the contradictory character of the significations embedded in their own Orientalist project consequently came increasingly to the fore. Thus, in his emphatically Orientalist work for *Le Minaret,* Poiret was widely regarded not as a dangerous, alien threat, but as precisely the opposite. In fact, although *Le Minaret* was entirely Orientalist in all its features, including the plot, the decors, and the costumes, the play was both produced and received as an expression of French nationalist sentiment. Indeed, in mounting the play, Cora Laparcerie intended from the outset to avoid the alien sensibility that French audiences identified in *Schéhérazade* and *Sumurun;* the staging of *Le Minaret* was designed, she said, to present "a Persia [that is] more French, . . . a Persia of the eighteenth century, or almost."[21] It was her opinion, declared in response to the impact of foreign works on contemporary stage practice in Paris, that "for French plays, a French *mise-en-scène* is required."[22] Criticizing the "disparate, loud colors [that] shock the eye," and the "deplorable contrast between the art of the set designer and that of the costume designer" that she said typified recent innovative work in the theater, Laparcerie blamed the influence of foreign artists whose conception of *mise-en-scène* "differs so much from ours." "France is the land of art and beauty," she declared. "It is the birthplace of the arts; its stature is reduced by the intrusion of foreign stage and costume designers. Finally, I had an occasion to give French art its due, and I seized it with alacrity . . . [commissioning Poiret and Ronsin,] two French artists, as original as possible, but simple. Their production . . . is marked by seductive charm and incomparable taste, by that taste which only the French possess, and which makes us the envy of all other nations."

Laparcerie's success in familiarizing the foreign and in creating a representation of the Orient that Parisian audiences would find compatible with traditional French sensibilities can be measured in the overwhelmingly positive responses of the critics, who praised both the sets and the costumes of *Le Minaret* for their relatively restrained and tasteful treatment of Oriental elements. This comes as something of a surprise almost a century after the fact, in light of what today appear to be unusual, even radical or bizarre, features of the female actresses' costumes (figures 3.4, 3.5, and 3.6). Many of them included bouffant trousers accompanied by bodices whose projecting, wired hems, or hoops, encircled the wearer's hips, creating a "lampshade" effect that was visually striking on stage but highly impractical if adopted in real life, particularly when it came to costumes whose multiple hoops created a tiered effect. Described as "improbable, startling, glittering, flashing, so rich, so numerous that each entrance of the actresses was greeted with applause," the costumes were accompanied by "colossal aigrettes studded with precious stones, and corselets and turbans with large, delicate pearls" that one critic noted would be the financial ruin of any husband whose wife might mistake them for items that could be worn outside the theater.[23] Given the creative license evident in the costumes "with their bouffant pantalons with metallic reflectors, their triple and quadruple wire hoops, their curved-toe Turkish slippers, their aigrettes like golden antennas,"[24] it is difficult to explain exactly why, in marked contrast to the marginalized, outsider role he was assigned in *Rue de la Paix* a year earlier and in Sem's critique of such fashions in *Le Vrai et le faux chic* of 1914 (both discussed in detail in the previous chapter), in 1913 Poiret emerged with *Le Minaret* as the champion of what many critics identified as typically French values: "For once it was appropriate that the name of the couturier figured on the [cover of the] program and one could even say that M. Paul Poiret was the real triumph of the evening. Throughout the three acts he paraded before us creations of a very piquant inventiveness and often of a most delicate taste: Persian costumes accommodated to the Parisian imagination,

Figure 3.4 ↄ

Cora Laparcerie as Myriem, in *Le Minaret,*
from *Le Théâtre,* 1913.

Figure 3.5

Marcelle Yrven as Zouz-Zuvabé in *Le Minaret,*
from *Le Théâtre,* 1913.

Figure 3.6

Mademoiselle Corbé as Maïmouna in
Le Minaret, from *Le Théâtre,* 1913.

fabrics, furs, headdresses, whose color and mixture formed living and clever *tableaux.*"[25]

The discourses of Frenchness that enabled an Orientalist play such as *Le Minaret* to be received as a work redolent of ancien régime French values also made it possible for Poiret to suggest that adaptations of his radical and extravagant costumes might be appropriate for the Frenchwomen in the audience. From the minute the play opened, Poiret used it as an opportunity to advertise his costumes to members of the fashionable Parisian *haute monde* who, in the wake of his "Thousand and

Second Night" extravaganza, were mounting comparably lavish Oriental fêtes of their own, for which they of course required appropriate costumes. Indeed, the play's premiere furnished an ideal setting in which to publicize a line of women's clothing designed in what soon became known as the Minaret style. In the audience, outfitted in a costume as daring as the ones on stage—it was made of transparent red and violet chiffon and topped by a wide-brimmed lampshade hat, also in violet chiffon, with a fringe of pearls—Madame Poiret completed the theatrical illusion by appearing, according to one observer, "to be dressed to enter the scene"[26] (figure 3.7). Her presence in a lampshade tunic over bouffant trousers thus allowed for a seamless transition between the stage fantasy—itself verging on a fashion show—and the female consumers in the audience, those who attended the theater not simply to see the play or to be seen in the audience but to view the latest fashions, the clothes they would like immediately to purchase for themselves. These women presumably experienced *Le Minaret* as a spectacle in which they might imaginatively take part, something Poiret's guests had literally been able to do when they attended his "Thousand and Second Night" fête, where Madame Poiret had also been dressed in a fringed lampshade tunic and bouffant trousers (figure 2.26), setting an example for the Oriental costumes of all the other female guests at this and subsequent parties with the same theme. Thus, in the blurred boundaries between *Le Minaret* as a theatrical performance and a real-life event, an aestheticized production with aspirations to high culture on one hand and an opportunity for fashion marketing on the other, Poiret worked both with and against the upper-class privacy and elitism he had claimed for his Orientalist costumes in 1911. This he did both to appeal to the ancien régime tastes of his wealthy clients (and presumably also their politics) and to exploit the theatrical core of prewar fashion, the way in which it mimicked contemporary theater as spectacle by constructing women to be seen—often at the theater, even as they were in the act of seeing. One might further argue that *Le Minaret* exposed Poiret's

Figure 3.7

Henri Manuel, photo of Madame Poiret
posing in the outfit she wore to the premiere of
Le Minaret, 1913.

contribution—if that is what it should be called—to the discourse of Orientalism in prewar France as an effort to transpose this complex and value-laden cultural expression onto the commodity form by repeatedly confusing the distinctions between self and "Other," producer and consumer, actor and audience, art and clothing, theater and real life. And the play met with widespread approval, as suggested by the fact that it was performed 142 times in Paris before it toured major cities in France and Switzerland, followed by twenty performances in Brussels. In addition, the second act was adapted for independent performance at London's Alhambra Theatre in May 1913 as "Flowers of Allah," part of a revue entitled *8d. a Mile.* Spoofs of Orientalist spectacles, such as "Phèdre," performed in Paris the following year in another revue called *Très moutarde* (figure 3.8),

Figure 3.8

Très moutarde, Act II, from *Le Théâtre,* 1914.

kept examples of Poiret's lampshade costumes before a broad range of theater audiences in the period following the premiere of *Le Minaret*.[27]

When *Le Minaret* opened to rave reviews in Paris, Poiret insisted, as was the custom of all his colleagues in the couture business, that he had no interest whatsoever in the commercial implications of his theatrical and related activities. He declared at the time, "I invented the [Minaret] tunic for a Persian play to be worn in a Persian garden in a spectacular ballet. I was astonished when my patrons called me on the telephone the morning after the premiere and begged that I fashion them such a tunic for social occasions. Naturally, I complied. . . ."[28] Indeed, he did much more than that. Not content to wait passively for women to come to him, he determined to build a new and far broader clientele by maximizing the publicity surrounding *Le Minaret* and the dresses he made for the play. This resolution bore fruit in September 1913, six months after the Paris premiere, when Poiret spearheaded an extensive public relations campaign to accompany the introduction of dresses inspired by his Minaret costumes to the American market. This transatlantic effort was carefully planned to coincide with his own tour of major cities in the Northeast and Midwest, including New York, Philadelphia, Baltimore, Boston, Buffalo, Toronto, and Chicago, where he lectured extensively, accompanied by films and portfolios filled with photographs of his mannequins parading in the garden of his Paris *maison de couture*,[29] and he received members of the press in the commodious suites he occupied at luxury hotels. In New York, for example, Poiret made appearances at major department stores, including J. M. Gidding, Gimbel Brothers (figure 3.9), R. H. Macy, and John Wanamaker (all of them boasted about the presence of "The Famous Fashion Dictator" in their ads).[30] He addressed female students of "practical art" and what were known as "household arts" at the Horace Mann School of Teachers College at Columbia University, and at the Pratt Institute.[31] He lectured at Carnegie Hall under the auspices of the Société des Beaux Arts. And he spoke to reporters in a room of his suite at the

Figure 3.9

Advertisements for J. M. Gidding and for
Gimbels, from *Women's Wear,* 26 September
1913.

Plaza Hotel that he transformed from a nondescript—if nevertheless luxurious—hotel interior into a small-scale version of his own *maison de couture*. The decorative accoutrements he brought from Paris for the purpose included a vividly colored "typical Poiret rug" on which he piled pillows in gold and silver brocades and other metallic fabrics. There was also a large screen decorated with a "Poiret rose," intended to be used as a backdrop for the dramatic appearance of Madame Poiret, who made her entrance and then reclined on the pillows "gowned in Oriental fashion" in a straight white brocaded silk sheath, a white turban, and emerald green satin shoes.[32] A photograph published in *Vogue* (figure 3.10)[33] indicates how the interior ensemble-cum-theatrical *mise-en-scène* was composed so

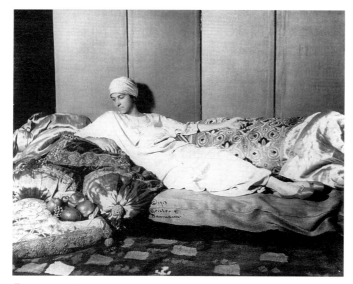

Figure 3.10

Geisler & Baumann, photo of Denise Poiret,
New York, 1913.

the screen would shut out background distractions, the rug was visible in the foreground, and Madame Poiret could assume the pose of an odalisque lounging across the pillows whose dense patterns and dark velvet surfaces created an effective contrast with her elegant white costume.

As Poiret toured the United States with his Minaret costumes, showing off his wife, delivering his lectures, giving interviews, and dining as the guest of department store executives, the couturier emphatically repeated the contention that his trip had nothing whatsoever to do with publicity. Two days after his arrival he declared to reporters "that he was 'very cross' at the advertisements that appeared in . . . newspapers exploiting his arrival. He said: 'I came to America on a social visit. I am merely a tourist. I think it is very bad form for my name to be used in a commercial sense just because I happen to be here. . . .'"[34] The fact that his wife brought with her 100 outfits for a visit lasting less than a month should not, he insisted, be taken as proof that she was there to serve as his mannequin. "Nothing could be further from the fact. We will be here in this country three weeks. Mme. Poiret must wear clothes. That is the only purpose for which she has brought her costumes. She is not to act as my model."[35] Poiret's denial of a commercial intent, his disdain for advertising and publicity, were part and parcel of his self-construction as an artist and an aristocrat, an individualist who rejected fashion because it smacked of mass production: "Women are wrong to adopt one style regardless," he told a *New York Times* correspondent. "They are not all made alike. They are different. They should wear different gowns."[36] While stressing individualism and originality, however, he was careful to distance himself from the reputation he had gained for stylistic extremism: "'Whenever there is anything sensational produced,' he said, 'people say "That is Poiret." Often it is something with which I have had nothing to do at all, out of character and beneath my style. So much that is outlandish has been credited to me that I have come to explain what my styles really are.'"[37] These, he said, could be described by two fundamental principles: simplicity and individuality. "Women must wear something simple, but personal or individual. It can be personal without extravagance. Simple things prove most original."[38] Thus Poiret sought to appeal to American clients interested in practical, functional clothes. While department stores were touting the extravagant and outlandish Orientalist costumes seen in *Le Minaret,* Poiret countered with the clothes visible in his film and photographs, which were, by comparison, relatively conventional and which supported his rhetoric of simplicity more credibly than did his most striking and critically acclaimed Minaret designs. Ultimately, the effect of this discursive reversal was to drain away the force of the aesthetic differences between Orientalism and classical simplicity, as each became a discursive marker signifying not so much a particular style, but rather, the distinction and fashionable elitism of Poiret's wealthy client base. Seeking to retain that base yet also expand it, especially by appealing to the broad spectrum of American department-store patrons, the couturier made sure to explain to American women that simplicity was neither a path to uniformity nor the result of designing according to a formula: "The mode does not come from a theory; it is a sort of feeling. I feel the tendencies which I cannot explain."[39] Steeping himself in the rhetoric of originality that characterizes modernist aesthetic discourse in general, Poiret appealed to the Romantic notion of the artist, not as a mere artisan or someone who had to hawk his own wares, but instead, as a creator and a dreamer who pursued inspiration without regard for commercial considerations.

The prohibition against mingling art with commerce was not Poiret's invention; it was, in fact, deeply ingrained in art discourse. Intended to ensure the elevated status of the artist, it was already inscribed in the mid-seventeenth-century statutes of the French Académie Royale de la Peinture et du Sculpture, whose members were forbidden to open a picture shop, display paintings in the windows of their houses, or otherwise suggest any engagement in mercenary affairs.[40] Poiret always insisted on this ancient distinction, and he spared no expense in presenting himself as an artist and an aristocrat who considered commercial matters beneath his dignity. Throughout his tour of North American cities, however, his actions belied that purity and disinterestedness he consistently claimed for himself. During the few weeks of his stay in the United States, where he was the guest of one department store magnate after the next, he addressed thousands of potential clients in the lectures he delivered in hotel ballrooms and department store theaters. He also closed deals with several American businesses, including a commitment to supply *Harper's Bazar* with a series of illustrated articles and an exclusive arrangement to provide "authoritative models" of blouses to Larrymade Waists.[41] Larrymade announced its arrangement with Poiret in *Women's Wear* in full-page, graphically arresting weekly advertisements in which Larrymade paired its trademark with the distinctive typography and imagery that Paul Iribe and Georges Lepape had designed for Poiret's labels, stationery, and deluxe albums (figures 3.11–3.15).[42]

The department stores made much of their association with the French couturier, often by trumpeting claims of having been the first to introduce Poiret's costumes from *Le Minaret*. Gidding's, for example, claimed to have been the first in the United States to have "announced" the play, and said it was the firm responsible for "the largest single collection [of Minaret dresses by Poiret] imported into this country."[43] Gimbels argued that, in fact, it took precedence, on the grounds that the first gown with a Minaret-style lampshade tunic that Poiret ever created "was brought to America and shown in the Gimbel La Promenade des Toilettes on Oct. 4, 1912."[44] Nevertheless, in fall 1913, Gimbels had to wait several weeks before it could show gowns from the eponymous play. In the meantime, the store mounted "a special exhibit of color-photographs on glass of the original Le Minaret Costumes Created By Monsieur Paul Poiret," each illuminated from below and displayed in "a cabinet draped with ruby velvet."[45]

Advertisements, reports, photographs, and drawings published in newspapers and trade journals indicate that Gimbels, Macy's, and

Figure 3.11

Advertisement for Larrymade Waists, from
Women's Wear, 10 October 1913.

Figure 3.12

Advertisement for Larrymade Waists, from
Women's Wear, 17 October 1913.

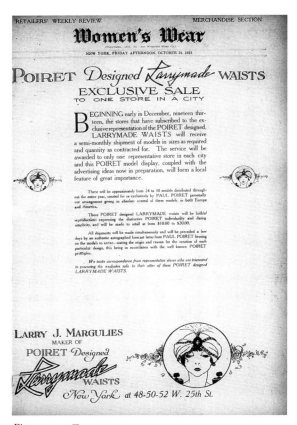

Figure 3.13

Advertisement for Larrymade Waists, from
Women's Wear, 24 October 1913.

Figure 3.14

Advertisement for Larrymade Waists, from
Women's Wear, 31 October 1913.

Figure 3.15

Advertisement for Larrymade Waists, from
Women's Wear, 28 November 1913.

Wanamaker's all installed special Oriental settings inspired by *Le Minaret* for the Fall 1913 fashion shows they mounted on their premises. The stores obviously competed with one another in adapting theatrical sets, props, and costumes from the Paris performance of *Le Minaret*. Macy's created a generic "Moorish Palace" on the eighth floor of its store, where the setting, "an arabesque mass of gold and red and green," occupied the greater part of the store's restaurant (an enormous space that could seat 2,500 people at once[46]) and provided a focus for a raised promenade on which live mannequins paraded in fashion shows. Gimbels and Wanamaker's went further, attempting to reproduce sets from the Paris production of *Le Minaret* to reinforce the authenticity of the Minaret-style dresses presented on the their stages—and sold in their Women's Gown Salons. Gimbels, for example, used "three scenes taken from 'Le Minaret' as it was staged in Paris" and spread them across the available space rather than through time (as would have been the case on an actual stage).[47] Thus, Gimbels management adapted the sets from the play's three acts to suit the auditorium, tea room, and piano showroom on the eighth floor of its New York store, where approximately 1,100 seats could be arranged, as at Macy's, along the perimeter of a raised promenade. The fall fashion display that Wanamaker's mounted, entitled "In a Persian Garden," must have resembled even more closely an actual theatrical performance, because it was presented to the accompaniment of organ music in the vast auditorium of Wanamaker's New York store, which was capable of seating 1,500 people (figures 3.16 and 3.17).[48]

The press gave ample coverage to these manifestations and, in at least one instance, press coverage came close to collapsing the distinction between the Paris production of the play in a professional theater and its adaptation in an American department store. Thus, in a special section devoted to "The Style Influence of 'Le Minaret'" published in *Women's Wear,* a double-page spread of photographs juxtaposed the fashion show on the stage at Wanamaker's with a scene from Act II of *Le Minaret* at the

Persian Garden Scene From Fashion Display of John Wanamaker, New York

Figure 3.16 ↻

Persian garden scene at Wanamaker's, New
York, 1913, from *Women's Wear,* 1913.

Théâtre de la Renaissance in Paris (figure 3.18). The evident similarities
between the two stage sets pictured in the images was brought home by
similar wording in the captions, which referred in both cases to a "Persian
Garden Scene." Other photographs in the same two-page spread showed
individual costumes as well as a scene from Act I of the Paris production
(one of the scenes adapted by Gimbels, as the caption noted) alongside the
"Moorish Palace Setting for the Fashion Show at R. H. Macy & Co., New
York." On another page, a photograph of a "Poiret Model with the
Minaret Tunic—White Satin and Black Velvet—From Gimbel Bros."
was reproduced in conjunction with a photograph labeled "Paul Poiret
Costume Worn by Mlle. Marcelle Yrven in 'Le Minaret'—From Gimbel

Bros."[49] The overall effect of all these juxtapositions of similar photographs and captions was to blur the distinction between professional
theatrical production and department store fashion show—and thereby to
suggest greater authenticity for the American adaptations of the original
Minaret costumes.

Wanamaker's show, described as "a dramatic presentation of the
newest Paris fashions for autumn and winter, in three tableaux," incorporated gowns by all the major Parisian couturiers, including Doucet,
Lanvin, Paquin, and Worth, although those of Callot Soeurs and Poiret
predominated. Given the "vividly Oriental and largely Persian" inspiration of the costumes, it is not surprising that Wanamaker's prominently
featured Poiret in its promotions of the fashion display: not only was he

Figure 3.17

Auditorium in the Wanamaker building, New
York, from *Golden Book of the Wanamaker
Stores*, 1911.

225

Figure 3.18 ⟩

"Oriental Influence on the Style Displays,"
two-page spread from *Women's Wear*, 1913.

invited to witness an evening rehearsal (a store employee announced that Poiret "had been much pleased" by what he had seen),[50] but his name was highlighted in the invitation issued by the store. Printed in Paris in gold and black on heavy paper, the invitation reproduced an inscription handwritten and signed by Poiret: "The sun rises from the East each day and it is in the East that all artistic revolutions are born."[51] He thus allowed his words and personal penmanship—indeed, his carefully constructed artistic identity—to sanction a fundamentally commercial occasion. The correspondent for *Women's Wear* was clearly not exaggerating when she or he remarked that "the visit of Paul Poiret to this country could not have been more timely for the leading shops and stores to take up the Minaret styles, and the leading houses were not slow in grasping the psychological moment."[52] In fact they competed avidly with one another, producing "[m]ore and more elaborate and costly . . . fashion displays . . . a result, no doubt, of the desperate effort of each store to hold the attention of the always fickle women in the face of the growing and already keen competition."[53]

Poiret's spectacular marketing campaign, which owed as much to the couturier as it did to the department store owners who underwrote his American trip, proved to be enormously effective, although it differed markedly from his customary practice, which was characterized by the privacy, intimacy, and elitism Poiret took great pains to assure his personal clients in Paris. The high visibility of Poiret's U.S. tour obviously responded to the particular conditions governing the merchandising of French fashions in North America, which took place in the public arena dominated by the large-scale department stores rather than in the carefully controlled environment of the couturier's private *hôtel.* Like Daniel-Henry Kahnweiler, who developed a discrete method of marketing cubism to a limited range of patrons in Paris while widely circulating and extensively publicizing his artists abroad, Poiret recognized the necessity of modifying his discursive and marketing practices for the American situation. In the absence of an aristocratic tradition, his Orientalism as well as his classical simplicity would be seen not just by those wealthy women who could afford to travel to Europe and patronize his couture house in Paris but, more crucially, by a vast, middle-class clientele.

In an effort to lure ever more customers and diversify the class origins of their patrons, department stores began at the end of the nineteenth century to expand the scope of their merchandise by offering more expensive items, and to appeal to more sophisticated customers by enhancing the aesthetic arrangement of the items on display.[54] At the same time the stores developed what *The Dry Goods Economist* described in 1903 as "spectacular methods of bringing people within their doors," including such free entertainments as "cooking lessons, automobile shows, stereopticon displays, moving pictures, or the presentation of some novel and interesting exhibit. . . . Very often these openings are held in the evening and partake of the nature of a reception, no goods being sold and visitors being treated as the guests of the concern."[55] It was, the author noted, an effective, though expensive, form of advertising. Thus, the department stores shared with Poiret some of the same strategies—though on a larger scale and often without his commitment to stylistic modernism—of covering their marketing with a veneer of culture or, in other words, promoting consumer interest and generating sales by means of theater, interior design, and the visual arts.[56]

John Wanamaker, who inaugurated an art gallery in his flagship Philadelphia store as early as 1881, was among the most aggressive of his contemporaries in this respect. By the early twentieth century Wanamaker and his son Rodman Wanamaker were importing hundreds of paintings each year from mainstream French Salon exhibitions and displaying and selling them in their New York and Philadelphia stores. In addition to embellishing his store interiors, the elder Wanamaker wanted department store buildings themselves be to be tasteful and socially uplifting models of store design whose architectural style and ornate decoration could become what a contemporary writer described as a civilizing force "for good to an extent that only the children of the coming generations will realize."[57] With paintings and other art objects presented in a manner and an environment that blurred the boundaries between morally uplifting aesthetic contemplation on one hand and banal material consumption on the other, Wanamaker's stores exemplified the ways in which American consumer culture integrated the arts into a larger promotional program, rather than using them—as did Poiret and other French couturiers following Worth's and, especially, Doucet's example—to project aristocratic disinterestedness. Indeed, Wanamaker's was quite explicit about the connection the store sought to draw between artistic culture and commodity culture, arguing in its jubilee book published in 1911 that, contrary to conventional wisdom, "exhibitions of fashions and fabrics [can be] as beautiful to look upon as a gallery of paintings," and suggesting that its staff included "women and men who are in their own metiers artists as worthy as those whose names are preserved in the catalogs of galleries today." Having likened the store's ordinary wares to art objects and compared its employees to fine artists, it was hardly a stretch for Wanamaker's to claim that the French paintings the store imported "have helped to convert the Wanamaker Stores into vast public museums, quickening the interest of thousands of visitors, and reaching a larger number than many of the museums owned and controlled by the city or state."[58]

Where Poiret sought to obfuscate the commercial aspect of his activities as a couturier and designer, the American department store magnate proudly proclaimed the union of art and commerce, and worked to make it visible in the physical environment and operating practices of his stores. If art and business had once been "looked upon as first-cousins only in the sense that they could not wed," according to the 1911 jubilee publication, "Wanamaker's denied the allegation." Instead, Wanamaker's boasted of its success in bringing art and commerce together: "And now none would even think of trying to divorce Art and Business thus happily mated!"[59]

As Susan Porter Benson has pointed out, department stores like Wanamaker's were designed to be "palaces of consumption, schools for a new culture of buying."[60] By providing art exhibitions, restaurants with live music, lectures, and other cultural amenities, as well as elaborate and often costly services in a spacious and luxuriously appointed environment, department stores conveyed to their clients the sense that consumption was not simply a means of addressing one's needs or even fulfilling one's desires, "but also a way of behaving that had links to class, particularly to urban gentility. The palace of consumption elevated prosaic goods and touched them with the aura of elegance while fostering a taste for luxury and encouraging the sale of finer goods."[61] Department stores sought the largest possible client base, using art and theater to make ordinary objects appeal to a wide spectrum of potential patrons. Poiret, on the other hand, stressed the high-end, luxury aspects of art and spectacle in order to build a relatively small, elite clientele through individual sales on the premises of his couture house in Paris; in coming to America, however, he entered the domain of the department store where art and especially theater operated more explicitly and on a much larger scale. As William Leach has pointed out, "The upper-class French trade . . . became an American mass market."[62]

Those who have written about the department store, whether in France or the United States, have frequently commented on the fact that theatricality of one sort or another is at the core of the shopping experience. Rachel Bowlby, for example, describes the department store sales transaction as a "remarkable performance. . . . That it is a drama, in the full, theatrical sense, is made explicit by the constant use of this word in presentations of the method of selling. . . . Salespersons are to think of themselves as acting a part and as endeavouring to carry a performance through to a happy ending."[63] Kristin Ross returns to one of the principal nineteenth-century accounts of such ideas, Emile Zola's novel about a fictional department store called *Au Bonheur des Dames,* noting that "the melodrama and posturing that characterized the urban theater of everyday bargaining" in the old commercial regime "was displaced onto the set. By creating a spectacle out of the store itself, early commercial pioneers . . . discovered that they could endow metonymically what were essentially nondescript goods with the fascination that was lacking in the merchandise."[64] David Chaney also makes this point in his discussion of what he calls "the dramaturgy of interaction in buying and selling."[65] He observes as well that when Selfridge's opened in London in 1909, it produced advertisements comparable to Poiret's deluxe albums insofar as they were designed by artists and avoided direct marketing of goods. "What is distinctive about consumerism," Chaney concludes on this basis, "is that the form of life accumulated through commodities is displayed as much through the means whereby the commodities become accessible and are acquired, as through what are held to be desirable features of particular commodities."[66] Or, as W. H. P. Barley of Wanamaker's decorating department put it succinctly when he repeated an adage in an article for *The Dry Goods Economist* in 1907, "People do not buy the thing; they buy the effect."[67]

William Leach has described in detail the theatrical dimension of American department store practices, whose origin he traces to the 1890s, "when merchants started to build their own auditoriums, [and] department stores literally became theaters, putting on plays, musicals, concerts, and, in some instances, spectacular extravaganzas. . . . Display managers used theatrical strategies inside and outside the stores. Windows not only were conceived as stage sets but also often depicted scenes from the latest theatrical productions. . . . Immersed in those theatrical, surreal settings, commodities themselves acquired new life, new meanings."[68] Leach points out that Orientalist themes—a pervasive feature of American popular culture, appearing in novels and films as well as on stage—were among the most widespread merchandizing vehicles because they provoked fantasies of sensuality and luxury that were particularly effective in the production of consumer desire. Leach relates the story of *The Garden of Allah,* a typically romanticized Orientalist novel published in 1904 by Robert

Hichens, which was adapted for the stage in 1907 and eventually inspired three movies. Around 1910, "[s]everal large department stores organized sensational fashion shows around the Garden of Allah theme." A spectacle mounted by Wanamaker's New York store in 1912 was by far the most lavish, with members of the cast of the Broadway play in Arab costume roaming through the store, not simply drawing attention to their own outfits but also encouraging clients to view similar gowns on the store's theatrical stage, where, to the strains of Oriental music played by a string orchestra, thirty mannequins modeled costumes said to have been inspired by Algerian designs.[69]

The effectiveness of just such machinations, enhanced by Poiret's active participation in them during his North American tour, had a direct and impressive impact on sales of Poiret's dresses in the United States. An article in *Harper's Bazar* noted that in the wake of Poiret's visit, Americans had seen "a perfect avalanche of minaret or Poiret costumes."[70] According to an account of the Minaret style that appeared in the American trade journal, *Women's Wear,* "Already its extremest expressions have been shown by the leading stores in the largest American cities to thousands of women, and judging by the intent faces, the bated breath of the onlookers, the modes of Le Minaret, at least in modified form, are considered neither entirely ridiculous nor wholly impractical."[71] Within six months *Vogue* declared it "a safe wager that every woman in the land possessed at least one of [Poiret's lampshade] tunics during the past season."[72] This is obviously an exaggerated claim, but it nevertheless alerts us to a problem of which Poiret became acutely aware while touring the United States. As he went about denying any commercial interest in his visit, and, indeed, suggesting that as an artist he was above commerce altogether, he discovered to his great dismay that in the United States his exclusive dress designs were being copied for sale at cut-rate prices. The story was recounted eighteen months later in the pages of *Vogue:* "During his visit to America, Mr. Poiret was much astonished to see advertised in various shop windows Poiret gowns which he himself had never seen before. Needless to say, Mr. Poiret quickly identified these gowns as never having emanated from his establishment and the labels which were sewed in them as nothing but counterfeits of his original label. He immediately placed the matter in the hands of his attorney, who started an investigation which revealed the fact that not only were Poiret labels being imitated and sold throughout the country by a number of manufacturers, but the labels of other prominent couturiers were also being duplicated. In fact, it was discovered that quite a flourishing trade in these false labels had become well established in America."[73]

The widespread manufacture and use of false designer labels was hardly a secret, as is evident from an article entitled "The Dishonest Paris Label" by Samuel Hopkins Adams. Published in *Ladies' Home Journal* in March 1913 (just over half a year before Poiret's arrival in the United States), the piece described precisely, according to its subtitle, "How American Women are Being Fooled by a Country-Wide Swindle."[74] In it, Adams reported that fraudulent labels were readily produced from photographs, their fidelity to the original was therefore assured and, moreover, their colors were often guaranteed by label manufacturers. In large cities such as Chicago and New York, numerous label factories offered dozens of counterfeit labels from stock on hand, or a potential buyer could order new ones to be made up in a matter of days. In addition to the labels manufactured in America, a large number of genuine French labels were being imported and sewn into American-made garments, "some of which, however," Adams reported, "are legitimately used with the designation, 'copied after.' Deducting for this use, and allowing a moderate output for the factories in this country, a conservative estimate would indicate that not fewer than two million and a half hats, gowns and cloaks are on sale, under fraudulent labels, to the American public. It is one of the most extensive swindles of modern business."[75] Manufacturers, wholesalers, and retailers across the county and at all levels of the wholesale and retail industry participated in fraudulent trade practices; indeed, according to Adams, the number of honest labels was "almost negligible." Thus, the overwhelming odds were that any woman in America who purchased a garment with a Paris label risked paying top dollar for a sham. Adams made this point when, addressing his readers directly, he concluded, "In purchasing a so-called imported cloak or gown in this country you have one chance out of fifty of getting what you pay for. In purchasing a so-called imported hat you have (possibly) one chance out of two hundred."[76] American women themselves played into the hands of design pirates, copyists, and false-label makers by uncritically accepting the notion that fashion necessarily emanated exclusively from Europe and, therefore, insisting on the purchase of imported clothes. Those who bought garments with Paris labels at what they must have known were impossibly low prices probably should have suspected that they were not getting genuine articles. "If our customers want the French-labeled goods," one label manufacturer told Adams, "we supply 'em. That's what we're in business for, to give 'em what they want. . . . Any woman knows that she can't get a new Paris hat for twenty dollars. If she doesn't she's a fool, and she deserves to get swindled." Ironically, high demand put the original French designers in an awkward position. Not only were there few legal means of stopping the dishonest practices, but trying to do so might make matters worse by driving away customers who at least purchased a small number of couture hats and gowns either for purposes of direct copying or in order to use as fronts for related illegal practices. There was thus a danger in taking any steps to prevent design piracy. As Adams pointed out, any French couture house that tried to stop it "would hit some of their own customers who buy here and there a gown and fake a hundred." Attempting to address this problem, Poiret's rival, Callot Soeurs, published a list of those American establishments that had made legitimate purchases from them in Paris and, therefore, were offering genuine articles for sale to American consumers (figure 3.19); but, according to Adams, Callot Soeurs's isolated

Figure 3.19

Announcement by Callot Soeurs concerning
sales in the United States, from *Women's Wear,*
1913.

practice did little or nothing to prevent unscrupulous enterprises from selling pirated copies into which counterfeit labels had been sewn. When Poiret was informed that counterfeit copies of his house label had been sewn into headgear for which he was not responsible, he decided not to follow Callot Soeurs's example but, instead, threatened to "turn the fullest punishment of the law upon those who offend in this manner." Since there were no legal remedies available to protect his clothing designs in America, Poiret's only recourse was to mount a campaign—including ads (figure 3.20) and open letters—to protect his label, which, he noted, "is now registered at Washington."[77]

Not until six months after Poiret first complained of fraud, and well after he had returned from the United States to Paris, did he finally get some satisfaction; William Fantel of the Universal Weaving Company was found guilty of passing counterfeit trademark in the form of false labels and sentenced to a $50 fine or ten days in jail.[78] But most problematic instances of copying, particularly where clothing rather than labels was directly concerned, did not come to such a satisfying conclusion, nor were all of them equally clear-cut. At issue was a spectrum of practices that extended from outright fraud to legitimate copying, very little of which was regulated and for which there appear to have been few systematic rules. It is, for example, difficult to determine the status of copies advertised by some of Poiret's own commercial clients, including stores that prided themselves on introducing his Minaret style. The ambiguity of just what it was that department stores were selling points up the ways in which originality and reproduction were confounded in the fashion industry—and particularly in the language that department stores used in their ads. For example, after its fall 1913 shows of French fashions, Macy's advertised that it would present "American-made copies of the Imported Gowns," claiming, "We are in a position to duplicate any of these models accurately at far less than the cost of the originals."[79] Similarly, Gimbels advertised Paris designs at one-tenth the usual price, proclaiming,

Figure 3.20

Paul Poiret, warning against false labels, from
Women's Wear, 1913.

"Without exception, these Suits are unapproached in New York or in Europe, for they are our latest specialty. Yes, we had the suits made in New York, but they are true to the original Paris models."[80] J. M. Gidding developed ads whose wording left it unclear whether the store was selling original Paris models or American "interpretations"—or both: "Individual ideas from those famed couturiers, Poiret, Worth, Paquin, Premet, Callot, Cheruit, Bernard, Drecoll, Lanvin and others of equal note—The styles worn in Paris, Deauville, Trouville, Ostend, Brighton and other famous European resorts are at your very door in New York— The *uncommon* effects produced by the noted *style-originators* of the world. . . . Our own exclusive interpretations of these new French modes form an interesting collection."[81] Another outlet which called attention to its genuine dresses by Poiret—"creator of this season's style"—along with a dozen other couturiers, also boasted, "Individual adaptations and Reproductions are assured. Chic style, perfect fit and superior workmanship at very moderate prices."[82] No mention is made in these advertisements of any authorization the stores might have obtained in order to sell their "adaptations" and "reproductions." Nor is it stated whether they paid a special price for the couture creations, one that could have included the right to make and market multiple copies of those garments. Such regulatory practices were only beginning to be put into place by the French couture industry during this period, and there is scant information about their nature and even less about the uniformity of their application. The fact that many American department stores openly acknowledged a distinction between authentic models imported from Paris and their own copies suggests that they were not guilty of the kind of dishonest copying and inclusion of false labels that Poiret discovered during his visit to the United States. Nevertheless, Poiret's own experience, Adams's article, and the department stores' advertisements are only the tip of a large mountain of evidence attesting to the serious problem that copying posed for Poiret and other couturiers.

Copying, it is important to keep in mind, is inherent in the very structure of haute couture, according to which the couturier produces a model that is then adapted to the needs of individual clients. In practice, as soon as a model left the atelier of the couture house to be presented for sale, examples (what might be called "original copies") could be purchased by, and sent to, both high-end retail establishments and large-scale manufacturers abroad. Elite retailers would copy the couture example, with or without alterations, and sell that copy legitimately as a "reproduction" or "adaptation" of signature French haute couture. Most often these legitimate copies would not be made by the couturier or another dressmaker in France but in the country of eventual sale. Thus, the importer could avoid taxes on the importation of finished goods, as well as the high price the couturier would demand for additional examples of his or her own models in order to support the creative work, skilled labor, and high-quality materials that were the hallmark of haute couture. The couturier also lost out when a design was purchased by a large-scale manufacturer who would typically use a carefully selected couture design as the basis for a series of garments made with cheaper fabrics, less costly decorative details, and inferior workmanship. Mass production and widespread distribution of inexpensive garments allowed the manufacturer to recoup costs without the risk that was assumed at the creative end of the industry. As a result, couturiers saw their markets diminishing; even when their designs were selling, someone else was reaping a much greater benefit than they. How much more difficult and complex the picture became when copying was done without acknowledgment or compensation.

Both American and French newspapers and fashion journals published many articles during this period that shed light on how copies were secured, for example by American buyers, several of whom might "unite in purchasing a limited number of gowns, to divide their expense and share the models in America," without paying any fees for copying privileges to the French couturiers who originated the designs.[83] Alternatively, unscrupulous foreign buyers who secured dresses directly from the couture houses might display them in their hotel rooms for carefully selected audiences of other buyers to copy on the spot at greatly reduced prices.[84] Forgeries were also produced by "the hundreds of little dressmakers who flourish everywhere in Paris, making a good living off copies of models, if they can secure them, and selling them at less than half the price that is asked by the large dressmakers. . . . The employees of the various big houses make a good living on the side if they will impart secrets, and the buyer who is interested in dresses, who really buys when he sees them, and therefore has an entree into the big houses, can give the most valuable information of all. He will enter a small establishment. He will explain a dress he has seen. He will even manage to have a sample of the material of which it is made. He will explain it all in a manner perfectly intelligible to those in the same line of business as himself and will go home with dresses that cost so little in comparison to the dresses from which they were copied that the customs man becomes doubtful and must have the matter explained in turn to him."[85] In addition to disloyal couture house workers who stole patterns and sold them to copiers,[86] another source of pirated designs was the *commissionaires* who facilitated the work of American buyers in Paris, consolidating their purchases, handling their shipments, and resolving customs issues. "[U]nfortunately, some are not satisfied with their 5 per cent and 10 per cent profits and do not scruple to open a package in transit for America and send for artists in the employ of various firms in America, London, Vienna and Berlin, who make drawings of the model. In this manner, a model sold to me by M. Doucet, for instance, for 1,500fr., might be copied five or six times before it left France, and the commissioner makes huge profits. What I paid 1,500fr. for, the five or six other firms would obtain from the commissioner for 500 or 600fr. each."[87] The negative impact of copying—on Poiret's business in particular—is suggested by an article published in 1912 in the *New York Times* reporting that French couturiers had decided not to send their mannequins to display the latest spring fashions at the opening of the races at Auteuil because they feared they would immediately be "copied by the smaller houses and wholesale dressmakers, who only vulgarize the models. The jupe-culotte, or harem skirt, which was intended to revolutionize women's dress last year, was instanced. It was declared that it would easily have lived down the first unfavorable reception at the hands of the public had it not been travestied by cheap houses, and thus exposed to ridicule."[88]

What all this agitation about copying suggests is that just as Poiret's entrepreneurial dream became reality, at the moment that, as *Women's Wear* put it, every woman possessed at least one of his designs, the dream was turning into a nightmare of uncontrolled proliferation and consumption. Poiret was neither effectively overseeing the latest developments in manufacturing and marketing, nor was he benefiting financially from them. Some of this may have been due to his own lack of business discipline, his apparent readiness to give away privileges for which he might have charged dearly, such as when he declared in an open letter to the American fashion press that copyists were welcome to work from his models, so long as they labeled their copies as such.[89] No mention was made of licensing agreements or other means of gaining financial compensation for allowing others to copy designs that originated in his couture house. Instead of following Callot Soeurs's lead and announcing exactly which stores were legitimately selling his designs, he posed as the magnanimous yet wronged artist seeking to punish those whose false labels made dishonest use of his name. The very strategies he had successfully employed to position his clothes as unique creations and to put his name at the pinnacle of Paris fashion—the exploitation of art, interior design, photography, architecture, and theater—had elicited the production of a profusion of examples destined for mass consumption, thereby effecting a popularization that simultaneously validated his fashionable status and destroyed his aspirations to elite culture.

Poiret was not alone in facing this dilemma, and he must have been aware of design piracy in the couture business before he went to the United States, for it was already widespread in France where well-established couturiers were fighting it in the courts. For example, in December 1910, Callot Soeurs had sued the directors and administrators of a fashion journal, *Le Grand Chic,* for publishing drawings that were forgeries of several house designs registered with the Secrétariat du Conseil des Prud'hommes de la Seine. However, it took more than a year and a half for a verdict to be handed down in the case, rendering its effectiveness all but moot as far as design protection was concerned. The court found that *Le Grand Chic* was actually aware that Callot Soeurs had registered its important models and was prepared to go to court to protect them, not only from copying by competing houses but also from unauthorized circulation in fashion journals. But *Le Grand Chic* was required to pay damages of only 1,000 francs for each pirated model, in addition to placing announcements of the judgment in twenty French and foreign publications, whereas Callot Soeurs had requested 15,000 francs and fifty announcements.[90] Around the same time, in 1912, a judgment was rendered in a case Paquin had brought against the Maison Boringer for stealing three of her designs. Although she lost on two counts, a judge found that in the third instance a kind of pattern called a *demi-toile* made by Boringer was an almost exact copy of a Paquin design; the *demi-toile* was therefore confiscated and Boringer was required to pay damages in an amount determined by the state.[91] Recognizing the import of these decisions, and acknowledging that many comparable cases were taking a toll on the work of French couturiers, in November 1912 the trade journal *Echos de l'Exportation* noted that the major Parisian couture houses had to "fight hard against their competitors who imitate their models, and the number of legal actions brought against them for counterfeiting is high." The problem was not limited to the making of copies by rival dressmaking establishments, or even to the reproduction of designs by journals such as *Le Grand Chic.* "Sometimes it is also the producers of 'patterns' and '*demi-toiles*' who take too much inspiration from registered designs. This is also a practice that seriously compromises the interests of the *maisons de couture.*"[92] This point was extrapolated from a case in which a middleman named Chollet—who produced *mousselines,* or models in muslin, based on couture designs and intended to be sold to manufacturers of actual dresses—tried to argue that even when his products were directly indebted to couture designs, indeed even when they were copies of them, this did not constitute piracy. Happily for couturiers, the court rejected Chollet's outrageous claim that the production of *mousselines* on the basis of couture designs "could be considered as *a preparatory act;* not until the buyer, with the aide of the *mousseline,* has reproduced the model [in an actual garment] could there be counterfeiting."[93]

While pursuing those who stole their designs in the courts, French couturiers also took action in other public venues, including opening day at the races. In April 1912, for example, they decided as a group to keep most of their models away from the "grand parade of mannequins" that traditionally inaugurated the spring racing season at Longchamp. The purpose, notably similar to that of Kahnweiler in protecting his stable of cubist artists from public view in Paris, was "to prevent the latest models from being copied by smaller firms."[94] Thus, at the same time that they were avidly pursuing distribution and sales in foreign markets, both Kahnweiler and French couturiers restricted access to their products at home in an effort to prevent copying and to maintain the elite character of their respective businesses.

In an article published in *La Vie Heureuse* in May 1912, that is, just when attention to the problem of piracy was reaching new heights, Jules Huret posed a serious question: Why was the government not taking action to prevent these widespread illegal practices? Huret noted that Callot, Doucet, Paquin, Poiret, and four other top couture firms represented a combined capital of at least 50 to 60 million francs, and did annual sales of nearly 70 million francs. Paquin alone employed 1,350 workers who earned 4 million francs per year. And this was just the pinnacle of the French couture-industry pyramid; in Paris alone there were more than 12,000 dressmaking businesses employing between one and one hundred workers, a figure that did not include the 15,000 *maisons de lingerie* or 4,000 seamstresses and shops handling alterations and repairs. Throughout the country there were more than a million people in the industry—940,000 women and 75,000 men—contributing more than 114 million francs annually to France's commercial export economy. Given the size and significance of these numbers, Huret wondered, why did the politicians do nothing about the stealing of clothing designs? The answer, he suggested, was simple: "Because out of all the owners and workers in the couture industry, there are not even 100,000 voters; a million more, being women, do not vote."[95]

Huret's condemnation of the political motivations behind what he saw as official disinterest in curtailing rampant piracy in the couture industry came at a time when the French government was, ironically, actively engaged in efforts to secure changes in American copyright and design patent laws. If successful, these changes could have a significant impact on the copying of dresses, and on many other so-called industrial arts, at least in the United States, which was at the time the world's largest producer of commodities protected against copying in most other developed countries but unregulated in the United States. An especially good opportunity to press for reforms presented itself when, on 2 February 1912, the American President William Howard Taft issued a proclamation inviting the nations of the world to participate in an international exhibition in San Francisco to celebrate the opening of the Panama Canal. (Initially planned for 1916, the Panama-Pacific International Exposition was eventually rescheduled for February through December 1915). Taft's invitation was reiterated by a delegation that traveled to Europe for three months in spring 1912 personally to press the case for foreign participation to heads of state and other representatives of national governments. It immediately became clear to the members of the delegation that a major obstacle to foreign participation was posed by "the long-standing grievance of European manufacturers against the pirating of their patterns, models, copyrights, patents, or trade marks, and the insecurity they should feel for this sort of property should they expose it to such piracy at an exhibition."[96] Accordingly, upon their return the delegation recommended "that steps be taken to secure legislation at Washington that should protect designs and copyrights,"[97] a proposition endorsed by President Taft later that year.

Although such major European countries as Germany and Great Britain declined to participate in the San Francisco exposition, France apparently accepted American assurances that its concerns would be addressed in forthcoming legislation and on 26 July 1912, became one of the first European countries to agree to take part. A period of active negotiation ensued during which Ambassador Jusserand of France and the Comité Français des Expositions à l'Étranger pressed for improvements in the copyright protection provisions that the U.S. government had adopted to cover objects shown at its last international exposition, held in Saint Louis in 1904. That law protected exhibited objects for two years, but covered only the fine arts (painting, drawing, sculpture, statuary, and models or sketches of works of art). It did not protect manufactured goods (as distinct from designs for them), nor did it specifically apply to what the French referred to as *oeuvres d'art appliqué à l'industrie*. While it proved possible in practice to register some works in this category, their protection, the French claimed, remained entirely arbitrary. In 1904, the American government promised that this provisional protection would be transformed before the end of the two-year period by a law offering definitive protection in the United States not only to fine art but to the industrial arts, as well. Eight years later, this still had not happened.[98]

The Kahn Law (named for its sponsor, Representative Julius Kahn of California) that was passed by the U.S. House of Representatives on 18 September 1913, intended to resolve these issues but seems to have presented almost as many problems as it resolved. The law allowed duty-free importation of articles to be shown in the Panama-Pacific Exposition and prohibited unauthorized copying, imitation, or reproduction of any pattern, model, design, trademark, copyright, or manufactured article protected by the laws of any foreign country for three years after the close of that event.[99] Nevertheless, neither French nor American trade organizations were satisfied with its provisions. The Paris Chamber of Commerce objected to the fact that the protections on offer were temporary and limited to objects exhibited in San Francisco. These were not the permanent changes to American copyright law that the French had been demanding for at least a decade. The group was especially displeased to find that once again the United States had managed to avoid longstanding demands that it conform to international standards of intellectual property protection. As a result, the Paris Chamber of Commerce, together with other French trade organizations, refused to take part in the exposition and, only a year before it was due to open, demanded that the French government postpone the appropriation of funds to support the nation's participation until acceptable modifications to the American customs regime were made. As reported in an American newspaper, "It is becoming generally understood that nothing short of official abstention from participation will now calm the opposition that has been raised."[100]

Meanwhile, in America, the Committee on Laws and Rules of the Patent Law Association of Washington drew up a long list of objections to the Kahn Law, which it described as "the most dangerous, ill-considered and inexcusable law which has ever been enacted in relation to patent, design, trademark and copyright property."

After enumerating its complaints, the patent law group asserted, "It was said to be necessary to enact legislation which would protect the foreign exhibitor from piracy. To do this the law permits the piracy of the inventions, designs, trademarks and business of our citizens, protects the pirate and penalizes his victim." Finally, the committee urged its readers to contact their representatives in Congress to demand amendments to the Kahn Law to ensure that American manufacturers would continue to support the exposition.[101]

By December 1913, the Patent Committee of the House of Representatives was considering replacing the Kahn Law with new, less stringent legislation, and the French ambassador was exerting strong pressure on the State Department to protest any changes. Exhibition organizers suspected the French were using the negotiations surrounding their official participation in the exposition to resolve longstanding copyright and customs disputes that had nothing to do with the exposition and which the French could not otherwise hope to settle in a manner favorable to their own interests.[102] "For a while domestic participation was threatened if [the Kahn Act] were not amended, foreign if it were. Ambassador Jusserand notified the State Department by letter that if the protection offered by the act should be withdrawn France would be compelled to withdraw her acceptance of the national invitation."[103] Congressional hearings stretched on for more than a month while exposition organizers worked through "proper channels" to convince members of the House Patent Committee to support the Kahn Law.[104] The controversy was resolved and French participation in the exposition assured when a vote taken in early 1914 resulted in support for the Kahn Act and rejection of the proposed amendments.

This episode makes clear the intensity of international debate and diplomacy surrounding copyright protection of foreign designs and manufactured goods entering the United States. These controversies may sound arcane but they had a direct impact on the French couture industry. As we have seen, piracy of couture designs and trademarks was rampant in both the United States and France. Although the several French prosecutions discussed above provide a sense of the range and complexity of illegal dressmaking practices in Paris, they may not adequately reveal the degree to which those practices were directed at foreign markets. While there were no doubt hundreds of independent dressmakers in Paris producing copies of couture clothing for individual clients at the local level,[105] the real threat to haute couture came from piracy that had a deleterious impact on sales abroad, especially in America. When *Echos de l'Exportation* decried the disorganized and ineffective measures taken by French couturiers to protect themselves, the problem was described in terms of "foreign buyers who purchase their models with the *sole aim of renting them out* for a modest sum in their own country to large manufacturers of readymade clothing, to tailors for women and to couture houses.

> Instead of selling the same model fifty or a hundred times, it too often falls into the hands of these exploiters and thereafter it is lost to the rest of the buyers and consequently to the *maison de couture* that created it.
>
> Another, equally important consequence is that the good buyer, the one who comes to Paris to compose his or her collection of French models, carefully avoids the acquisition of the model that he knows has been purchased by professional copiers.[106]

All the major French couturiers recognized the double-edged sword of the American marketplace. Traditionally, they made their most lucrative sales in America but they were now also losing increasingly higher sums due to largely unregulated imitators engaged in rampant copying. It was in response to this crisis, in the spring of 1914—just after the problems of copyright protection at the Panama-Pacific International Exposition had finally been resolved—that Jeanne Paquin decided to send her sister-in-law and business partner, Suzanne Joire, and a small group of mannequins to follow the path beaten across America by Poiret and his wife the year before.[107] "Yes, this tour is necessary," Paquin told a reporter for the French magazine *Femina*; "it is time to react and to combat the danger that threatens French haute couture. Of course, our taste is unparalleled in the world, there is no dispute about that . . . [W]e know how to renew the invention of form with an infinite delicacy, we have ideas; in a word, we are creative artists. However, a commercial phenomenon has developed that affects our possibilities for expansion. . . ."[108] Paquin went on to recount the problems posed by indiscriminate copying and mass production, which enabled American manufacturers to sell what passed for French designs at unbeatable prices. As a result, French couturiers were losing ground in the American market which, Paquin observed, "as everyone knows, is the most important in the world. Of course a clientele of substance always remains," she acknowledged, referring to those clients who traveled to Paris to replenish their wardrobes each year, "but an entire sector of the overseas population, the most numerous sector, those who do not leave their homeland, should by no means [be allowed to] fall into the trap that has been set for them. And that is why we are going to America with our mannequins, a hundred gowns, a hundred hats, a hundred umbrellas and our theater" (figure 3.21). At this point in the interview the reporter interrupted Paquin to ask, "What? A theater?" And Paquin responded, "Yes of course, a theater: these are truly elegant presentations that I am going to give in the United States: the spectators will witness the tragedy of beauty, the comedy of prettiness, I will recount to them the eternal dialogue of the body and of chiffon. Believe me, the most spiritual dialogues do not have the accent of a hip that a turn of the skirt brings out or the piquant irony of an arm that disengages itself from a wavy tulle fabric." As testimony confirming the collapse of theater conceived as high art into the debased spectacle of fashion, one can scarcely imagine a more cogent statement than this one, which compares classical comedy and tragedy with the contemporary well-dressed body and suggests that fashion will always beat out "the most spiritual dialogues" in making a theatrical point.

Figure 3.21 ↺

Paquin fashion show, Chicago, 1914, from
Femina, 1914.

Paquin appears to have been right on the mark. So many visitors
thronged the presentations of Paquin costumes at the Ritz-Carlton Hotel
that a special presentation had to be scheduled to accommodate the hundreds who were turned away. After the tour, when the gowns were exhibited at Altman's, the New York department store that ultimately
purchased them, 60,000 people lined up to see them over a period of only
three days. Yet the huge numbers of women who mobbed hotels and
department stores in order to view Paquin's garments testified at once to
the success and to the failure of her enterprise. While they were undoubtedly drawn in part by the theatricality of the presentations, which I have
argued marked both the high-culture ambitions and the commercial

potential of haute couture, these women constituted a mass audience, not the discrete individual clients who were in a position to sustain the elitism that continued to characterize the practices of Paquin and Poiret, and those engaged in haute couture generally, in Paris. The irony in this situation was that Paquin, like Poiret, in fact embraced a vulgarized form of theater—the fashion show—in order to stave off a parallel vulgarization of haute couture.[109] In both cases, the compelling purpose was to marshall a form of expression that could be associated with high culture in the effort to protect haute couture as an art form from the menace of uncontrolled commerce.[110] At the same time, however, the theater was invoked precisely because it did appeal to such a broad audience and, therefore, assured that couture designs would reach a vast new clientele—precisely the circumstances that would ultimately compromise the elite status that was considered crucial to the viability of haute couture.

The contradictions inherent in this situation suggest that, according to the logic of fashion, just as the original could not be defined in isolation from the reproduction, so elite culture was embedded in the commercial domain from which it sought to distinguish itself.

The collapse of these supposed oppositions is confirmed by another episode in which Poiret contributed to a theatrical production at Cora Laparcerie's Théâtre de la Renaissance in Paris. The play in question, entitled *Aphrodite,* was a five-act drama in verse written in 1914 by Pierre Frondaie, based on a Symbolist novel about love, sexual desire, and betrayal by Pierre Louÿs, and set to music by Henry Février. The characters and setting, Alexandria during the reign of Queen Bérénice, mingled aspects of classical and Orientalist cultures, suggesting once again the degree to which sensuality and decadence were equally embedded in both discourses and the two often coincided, or at least overlapped, in early twentieth-century France. In the opening scene, the principal male character, a sculptor named Demetrios, is creating a nude statue of Aphrodite (visible in figure 3.22), indicating the classical dimension of the story; on

Figure 3.22

Aphrodite, scene 4, from *Le Théâtre,* 1914.

the other hand, the fifth scene presented a fête with distinctly Orientalist features (figure 3.23), including, according to the program, the customary and by now familiar "black slaves, music, banquet, [and] orgy."[111] In this instance the sets were not designed by Poiret but, again according to the program, he was responsible for no less than 300 costumes.[112] As was the case in the staging of *Le Minaret* a year earlier, *Aphrodite* was described as "less a play, in the dramatic sense of the word, than a spectacle"; in the absence of a convincingly sustained narrative, what action took place was

Figure 3.23

Aphrodite, scene 5, from *Le Théâtre*, 1914.

said to provide no more than a pretext or frame for the "picturesque and ostentatious *mise en scène.*"[113] As one critic observed, "If the play itself is rather thin, the spectacle, in contrast, is plentiful, well got up, opulent."[114]

This time, however, the main attraction and focus of critical condemnation was neither Poiret nor any potentially deleterious foreign influence but a recognized master of French modern art, the sculptor Auguste Rodin. At Laparcerie's request—indeed, she admitted that she had used flattery to convince him—Rodin had agreed to lend a life-size plaster-cast sculpture of a female nude entitled *Aphrodite* to embody the work of the sculptor Demetrios. "A theater that strives to realize the work of a great artist by means of all the arts—painting, music, decorative art, drama—can lay claim to the honor that is accorded a museum," Laparcerie told Rodin.[115] Obviously seeking the sanction of behavior modeled on high-art institutional practices, before the play opened Laparcerie arranged to unveil Rodin's plaster with great fanfare at an event that was compared to "a vernissage of the Salon (figure 3.24)."[116] (The occasion was preceded by a visit from the Minister of Public Instruction who duly praised Rodin's sculpture.) Despite this attempt to mimic an art-world style opening in the lobby of the Théâtre de la Renaissance for the purpose of presenting Rodin's sculpture to the press as well as invited guests, Rodin himself was severely criticized for pandering to publicity. It was said he compromised his greatness as an artist by permitting an enlarged cast of a neglected, much earlier, and possibly unfinished sculpture to be made for inclusion in the play. "Where will we stop with what we call the *mise en scène,*" one critic asked rhetorically. "Here is M. Auguste Rodin, our greatest glory, who consents to being, so to speak, a supplier of theatrical props."[117] But the problem with enlarging Rodin's forgotten sculpture so that it could be presented on the popular stage was not simply a matter of the spectacle thus created; it also involved the evident willingness of the artist to sanction a copy of questionable quality for

Figure 3.24

Auguste Rodin, *Aphrodite,* 1913, from
L'Illustration, 1914.

a theatrical purpose. The sculpture was, Arsène Alexandre complained, "a beautiful figure, for sure, but closer to works of the decadent period . . . than to the great conceptions of antique perfection. . . . Our time," he continued, "by dint of going from bad to worse, from parodies to pastiches, and from pastiches to lies, has completely changed the notion of Aphrodite and simultaneously of statuary itself. In short, we certainly see Aphrodite at the Renaissance, but we are not witnessing the renaissance of Aphrodite." Acknowledging his admiration for Rodin as a master whom he had defended decades earlier when Rodin had created his greatest works, now, Alexandre lamented, "we must consider this sketch borrowed from his atelier as a work by him, but not as the perfect image that a temple would demand." At first Alexandre had found it agreeable, but then, he wrote, "on second sight, it appeared that there was nothing in it that was really characteristic of Rodin himself, and that any old cast from an antique work in our museums would have produced the same effect." The problem, as far as Alexandre was concerned, was that the enlargement of Rodin's "charming study" rendered it "weak, a piece of flattery, [and only] partially representative of Rodin. . . ."[118]

For Alexandre and others, then, *Aphrodite* raises the issue of reproducibility which, Rosalind Krauss argues in a groundbreaking essay of 1981, was not only a characteristic feature of Rodin's sculptural production but a central problem for modernism itself, as Walter Benjamin already suggested in 1936.[119] In her essay, Krauss draws attention to an earlier discussion by Leo Steinberg devoted to the status of Rodin's many copies, including those in marble or stone: "Having signed them," Steinberg there observes, "the master is legally responsible for them; and of course morally, since he ordered, supervised, and approved them for sale. But he did not make them . . . they are dulcified replicas made by hired hands."[120] By allowing his name to be attached to marbles actually produced by his assistants, Steinberg suggests, Rodin enabled these objects, some of which exist in multiple versions, to assume the status of original works of art. Steinberg infers that indifferent commodities were thus transformed by the addition of a signature; it is a process that has much in common with the transformation of mass-produced copies of Poiret's dresses into what passed for couture fashion simply by the addition of his name in the form of the house label, or counterfeit versions of that label. Jean Chatelain's phrasing of the problem in relation to Rodin's art makes evident the parallel with the diffusion of haute couture through quantity production: "Originality implies uniqueness; an edition implied diffusion, multiplication and series. From this point of view alone the very formula 'original edition' defies logic and linguistic accuracy."[121]

The problematic status of the multiple, the object oscillating between the poles of art and industry, is something both Steinberg and Krauss find especially compelling in the work of Rodin. According to Steinberg, who drafted most of his essay in the early 1960s, a time when Rodin's work was being reevaluated after a long period of neglect on the part of modernist critics, the plaster and bronze multiples are crucial works that must be appreciated if we are to achieve an adequate understanding of Rodin's contribution to the development of modern sculpture: "In Rodin's maturity the constant multiplication of identical forms again helps to remove his art in two directions from the position of the *Bronze Age* [of 1876]: towards the work of art as an industrial object, made and makable again and again; and towards art as the inside-out of a private obsession. Only by such departures could the art of sculpture be reconstructed into a potentially modern art form."[122]

Krauss's emphasis differs from Steinberg's insofar as she views Rodin's copies (for example, *The Three Shades* at the apex of *The Gates of Hell,* figure 3.25) not so much as a measure of his contribution to modernist sculpture, but as evidence to support her assertion that the lack of a singular, original object is a feature that unites rather than separates early

Figure 3.25 ↺

Auguste Rodin, *The Gates of Hell (detail—The Three Shades),* 1880–1917.

twentieth-century modern art and its contemporary postmodern counter-part. She offers Rodin's oeuvre as an example of the importance of the copy in the arena of modernist production, where, according to the nor-mative rhetoric of modernist originality, one should be surprised to find it. "Rodin's relation to the casting of his sculpture could only be called remote," Krauss has pointed out. "Much of it was done in foundries to which Rodin never went while the production was in progress. . . . The ethos of reproduction in which Rodin was immersed was not limited, of course, to the relatively technical question of what went on at the foundry. It was installed within the very walls . . . of Rodin's studio. For the plas-ters that form the core of Rodin's work are, themselves, casts. They are thus potential multiples. And at the core of Rodin's massive output is the structural proliferation born of this multiplicity." Indeed, for Krauss, Rodin's work embodies "the ever-present reality of the copy as the *underlying condition of the original,*" a formulation that in turn suggests how closely the originality of Rodin compares with that of Poiret. For one could easily say the same about haute couture: not only is any original couture creation based on a model designed for reproduction, but in order for that model to become an established fashion, it must first be circulated in the form of multiple copies. Moreover, as far as the theater is concerned, because the inclusion of Rodin's work was orchestrated so as to impart the aura of high art to the theatrical spectacle of fashion that *Aphrodite* exemplified, the critical response to that particular episode indicates that in 1914, at least, high art could no longer be counted upon as a defense against the culture of commodities, since the reproducibility of the commodity was arguably a feature of the so-called original artwork as well.

And indeed, for his part, Poiret quickly recognized that the discourses of high art would be no match for the forces unleashed by modern commerce. Compelled to do battle on a field that, in America at least, was structured in ways that benefited industry rather than art, Poiret appealed to United States law by publicly threatening to "prosecute to the full extent of the law anyone who places a false label in imitation of my trademark on any article of merchandise."[123] By invoking trademark law, which applied only to the couture label attached to his garments and not to the garments themselves, Poiret tacitly acknowledged that American intellectual property law did not protect him against many types of design piracy, nor did it accord him the status of a creative and original artist to which he continually laid claim. Trademarks are not a matter of originality, but "mere adjuncts or appurtenances of articles of trade;" as such they are distinct from the domain of copyright, which covers "things whose value in exchange resides in themselves, viz., works of literature, science, and the fine arts" where issues of originality and authorship come prominently into play.[124]

As several scholars of law and literature have pointed out, and as Michel Foucault most influentially observed, authorship is "a culturally, politically, economically, and socially constructed category rather than a real or natural one."[125] The modern concept of the author matured simultaneously with the capitalist system in the eighteenth century when copyright laws linked creativity and originality with the property rights of individual authors and artists.[126] In the United States, early copyright law emphasized consumer welfare and the protection of utilitarian products such as maps and charts, as well as books. However, even that category was, according to Paul Goldstein, filled with works of low creativity such as grammars, dictionaries, and similar publications addressed to the practical needs of life in a new nation. "Courts gave these utilitarian works only the narrowest scope of protection, protecting them against literal copying—what we would today call piracy."[127] It was not until the middle of the nineteenth century that United States copyright law began seriously to concern itself with works of creative authorship, and only in 1870 did Congress revise the copyright law to embrace three-dimensional objects such as sculptures, molds, designs, and other works of fine art. Pressures to extend American copyright protection to foreign authors developed over the course of the nineteenth century, but the United States remained a major importer of intellectual property and it was, therefore, thought to be in its best interest not to join the ten countries whose representatives met in Berne in 1896 to form the International Union for the Protection of Literary and Artistic Work. Indeed, the United States maintained its independence from the Berne Union until 1971. Although the 1909 Copyright Act introduced a number of significant changes to American law, it did not extend copyright protection to foreign nationals, nor did it cover utilitarian objects or functional designs of any kind. The fundamental differences between American and continental copyright law had significant implications for international economic relations which defined the debate over passage of the Kahn Law enacted in 1913. These legal differences bear on cultural issues, as well.

American copyright law traditionally drew a sharp distinction between fine art on one hand and, on the other hand, applied art or industrial design—anything functional or utilitarian in purpose. The former category was subject to copyright registration while the latter was not. Although the Copyright Act of 1909 seemed to weaken the distinction by omitting the term "fine" from the phrase "works of art" in stipulating what it covered, the Copyright Office, which was responsible for carrying out the regulations, specifically stated in 1910 that "[n]o copyright exists in . . . embroideries, garments, laces, woven fabrics, or any similar objects."[128] Such utilitarian objects were relegated to the domain of design patent laws; these, however, had been developed to deal primarily with mechanical rather than aesthetic innovation. As a result, United States design patent laws were ineffective in protecting garments against piracy, if only because most articles of clothing lacked the kinds of innovative functional features that would enable them to rise to the level of protectible works of applied art. "The design patent statutes," Rocky Schmidt explains, "grant protection to 'a new, original and ornamental design for an article of manufacture.' . . . In order to be eligible for design patent protection, however, the design of an article of manufacture must be novel, non-obvious, original, ornamental, and meet the test of invention. Courts have consistently held that garment designs do not meet these requirements. Moreover, even if the design patent laws were amended to cover garment designs, the process required to obtain a design patent makes impracticable its application to garment designs."[129] The thorough search of existing designs, required to demonstrate that a candidate for design patent is indeed innovative, is far too lengthy to be practicable, since it generally exceeds what is called the "style life" of the garment, that brief period in which a new style retains its salability as fashion. Thus, in contemplating how to protect his designs from piracy in the American marketplace, Poiret discovered that he could not appeal either to copyright or to patent law. American copyright law refused to recognize his garments as works of art and denied his status as an artist; with similar implications, American patent law failed to acknowledge that originality and invention were embodied in his work. The only recourse that remained was the protection of his trademark, the label that bore his name, which was also the name of his company. Although he had succeeded in making that name distinctive, in the eyes of the law, as a trademark it was neither creative nor original; it simply identified his business. As Paul Goldstein has explained, "If copyright is the law of authorship and patent is the law of invention, trademark is the law of consumer marketing."[130] In America, then, Poiret could lay claim neither to authorship nor to invention; United States law ignored his self-construction as an artist and as an inventor, according him status only as an entrepreneur—a designation he had always sought to avoid and repress.

Since its inception, American copyright law has been driven by economic objectives and the exploitative interests of users, rather than by concern for the creators of protected works; French copyright law, on the other hand, has traditionally stressed the moral rights of the author, developing the Romantic assumption that the work of art is the extension of the artist's personality, the expression of his or her innermost being. Far broader in scope than American copyright law, the French doctrine of *droit d'auteur* concerns itself not only with the pecuniary rights of authors and artists, but more importantly, with their inalienable intellectual and moral interests as creators. While pecuniary rights may be transferred or sold, in France the moral rights of the author are personal, perpetual, and unassignable. According to French doctrine, copyright law recognizes the individuality and creativity of the author or the artist, in whose person the moral rights remain vested, even after the protected object itself has been transferred.[131] This being the case, the question arises as to what status French law accorded Poiret's work as a couturier, and whether in France he could legitimately claim to be an artist, that is, the author of intellectual property to which copyright law applied.

Throughout the nineteenth century, the French judicial system struggled to maintain a rigorous distinction between fine or "pure" art, protected by France's first copyright law of 1793, and applied art, which was subject to a special design law passed in 1806. According to J. H. Reichman, "Between 1806 and 1902 France experimented with five different criteria for distinguishing the subject matter of these two regimes." Reichman points out that the difficulty faced by the French courts in establishing the boundaries between pure art and applied art attests to the instability of the operative definition of art itself, which was also reflected in art institutions and art practices of the period. With artists and craftsmen increasingly addressing themselves to hybrid categories of applied art such as decoration and the decorative arts (and in response to the growing pressure of industrial manufacturers), in 1902 the government finally acceded to those who attacked the validity of any demarcation whatsoever between fine and applied art. The reform movement was led by lawyer and legal scholar Eugène Pouillet. "Pouillet and his followers argued that there could be no discrimination as to the degree of legal protection accorded different forms of aesthetic creativity, and that all creations were entitled to protection in the law of literary and artistic property. . . . Viewing attempts to establish a rational line of demarcation between the design law and the copyright law as futile, Pouillet maintained that decorators, painters, sculptors, and fashion designers were all artists whose works uniformly deserved to be governed by the copyright paradigm."[132] This so-called unity of art thesis was embodied in the French law of 11 March 1902, which extended the protections of copyright beyond the traditional fine arts to "designers of ornaments, whatever may be the merit and the purpose of the work." This did not obviate the design statutes of 1806, which were, in fact, confirmed and strengthened in 1909. Instead, the copyright law and the special design law were gradually integrated so they supported one another in "what is technically described as *a regime of absolute or total cumulation*."[133] Nevertheless, legal recognition did not solve the problem of design piracy in France. Garments may have been protected under French law, but the process involved in litigating cases of piracy was too cumbersome and time-consuming to be efficacious; moreover, the penalties imposed were often insufficient to deter copiers from their fraudulent practices, as demonstrated by the Callot Soeurs and Paquin cases described earlier.[134]

In France, then, Paul Poiret could invoke copyright law to protect his designs. In the eyes of the law, at least, he was an artist, although it is not clear whether he was fully aware of that fact. "There exists a law in France protecting artistic creations from imitation," he told a reporter for The *New York Times* in 1914. "We must see to it that this law is put into operation to protect new designs in dress."[135] Was he referring in this last phrase to French or American law? The answer remains unknown. What is clear is that in the United States, Poiret was legally defenseless against design piracy, and because U.S. law did not recognize the artistic character of his work, he could not legitimately claim to be an artist. In America not only were his designs stolen but his cherished and carefully constructed identity was put into question, as well. The constant effort to establish his status as an artist—an important means of maintaining his position as a purveyor of fashion to the elite, as well as to broader American audiences—was undermined by the conditions and the legal structures that promoted industrial and commercial culture in the United States. Unable to invoke copyright to shore up his elitist position as an artist in the world of fashion, Poiret had to resort to laws against trademark infringement, which allowed him to protect his name only because it was the name of his business. Poiret, therefore, found himself forced to take action that betrayed his identity as that of a businessman and made manifest his deep engagement in the world of commerce. This experience appears to have had a profound impact on him, which became evident as soon as he returned to Paris, where he began to acknowledge his entre-preneurial activities and the need to protect his own business interests, as well as those of the couture industry in general.

Four

The Readymade and the Genuine Reproduction

Paul Poiret's visit to the United States in the autumn of 1913 occurred at a time when many European artists and intellectuals were fascinated by American industrial and consumer culture. In contrast to the entrenched American conception of Europe as the seat of the arts, culture, and taste, Europeans at the turn of the century and after constructed a myth of America as a primitive yet modern landscape populated on the one hand by cowboys and on the other by engineers. American architecture in the form of grain silos and skyscrapers circulated in European avant-garde journals as testimony to the raw energy and vitality of an industrial powerhouse whose modernity supposedly developed without regard for the centuries-old aesthetic traditions that were thought to stifle innovation at home.[1] When Francis Picabia went to New York at the time of the Armory Show in 1913, and when Marcel Duchamp followed suit two years later in self-exile from the First World War, they both arrived, as Wanda Corn has observed, with culturally conditioned expectations of what they would find: "They came prepared to indulge in New York City's modernity—and to be blind to, and uninterested in, other parts of the vast American continent. Their America was a European schema for the New World, a land of skyscrapers, plumbing, mass culture, industry, efficiency, and American girls."[2] Corn argues that European-bred preconceptions of American modernity, or *américanisme,* structured the work of Picabia, Duchamp, and other modern artists active in New York during the war years. Of Picabia's mechanomorphic object portraits—for example of a generic "young American girl"—whose forms were drawn from images of industrial commodities in magazine and newspaper advertisements, she writes, "Only a European . . . could possibly have seen the United States so reductively and unidimensionally in 1915."[3] Corn's discussion of Duchamp, and in particular of the objects he selected as readymades while in New York, indicates that he too experienced New York from a perspective steeped in European stereotypes of American industrial production and female-dominated consumer culture. This insight is valuable because it underscores the extent to which the wartime and post-war work of French modern artists, no less than that of French couturiers, was conditioned by the myth and the reality of American industry, consumerism, and the "new" American woman. Those aspects of American culture are precisely what Poiret's trip to America drove home to him. Just as Duchamp's work of this period can best be understood within the cross-cultural context of his New York experience, so Poiret's work as a dress designer and businessman was conditioned by his discovery of the vast American marketplace, the contradictions engendered by American consumerism, and the needs and desires of American women. Comparing Duchamp, the fountainhead of conceptual art who abjured art-world professionalism and its marketplace and who distrusted anything that smacked of good taste, with a couturier and entrepreneur who reveled in material goods and promoted his designs as artistic examples of elegance, taste, and discernment—as this chapter sets out to do—not only challenges traditional biases of art historical inquiry in general, it goes against the grain of the hagiography associated with the study of Duchamp's work in particular. I intend to show, however, that Duchamp and Poiret, despite their markedly different social positions and wartime commitments, and despite their widely divergent perspectives on issues of aesthetics, nevertheless shared certain fundamental experiences and concerns, beginning with the cultural dislocations that accompanied their transatlantic travels and culminating in a surprising convergence of their work during the war years, especially around issues of originality and reproduction. Indeed, the ambiguities, contradictions, and even the word play characteristic of Duchamp's readymades and related works—several of which directly engaged issues central to fashion—are also to be found in the logic of fashion as Poiret experienced it in the wake of his trip to America in 1913.

Poiret's trip made him acutely aware of the necessity to respond effectively to the ready availability in the United States of counterfeit labels and pirated copies of couture dresses. Upon his return to Paris Poiret broadened his sphere of activity beyond the semi-private domain of his couture house and other business operations to the public arena. Even before the outbreak of war, he was becoming an outspoken champion of policies designed to protect French haute couture in the rapidly industrializing international marketplace. When war intervened in August 1914, he immediately joined the French army and, as this chapter will show, he also continued to campaign vigorously for couture industry regulations that he now aligned with the national defense against German military encroachment. Recognizing the importance of the American market in particular to the survival of French haute couture, he spearheaded efforts to ensure that American consumers would have access to examples of the finest French couture clothing, despite the extraordinary difficulties posed by transatlantic commerce under wartime conditions. At the same time that he was taking steps to shore up the elite French couture industry, however, he was also making plans to challenge it by exploiting the American mass-market thirst for cheaper copies of authentic couture dresses. The strategy he devised in 1916, when he announced a spring 1917 line of relatively inexpensive, readymade clothing specially designed to satisfy the practical and economic demands of American female consumers, responds to the same concerns—about the colliding forces of art and industry, the ambiguous relationship of original and reproduction, and the tensions between French and American culture—that informed not only his work and that of every other couturier, but also the very different work of Duchamp that is associated with the wartime Dada movement in New York. The complex and contradictory logic of fashion that Poiret's career unveils emerges as a potent tool for understanding what appears to be a deep, structural relationship between fashion and art during this period, which even the most intense visual analysis cannot reveal.[4]

Rebounding from his shock upon discovering his dresses were being copied and his label counterfeited, back in Paris at the end of 1913 Poiret organized a select group of the most prominent couture houses, as well as several representatives of related industries (notably Lucien Vogel, publisher of *Gazette du Bon Ton*), into an association known as Le Syndicat de Défense de la Grande Couture Française et des Industries s'y Rattachant (the Syndicate for the Protection of the Great French Couture and Related Industries). Officially founded on 14 June 1914 (see figure 4.1), the Syndicat was dedicated to protecting the top echelon of couture houses from the piracy, copying, and other bootlegging practices that threatened them all. This new organization was far more elite than the older and larger Chambre Syndicale de la Couture Parisienne, whose members were drawn from the full spectrum of businesses in the women's tailoring industry, not only haute couture. Headed by Poiret as president and Jacques Worth (business manager in the third generation of family members to run the Worth firm) as vice-president, the Syndicat had close

COPYRIGHTING CLOTHES

Led by Paul Poiret, the French Dressmakers Establish in New York an Association to Protect and Copyright Their Designs

AN interesting result of the visit Mr. Paul Poiret, the well-known French designer, made to America in the autumn of 1913, has recently developed in the decision rendered by the court of Special Sessions on the eighteenth of December in the case of Mr. Poiret against William Fantell of the Universal Weaving Company, accused and convicted of having manufactured and sold to the fashion trade imitations of Mr. Poiret's labels. During his visit to America, Mr. Poiret was much astonished to see advertised in various shop windows Poiret gowns which he himself had never seen before. Needless to say, Mr. Poiret quickly identified these gowns as never having emanated from his establishment and the labels which were sewed in them as nothing but counterfeits of his original label. He immediately placed the matter in the hands of his attorney, who started an investigation which revealed the fact that not only were Poiret labels being imitated and sold throughout the country by a number of manufacturers, but the labels of other prominent couturiers were also being duplicated. In fact, it was discovered that quite a flourishing trade in these false labels had become well established in America.

WAYS AND MEANS FOR PROTECTING COUTURIERS

As an outcome of Mr. Poiret's report on this matter to his colleagues upon his return to Paris, there was a general movement among the leading French couturiers to devise some means to protect themselves against this spurious exploitation of their names. Accordingly, last June, at the suggestion of Mr. Philippe Ortiz, a Frenchman who has long been resident in America, and who is the representative in this country of Braun et Compagnie of Paris, Mr. Poiret and his colleagues formed an association styled, "Syndicat de Défense de la Couture Française" (Association for the Protection of French Dressmaking), with a branch in New York City, the direction of which was placed in the hands of Mr. Ortiz.

Immediately following the installation in New York of a branch of the Paris Syndicat, it was expected by those who were familiar with the situation that a great number of trials would follow and that the Syndicat would be inclined to press every charge against the false label manufacturers and fashion dealers; but on the contrary, the representative of the Syndicat acted very generously in the matter and issued a public warning to the effect that the manufacture of these imitation French labels must immediately cease, and that those who failed to heed this warning would be (Continued on page 100)

The above is a facsimile of the statement signed by the French couturiers thanking Mr. Paul Poiret for his efforts to prevent the fraudulent manufacture and use of the labels of French couturiers

Figure 4.1 ↺

Article reproducing a statement of support for Paul Poiret's efforts to prevent American piracy of French fashions, signed by leading French couturiers, from *Vogue,* 1915.

ties in America, where an associate of *Vogue* magazine, Philippe Ortiz, represented the organization in New York.[5]

The connection with *Vogue* is intriguing, as it indicates that the semi-monthly American women's magazine shared the couturiers' interests in promoting a robust French fashion industry and restricting design piracy at home and abroad. This is not surprising, given the fact that Americans in general and *Vogue*'s editors in particular saw Paris as the undisputed source of fashion and stylistic cachet. While the French viewed America in stereotypical terms as a locus of modern experience, Americans saw France in similarly simplistic terms as the fount of high culture and art, the same terms in which Poiret and Paquin had presented it when showing their dresses to audiences in the United States. *Vogue*'s motivation in joining with French couturiers' efforts to control piracy was equally self-interested, designed to protect its own financial investment in the fashion photographs and drawings it published, and in the fashion merchandising business it controlled, which included the sale of patterns based on the designs illustrated in the magazine. In 1914, when the new Syndicat was founded, *Vogue* was advertising three kinds of patterns through its own Pattern Service, ranging from inexpensive stock designs in standard sizes to "cut-to-individual-measure" patterns made for every garment illustrated in the magazine, whether in a drawing or a photograph. *Vogue* was thus heavily invested in the continuing efficacy of French haute couture, the subject of most of its images and editorial pages, as well as the principal source of the cachet that helped the magazine to secure its circulation amongst wealthy bourgeois readers in America, whose potential patronage attracted advertising revenue. When the high-end *Gazette du Bon Ton* was forced to discontinue publication during the war, *Vogue* publisher Condé Nast stepped in to produce a special American edition of the *Gazette* to accompany the exhibition of French haute couture at the Panama-Pacific Exposition of 1915.[6] (Many of the artist-illustrators originally associated with the *Gazette du Bon Ton* subsequently published drawings in *Vogue.*) Nast also published an American edition of the *Gazette du Bon Ton* after the war.[7] He recognized that only a fraction of his potential audience would pay the $4.00 price per issue of the *Gazette du Bon Ton,* just as few *Vogue* readers could afford to purchase couture creations. But, like the couturiers themselves, Nast played to both ends of the economic spectrum, addressing a wealthy clientele as well as the needs of women with "limited incomes," for example by developing *Vogue*'s Pattern Service for those who wished to copy designs seen in the pages of the magazine. The language used in advertising this service mimicked that of the couturiers and department stores in stressing originality and uniqueness, even while promoting what was, after all, a mechanism for the copying of designs: "Vogue Patterns are unique. They are the replicas, in different colored papers, of the models you select. The gown is of gray paper, the trimming of green paper, and the lining of brown paper; hand made and hand cut."[8] But if, like the couturiers, *Vogue* was to profit by selling not only its magazine but also "unique" and supposedly hand-made patterns to its readers, the company had to protect its investment by preventing others from stealing the images on which those patterns were based. This was the strategy behind the magazine's announcement in 1915 that, in order to protect its "originality," *Vogue* had sued a number of newspaper publishers, department stores, and advertising services who had appropriated images from *Vogue* without permission. Though supposedly reluctant to take legal action, the magazine nevertheless went ahead because, it said, "so much of Vogue's charm depends on the originality and distinctiveness of its illustrations," here formulating an argument whose logic and rhetoric are identical to those repeatedly made by Poiret and the other members of his Syndicat.

Securing copyright protection was a major goal of the Syndicat de Défense de la Grande Couture Française. According to an article in the *New York Times*, the organization aimed "in particular, to prevent the copying or pirating of their models by foreign houses. This they propose to accomplish by copyrighting each model, the same as if it were a picture or a book."[9] *Vogue* too was not only committed to battling copyright infringement but, like the Syndicat, it wanted to limit use of its name by manufacturers who, according to the magazine, produced "'Vogue' candies, and 'Vogue' toilet articles, and 'Vogue' hats, and various other things, good, bad, and indifferent, all labeled 'Vogue.'" These firms, it was argued, did not simply or innocently use the word "vogue"; rather, they "trade on the reputation and prestige of Vogue, the magazine." Yet the magazine acknowledged that it could not prevent others from using the term because, unlike a couturier's name (the name on Poiret's couture house label, for example), "vogue" was a word in general circulation and, therefore, could not be claimed as an exclusive trademark in connection with goods other than those directly associated with the magazine.[10] Nevertheless, *Vogue* found itself in deep sympathy with the French couturiers, caught between the need to protect their elite business status and high-priced designs from copying, and the equally urgent, though antithetical, pressure to produce lower-priced copies to appeal to an American mass market that had shown its readiness to spend its money on the pirated copies that had such a destabilizing effect on the precarious relationship between originality and reproduction at the heart of haute couture.

Strengthened by its affiliation with *Vogue* and operating under the energetic direction of Poiret, during the year after its establishment the Syndicat de Défense de la Grande Couture Française promulgated a set of controversial rules designed to regulate access to the members' seasonal shows, to control the publication of photographs of new models, and to prevent shipments bound for legitimate clients and commercial outlets from falling into the hands of illicit copiers in Paris or the United States. However, the anti-piracy measures taken by this elite trade organization to control copying should be understood less as means of prevention than as opportunities for exploitation. After all, Syndicat regulation of copying

not only acknowledged but sought to profit from the centrality of reproduction in the rapidly changing economy of the couture industry.
Through the measures it instituted, the organization envisioned the division of the vast American dressmaking and marketing sectors into five categories according to the manner and scale in which copies of couture
originals were to be produced and distributed by American garment manufacturers. Licenses would be strictly policed; a charge of five dollars was
imposed on every model rented or lent out for reproduction, and twice
that amount was charged for every copy that an American manufacturer
sold. In addition, special labels indicating that a reproduction was authorized by the Syndicat cost one dollar apiece.[11] These and other regulations
intended to curb piracy and fraud at the same time enabled the couturiers
to profit from mass production of their designs. The program provoked a
storm of protest amongst professional buyers, many of whom regarded the
new rules as an assault on their honesty and good faith—not to mention
the measures' negative impact on profits being reaped by unscrupulous
buyers from widespread, legally suspect, copying practices.[12] Nevertheless,
the Syndicat's regulations were put into place in the months following the
outbreak of war in August 1914, when strains between French couturiers
and their American corporate clients were on the increase. These strains
were due, in part, to French fears that neutral Americans would use the
occasion of the war in Europe to disengage themselves from their long-
standing dependence on French haute couture and develop a viable fashion industry of their own. Jacques Worth had already foreseen this
possibility in 1912, when he spoke out against design piracy and false label-
ing practices in America but, according to the *New York Times,*
"declin[ed] to discuss the problem of American fashions for American
women, against which he is plainly arrayed . . ."[13] As damaging to French
interests as were the fake couture labels and the sale of American copies
passed off as imported dresses, Worth believed these practices had little
actual impact on the high end of the Paris couture industry. He regarded

as a more serious danger the possibility that American designers might improve the quality and allure of their dresses, making them attractive to American women and, therefore, a competitive threat to the French. As the *Times* reporter noted, "Here at last is a really inside view of this question from the French trade point of view! It fully bears out the suspicion that this is really not at all a conflict between a nation of taste and a nation without taste; but a race between two business rivals, with the Frenchman so far in the lead that he is nearly out of sight, but panting painfully, and the American, strong and fresh, and just waking up to the fact that he can easily win if he will but try."[14]

Worth's prediction that one day American dress designers would successfully compete with French couturiers for American trade exposed a deep ambivalence about American economic power and its potential for cultural domination. This became an almost palpable threat under wartime conditions that made the United States both more difficult to access and more important to the French economy. As Poiret wrote "from the trenches" in an article published in early 1915:

> And the magazines! Here is one that has just come from America. It seeks to explain that the great fashion houses of Paris are actually closed; paralyzed by the war, and that Paris will not create the styles for the coming spring. It adds that a number of the New York dress-making houses have grouped themselves together (it seems incredible) with the object of instituting what they call American Styles!
>
> This is sensational news! Thus Americans seek to throw off the yoke of Paris.[15]

Poiret may well have been reacting to news of a "Fashion Fête" produced at the Ritz-Carlton Hotel in New York in November 1914, in which American dress designers sought to fill the void created by the war-induced closure of many Paris couture houses, including his own, in the late summer and autumn of 1914. A charitable event patronized by the leaders of American high society from Mrs. Vincent Astor to no less than five members of the Vanderbilt family,[16] the "Fashion Fête" was organized under the auspices of Poiret's own ally, *Vogue*—which accounts for the tone of betrayal conveyed in his words quoted above. In fact, *Vogue* played a leading role in organizing the display of 125 American models that was preceded on stage by a dialogue between two characters, a male "artist" and a woman described as "Miss Vogue herself." Their debate over whether New York was capable of producing a fashion season without help from Paris ended in a wager, and the models presented in the mannequin parade that crossed the stage and descended into the audience were the proof offered by Miss Vogue that American designers could rise to the challenge.[17] The three-day run of performances received a great deal of attention in *Vogue,* whose editor, Edna Woolman Chase, actually conceived and orchestrated the series as a society and fashion extravaganza in order to offset the wartime loss of editorial content normally generated by the Paris fashion scene.[18]

Several of the articles *Vogue* published about the "Fashion Fête" emphatically stated that the event was not intended to support an American couture industry independent of Paris: "To break away from the influence of France was not the object of the exhibition; it was rather to uphold the traditions of smart dress endangered by the conditions existing abroad."[19] The principal participants were said to be New York shops that traditionally imported a substantial number of models by French couturiers and merely supplemented these imports with models of their own design:

> Their art and their sympathies are strongly French. They hope, not to equal Paris, but to be worthy of her teaching; not to compete with her art and her trade, but to supply the need for them while she is

incapacitated, and, perhaps, some day to contribute their share toward the art of fashion.

American fashions for American women is no part of their platform. There is, we hope, no such thing as an American fashion.[20]

Poiret and the French clearly viewed such reiterated disclaimers as evidence that the opposite was actually the case. Even *Vogue* acknowledged that the success of this highly visible series of performances, with their theatrical setting and valuable stamp of social approval, gave Americans confidence in their own taste and their ability to meet the demand for fashionable clothing. All this translated into sales for American dressmakers, most of which would otherwise have gone to French couturiers. But if the French were apprehensive about the threat of competition from newly emboldened New York dress designers, they were equally agitated about the prospect that more immediate rivals in the enemy capitals of Berlin and Vienna might succeed in attracting a large measure of the trade that Americans had traditionally done in Paris. The *New York Times* published numerous articles on this topic during the war years, reporting on the "special efforts" that German and Austrian dressmakers and milliners were making "to capture trade which in this season of the year [February 1915] Americans would be doing with Paris and London."[21]

In response to these war-related apprehensions, the anti-piracy measures promoted by the Syndicat were made to do double duty, which is to say that Poiret deployed them to deter or regulate copying and also to support France's war effort. In a sternly worded speech soliciting support from Syndicat members and their sympathizers, Poiret declared war on foreign dressmakers: "It will be fought not only against Austro-German firms, but also, and especially, against all the false firms under which Austrians and Germans lie concealed, and against all the cheating trademarks which provide cover for them." Conflating France's enemies in the First World War with those who practiced design piracy, he lashed out against all of them, including the Americans: "It is not only against Germans, Austrians, or Turks that we must aim our blows, but against the counterfeit Swiss, the false Americans, the pseudo-Poles. . . . [T]he sudden attack which we shall soon make will restore to us the ground which we have lost and the position abandoned by us owing to negligence due to our naïve trustfulness and loyalty."[22]

That Poiret so stridently proclaimed this nationalist rhetoric might seem peculiar in light of the defining characteristics of his prewar posture, marked by his sophisticated cosmopolitanism in general and, in particular, his support for advanced tendencies in the visual arts, his intensive involvement and close identification with Orientalist themes associated with the Turkish Empire, and the fact that he had traveled on several occasions to both Germany and Austria, where he had been favorably received and where he had found a good deal of inspiration for some of his most acclaimed work in couture and interior design (which was also, it must be said, his most controversial). As Sem's vitriolic diatribe in *Le Vrai et le faux chic* suggested in spring 1914, all of these engagements became a distinct liability for Poiret in the ideologically charged atmosphere of Paris immediately before and during the First World War.

Where Sem's caricatures had a humorous dimension and his text acknowledged their tendency toward exaggeration, little more than a year later Poiret was being singled out in extremely aggressive terms as a lightning rod for conservative antagonism to the internationalism of French avant-garde culture in the pages of the magazine *La Renaissance Politique, Économique, Littéraire, et Artistique.*[23] The fact that Poiret dresses might have remained attractive to German consumers during the war (as suggested by a cartoon in the German humor magazine, *Simplicissimus*) was sufficient grounds for the editor of *La Renaissance,* Ingres scholar Henri Lapauze, to condemn Poiret for "*boche* taste" and to accuse him of harboring anti-French sympathies. When the attack was broadened in October 1915 to include "the disgusting taste of Mlle. Martine, of the Ecole Martine, of the Maison Martine," Poiret felt compelled to defend himself by suing *La Renaissance* for defamation of character. At this point, Kenneth Silver has shown, *La Renaissance* felt justified in letting out all the stops, publishing the complete text of the court summons along with an editorial reply that welcomed Poiret's lawsuit for providing an occasion "to explain what we mean by *boche* art, or, if you prefer, by German influence on the French decorative arts and fashion." Faced with accusations that linked him to what many conservative cultural critics regarded as dangerous foreign influences in avant-garde art and design, Poiret refused to be cowed. In July 1916, he hosted a large exhibition of works by some of the most advanced artists in Paris in his couture house, which was otherwise closed for the duration of the war. Organized by André Salmon, the exhibition, "L'Art Moderne en France," included works by many of Poiret's closest artist friends, Jean-Louis Boussingault, André Derain, Raoul Dufy, André Dunoyer de Segonzac, Kees van Dongen, Guy Fauconnet, André Lhote, and Luc-Albert Moreau, as well as by Fernand Léger, Henri Matisse, and Pablo Picasso, whose *Demoiselles d'Avignon* made its first public appearance on this occasion. Critics treated the show with grudging respect, although several disparagingly noted the large number of non-French exhibitors—"foreign riffraff" who copied their French counterparts, "floundering in the most ludicrous sorts of imitations."[24]

Fourteen months later, when Poiret agreed to a settlement with *La Renaissance,* dropping his lawsuit in return for a public apology by the journal, all the letters supporting the opposing sides in the dispute were published. Among Poiret's backers were several artists who had been included in the Salon d'Antin: Boussingault, Derain, Dufy, Dunoyer de Segonzac, and Fauconnet; many more signed a petition (published with the letters backing Poiret) that had been circulated by Sébastien Voirol in support of a new organization called Art et Liberté, the purpose of which was to defend modern artists, architects, designers, writers, and others— including Poiret—whose work had been accused of germanic affiliation.[25] But by 1917, when these expressions of support appeared in print, the damage to Poiret's reputation had already been done. As Silver observes, ". . . [L]ittle could be worse than a public accusation of treason in the midst of war."[26] Indeed, the repercussions of this experience can be seen in Poiret's professional conduct, not only in the attention he continued to devote during the war to cultivating an American audience, or in the ways he sought to align the Syndicat de Défense de la Grande Couture Française with France's war effort, but also in the diminishing influence he exercised over members of the Syndicat from November 1915 on, when the regulations Poiret advocated themselves became a public relations problem precisely in the American market that was so valuable to the Syndicat.

In January 1916, the *New York Times* reported that the rules imposed by the Syndicat "created a cyclone of trouble and comment in New York . . . [and] may cause an upheaval in the conditions of our trade in women's apparel with France."[27] Exactly this had been threatened three months earlier, when, at the height of the controversy over Poiret's patriotism, the Syndicat blacklisted two American customers with German names, and, as a result, French haute couture houses, many of which were by then back in business, were compelled to refuse their orders. One of the buyers turned out to be Charles Kurzman, the American department store owner (a naturalized U.S. citizen) who was also the agent responsible for purchasing the trousseau of President Woodrow Wilson's fiancée, Edith Bolling Galt. As head of the Syndicat, Poiret had to deal with the uproar the incident ignited in the United States. This he did by announcing that members of the Syndicat would be honored to "make all [Edith Galt's] gowns for her wedding and present them to her with our compliments," thereby attempting to buy good will while, at the same time, obviating the need to deal with Kurzman in his role as intermediary.[28] Nevertheless, the situation caused considerable embarrassment to everyone involved: Galt denied placing any orders through Kurzman; he contended that the entire story was false; couturiers on the rue de la Paix and elsewhere in Paris expressed "regret that such an incident has come up and state they hope it will cause no annoyance to President Wilson."[29] It appears to have been precisely such fears of the Syndicat's potentially negative impact on their businesses that led several members to consider resigning. Their resolve to withdraw was only strengthened by the draconian measures Poiret proposed at the end of 1915, when he was grappling with just how to defend himself against the accusations of Henri Lapauze in *La Renaissance:* Poiret's idea was to initiate a series of boycotts, blacklistings, lawsuits, and the creation of what was described as "a police organization for the purpose of running down all counterfeiters and denouncing them to the parties interested and to the Syndicate. The seriousness of the danger may make this organization a veritable counter-espionage agency."[30] Callot Soeurs was the first to withdraw, several others followed suit, and in February 1916, Paquin was said to be "wavering and undecided as to whether she would stay in."[31] Rumors circulated that Poiret, clearly damaged by adverse publicity on all sides, would resolve the Syndicat's problems "by abandoning the dressmaking business altogether and launching out independently as a theatrical costumer and designer," which his associates regarded as "a branch especially suited to his abilities."[32] In the end, the troubled organization was superseded by the larger, more inclusive Chambre Syndicale de la Couture Parisienne which, according to *The New York Times,* included "all members of the Couture Defense Syndicate except Poiret and Worth." The newspaper further reported that the Chambre Syndicale was sympathetic to the purposes of Poiret's organization, but not to its methods; it accordingly sought an agreement between French and American interests that would ensure the elimination of the organization headed by Poiret.[33]

Although the efficacy of the Syndicat de Défense de la Grande Couture Française was probably compromised from the start by the repeated attacks on Poiret's reputation in *La Renaissance,* and the organization eventually did succumb to the outrage that greeted his overzealous efforts at protection of the high-end French dress trade, the Syndicat did meet with some success as far as its efforts to maintain and promote awareness of French fashions in the United States were concerned. Especially during the first eighteen months of the war, access to the American market gained new urgency for French couturiers who were hard pressed to maintain adequate business activity. Faced with the virtual collapse of domestic markets, as well as drastic reductions in foreign trade, Poiret and his colleagues redoubled their efforts to appeal to American buyers. A climax of sorts was reached in late November 1915, just as the Syndicat was beginning to enforce its regulations—and show signs of serious internal dissension—when the organization surmounted a myriad of war-induced shipping delays and other obstacles to stage a week-long "Fête Parisienne" in the ballroom of the Ritz-Carlton Hotel in New York. A reprise, more or less, of the "Fashion Fête" that *Vogue* had promoted the year before (with many of the same patronesses), this event focused not on American but on French designs, and the money raised was intended to benefit the orphans of French workers in the dressmaking trades. Caroline Seebohm suggests that French couturiers had been furious with *Vogue*'s publisher, Condé Nast, for his endorsement of the hugely successful fashion show put on by their American rivals. Therefore, it made good business sense for Nast to allay their anger by offering *Vogue*'s patronage and organizational expertise to produce the Syndicat's own fashion event.[34] Like the 1914 "Fashion Fête" starring Miss Vogue, the French show was constructed as a series of theatrical presentations. Poiret commissioned his friend Roger Boutet de Monvel (a writer, historian, and Assistant Director of the Musée Carnavalet in Paris who had been wounded at Ypres early in the war) to compose a two-act play that would serve as a culturally acceptable vehicle for the twice-daily presentation on the Ritz-Carlton's ballroom stage of 100 examples of the latest, genuine French fashions designed by the members of the Syndicat. As initially reported in the *New York Times* a month before it was staged, "The comedy is entitled, 'Talking Rags,' and is written around the return of a young American heiress from a visit to the Rue de la Paix with her chaperon [*sic*]. She describes her purchases to envious friends, thus creating the opportunity for the introduction of the names of the houses belonging to the syndicate and the various models which will be worn by American actresses."[35] When the *Times* reported on the actual performance, its title had been changed to the more prosaic *Betty's Trousseau,* but the thrust of the "comedietta" as an advertising vehicle remained the same.[36] Here the Orientalism and classical themes so pervasive in the prewar theatricalization of fashion were abandoned as shopping itself became the theme as well as the raison d'être of the play.

By asking Boutet de Monvel to create the play in which actresses familiar to New York audiences would act as mannequins, Poiret once again pursued a marketing strategy for haute couture that collapsed the boundaries between art and advertising, between dramatic theater and the fashion show. According to the *New York Times,* some of the gowns were inspired by historical paintings, and in those cases the models "took the names of the artists of the brush for their creations. There was Pietro Longhi, the Venetian painter, and the gown suggested his time. There were Velasquez and Goya, and an evening wrap was Beardsley."[37] Boutet de Monvel had apparently struggled to find ways of handling the problem of integrating the competing demands of the occasion, for as he himself acknowledged, "It is a difficult problem, indeed, an arduous and delicate task at the same time to conform to the laws of dramatic art and to meet the needs of French industry."[38] He seems to have managed it well, for the play he wrote and came to New York to direct was not simply a spectacle devoid of meaningful content but, rather, a finely tuned vehicle specifically crafted to convey crucial information about French haute couture to the industry's American clientele. Thus, as the contents of the ingenue's trousseau were displayed, the dialogue suggested that dressmaking was not moribund in Paris but, in order to maintain its vitality during the war, it simply needed orders from Americans, who should not try to create fashion independently but, instead, should rely on the French to provide chic clothes that would be both comfortable and practical, as American women demanded. Boutet de Monvel even managed to include the point that Americans should make their purchases from a *grand couturier* rather than from a mere copyist.

The issues surrounding copying and copyright protection were matters of great concern to French couturiers during the early twentieth century, because, as has been shown, they raised crucial questions involving the legally and culturally constructed relationship between art and industry. They also played a part in the international economic rivalries that were intensified by the war, distorted the creative process, and destroyed the trust once shared between dressmakers and their clients, both commercial and individual. But the questions of originality and reproduction, art and industry, nationalism and internationalism, commerce and culture were also relevant to many artists during this period, for example, the salon cubists and their counterparts represented by the dealer, Daniel-Henry Kahnweiler. During the teens, these issues were of particular interest to Marcel Duchamp. Indeed, the point at which the interests of Poiret and Duchamp intersect is marked by the unstable juxtaposition of art and reproduction. Here—where haute couture confronts the copy and the individual art object can no longer be distinguished from the mass-produced commodity—is the point where elite culture and what Molly Nesbit has called "industrial culture" overlap and interpenetrate: readymade clothes and the art of the readymade encounter one another on a field defined by French-American cultural and economic relations during the First World War.

A great deal has been written about the significance of Duchamp's readymades of the middle and late teens: a small number of industrially produced, individual objects that the artist selected at random (or so he said) in a spirit of what he described as "aesthetic indifference" and which, by virtue of that selection, were removed from circulation in the commercial realm. Inscribing each with a word or phrase and his signature,

Duchamp destabilized their functional purpose by treating them in a manner similar to works of art. Scarcely altered physically from the state in which Duchamp found them, the readymades were nevertheless transformed conceptually by this process, which stripped them of their use value while confirming their status as reified commodities.

Duchamp's first "unassisted" readymade was a metal rack for drying wine bottles that he purchased in 1914 at a Paris department store, the Grand Bazar de l'Hôtel de Ville (figure 4.2).[39] But it took some time and

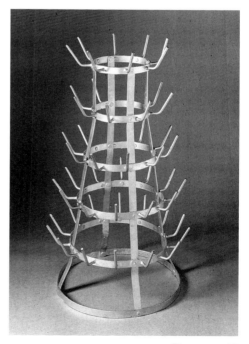

Figure 4.2

Marcel Duchamp, *Bottle Rack,* 1963 (replica of 1914 original).

a stay in the United States before this bottle rack would assume its new and intentionally unstable status as a work of art. Writing to his sister in mid-January 1916 from New York, where he had been since June 1915 (his health having prevented him from serving in the French military), Duchamp explained,

> Now, if you have been up to my place, you will have seen, in the studio, a bicycle wheel and a *bottle rack*. I bought this as a ready-made sculpture [*une sculpture toute faite*]. And I have a plan concerning this so-called bottle rack: Listen to this.
>
> Here, in N.Y., I have bought several objects in the same taste and I treat them as "readymades" [here Duchamp used the English word]. You know enough English to understand the sense of "*readymade*" [here Duchamp used the French "*tout fait*"] that I give these objects. I sign them and I think of an inscription for them in English. . . .
>
> Take this bottle rack for yourself. I'm making it a "Readymade" [again, he used the English term], remotely. You are to inscribe it at the bottom and *on the inside* of the bottom circle, in small letters painted with a brush in oil, silver white color, with an inscription that I will give you herewith [Duchamp's intended inscription is lost and therefore remains unknown], and then sign it, in the same handwriting, as follows:
>
> [after *(here, in brackets, Duchamp used the French* d'après*)*] Marcel Duchamp.[40]

In several articles dealing with the readymades, Nesbit has stressed their strangeness, their difference from works of art. She notes that Duchamp made them "not for public but for private distraction," and that he was at best ambivalent about their exhibition.[41] Paradoxically, perhaps, he thus confirmed his status as an artist by distancing himself from the commercial world and refusing to earn a living through the sale of his work. By displaying some of the readymades in peculiar positions in his studio [(*Fountain*, the infamous readymade in the form of an upended urinal, for example, was suspended in a doorway (figure 4.3); the snow shovel, *In Advance of the Broken Arm*, hung from the ceiling (figure 4.4); and *Trébuchet*, originally a coat rack, was nailed to the floor (figure 4.5)],

Figure 4.3

Henri-Pierre Roché, photo of Marcel Duchamp's New York studio with *Fountain* suspended in the doorway, 1917–1918.

Figure 4.4   ↻

Marcel Duchamp, *In Advance of the Broken Arm,*
1946 (replica of 1915 original).

and presumably anticipating that two of them would be overlooked when
he encouraged their exhibition not on conventional sculpture pedestals
but in an unmarked umbrella stand at the entrance to a New York art
gallery in 1916, Duchamp did not simply alienate these objects from their
functional contexts in order to locate them securely in the sphere of fine
art, he placed them in an ambiguous, seemingly contradictory conceptual
zone that corresponded entirely neither to conventional expectations for
art nor to commonly held notions of the industrially produced commodity.[42] Belonging equally yet nevertheless problematically to both or neither
realms, the readymades testified to what Duchamp regarded as the crisis
of traditional art-making brought on by industrialization. They embodied
his rejection of the retinal rather than conceptual character of modernist

painting and its emphasis on formal innovation as practiced by the circle of salon cubists (his brothers Jacques Villon and Raymond Duchamp-Villon, as well as Gleizes, Metzinger, Le Fauconnier, et al.) with whom he had been associated as an artist for several years in the early teens. As he famously said to Constantin Brancusi and Fernand Léger in autumn 1912 when together they looked at the airplanes exhibited at the fourth Salon de la Locomotion Aérienne in Paris, "Painting is finished. Who can do anything better than this propeller? Can you?"[43]

"It was in 1915," Duchamp later recalled in an interview with Pierre Cabanne, "especially, in the United States, that I did other objects with inscriptions, like the snow shovel, on which I wrote something in English. The word 'readymade' thrust itself on me then. It seemed perfect for these

Figure 4.5

Marcel Duchamp, *Trébuchet* seen in
Duchamp's New York studio, c. 1917–1918,
from *Boîte-en-Valise,* 1941–1942.

things that weren't works of art, that weren't sketches, and to which no art terms applied. That's why I was tempted to make them."[44] Having left France for New York in the summer of 1915, Duchamp was soon introduced to Walter and Louise Arensberg, who became his close friends and lifelong supporters of his work. The Arensbergs had recently begun to collect contemporary art in a concerted fashion, and during the war their apartment on West Sixty-seventh Street "served as a virtual open house" where Duchamp encountered other French as well as American artists, writers, and intellectuals.[45] Walter Arensberg was supported financially by his own family's wealth and by money Louise had inherited, and he was therefore free to pursue interests in literature: writing his own poetry (in French and in English), translating that of others, and nurturing a serious preoccupation with cryptography, that is, the art of writing or deciphering writing in secret code. "His system," Duchamp explained to Cabanne, "was to find, in the text, in every three lines, allusions to all sorts of things; it was a game for him, like chess, which he enjoyed immensely."[46] In this atmosphere, Duchamp, who spoke little or no English when he first arrived in America, could not help but become intensely aware of language. It was a realm of signification he had apparently already begun to explore in Paris. Again in conversation with Cabanne, Duchamp recalled how "the poetic aspect of words" had already been affecting his thinking about his masterwork of this period, *The Large Glass,* which he called "a delay in glass" in order not to have to explain it in merely descriptive, rational terms as "'a glass painting,' 'a glass drawing,' 'a thing drawn on glass,' you understand? The word 'delay' pleased me at that point, like a phrase one discovers. It was really poetic, in the most Mallarméan sense of the word, so to speak." And he went on, "Titles in general interested me a lot. At that time, I was becoming literary."[47] Indeed, in New York he behaved like a dandy, circulating amongst a small circle of avant-garde writers and artists and enjoying financial support from members of an economically privileged elite. As Nesbit and

Naomi Sawelson-Gorse have observed, "He wrote a little word piece based on the genderless article, or rather its omission and called it 'The.' At first it looked like a puzzle solved with little effort by the substitution of the definite article for the star. Except that the sentences were senseless, though grammatically correct."[48] Eventually, they argue, Duchamp's play with words and language, encouraged by Arensberg, led him to "the inscrutable sentences that would be taken over as inscriptions for the readymades."[49] Thus the phrases "In Advance of the Broken Arm" and "Pulled at 4 Pins" that Duchamp inscribed on two of his readymades, or even such titles of readymades as *Fountain* and *Trébuchet,* were intended—like the readymades themselves—to deflect any functional, referential, or otherwise rational consideration from the objects to which these words were applied. The goal, if it could be described as anything so consciously motivated and directed, was to drain the industrially produced commodity of its sense and purpose in the physical world by transposing it into the abstract realm of poetic language. And this, strangely enough, brings us back to the subject of haute couture, whose practitioners—Paul Poiret and Lady Duff Gordon, for example—also used allusive words and phrases for the titles of their couture models in order to encourage their clients to make poetic associations rather than merely functional or straightforward, commercial connections with the dresses. Furthermore, the ways in which their couture labels functioned in a process that Bourdieu has likened to magic, as signatures that inscribe artistic distinction in salable commodities, bears comparison with the function of the signature in Duchamp's readymades and related works.[50] That a couture label could be counterfeited, thereby destroying any transparent relationship between the name and the individual creative designer, suggests further parallels to Duchamp's activities and interests at the time, as we shall see.

The comparison I am presenting here is not intended to suggest that there was an exchange of influence or significant personal connection between Duchamp and the leading figures in the world of haute couture, although Duchamp may well have known Poiret.[51] But it is, I believe, significant that, according to Francis Naumann, Duchamp was thinking of the clothing industry when in America he hit upon the term "readymade,"[52] which was the focus of so much anxious attention amongst French couturiers at this time. Furthermore, Naumann notes, as the son of a French notary, Duchamp was from a young age "keenly aware" of the differences that distinguished originals and copies in the eyes of the law.[53] Titles, signatures, labels, trademark, copyright, and the status of art and the artist in an international cultural context marked by the production, circulation, and consumption of industrially produced commodities all raised issues of profound interest to both Duchamp and Poiret. This suggests that Duchamp and Poiret operated not in two entirely different spheres hermetically sealed off from one another, as the dominant discourses of fashion and art history might lead us to believe. Rather, each in his own way, in his own intellectual or professional arena, confronted the same problem, one that was arguably among the most recalcitrant (and compelling) of the modern period: the instability of the authorial subject faced with the collapse of distinction between originality and reproduction, the work of art and the object of mass production.

As we have seen, each of Duchamp's readymades thematized this original/copy dichotomy by using a title or phrase and a signature to transform an industrially produced commodity into something approaching a unique object. Duchamp was concerned to sustain this practice on a programmatic level, as he himself noted in 1961: "I realized very soon the danger of repeating indiscriminately this form of expression and decided to limit the production of 'readymades' to a small number yearly." Not unlike the couturier, the artist recognized a danger inherent in making available too many models of his extraordinary conception. Yet in limiting the number of readymades, Duchamp never intended to condemn them to a stable status as works of art, as Nesbit has pointed out.[54] "I was aware at that time," Duchamp later recalled, "that for the spectator even more than for the artist, *art is a habit forming drug* and I wanted to protect my 'readymades' against such contamination."[55] Characteristically, he dispelled any possible misconception that the readymades might be singular or unique, like the traditional work of art: "Another aspect of the 'readymade' is its lack of uniqueness . . . the replica of a 'readymade' delivering the same message; in fact nearly every one of the 'readymades' existing today is not an original in the conventional sense."[56]

This notion of the readymade as limited in production yet neither original nor unique corresponds surprisingly closely to the inherently contradictory terms in which Paul Poiret described the dresses he designed for the American market in 1916, at precisely the same time that Duchamp, a Frenchman in America, was designating his readymades. As physical objects the readymades retained the form of the multiple, yet their titles, signatures, and inscriptions functioned like the couturier's often-forged *griffe,* or the titles assigned to dresses, to charge with aura things that would otherwise be unexeceptional, widely available, industrially produced commodities. The result in each case was an object that articulated a contradiction, an oxymoron, an instability, a constant oscillation between opposite poles—an object occupying an alternative position that both exposed and reconciled without denying the underlying dualities of art and industry, original and reproduction.

Yet Duchamp did not always affix his own name to the objects he appropriated; indeed, perhaps the most notorious readymade, *Fountain,* was signed and submitted for exhibition in 1917 by R. Mutt (figure 4.6).[57] Three years later, back in New York after an absence of almost 18 months, Duchamp created another alter ego, this time a female—Rose Sélavy—whose name and claim to copyright protection are boldly affixed to her inaugural work, which is not a readymade but a reduced scale model of a

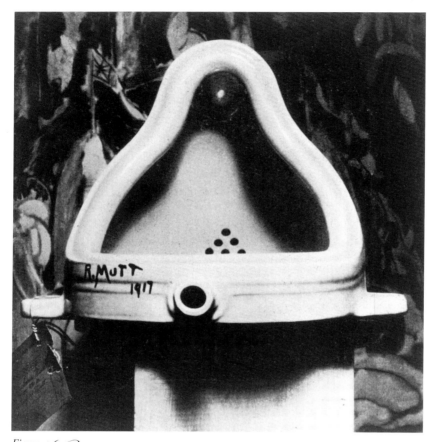

Figure 4.6 ↻

Marcel Duchamp, *Fountain*, 1917.

French window in which each pane of glass is covered with black leather. In this enigmatic object, entitled *Fresh Widow* (figure 4.7), according to Nesbit,

> the French has gone fresh; the window is a widow; the panes are made of leather; and it has been translated into English. The design was given to an American carpenter to get this small-scale model in blue. So the design is repeated and manufactured like a model for a patent office. It makes a joke at the expense of the French war widow. But this time around, Duchamp has inserted a bona fide word that takes the visual language into another order of discourse: the *Fresh Widow* is declared copyrighted by Duchamp's alias, Rose Sélavy. . . . Duchamp has claimed copyright for a window that is not only plagiarized but by definition not eligible for copyright: the window is an industrial good in the eyes of the law; if suitably innovative it might be patented but never given the *droit d'auteur*, not even in America. The copyright was a bluff. But with it, Duchamp subjugated the culture of the patent in no uncertain terms: by means of that one word, he pulled the culture of the patent over into the culture of copyright, the traditional culture, the culture of artists.[58]

This, it should be noted, is precisely what Poiret repeatedly tried to do when he sought to protect his dress designs under copyright law and defended his couture house label—which was also his name—by suing William Fantel for trademark infringement.

Fresh Widow was like Duchamp's readymades insofar as it, too, posed the question of the nature of art itself. Such works left unanswered the paradigmatically modernist question Duchamp asked in 1913, "Can one make works which are not works of 'art'?" And as Thierry de Duve has argued with reference to *Fountain,* in their manner of doing so the

Figure 4.7 ↻

Marcel Duchamp, *Fresh Widow,* 1920.

readymades signaled the end of modernism: "Perhaps it doesn't even matter whether the pissoir is an 'objet d'art' or an object of non-art, or whether its ambiguous status of *objet-dard* [a punning term coined by Duchamp] will keep the question open. Too many answers have been given already. *Fountain* is hard to dislodge from the patrimony of avant-garde art, while it has not yet found its legitimate place among the practices of *art tout court*."[59] But if for Duchamp the question was an end in itself, for Poiret, who was motivated by professional interests far removed from Duchamp's professional indifference, neither the ambiguous status of the readymade (the genuine reproduction dress) nor his own problematic status as an artist (lacking intellectual property rights over his designs) were disinterested issues that he could afford to leave unresolved. As we have seen, he had staked his self-representation and his business success upon particular responses to these very questions.

For Duchamp, on the other hand, authorial self-representation was multiple, enigmatic, and unfixed, as his creation of a female persona would suggest. Yet there are significant correspondences between her identity and the fashionable world of Paul Poiret. Rose (she soon became Rrose) Sélavy was born in the Franco-American context in which Duchamp circulated during and after the First World War. In French, her name is a pun on the phrase *Eros, c'est la vie;* in addition, Duchamp later recalled, "Rose is for me—or was, in France—the most common (not vulgar), but the most popular name of the time, one you wouldn't think of giving to a girl."[60] In English too the name Rose was something of a cliché that in 1920 called to mind the many French flower names found in commercial advertisements aimed at women. As Nancy Ring has observed, "The name 'Rose' was used extensively in the United States to refer to mass-market beauty products . . ." Furthermore, she notes, "Throughout the 1910s and 1920s, manufacturers and copy writers began to combine flower names with French phrases, partly on the grounds that French was 'one of the most graceful languages, possessing exceptional feminine beauty.'"[61] Thus even in this act of naming, Duchamp engaged the rhetoric of French fashion marketing as it entered the sphere of American mass consumption. In this context it bears noting that Poiret, too, was closely associated with the rose, an image of which appears alongside his name on the couture house label that Paul Iribe had designed for him around 1909. Moreover, the name of his perfume line, Rosine, is a variant of the same word that Duchamp chose to name his alter ego. In fact, her name was arguably Rose (or Rrose) Sélavy's most important feature, as it was written on readymades, letters, photographs, and other objects, "authenticating them by inscribing them with 'her' name (a name that, nonetheless, takes its value through that of the *master,* Duchamp)," as Amelia Jones has observed.[62] Rrose Sélavy did actually take shape in 1921 in several portrait photographs made by Man Ray of Duchamp in drag, wearing a hat, a fur-trimmed coat, eye liner, and lipstick, and assuming poses made familiar by actresses and fashion models seen in women's magazines or advertisements of the period for perfume and make-up (figure 4.8). Her image is similar to the photograph of the actress Musidora who endorsed Aladin perfume in the Rosine catalogue published at about this time (figure 4.9).[63] Duchamp was obviously aware of such commercialized tropes of feminine celebrity emanating from the world of contemporary fashion that Poiret so prominently occupied during this period. Duchamp made direct reference to that world in another work by Rrose Sélavy: an assisted readymade entitled *Belle Haleine, Eau de Voilette* (figure 4.10) composed of a repackaged bottle of perfume manufactured not by Rosine (whose artfully crafted, hand decorated, and often unconventional bottles would not have served Duchamp's purposes) but by the better known Paris firm of Rigaud. To Rigaud's bottle he affixed a new label, created in collaboration with Man Ray.[64] This label includes another photograph of Duchamp in drag, beneath which it prominently displays the words "BELLE HALEINE," or "beautiful breath," a pun that plays on the closeness of the French word for breath—suggesting a perfumed scent—

Figure 4.8

Man Ray, *Rrose Sélavy,* gelatin silver print, 1921.

Figure 4.9 ↺

Henri Manuel, photos of the actress Musidora
and of Aladin perfume, from *Les Parfums de
Rosine.*

and Hélène—conjuring up the beautiful woman of Greek myth, Helen of
Troy. Thus, in the condensed form of this work Duchamp explored several of the devices that were Poiret's stock in trade: on the label Duchamp
employed the strategy of cross-dressing to create a parodic image of female seduction and allure and, at the same time, through the trademark,
Belle Haleine, he referenced the role of feminine beauty in classical antiq-
uity. On the back of the cardboard box that holds the bottle Duchamp

Figure 4.10

Marcel Duchamp, *Belle Haleine, Eau de Voilette,* 1921.

later inscribed this readymade with the name Rrose Sélavy, whose initials already appear on the label as if signing the work. This further complicates the authorial role of the artist whose identity is splintered across multiple names, as well as gender positions.[65]

Just as the readymades embodied Duchamp's investigations of what Nesbit has called "the language of industry" in the context of his experience of the encounter between French and American languages, cultures, debates over intellectual property, and attitudes toward fashion and commerce, so Poiret's commercial practices responded to the unique conditions of French fashion marketing in America. Although he was forced to scale back his business operations drastically during the First World War, in October 1916, in the pages of *Vogue*, Poiret advertised a new clothing collection "produced exclusively for the women of America." He described the models as "genuine reproduction[s]," which, he claimed, gave American women "the opportunity to own a PAUL POIRET creation without paying the usual excessive price"[66] (figure 4.11). Here was a solution to the crisis of fashion caught between art and industry that could make everyone happy. Poiret would benefit financially from the reproduction of his models in a process that he supposedly supervised (in fact the garments were to be manufactured by the Max Grab Fashion Company in New York, where their production was to be "superintended by Monsieur Poiret's artistic representative, whom he sent here for that purpose from France"[67]); the seller would be legally sanctioned to sell the copy, which would bear a version of the Poiret label indicating that it was indeed an "authorized reproduction of the original from Paul Poiret in Paris"; and the buyer would acquire a "genuine" item, admittedly a reproduction, but one with a pedigree, at a greatly reduced price.

As a hybrid devised, like Duchamp's readymades, to reconcile (as it exposed) the contradiction between art and industry, the genuine reproduction preserved the modernist fictions of originality and authorial prerogative; at the same time it acknowledged the modern realities of industrial reproduction and consumer demand. By licensing Max Grab,

Figure 4.11

Advertisement for Paul Poiret authorized
reproductions, from *Vogue,* 1916.

Poiret was doing no more (but also no less) than following the lead of Rodin when the sculptor paid an assistant to reproduce a small plaster as a larger-scale *Aphrodite,* or Duchamp when he wrote to his sister with instructions for inscribing and signing his bottle rack as a readymade. However, unlike Duchamp, Poiret never reveled in the ambiguities his actions brought to the fore. Propelled by his own pre-war success with haute couture into the very different yet nevertheless related realm of mass-production, Poiret clung to his identity as an "artist and innovator," the terms in which he was described in the brochure advertising his new line of fourteen genuine-reproduction models to American women. The rhetoric of this publication is familiar from all his pre-war self-constructions and promotional materials: "To think of Poiret as a dress-maker is to miss the essence of his personality. Paul Poiret is an artist of many arts, and an innovator in each. It is not by accident that he is a land-scape painter full of color, a poet full of charm; that he is a musical com-poser, a singer and an amateur of the violin; it is not by chance that he excels in the combination of line and color in decoration, nor that the same gift which has produced beautiful dresses has produced also furni-ture of beauty, rugs and *objets d'art* and perfumes, all of the same quality of originality, charm and daring."[68]

The brochure in which this text appeared was enclosed in a soberly colored yet elegant paper wrapper designed by the graphic artist Benito (figure 4.12), but it was otherwise printed entirely in black and white on ordinary semi-glossy paper stock. With four simple and unobtrusive little line drawings by Benito interspersed throughout the booklet, the fourteen costumes were presented as worn by mannequins posing in straightfor-ward black-and-white photographs (figure 4.13). The most striking feature of the publication for the reader today is the constantly reiterated appear-ance of the "authorized reproduction" label, which is presented in four slightly different versions (one each for dresses, skirts, suits, and coats) stacked one above another on the inside of the wrapper (figure 4.14) and

Figure 4.12

Benito, design of wrapper for *Les Modèles de
Paul Poiret, Printemps 1917*, 1917.

again, individually, alongside each of the fourteen models presented in the
brochure. Altogether, it is a far cry from the deluxe, limited edition
albums by Iribe and Lepape that Poiret had been able to publish before
the war, or from the publication as it was announced in an ad in *Vanity
Fair* in March 1917. There the "style brochure" was described as "a book
of Paul Poiret's own conception, decorated by the foremost French col-
orists and artists, printed on fine paper, and bound in such a manner as to
make this, without question, The Most Exquisite Style Brochure ever
published in America."[69] That vision of elegance and luxury, typical of
Poiret products before the war, had not yet been realized when the ad
was published and subsequently it must have succumbed to wartime exi-
gency; in any case, it would have been at odds with the character of the

LAVEUSE

THIS dainty and piquant summer skirt for town or country, for the canoe or for the beach, disproves the old reproach to washable skirts, that they sacrifice individuality to practical needs.

The contrast of two colors, which gives it originality, marks its essential youthfulness of character, by reflecting the jocund tones of springtime. The crenelated effect above the band breaks the usual hard line of the waist, which is further softened by tassels attached to gleaming buttons.

Washable cords passing over the shoulders seem to sustain the whole. A pocket at the meeting of the two colors adds its note of usefulness.

Laveuse is equally charming worn with a blouse alone, or with a sweater jacket.

LAVEUSE.   Price $7.50. The lower part of the skirt is of white washable gabardine, surmounted by linen in any one of the following colors: Green, gold, delft, mauve, tan or white.

PAUL POIRET PRINTEMPS 1917

[7]

Figure 4.13

Paul Poiret, "Laveuse," from *Les Modèles de
Paul Poiret, Printemps 1917*, 1917.

merchandise the brochure was intended to advertise—garments aimed at "the American woman at large," offered at prices comparable to those of "ordinary garments manufactured in the ordinary way."[70]

If the constant reiteration of the "genuine reproduction" label and the quality of the brochure in terms of its materials and style suggest some of the ways in which Poiret was adapting to the American marketplace, a letter in French from the couturier that was both reproduced and translated in the brochure provides further indications of how he sought to appeal to American women (figure 4.15). Explaining his view that all

DRESS LABEL

SKIRT LABEL

SUIT LABEL

COAT LABEL

EVERY GENUINE REPRODUCTION
MUST HAVE
ONE OF THESE LABELS

Figure 4.14

Labels for Paul Poiret "genuine reproductions,"
from *Les Modèles de Paul Poiret, Printemps 1917,*
1917.

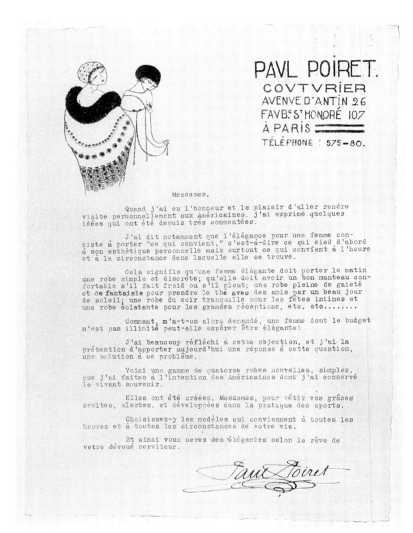

Figure 4.15

Paul Poiret, letter addressed "Mesdames," from
Les Modèles de Paul Poiret, Printemps 1917, 1917.

women of elegance require clothing appropriate for particular occasions—
"in the morning a dress which is simple and discreet; . . . a good, comfortable cloak for chill or rain; a dress full of gaiety and fantasy to go out
to tea with her friends on a beautiful sunny day; a quiet evening dress for
intimate parties, and a stunning gown for great receptions, etc., etc."—he
also repeated a question posed to him when he visited America: "How
then, I was asked, can a woman whose budget is not limitless hope to be
elegant?" The answer, he said, was embodied in the models presented in
the brochure: "Here is a gamut of fourteen garments—original yet simple, which I have made for the service of those American women of whom
I have retained so warm a memory. They have been created, Mesdames,
to clothe your grace—slender, alert and developed in the practice of outdoor sports."[71] Poiret made it clear that in designing the "genuine reproduction" garments he drew on his first-hand familiarity with the practical
needs and simple desires of America's female consumers. Yet in this personally signed letter, typed on couture-house stationery with letterhead
adapted from *Les Choses de Paul Poiret vues par Georges Lepape,* he reinforced the link between those readymade, moderately priced designs and
the personal commitment to elitist elegance characteristic of his Paris couture business. A second letter, included on the last page of the brochure
and addressed in English "To the Women of America," also made this
connection—and, at the same time, called it into question (figure 4.16).
The stationery on which this letter was typed prominently displays a different image lifted from Lepape's 1911 album, thus drawing another visual
connection between the "genuine reproductions" to be marketed by
Poiret's American collaborators and the more exclusive and costly dresses
produced in his prewar Paris couture house, the address of which is
printed in the upper right corner. However, just below the Paris address,
an address on Broadway is given for a New York Business Office, while in
the upper left are printed in large letters the words, "Poiret Inc," and "Paul
Poiret President." Thus the commercial nature of the new, American

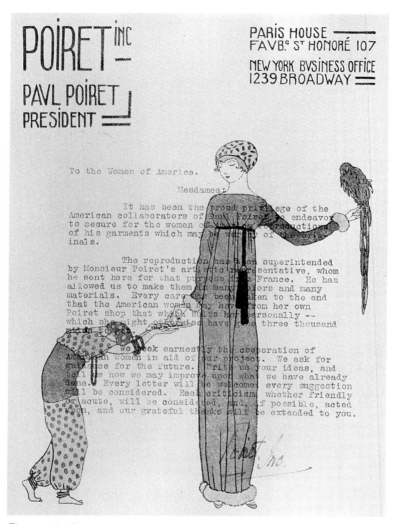

Figure 4.16 ☉

Paul Poiret, letter addressed "To the Women of
America," from *Les Modèles de Paul Poiret,
Printemps 1917*, 1917.

enterprise is clearly stressed, not only in the letterhead, where Poiret Inc. takes precedence over Paul Poiret President (as might be expected), but also in the signature, written in pen not by the individual Paul Poiret, but by Poiret Inc. Here the personal identity of Poiret, the man, and the creative identity of Poiret, the couturier-artist, are superseded by a corporate entity, Poiret Inc., formed to facilitate the sale of readymade Poiret designs to the American mass market.

Poiret's American financial backers, led by a man named Crane and a New York lawyer named Swinburne Hale, were extremely optimistic about the new enterprise, whose capitalization was projected at $100,000 divided into 1,000 shares at $100 each, with Poiret as the majority stockholder. In January 1917, Hale described plans for distributing no less than 1 million copies of the "genuine reproduction" brochure by selling it to department stores across America, thereby more than recuperating its production costs. His strategy called for the stores, in turn, to mail the publication to selected lists of female clients. According to Hale, "the reasonable expectation of sales of dresses is one sale per five catalogues. . . . This is the situation for the spring business, and the fall business will probably be greater, because it always is in the trade." Thus Hale foresaw sales of some 200,000 garments for the Spring 1917 season alone; using an average of the retail sales price of the fourteen garments on offer of about $45 per item, Poiret Inc.'s gross income would amount to $9 million.[72] No wonder Poiret saw value in cultivating the American readymade market!

Despite the existence of the "style brochure" and the outline of Hale's marketing strategy, it is unlikely that Poiret Inc. sold a great deal from its new line of "genuine reproductions" for American women.[73] In 1917, Poiret was still in the army and the French War Ministry refused him permission to pursue his grandiose plans for expansion which involved the sale in America not only of dresses but also perfumes, furniture, fabrics, and glassware.[74] The New York office of Poiret Inc. was short-lived, and the dreams described by Poiret's American backers of seeing a substantial return on their money were presumably dashed when the United States entered the war on 6 April 1917. Poiret appears to have been devastated by this failure; although his career in the world of fashion was far from over, he seems never to have recovered the dominant position he occupied in the couture industry before the war. Neither did he develop the potential benefits of the readymade that he introduced in the form of his genuine reproduction designs. The reasons were financial as well as structural. They also involved Poiret's vision of fashion, which by the early 1920s had already veered away from the moderate pricing, licensed mass production, and sporty styles he had designed for American women during the war. Having been frustrated in that experiment, he quickly reverted to the ways in which he had always privileged originality, individuality, and art, even when he had grappled directly with the challenges posed by American models of marketing in an environment increasingly characterized by large capital investments that allowed for mass production and encouraged consumption on an unprecedented scale.

To support himself and his family during the war, Poiret had been forced to give up such markers of elite status as his chauffeur-driven limousine as well as the Pavillon du Butard, where he had earlier staged the *Festes de Bacchus* and other entertainments for his friends. When he returned to Paris after the armistice, he reassembled his employees and reopened his couture house but found that most of his assets were still tied up in real estate while his couture, interior design, and perfume businesses desperately needed infusions of capital. In 1918, he sold the building he owned at 39, rue du Colisée adjoining his other properties. The following year he parted with one of his most treasured sculptures, a Chinese Bodhisattva from the Tang dynasty, which was acquired by the Metropolitan Museum of Art in New York.

Poiret obviously knew that the fashion business was being transformed by new production and marketing paradigms, some of which—the licensing of models for reproduction by wholesale manufacturers, for example—he had pioneered himself, but after the war he lacked the financial resources and, apparently, the will to make the changes required to profit from that knowledge. Most who lived through the war were aware that the lives of European and American women had been changed by the necessity of assuming responsibilities and positions outside the home that had previously been reserved for men. Nevertheless, Poiret resisted the practicality, simplification, and rationalization to which other couturiers—most notably Coco Chanel and Jean Patou—more readily adapted their styles. Poiret rejected these developments despite the fact that his 1917 marketing brochure emphasized what were understood to be typically American qualities of comfort and adaptability. The brochure stressed the youthful character and appropriateness of his clothes, for "the business girl" or "the athletic girl." The latter idea was reinforced by the many photographs in which mannequins held sporting accessories such as tennis rackets, golf clubs, or walking sticks (figures 4.13 and 4.17). Yet Poiret rejected this same rhetorical and stylistic discourse when, during the early 1920s, it came to dominate the couture profile of his increasingly successful rival, Coco Chanel.

Chanel got her start as a designer of hats before the war when her wealthy English boyfriend, Arthur (Boy) Capel, set her up in business on the rue Cambon, located just west of the rue de la Paix in the most fashionable area of Paris; her work received its first public recognition in *Comoedia Illustré* in 1910. Three years later, she opened a boutique to sell hats and sportswear in the resort town of Deauville where many wealthy Parisians went to escape the war zone after August 1914. This was the genesis of the loose-fitting, casual style that eventually characterized Chanel's most admired designs (figure 4.18), many elements of which were inspired by men's wear and appealed to women who moved more freely in public and required clothes appropriate to their new-found independence. In 1915, Chanel opened a couture house in Biarritz, a resort near the French border with neutral Spain, which became an important source of

Figure 4.17

Paul Poiret's "Croisade" dress, from *Les Modèles
de Paul Poiret, Printemps 1917*, 1917.

materials, as well as wealthy clients. The next year she was able to return
to Paris, leaving her sister to run the operation in Biarritz. In 1919 she
established a couture house at 31 rue Cambon, and by the early 1920s her
clothes, especially what is now called sportswear—often made of jersey or
other supple, knitted fabrics with simple lines and relatively short hems—
had become enormously popular. Whether she drew inspiration from
Poiret or, conversely, the styles of his "genuine reproductions" were
indebted to Chanel's informal and sportive clothes is difficult to determine. In any case, the coincidence of their trajectories was short-lived.

Although he had been perhaps its earliest champion, Poiret soon rejected the implications of sportswear for the new American woman; this would, instead, become the hallmark of Chanel's overwhelming success in the two decades that followed the First World War.

While most astute couturiers took notice and adapted to the trend toward youthful, simple, and functional clothes, Poiret rejected the sporty style he himself had pioneered in 1916–1917. He railed against the boyish fashion silhouette, nicknamed "*la garçonne*" after a 1922 novel by Victor

Figure 4.18

Coco Chanel modeling a Chanel suit, 1929.
© 2002 Hulton Getty/Archive Photos.

Margueritte whose heroine "personified the emancipated, uninhibited modern woman."[75] In remarks published that same year, Poiret declared his disdain for such "cardboard women, with hollow silhouettes, angular shoulders and flat breasts. Cages lacking birds. Hives lacking bees . . ."[76] Instead of the impersonal simplicity of what would become Chanel's signature "little black dress" (figure 4.19), in the early 1920s Poiret often turned for inspiration to historical and regional folkloric styles and, although some designs were relatively simple and straightforward, too many others were eccentric or richly spectacular. Thus, although Chanel had not gone to America or appealed directly to American women as Poiret had done, she succeeded where he failed in creating a style that responded to the desires those women were said to have expressed for practical, adaptable, and comfortable clothes. The simplicity of a Chanel dress assured not only that it could be adapted to suit virtually any woman—in 1926 *Vogue* described one of her designs as a uniform for all women of taste—but that it would also be easy to copy and distribute in the burgeoning postwar ready-to-wear market. In fact, unlike Poiret, Chanel apparently did nothing to resist the wholesale copying of her couture clothes, whose style gave aesthetic expression to the industrial and commodity character of the readymade in a manner antithetical to Poiret. Comparing the little black dress to an American mass-produced automobile, *Vogue* declared that its quality was assured by its brand name, just as the Ford name guaranteed the quality of the company's cars: "Here is a Ford signed 'Chanel.' "[77] Once again we find in haute couture an articulation of the contradiction imbedded in Duchamp's readymades between the mass-produced object and the signed work of an individual author.

Although his own name was being subjected during these years to a process of degradation through which it would become no more than a brand name itself, Poiret seems scarcely to have noticed. Instead, he continued to rely on the theatrical strategies that had assured his elite, artistic status before the war. Declaring his contempt for what he saw as Chanel's

Figure 4.19

Coco Chanel, "The Chanel 'Ford'—The Frock
That All the World Will Wear," from *Vogue,*
1926.

"poverty de luxe,"[78] Poiret spent vast sums of money to open an outdoor nightclub called L'Oasis—he turned it into a theater for the summer of 1921—in the garden of his couture house. Rejecting the practical alternative of transforming the space permanently, he took the more extravagant step of commissioning the Voisin firm (manufacturers of automobiles and airplanes, the company later lent financial support to Le Corbusier's 1925 plan for the redevelopment of the center of Paris) to devise a special, inflatable roof, made of the same material as a dirigible. The roof could be filled with compressed air and hoisted up every evening, only to be dismantled before dawn (figures 4.20 and 4.21).[79] Despite his efforts to pro-

Figure 4.20

Poiret's nightclub, L'Oasis, from *L'Illustration,* 1921.

Figure 4.21

Roof of L'Oasis deflated, from *L'Illustration,*
1921.

vide lively programming, L'Oasis proved to be an extravagant failure. The
wealthy clientele that Poiret hoped to attract spent the summer months
away from Paris and, in any case, night spots in other neighborhoods such
as Montparnasse, as well as more conventional theaters, proved to be
either more fashionable or more popular—or both. In a last-ditch attempt
to bring in audiences, in July 1921 Poiret began showing examples of his
coming winter fashions during intermissions, and invited those in attendance to visit the Galerie Barbazanges, where exhibitions related to the
theatrical performance would be on view. At the same time that he thus
aligned his theater, art, and couture interests in another attempt at syn-
ergy, he made a pathetic appeal to those who were in attendance in an
effort to understand why so many stayed away. As reported by one critic,
"The show began with a little speech by the director of L'Oasis who is
rather disappointed. Except for the evenings of the premieres, when

invitees are hard-pressed to find a seat, the theater is empty. No one comes. 'Why, honorable judges?' asks M. Poiret, who passes out blank paper to this invited public, asking them to fill the pages with comments on the program and the reasons for its lack of success."[80]

In his memoirs, Poiret recalled that the Oasis theater was a "fiasco" in which he lost half a million francs.[81] Faced with such a huge financial drain while at the same time investing in new branches of his perfume and interior design outlets in fashionable French vacation resorts and still planning to build a large private villa designed by Rob Mallet-Stevens on land he had purchased in 1920 near Paris in Mézy, Poiret revisited the idea of marketing his clothes in the United States. During a trip to America in late summer and early fall 1922, *Women's Wear* announced that Poiret intended to open a branch in New York. But when he returned to Paris, he discovered that one of his principal designers, Alfred Lenief, had left to open his own couture house, taking with him three of Poiret's most valued employees. Faced with the loss of his dominant position in the Paris fashion hierarchy as well as his grip on his own business operations, Poiret was compelled to take on a business administrator who began to reorganize his couture house and who assumed control of bookkeeping and the management of Poiret's financial affairs. In 1924, still in need of cash to support the lavish expenditures that he hoped would prop up his failing businesses, Poiret allowed himself to become allied with an investor named Georges Aubert, who turned the couture house into a stock company backed by a large bank and chaired by the senator, Lazare Weiler: Paul Poiret became a Société Anonyme. The house label now no longer signified a singular author who could convincingly lay claim to the status of creative artist; instead, it referred to a corporate entity that was in the process of displacing the individual designer. In this context, Poiret's revival of historical styles, his regional references, and the ostentatious display of expensive materials that characterized many of his dress designs of the period must be seen as a fantasy of return to the preeminent position he once occupied in the couture industry. His rejection of the simplified, standardized feminine silhouette went hand in hand with his repeated attempts to stave off the rationalization of his postwar business practices.

During this period, the group of investors that underwrote Poiret's stock company was also buying up other couture houses, including that of Doucet, which it fused with Doeuillet. (It had already provided the financing that enabled Lenief to leave Poiret and set up on his own.) Rumors circulated that Aubert was the Paris representative of an international trust owned by Standard Oil or J. Pierpont Morgan. Although such stories proved to be untrue, the specter of American monopoly capitalism hung over French haute couture, providing yet another discursive axis around which the French-American couture-culture relationship would revolve. Poiret claimed he had been naively trusting in his business dealings and failed to realize that he was loosing control over his affairs by entering into complicated arrangements with outside investors. "I was promised a million [francs] in fresh cash. Only a few knew that this million would be divided between Monsieur Galibert [the pseudonym Poiret gave to Aubert in his memoirs] and another person from the Banque de Prusse, and that this would constitute their legitimate commission. As a result, I never saw a cent."[82] As far as Poiret was concerned, Aubert cared nothing about the couture business except insofar as it affected the interests of the stockholders; where Poiret was inclined to spend money to attract attention and clients, Aubert and his partners reined in the couturier, for example, by refusing to finance any part of Poiret's extravagant display of three specially designed barges moored on the banks of the Seine at the 1925 Art Deco exhibition (figure 4.22). When later that year Poiret agreed to play a role in a theatrical production conceived by Colette, Aubert prevented him from doing so. Thus, outside interests not only controlled the couture house, perfume, and design businesses with which Poiret had always been personally associated, they were also in a position to limit his artistic freedom and prohibit the association of his

Figure 4.22 ◯

Poiret's barges at Exposition Internationale des
Arts Décoratifs Industriels et Modernes, Paris,
1925.

name with any person or practice they deemed undesirable. Modern business practices modeled on American monopoly capitalism thus displaced
the personalized, laissez-faire operation that had underwritten Poiret's
success as the premier couturier of the prewar period. Eventually Poiret
was totally isolated: the directors of Paul Poiret avoided discussing anything of substance at meetings he attended, and none of the company
employees were permitted to consult him in his office; he claimed he was
even prevented from seeing his clients. On 18 November 1925, Poiret put
his art collection, including two paintings of his own creation, up for auction at the Hôtel Drouot;[83] within months, the remainder of his assets was
liquidated.

Nevertheless, throughout the 1920s, Poiret continued to act and to
pose for the press as a couturier. In published interviews, he reiterated his

critique of the boyish, straight silhouette, which he said lacked fantasy and made all women look alike. He even drew a direct connection between the standardization of the female image predicated on the stereotype of the new American woman and American methods of production and merchandising. American manufacturers came to Paris, he complained, in search of "dresses that are easy to wear, easy to make, and little by little they led our couturiers to a type of dress, almost standardized, that each woman dons like a uniform without thinking of her personality, or even of her silhouette!"[84] In a business context dominated by standardization, mass production, and mass consumption, his couture label became little more than a vestigial fetish deployed in protest against an inexorable process of de-individualization. This characterization is even more appropriate for the label that another colleague in haute couture, Madeleine Vionnet, introduced in 1923. Bearing not only her signature but also the imprint of her right thumb (figure 4.23), Vionnet's label is a physical expression of French couturiers' continuing attempts in the face of stylistic conformity and rampant copying to invest their dresses with an aura of uniqueness and creative individuality.[85]

In fall 1927, during his third and last trip to the United States, Poiret made some disparaging remarks in public about the difficulty of designing

Figure 4.23

Madeleine Vionnet label, mid-1920s.

clothes for American women that were reported to his business partners in Paris. The director of the company used this opportunity to disavow Poiret in a public letter addressed to the American press, stating that Poiret did not represent the company's views, that he was traveling as a private citizen and speaking personally when he aired his opinions about American women. Having been publicly humiliated as well as distanced from the company that bore his name, Poiret was also refused the funds that he had been promised to cover the expenses he incurred in America. Little more than a year later, in 1929, he quit the couture house that continued to bear the Paul Poiret name until it closed and was liquidated in 1933. In the meantime, without legal recourse to his own name or to his signature label, Poiret briefly operated a new couture business called "Passy-10-17," a name that corresponded to his telephone number. The couturier who had always eschewed the anonymity of numbers in favor of individual names for his dresses thus responded with sardonic humor to his loss of identity and authorial control, a loss that might be described as the inverse of Duchamp's experience in creating Rrose Sélavy as a supplemental identity that possessed a powerful authorial presence. Alternatively, one might argue, by superimposing another identity on himself, Duchamp had fractured and dispersed his subjectivity in a manner that found an unwilling parallel in Poiret's loss of identity and control.

When in the early 1930s Poiret regained rights to the commercial use of his name, his first application of it was to a spring 1933 collection of inexpensive ready-to-wear models for the Printemps department store, which singled out two outfits as "Paul Poiret Creations" from amongst all the other clothes reproduced anonymously in one of its advertising circulars (figure 4.24). The featured garments, a light overcoat for seaside wear and a sports ensemble in opposing colors, were anything but radical or transgressive, eccentric or spectacular. Without the special attention paid to them in the typography of the brochure and the written words that accompanied the illustrations, there is nothing in particular that distin-

Figure 4.24

Advertising circular for the department store
Au Printemps, showing two designs for readymade women's outfits by Paul Poiret, 1933.

guished Poiret's clothes either technically or stylistically from the other
models amongst which they were shown. Even their prices were well
within the range of the other models, whose silhouettes they shared. Thus
the garments designed by Paul Poiret were no longer individual creations,
hardly even "genuine reproductions," and they could no longer be described as art. But his name, despite its considerable loss of aura, would
only have appeared in the circular because it retained some degree of special

signification, some slight added value, in the world of fashion. What else would explain why Poiret's was the only name to appear in the ad? Operating now at the low end of the fashion spectrum, at the level of mass production, for a brief moment—no more than two fashion seasons, after which he argued with his employer and they parted ways—Poiret's signature was still being called upon to work some of its old magic. It is as if by affixing his name to these nondescript and uninteresting garments, Poiret reactivated the logic of fashion in a Duchampian mode, designating as readymades what would otherwise have been anonymous and quite ordinary ready-to-wear clothes.

Conclusion

On 2 August 1921, French couturière Madeleine Vionnet published a terse statement in the trade journal, *Women's Wear,* in which with evident exasperation she warned her American clients not to be fooled into purchasing counterfeit copies of her clothes:

> We again inform our New York customers that Madeleine Vionnet does not sell to Agents or Dressmakers; that her models are registered according to the Law; that nobody has the right to copy them or to have them copied and that no one has the right to sell them without special license from Madeleine Vionnet.
>
> No firm whatsoever holds such a license and those who state they are selling Madeleine Vionnet models are merely imitators and are deceiving the Public.
>
> Madeleine Vionnet kindly requests American Ladies to inform their friends of these facts and to spread the truth abroad that

Madeleine Vionnet creations are only to be obtained in Paris, 222, rue de Rivoli.[1]

Vionnet's statement is noteworthy, but not because she was unique in discovering that her designs were being copied without her authorization for sale in American department stores. As we have seen, all the major French couturiers struggled to protect their creations from the rampant piracy that characterized the American trade in high-end women's clothes. What makes Vionnet's case particularly interesting is that her designs (figure 5.1), more than those of any other French couturier, have been regarded as especially difficult to copy. For example, in her monograph on Vionnet, first published in 1990, Jacqueline Demornex noted that Vionnet's designs "have an enigmatic, indefinable quality." The dresses (especially those of the 1930s) were not only difficult to describe, they were difficult to put on: "Some clients became quite hysterical when leaving for a soirée. How should they tie the belt—where should it be placed? And what about that long panel which fell to the ground? Should it be twisted or draped up around the waist?"[2] Demornex notes that another Vionnet scholar, Betty Kirke, spent more than twenty years trying to unravel "the mystery of the Vionnet cut," conducting research which Kirke herself likened to "a police enquiry."[3] Kirke's own book on Vionnet presents the fruits of these labors in a series of patterns which she herself painstakingly created in an effort to understand the technical basis of Vionnet's distinctive style. She succeeded in uncovering how Vionnet's innovative use of the bias cut exploited the physical characteristics of textile structure; she also discovered many other exquisitely refined dressmaking techniques Vionnet employed to create clothes of a simple mathematical logic whose stunning effects often made them appear to be extraordinarily complex. When Kirke asked herself why, given the high quality of Vionnet's work and the creative originality it consistently displayed, Vionnet never

Figure 5.1

Madeleine Vionnet, dress from an album of
registered models, summer 1921.

achieved the level of reknown enjoyed by her contemporaries, the explanation Kirke initially offered was that the couturière found publicity distasteful. But the real reason Vionnet was overshadowed by Coco Chanel, Paul Poiret, and Elsa Schiaparelli, according to Kirke, was that "her designs, due to their unique cut, were just too difficult to copy."[4]

That Kirke should have come to this conclusion is peculiar because in her own book she provides ample evidence that copying actually structured Vionnet's approach to the development and growth of her couture business after the First World War. In this respect Vionnet's experience may be taken as emblematic of the contradictions embedded in the logic of fashion as exemplified by the works of Paul Poiret, Jeanne Paquin, and their contemporaries. Just as they had arrived at the pinnacle of elite prewar fashion only to realize that the armature of their success was built on a framework of popular appeal that required them both to woo and to reject a mass market, so Vionnet emerged as a powerful player on the postwar fashion scene and immediately confronted even more powerful forces in the form of American industry and consumer culture. In 1921, she successfully sued two Parisian copy houses and named three American department stores as outlets where unauthorized dresses claimed to be by Vionnet, or in the Vionnet style, were sold.[5] The following year she sued another American firm for selling patterns made illegally from her models.[6] By early 1923, a lawyer named Louis Dangel had been installed as the business manager of Société Madeleine Vionnet & Cie, the company formed in 1922 to raise the capital required by Vionnet's growing business. Vionnet now had a branch in Biarritz and would soon move her Paris headquarters to a large and luxuriously redesigned private *hôtel* near the Champs-Élysées at 50, Avenue Montaigne. Dangel appears to have been Vionnet's spokesman and agent where issues of copying were concerned. In 1923, he founded a new anti-piracy group, the Association for the Defense of the Plastic and Applied Arts, and formally demanded that the French government "move for international copyright to protect the creative brains of the Paris fashion designers." Poiret and Worth were also members of this organization but, *Women's Wear* observed, several other couture houses declined to join because their attitude was "considered to be on the contrary, in favor of American volume methods of production."[7] Like Poiret and Paquin, Vionnet herself, while forcefully pursuing protection of her designs as intellectual property throughout the 1920s and 1930s, could be counted among the many French couturiers who were trying to devise effective means of exploiting the American market for copies and, at the same time, continuing to offer made-to-order garments to wealthy patrons in France, the United States, and elsewhere abroad. Already in November 1921 *Women's Wear* reported that Vionnet—whom it described as the "inspiration of copyists and bete noir of commissionnaires, a succes fou among the younger school of French dressmakers sprung up since the war"—had sold reproduction rights for her models to another dressmaker, Eva Boex. Thenceforth, she would have the exclusive right to sell Vionnet models to the trade: ". . . these models will be signed by a label carrying the name of Eva Boex, followed by 'licensed by Vionnet' or some phrase to indicate that the garment is an official and approved copy."[8]

Thus Vionnet, like Poiret and the other couturiers whose work is explored in this book, found herself caught in the web of contradictions that I have described as the logic of fashion: attempting, on the one hand, to prevent copying while, on the other hand, seeking to exploit the practice by licensing designs, controlling their reproduction and circulation, and demanding a royalty for each copy sold. The problem for Vionnet and every other couturier—including Chanel, who is said to have reveled in the recognition and acclaim that the mass-production of her simple dresses signified[9]—was that quantity production of couture designs, even under a licensing agreement, would ultimately destroy the exclusivity of haute couture. No client would be willing to pay 4,000 to 5,000 francs for a made-to-order Vionnet dress if good quality authorized reproductions were available for half that price.[10] Yet, in order to support her exclusive work for wealthy women, for whom she preferred to design dresses, Vionnet was forced to expand her client base and appeal to a larger market. As she herself later recalled in terms reminiscent of Poiret, whose spectacular success in a wider spectrum of fashion-related fields eventually led him into a similar commercial cul-de-sac, "I wanted to dress women well, and the idea of the anonymous clientele was the opposite of what I had in mind. As soon as I set up in avenue Montaigne, I was obliged to accept orders from foreign buyers. . . . [Even] though business was excellent, the overhead was heavy. Think of it, twelve hundred employees, not divided . . . among sidelines that have nothing much in common with couture. . . . I had a large fur department, but apart from that, we made nothing but dresses and coats."[11] Kirke has noted that in the early- and mid-1920s Vionnet produced 300 to 350 new models each season. Typically, however, only two or three clients might purchase the same couture dress. If ten women ordered a given design, it was considered a success; twenty would be sensational. But the lesson of mass marketing was not lost on Vionnet after one design that elicited an extraordinary fifty orders in the Paris couture house was purchased by an American manufacturer who reportedly sold the much more impressive number of 1,000 copies to American women.[12] This experience and perhaps others like it forced Vionnet to acknowledge that her own business ought to reap the benefit of such sales, rather than cede that income to others. The excuse she gave when in 1926 she produced a line of ready-to-wear clothes destined for the wholesale market was that buyers "found the intricacy of her dresses too difficult to copy;" she therefore decided to copy them herself.[13] That she was also selling her made-to-order couture dresses with labels specifically designed to discourage copying—each one bore the imprint of her finger as an indexical mark of its authenticity (figure 4.23)—clearly indicates the extent to which originality and reproduction constituted the polar yet overlapping constraints between which Vionnet, like every other couturier, was operating at the time.

Vionnet's situation during the post–World War I period, when she was at the height of her success, encapsulates the problem that has motivated this book. Her interest as a couturière resides, I would argue, not simply in the particular features of her beautiful dresses, which have been studied in detail by costume historians, but more fundamentally in the dilemma she faced as a creative designer of individual objects. Vionnet perfected her art through the production of models from which the dresses made for each of her clients were copied. Like Worth, Doucet, Paquin, and Poiret, her business depended upon the circulation of her designs through a network of diverse and interrelated media. In Vionnet's case, that included seasonal presentations on the stage located at one end of the large and opulent salon of her avenue Montaigne couture house, drawings and photographs reproduced in elite and popular women's magazines, commentaries in trade journals, her own advertisements, and the appearance of celebrity clients in theatrical plays and films, at the races, and at fashionable summer resorts. More pointedly, her success as a couturière and as a businesswoman depended upon the capacity of a given model to command attention, generate interest, and elicit a demand for copies. The problem arose when Vionnet was unable to control this demand after it had been unleashed in the venues enumerated above, through which her designs became accessible to a large public audience.

Like any artisanally based enterprise, the couture industry was capable of creating only a limited quantity of its high-quality, work-intensive product; once demand exceeded that limit, rationalized and standardized methods of quantity production, for which couturiers were ill-adapted, were inevitably set into motion. As other manufacturers better equipped to satisfy a mass market began to exploit large-scale consumer demand, the couturière found herself in a problematic bind: faced with uncontrolled and often illegal or unauthorized copying of unique models, she was compelled to prohibit or, more realistically, try to limit mass production in order to protect her elite business. At the same time, she was forced to enter the mass market to support her high-end trade and to protect her financial interest in the exploitation of her own designs. Both of these options were losing propositions; in the first instance, it proved impossible to prevent illegal or unauthorized copying and, in the second, once the couturière offered less expensive garments to a mass market, exclusive, high-end clients would refuse to pay the top prices required for the production of made-to-order merchandise.

This, then, is the essence of the fashion conundrum, the contradiction that characterizes the (supposedly) unique and auratic object when it is subjected to the conditions of mass consumption in an industrialized economy. I have indicated how this situation resonates with the problem faced by the modern artist, exemplified by the cubist painter, who seeks an audience and a market for his work. As the salon cubists who showed in public venues and the gallery cubists represented by Daniel-Henry Kahnweiler learned from the experience of exhibiting their paintings, it was not sufficient (despite Kahnweiler's protestations to the contrary) to present simply or indifferently an individual work of art. Rather, it was necessary to create conditions in which that work could be understood in relation to others like it and as distinct from everything else. Only because the salon cubists showed their paintings alongside one another was it possible for critics and others (including the artists themselves) to recognize the qualities shared by those individual works, to see amongst them a commonality of formal characteristics that could be understood as the expression of shared intellectual commitments brought together to forge a coherent movement. One might argue that it was the proliferation of examples in the public sphere that allowed cubism to become visible and enter into discourse, to circulate and be consumed. Kahnweiler, however, clearly relegated salon cubism to the debased position of the fraudulent copy whose public orientation posed a threat to the version of cubism defined in his gallery, whose status as unique and original he promoted through a discourse of privacy, elitism, and distinction. To create and maintain the cachet attached to Picasso and Braque as creators of true or original cubism, to resist the deleterious impact that a supposedly derivative version of cubism might have on his artists, Kahnweiler astutely controlled access to their works and actively sought to influence what might be written about them. It is here in the tension between the discourses of elitism and originality versus publicity and reproduction that the logic of fashion (as distinct from its look) emerges as a mechanism for understanding the impact of commercial considerations in the realm of fine art.

The example of cubism demonstrates that, like fashion, fine art in the modern period requires an audience, a discourse, a profile in the public sphere. The purity and disinterestedness often claimed for modernist art is, in this sense, a fiction that masks art's dependence upon socially constituted—even if buried or invisible—discourses of authorship, display, and reception, the existence of which is necessary in order for art to be seen and understood as art. Elaine Sturtevant might be said to exemplify this situation in a more contemporary context: her work, consisting of copies of paintings, sculptures, and related works by prominent Pop artists, was either greeted with indifference or condemned as a fraud when she first exhibited it in 1965. Unlike Duchamp in the late teens, when the two readymades he showed publicly were entirely ignored in the press and his *Fountain* (though never exhibited) created a scandal, Sturtevant at the time she began making copies had no previously secured public stature as an artist. Not until the 1980s, with the emergence of Sherrie Levine, Mike Bidlo, and others engaged in practices that only then became known as "appropriation," did the art world develop a discourse in which Sturtevant's copies could be widely understood not as naive expressions of intellectual homage nor as illegal infringements of intellectual property rights, but as sophisticated and creative statements in their own right. This discourse had to exist, or be created, in order for Sturtevant's work to be regarded and broadly appreciated, retrospectively, as art.[14]

Like art, whether in the guise of cubism, appropriation, or another form, fashion also requires a discursive frame. It cannot be separated from the public arena in which it circulates, not only because clothing is a crucial component of the public display of self, but also because clothing design interacts with the complex marketing mechanisms of the consumer economy in direct and explicit ways. Fashion is, thus, inherently theatrical and in the modern period it is also fundamentally commercial, and it therefore reveals especially clearly the discourses that linked the arts to commerce in the early twentieth century. The ever-closer relationship during this period between theater and fashion has been examined here in order to expose the commercial dimension they shared and the ways in which both exploited the interconnected and ideologically charged discourses of Orientalism and classicism for frankly commercial ends. These issues are relevant to the visual and cultural histories of the period, as well as the history of art because they reinforce the notion that the Orientalizing and classicizing dimensions of artistic practice had complex social and cultural resonances. Their reach went beyond the limited audience for (or against) avant-garde art to engage both wealthy aristocrats and the broad spectrum of the middle-class public to which fashion appealed. More than just markers of revolutionary or retrograde cultural politics, Orientalism and classicism circulated as signifiers of fashion *tout court* in a commercial realm dominated by the interests of commodity capitalism.

Nowhere was this more clearly the case than in the American department store, where theatrical presentations made what began as elite and aristocratic Orientalist fashions available to a bourgeois mass market. This is the point at which the modernist discourse of originality that posited the artist as creative genius and the couturier as purveyor to the wealthy elite were most forcefully exposed to the commercial pressures of reproduction that dramatically and abruptly leveled the societal playing field. In the department store, haute couture, which had always been based on the circulation of copies, was compelled to come to grips with this unacknowleged fact and, more urgently, with the realities of fraud and piracy that accompanied—as they fed and enabled—the rise of mass marketing and mass consumption. The compromise between original and copy that couturiers developed in response to this situation was a hybrid form that Poiret called a "genuine reproduction" and Vionnet described more straightforwardly (but with perhaps less marketing savvy) as "an official and approved copy." Both phrases referred to an industrially manufactured product intended for an anonymous bourgeois market that, although disdained by Poiret and Vionnet, dominated the couture industry and the French artistic imagination after the First World War. This was reflected particularly in the work of Coco Chanel and of the architect Le Corbusier, to name just two examples of figures identified with rationalization and standardization during the 1920s.

Where couturiers in general and Poiret in particular consistently marshaled the discourse of originality in order to resist or (equally unsuccessfully) to redirect for their own benefit the commercial power represented by the reproduction, Marcel Duchamp actively embraced the idea of reproducibility, making it a central and enduring focus of his work. Duchamp's readymades played upon the imbedded interrelationship of originality and reproduction that lies at the heart of the logic of fashion. He appears, however, to have eluded the commercial dimensions of the problem because as an artist he operated outside the market economy (while creating readymades and related works that commented incisively upon it[15]). Yet, by relying in part on the patronage of the Arensbergs for his modest living expenses, Duchamp indirectly reaped the benefits of capitalism, as he also did when dealing discreetly in works of art by family members and friends. Acknowledging this does not lessen the significance of his art as a commentary on the contradictions and dislocations engendered by the transformation from an artisanal to an industrial economy. It does, however, expose the degree to which even Duchamp was unable to escape the implications of those ruptures, any more than Poiret, Vionnet, and the other couturiers who have been the focus of this book.

Notes

All translations are by the author unless otherwise indicated.

Introduction

1. By demonstrating the importance of fashion for modern architects, architectural historians Mary McLeod and Mark Wigley have shown that the reigning paradigm needs to be reevaluated. In particular, Wigley has exposed a pervasive—though vexed and heretofore largely untheorized—discourse of fashion in modern architecture and architectural criticism. In addition, Tag Gronberg has focused attention on how the luxury boutique and the circulation of female fashion defined and articulated the urban experience of Paris in the 1920s. See Mary McLeod, "Undressing Architecture: Fashion, Gender, and Modernity," in *Architecture: In Fashion,* ed. Deborah Fausch, Paulette Singley, Rodolphe El-Khoury, and Zvi Efrat (New York: Princeton Architectural Press, 1994): 38–147; Mark Wigley, *White Walls, Designer Dresses: The Fashioning of Modern Architecture* (Cambridge, MA: MIT Press, 1995); Tag Gronberg, *Designs on Modernity: Exhibiting the City in 1920s Paris* (Manchester: Manchester University Press, 1998).

2. For example, see Elizabeth Ann Coleman, *The Opulent Era: Fashions of Worth, Doucet and Pingat* exh. cat. (New York: Brooklyn Museum, 1989); Dominique Sirop, *Paquin* (Paris: Adam Biro, 1989); Paris: Musée de la Mode et du Costume, *Paul Poiret et Nicole Groult: Maîtres de la mode Art Déco,* 1986.

3. See the catalogues that accompanied these exhibitions: Biennale di Firenze, *Looking at Fashion,* ed. Germano Celant, 1996; New York: Guggenheim Museum Soho, *Art/Fashion,* 1997; London: Hayward Gallery, *Addressing the Century: 100 Years of Art & Fashion,* 1998.

4. Even Richard Martin, author of a pioneering work in this arena (the exhibition at the Fashion Institute of Technology and accompanying catalogue, *Fashion and Surrealism* [New York: Rizzoli, 1987]) was content to make formal and stylistic comparisons between the construction of clothing or the design of fabrics, on one hand, and works of art by cubist painters and sculptors, on the other, in his *Cubism and Fashion* at the Metropolitan Museum in 1998. Nevertheless, in

the last chapter of the accompanying catalogue (Richard Martin, *Cubism and Fashion* exh. cat. [New York: Metropolitan Museum of Art, 1998]), Martin expresses skepticism about exhibitions that explore the art-fashion connection by presenting "a few utopian tokens of fashion or a few crossover works by artists making clothes." Arguing that the relationship between art and fashion is to be found "in another level of understanding," he insists upon "the immensity of art, its full compass, its compelling example to every human being, and especially every visual person. If art and fashion are conjoined, it is because of the magnanimity of art, its big spirit for all things created." Privileging the formal and intellectual aspects of works of art (an approach that is not surprising given that the exhibition and accompanying catalogue were organized by one of the world's greatest art museums), Martin focuses on stylistic affinities between cubist painting and early twentieth-century fashion, leaving unexplored the institutional frameworks and commercial imperatives that I examine in this book.

5. See Judith Butler, *Gender Trouble: Feminism and the Subversion of the Body* (New York: Routledge, 1990) and Judith Butler, *Bodies that Matter: On the Discursive Limits of "Sex"* (New York: Routledge, 1993); Kaja Silverman, "Fragments of a Fashionable Discourse," in *Studies in Entertainment: Critical Approaches to Mass Culture,* ed. Tania Modleski (Bloomington: Indiana University Press, 1986), 139–152; Ewa Lajer-Burcharth, *Necklines: The Art of Jacques-Louis David after the Terror* (New Haven: Yale University Press, 1999), esp. ch. 3, "The Revolution *Glacée.*"

6. Anne Hollander, *Seeing through Clothes* (1975; New York: Avon Books, 1980).

7. For a fascinating discussion of the range of possible North American market destinations for couture clothing, as well as numerous kinds of copies—focused, however, on a somewhat later period—than the present book, see Alexandra Palmer, *Couture and Commerce: The Transatlantic Fashion Trade in the 1950s* (Vancouver: UBC Press in association with the Royal Ontario Museum, 2001). I am indebted to Palmer for allowing me to read a pre-publication copy of her manuscript.

8. For this reason, I do not discuss the work of Sonia Delaunay, who began to make unique textiles, clothing, and decorative objects before World War I, in the context of her exploration together with her husband, Robert Delaunay, of what they described as the simultaneous contrast of colors in painting. As Delaunay herself recalled, ". . . there was no gap between my painting and my so-called

decorative work. . . . It was the application of the same research" (Sonia Delaunay, *Nous irons jusqu'au soleil* [Paris, 1978], 96, quoted in Elizabeth Morano, intro. *Sonia Delaunay: Art into Fashion* [New York: Braziller, 1986], 13). Her dressmaking activities became an important source of income for the Delaunays after the Russian Revolution cut off Sonia's income from real estate holdings in St. Petersburg; she eventually opened a clothing boutique on the Boulevard Malesherbes in Paris in 1924. According to Yvonne Brentjens, Sonia Delaunay's dressmaking and textile design business grew to employ about thirty workers before the boutique was closed in 1931, but the simple, rectilinear patterns of the clothes remained fairly constant (the significant innovations were in her textile designs). It is not known if Delaunay produced a new line of dresses each season or year, and her status as a couturière remains ambiguous: "In the existing literature, there are differing opinions over the degree to which Sonia Delaunay was inspired by other couturiers," Brentjens writes. "On the one hand there are indications that the artist worked somewhat apart, outside the proper zone of the Parisian haute couture. On the other hand, her participation in the Universal Exposition of 1925 suggests a mature professional position. In general, the dominant opinion is that she was never a couturière in the strictest sense of the word." Yvonne Brentjens, *Sonia Delaunay: Dessins* exh. cat. (Tilburg: Nederlands Textielmuseum, 1988), 75. See also *Sonia Delaunay: A Retrospective* exh. cat. (Buffalo: Albright-Knox Art Gallery, 1980).

9. On fashion and the theater in late nineteenth- and early twentieth-century England, see Joel H. Kaplan and Sheila Stowell, *Theatre and Fashion: Oscar Wilde to the Suffragettes* (Cambridge: Cambridge University Press, 1994). On the French art market in the early twentieth century, see Malcolm Gee, *Dealers, Critics, and Collectors of Modern Painting: Aspects of the Parisian Art Market between 1910 and 1930* (New York: Garland, 1981).

10. See Rosalind E. Krauss, "The Originality of the Avant-Garde," as well as the related and more polemical "Sincerely Yours," both reprinted in Krauss, *The Originality of the Avant-Garde and Other Modernist Myths* (Cambridge, MA: MIT Press, 1985), 151–194, from which the quotations that follow in this paragraph are drawn.

11. Douglas Cooper and Gary Tinterow, *The Essential Cubism: Braque, Picasso & Their Friends, 1907–1920* exh. cat. (London: Tate Gallery, 1983).

12. Pierre Assouline, *An Artful Life: A Biography of D. H. Kahnweiler, 1884–1979*,

trans. Charles Ruas (New York: Fromm International Publishing Corporation, 1991), 90.

13. A valuable exception is Valerie Steele, *Paris Fashion: A Cultural History* (New York: Oxford University Press, 1988). For an overview of the field and of recent revisionist projects, see Alexandra Palmer, "New Directions: Fashion History Studies and Research in North America and England," *Fashion Theory* 1, no. 3 (September 1997): 297–312; and the special issue of *Fashion Theory* 2, no. 4 (December 1998), ed. Anthea Jarvis and devoted to issues of methodology.

14. Nancy L. Green, "Art and Industry: The Language of Modernization in the Production of Fashion," *French Historical Studies* 18, no. 3 (Spring 1994): 722.

15. Roland Barthes, *Système de la mode* (Paris: Editions du Seuil, 1967); *The Fashion System*, trans. Matthew Ward and Richard Howard (Berkeley: University of California Press, 1990).

16. Philippe Perrot, *Les Dessus et les dessous de la bourgeoisie: Une histoire du vêtement au XIXe siècle* (Paris: Fayard, 1981); *Fashioning the Bourgeoisie: A History of Clothing in the Nineteenth Century,* trans. Richard Bienvenu (Princeton: Princeton University Press, 1994): 8.

17. Leila Kinney, "Fashion and Figuration in Modern Life Painting," in *Architecture: In Fashion,* ed. Deborah Fausch, Paulette Singley, Rodolphe El-Khoury, and Zvi Efrat. (New York: Princeton Architectural Press, 1994), 270–313.

18. Ibid., 276. See also Ulrich Lehmann, *Tigersprung: Fashion in Modernity* (Cambridge, MA: MIT Press, 2000), especially ch. 1: "Baudelaire, Gautier and the Origins of Fashion in Modernity."

19. For a lucid discussion of these developments in the United States, see Claudia B. Kidwell and Margaret C. Christian, *Suiting Everyone: The Democratization of Clothing in America* (Washington, DC: Smithsonian Institution Press, 1974). On the circulation of fashion in women's magazines, see Christopher Breward, "Femininity and Consumption: The Problem of the Late Nineteenth-Century Fashion Journal," *Journal of Design History* 7 (1994), 71–89.

20. Honoré de Balzac, "Traité de la vie élégante" (1830), quoted in Kinney, "Fashion and Figuration," 279.

21. Richard Sennett, *The Fall of Public Man* (1977), quoted in Hollis Clayson, *Painted Love: Prostitution in French Art of the Impressionist Era* (New Haven: Yale University Press, 1991), 58.

22. Clayson, *Painted Love.*

23. Kinney, "Fashion and Figuration," 291.

24. Brendan Holley, "The King and I," *GQ* 71, no. 2 (February 2001), 186.

25. Paul Goldberger, "25 Years of Unabashed Elitism," *New York Times* (2 February 2000), sec. 2, 1.

26. Ibid., sec. 2, 34.

Chapter 1

1. Clayson, *Painted Love,* 59.

2. See Diana de Marly, *Worth: Father of Haute Couture* (1980) 2nd ed. (New York: Holmes & Meier, 1990).

3. Peter Wollen makes this point in "Addressing the Century," in Hayward Gallery, *Addressing the Century* exh. cat. (London, 1998), 8.

4. Coleman, *The Opulent Era,* 33. On Worth's growing business after mid-century, see Françoise Tétart-Vittu, "Naissance du couturier et du modéliste," in Musée de la Mode et du Costume, Palais Galliera. *Au paradis des dames: Nouveautés, modes et confections 1810–1870* exh. cat. (Paris, 1992), 36–39.

5. Ibid., 33–34.

6. Palmer White, *Poiret* (New York: Clarkson N. Potter, 1973), 51.

7. de Marly, *Worth,* 100. In conversation with F. Adolphus in the early 1870s, Worth commented on the amount of money that women spend on dress: "There are quantities of very respectable women in Paris who don't spend more than £60 a-year on their toilet, and who, for that sort of type, really don't look bad. But you mean, of course, the women who come to me, who are of a different class. Well, they get through anything you like, from a minimum of £400 to a maximum of £4000. . . . Some of the Americans are great spenders; all of them (all of them that I see, I mean) love dress, even if they are not extravagant over it. And I like to dress them, for, as I say occasionally, 'they have faith, figures, and francs,'—faith to believe in me, figures that I can put into shape, francs to pay my bills. Yes, I like to dress Americans." F. Adolphus, *Some Memories of Paris* (New York: Henry Holt and Company, 1895), 193–194.

8. *Harper's Bazar* (23 December 1871): 820, quoted in Coleman, *The Opulent Era,* 15.

9. Jean-Philippe Worth, *A Century of Fashion,* trans. Ruth Scott Miller (Boston: Little, Brown, 1928), 86–87.

10. Coleman, *The Opulent Era*, 12.

11. C. F. Worth, quoted in ibid., p. 191. See also de Marly, *Worth,* 101. According to Coleman (p. 21), in 1900 the House of Worth employed far fewer, though still more than 500 people. Worth's sons, Jean-Philippe and Gaston, were active in their father's couture house well before his death in 1895, after which they ran the business, with Jean-Philippe as designer and Gaston as financial administrator. See Coleman, 29–32.

12. For a description of the division of labor involved in the construction of a single dress by numerous needleworkers distributed across multiple ateliers, see Arsène Alexandre, *Les Reines de l'aiguille: modistes et couturières (étude parisienne)* (Paris: Théophile Belin, 1902), esp. 80–83.

13. Zuzanna Shonfield, "The Great Mr. Worth," *Costume: The Journal of the Costume Society,* no. 16 (1982): 57–58.

14. Coleman, *The Opulent Era,* 34.

15. Ibid., 108.

16. Alan Trachtenberg, *The Incorporation of America: Culture and Society in the Gilded Age* (New York: Hill & Wang, 1982), 137–138.

17. Pierre Bourdieu with Yvette Delsaut, "Le Couturier et sa griffe: contribution à une théorie de la magie," *Actes de la recherche en sciences sociales,* no. 1 (1975): 21, 23. I thank Yve-Alain Bois for bringing this essay to my attention.

18. Jacques Derrida, "Signature Event Context" (1977), trans. Samuel Weber and Jeffrey Mehlman, in Jacques Derrida, *Limited Inc* (Evanston: Northwestern University Press, 1988), 1–23.

19. Hillel Schwartz, *The Culture of the Copy: Striking Likenesses, Unreasonable Facsimiles* (New York: Zone Books, 1996), 219.

20. Bourdieu with Delsaut, "Le Couturier et sa griffe," 23.

21. Ibid., 21.

22. In this context it may be significant that initially many couturiers of this period, including Worth, Jacques Doucet, and Jeanne Paquin, used only block print letterforms in their labels but eventually developed labels that conveyed their individual identities by featuring their names in cursive forms suggestive of—presumably inspired by—their handwritten signatures. Conversely, when in the 1920s Coco Chanel introduced straightforward, simpler couture designs inspired by sports clothes (in 1926 one of her dresses was compared to the mass-produced Ford automobile; see ch. 4), her label returned to the block letter

format, perhaps in order to evoke associations with contemporary industrial design even as the couture label laid claim to the authenticity and individual authorship of Chanel clothing.

23. This change in Worth's self-representation was first pointed out by de Marly, *Worth*, 110, and is also mentioned by Elizabeth Wilson, *Adorned in Dreams: Fashion and Modernity* (Berkeley: University of California Press, 1987), 32.

24. As Peter Wollen observed, Worth succeeded in overturning traditional dress-making practice by having his clients come to his premises, rather than vice versa, "just as a patron might visit an artist's studio." Wollen, "Addressing the Century," 8.

25. de Marly, *Worth,* 101.

26. *Souvenirs de la Princesse de Metternich 1859–71,* notes by M. Dunan (1922), quoted in de Marly, *Worth,* 198.

27. Adolphus, *Some Memories of Paris* (1895), quoted in de Marly, *Worth*, 198.

28. Edmond and Jules de Goncourt, *Journal* (1892), quoted in de Marly, *Worth*, 200.

29. See François Chapon, *Mystère et splendeurs de Jacques Doucet* (Paris: Éditions J.-C. Lattès, 1984).

30. Coleman, *The Opulent Era,* 152.

31. F. F. [Fenéon], "Les grands collectionneurs: IX.—M. Jacques Doucet," *Bulletin de la vie artistique,* no. 11 (June 1921): 313.

32. Worth*, A Century of Fashion,* 87.

33. According to F. F., "Les grands collectionneurs," 314, Doucet's tiny office with just one window, a table, and two chairs was entirely devoid of pictures, "and its austerity contrasted knowingly with the magnificence of the apartment on the avenue du Bois . . ."

34. Chapon, *Mystère et splendeurs de Jacques Doucet,* 71.

35. Ibid., 53.

36. F. F., "Les grands collectionneurs," 315.

37. André Breton, quoted in Jean-François Revel, "Jacques Doucet couturier et collectionneur," *L'Oeil,* no. 84 (December 1961): 51, 81.

38. Revel, "Jacques Doucet couturier et collectionneur," 50.

39. Paul Poiret, *My First Fifty Years,* trans. Stephen Haden Guest (London: Victor Gollancz, 1931), 78.

40. See the discussion of Poiret's collection in Gee, *Dealers, Critics, and Collectors*

of Modern Painting, 194–196. Gee notes that from the perspective of 1925, Poiret's collection was "firmly anchored in the middle ground of modern art, as it had developed over the previous twenty years, a period which corresponded with the high point of Poiret's own professional life" (194). He qualifies this assessment of "the relative conservatism of his collection" by noting as well that it "reflected the advanced taste of 1913–4, when Poiret was at the height of his success" (196).

41. See Palmer White, *Elsa Schiaparelli: Empress of Paris Fashion* (New York: Rizzoli, 1986), 39, on Poiret and Picabia; and White, *Poiret,* 64–66, on Poiret, Derain, and Vlaminck.

42. One such program is reproduced in René Jean, "Bernard Naudin," *Art et Décoration* 32 (November 1912): 136, together with a drawing (133), presumably from the same program; both are listed as belonging to Paul Poiret. On Naudin, see Marie Berthail, *Bernard Naudin: Catalogue raisonné de l'oeuvre gravé* (Paris: Librairie Auguste Blaizot, 1979); and Paul Cornu, *Bernard Naudin: Dessinateur & graveur* (n.pl.: Les Cahiers du Centre, quatrième série, March 1912).

43. On Poiret's couture house label, see "Note: Les Griffes de Paul Poiret, Nicole Groult, Germaine Bongard." In Musée de la Mode et du Costume, *Paul Poiret et Nicole Groult: Maîtres de la mode Art Déco*. Text by Paul Guillaume. Exh. cat. (Paris, 1986), 242–243. See also the discussion of labels and signatures in ch. 4.

44. On Dufy's collaboration with Poiret, see Hayward Gallery, *Raoul Dufy 1877–1953* exh. cat. (London, 1983).

45. See Galerie Barbazanges, *La Collection particulière de M. Paul Poiret* exh. cat. (Paris, April 26–May 12, 1923); this show included 151 numbered items including sculptures, paintings, and works on paper; and Hôtel Drouot, *Catalogue des Tableaux Modernes . . . de la collection de M. Paul Poiret* sale cat. (Paris: 18 November 1925), which includes a painting by Benito, who designed the cover for a spring 1917 catalogue of Poiret dresses (see ch. 4). The works put up for sale in 1925 correspond only partially to those included in the exhibition two years earlier.

46. On Boussingault, see André Dunoyer de Segonzac et al., *Boussingault par ses amis* (Paris: La Colombe, 1944). The decoration Boussingault painted for Poiret's couture house is reproduced on page 13.

47. Poiret owned numerous paintings by Dunoyer de Segonzac, the most important of which, *Les Buveurs,* he purchased in 1910, the same year it was exhibited at the Salon d'Automne (where it was titled *Un Cabaret*). In 1911, Poiret arranged

for Dunoyer de Segonzac to design the sets for a play, *Nabuchodonosor,* for which Poiret designed the costumes. The following year he asked the painter to create the curtain for a performance at one of his parties, *Les Festes de Bacchus* (see ch. 2).

48. This exhibition is announced in "Expositions ouvertes, Paris," *Art et Décoration,* 29 (March 1911), Supplément, 9.

49. These works are reproduced in the 1925 auction catalogue (see note 45) and can therefore be identified as catalogue numbers 199 and 260 in Pierre Daix and Joan Rosselet, *Le Cubisme de Picasso: Catalogue raisonné de l'oeuvre peint, des papiers collés et des assemblages, 1907–1916* (Neuchâtel: Ides et Calendes, 1979).

50. The Brancusi purchase is mentioned in Billy Klüver and Julie Martin, "Man Ray, Paris," in Merry Foresta et al. *Perpetual Motif: The Art of Man Ray* (New York: Abbeville, 1988), 98. However, according to André Dunoyer de Segonzac in the preface to White, *Poiret,* 9, Poiret purchased the sculpture (White misidentifies it as *Bird in Space*) from Brancusi's studio in 1911. I discuss the other purchases in Nancy J. Troy, *Modernism and the Decorative Arts in France: Art Nouveau to Le Corbusier* (New Haven: Yale University Press, 1991), 119.

51. "Poiret's New Kingdom," *Vogue* 40, no. 1 (1 July 1912): 16.

52. Poiret, *My First Fifty Years,* 157.

53. See the discussion of Macy's advertising policy as an expression of the store's attempts to distinguish itself from the commonplace practices of its rivals, in Edward Hungerford, *The Romance of a Great Store* (New York: Robert M. McBride & Co., 1922), 172–173.

54. Nozière (pseud. of Fernand Weyl), preface to *Les Parfums de Rosine* (Cannes: Imprimerie Robaudy, n.d.), n.p. A copy of this brochure is in the collection of the Musée de la Mode de la Ville de Paris. My thanks to Annie Barbera, Librarian, for help in gaining access to this publication and obtaining photographs of it.

55. Paul Poiret quoted in "Paul Poiret Here to Tell of his Art," *The New York Times* (21 September 1913): sec. 1, 11.

56. Aaron Jeffrey Segal, "The Republic of Goods: Advertising and National Identity in France, 1875–1914," Ph.D. dissertation, University of California, Los Angeles, 1995, esp. 47–50.

57. Ellen Gruber Garvey, *The Adman in the Parlor: Magazines and the Gendering of Consumer Culture, 1880s to 1910s* (New York: Oxford University Press, 1996), 94.

58. White, *Poiret,* 72.

59. *Women's Wear* (4 March 1912): 1.

60. "Poiret, Creator of Fashions, Here," *The New York Times* (21 September 1913): sec. 7, 3.

61. J. Arren, *Comment il faut faire de la publicité* (Paris: Pierre Lafitte, 1912), 14–15.

62. White, *Poiret*, 53, states that around 1909, Poiret "employed from 325 to 350 persons, including the business staff, mannequins, sales ladies, seamstresses, modistes, and stockroom and receiving and shipping clerks." On the previous ownership of Poiret's headquarters, see James Laver, "The Poiret Ball," in *Memorable Balls*, ed. James Laver (London: Derek Verschoyle, 1954), 109. On all of Poiret's adjoining property holdings at 26, avenue d'Antin, 107 rue du Faubourg St.-Honoré, and 39, rue du Colisée, and the location of Galerie Barbazanges at 109, rue du Faubourg St.-Honoré, see Billy Klüver, *A Day with Picasso: Twenty-Four Photographs by Jean Cocteau* (Cambridge, MA: MIT Press, 1997), 62–65. It is Erté who notes that Poiret lived in the adjoining property fronting on the rue du Colisée, in *My Life/My Art: An Autobiography* (New York: E.P. Dutton, 1989), 29.

63. Poiret, *My First Fifty Years,* 295.

64. "Poiret and Paquin Cling to Barbaric Colors," *The New York Times* (15 October 1911): sec. 8, 3.

65. Gustave Babin, "Une Leçon d'élégance dans un parc," *L'Illustration,* no. 3515 (9 July 1910): 21. Babin's article is preceded by an editorial note in which it is stated that the accompanying photographs (made especially for *L'Illustration* by Henri Manuel) "constitute, for a great Parisian couturier, publicity of the first order." The note goes on to state that this publicity was free; the couturier owed the journal nothing. In fact, "perhaps it is us who owe him for the rights of reproduction. He is not even named in the article you are about to read: let's at least give his name in full here: Paul Poiret. . . . so, now we are even."

66. Iribe also designed two kinds of stationery for Poiret's wife, Denise. See Raymond Bachollet, Daniel Bordet, and Anne-Claude Lelieur, *Paul Iribe,* with a preface by Edmonde Charles-Roux (Paris: Denoël, 1982), 91.

67. The album is described and discussed in ibid., 85–91. In addition to distribution to his best clients, Poiret envisioned sale of the album at 40 francs each.

68. Quoted in Bibliothèque Forney, *Paul Iribe: Précurseur de l'art déco* exh. cat. (Paris, 1983), 52, no. 123. On the technical aspects of pochoir production, see the beautiful book by Jean Saudé, *Traité d'enluminure d'art au pochoir* (Paris: Aux Éditions de l'Ibis, 1925).

69. See Grand Palais, *Salon d'Automne,* exh. cat. (Paris, 1909): Exposition du Livre, no. 85. That the album was also intended for sale underscores its location not strictly in the realm of advertising but closer to art, in the domain of the bibliophile and collector.

70. Regarding the exhibition, see Musée de la Mode et du Costume, *Paul Poiret et Nicole Groult,* 180. Regarding sales of the album, see the advertisement in *Comoedia Illustré* 3, no. 10 (15 February 1911): back cover. It seems likely that the timing of the exhibition was calculated to enhance sales.

71. *Les Parfums de Rosine,* n. p.

72. *Almanach des lettres et des arts* (Paris: Martine, n.d. [1916]).

73. Assouline, *An Artful Life,* 28.

74. The association with Kahnweiler should not be understood to suggest that Picasso was totally unaffiliated with Poiret who, it has been noted, owned several works by Picasso. According to Klüver, *A Day with Picasso,* Picasso's lover Fernande Olivier ran the Martine shop soon after it opened in 1911, and five years later Picasso appears to have been on intimate terms with one of Poiret's mannequins when, in the summer of 1916, his painting, *Les Demoiselles d'Avignon,* was publicly exhibited for the first time at the Salon d'Antin, held on the premises of Poiret's couture house.

On Kahnweiler's role in establishing his brand of cubism as the reigning paradigm, see Daniel Robbins, "Abbreviated Historiography of Cubism," *Art Journal* 47 (Winter 1988): 277–283. See also the discussion of the historiography of cubism in Eve Blau and Nancy J. Troy, introduction to *Cubism and Architecture,* ed. Eve Blau and Nancy J. Troy (Montreal: Canadian Centre for Architecture; Cambridge, MA: MIT Press, 1997), 4–7.

75. Gee, *Dealers, Critics, and Collectors of Modern Painting,* 21, n. 2.

76. D.-H. Kahnweiler, with Francis Crémieux, *My Galleries and Painters,* trans. Helen Weaver (London: Thames and Hudson, 1971), 41.

77. See the documentation of exhibitions outside Paris in which works by Picasso and/or Braque were shown during these years in Donald E. Gordon, *Modern Art Exhibitions 1900–1916: Selected Catalogue Documentation.* 2 vols. (Munich: Prestel, 1974).

78. See Patrick-Gilles Persin, *Daniel-Henry Kahnweiler: L'Aventure d'un grand marchand* (Paris: Solange Thierry, 1990), 11–12; and Werner Spies, "Vendre des tableaux—donner à lire," in Musée National d'Art Moderne, *Daniel-Henry Kahnweiler,* exh. cat. (Paris, 1984), 20.

79. David Cottington, *Cubism in the Shadow of War: The Avant-Garde and Politics in Paris 1905–1914* (New Haven: Yale University Press, 1998).

80. According to Gee, *Dealers, Critics, and Collectors of Modern Painting,* 14, there were 1,182 exhibitors, most with multiple entries, in the Salon des Indépendants of 1910; 1,320 painters exhibited in 1914.

81. Albert Gleizes, *Souvenirs: le cubisme 1908–1914.* Cahiers Albert Gleizes I (Audin: Association des Amis d'Albert Gleizes, 1957), 12. The following account of the 1911 Salon des Indépendants is based on this publication, 15–18.

82. Ibid., 20.

83. Ibid., 20.

84. Assouline, *An Artful Life,* 84, 86.

85. D.-H. Kahnweiler, quoted in Jacques de Gachons, "La peinture d'après-demain (?)," *Je Sais Tout* (15 April 1912), repr. in Spies, "Vendre des tableaux—donner à lire," 28.

86. Kahnweiler with Crémieux, *My Galleries and Painters,* 36.

87. Martha Ward, "Impressionist Installations and Private Exhibitions," *The Art Bulletin* 73 (December 1991): 599–622.

88. It would be interesting to compare Kahnweiler's strategy with the one Stieglitz was developing at the same time in his 291 Gallery in New York. The two appear to have had much the same opinion of the uninformed public. Photographs of Stieglitz's exhibition installations suggest that he devoted significant attention to the character of these displays; they also show that he used a sack-cloth wall covering similar to Kahnweiler's and kept the interior decoration to a minimum.

89. See the four photographs made in Kahnweiler's apartment on the rue George-Sand in 1913 reproduced in Spies, "Vendre des tableaux—donner à lire," 115–116.

90. "Poiret: Une silhouette Parisienne," *Le Miroir des Modes* 64, no. 6 (June 1912): 242.

91. Ibid., 242.

92. Paul Cornu, "L'Art de la robe," *Art et Décoration* 29 (April 1911): 112.

93. "Exclusive Poiret Costumes," *Harper's Bazar* 48, no. 5 (November 1913): 36.

94. "Poiret Talks about his Art," *Women's Wear* (23 September 1912): 1, 9.

95. Paul Poiret, *Art et phynance* (Paris: Lutetia, 1934), 142–143, quoted in Gee, *Dealers, Critics, and Collectors of Modern Painting,* 194.

96. The most important of these new publications, along with the *Gazette du Bon Ton,* were the *Journal des Dames et des Modes,* which took its title, format, and layout from a fashion journal of the late eighteenth century, and *Modes et Manières d'aujourd'hui,* also inspired by that earlier period and based on the similarly titled *Modes et Manières du jour,* published between 1798 and 1808. The *Gazette du Bon Ton,* too, borrowed its title from publications of that earlier period. These prewar publications participated in a reinvigoration of fashion illustration, initiated by the albums Poiret had commissioned from Iribe and Lepape, in reaction against the mechanical processes of illustration that had proliferated in women's magazines which, in turn, had themselves appeared in increasing numbers during the second half of the nineteenth century. See Raymond Gaudriault, *La Gravure de mode feminine en France* (Paris: Editions de l'Amateur, 1983).

97. "Beau Brummels of the Brush," *Vogue* 43, no. 14 (15 June 1914): 35–37, 88.

98. Henry Bidou, "Le Bon ton," *Gazette du Bon Ton* 1, no. 1 (November 1912): 1. On the *Gazette du Bon Ton,* see Shane Adler Davis, "Lucien Vogel," *Costume: The Journal of the Costume Society* 12 (1978): 74–82, and Edna Woolman Chase and Ilka Chase, *Always in Vogue* (New York: Doubleday, 1954), 110–113.

99. Bidou, "Le Bon ton," 1.

100. Henry Bidou, "Le Dîner de la Gazette du Bon Ton," *Gazette du Bon Ton* 2, no. 7 (July 1914): 225–228.

101. Charles Baudelaire, "The Painter of Modern Life," in *Baudelaire: Selected Writings on Art and Literature,* trans. P. E. Charvet (London: Penguin Books, 1972), 390–435. The essay was originally published in French in November and December 1863. On Baudelaire's interest in fashion in the context of theories of modernity and fashion from the mid-nineteenth century through the 1930s, see Lehmann, *Tigersprung.*

102. Baudelaire, "The Painter of Modern Life," 402.

103. Ibid., 402.

104. Ibid., 392.

105. Ibid., 395.

106. Bidou, "Le Bon ton," 1. As remarked of Bidou's definition of *le bon ton* by Peter Schertz in a paper on the *Gazette du Bon Ton* written for a seminar I taught at the University of Southern California in 1998, ". . . the term acquires an eternal (unchanging) quality as the underlying principle that governs elegance, fash-

ion, and even taste. This principle, I would argue, corresponds to the 'element that is eternal and invariable' which Baudelaire identified in beauty. *Le bon ton,* like beauty, can be extracted from the present. Impossible to represent as itself, because impossible to define with any precision, *le bon ton* can only be expressed via the 'relative circumstantial element' of beauty which Baudelaire called 'contemporaneity, fashion, morality, passion.'"

107. Baudelaire, "The Painter of Modern Life," 420.

108. Ibid., 419.

109. Ibid., 426.

Chapter 2

1. Hugette Garnier, "Un Théâtre de verdure va s'ouvrir cet été au coeur même de Paris." Clipping (27 May 1921) in Bibliothèque de l'Arsenal, Paris, Rt 4278.

2. Gilles Lipovetsky draws an even closer parallel between fashion and the star system, which, he argues, are based on the same values, that is, "on the sacralization of individuality and appearances. Just as fashion is the apparent personalization of ordinary human beings, so the star is the personalization of the actor: just as fashion is the sophisticated staging of the human body, so the star is the media staging of a personality. The 'type' personified by a star is her identifying mark, just like a couturier's style; the cinematographic personality proceeds from a surface artificiality that is of the same essence as fashion." Gilles Lipovetsky, *The Empire of Fashion: Dressing Modern Democracy,* trans. Catherine Porter (Princeton: Princeton University Press, 1994), 182.

3. Charles Castle, *Model Girl* (Newton Abbot, England: David & Charles, 1977), 17. On the widespread contemporary practice of fashion product placement and the breakdown of distinctions between entertainment and advertising that it fosters, see Ruth La Ferla, "A Star Is Worn," *New York Times* (14 December 1997): sec. 9, 1, 4.

4. Charles Eckert, "The Carole Lombard in Macy's Window," in Jane Gaines and Charlotte Herzog, eds. *Fabrications: Costume and the Female Body* (New York: Routledge, 1990), 100–121.

5. Marie Monceau, "Dressmaking Openings will Shortly be Held by Noted Paris Firms," *Philadelphia Inquirer* (8 February 1912): sec. 3, 3.

6. Robert Forrest Wilson, *Paris on Parade* (Indianapolis: Bobbs-Merrill, 1924), 56.

7. Erté [Romain de Tirtoff], *My Life/My Art: An Autobiography* (New York: E. P. Dutton, 1989), 34, 47.

8. Castle, *Model Girl,* 17.

9. For other photographs of Spinelly posing and a brief description of some of the interiors, see "Chez Spinelly," *Harper's Bazar* 51, no. 8 (August 1916): 41. Poiret's biographer, Palmer White, describes the unusual qualities of the couturier's perfumes: "He wanted heady, exotic scents. Ambergris, musk, and civet numbered among his favorite ingredients, and he pioneered the use of geranium and balsam. Through the exotic names he thought up for his scents—'L'Etrange Fleur', 'Le Fruit Défendu', 'Antinéa ou le Fond de la Mer'—he evoked mystery, forbidden sensations, and senuous qualities and, with 'Toute la Forêt', the freshness of nature in the countryside." White, *Poiret,* 111.

10. Alexandre, *Les Reines de l'aiguille,* 105.

11. Ibid., 37ff.

12. Paul Reboux, *La Rue de la Paix* (Paris: Pierre Lafitte, 1927): 15.

13. James Laver, *Taste and Fashion: From the French Revolution to the Present Day* (London: George G. Harrap & Co., 1937; rev. ed. 1945), 91.

14. "Drecoll and Beer Show Conservative Styles," *New York Times* (15 October 1911): sec. 8, 4.

15. Susan Day, *Louis Süe: architectures* (Brussels: Pierre Mardaga, 1985), 15.

16. "Le Théâtre du grand couturier," *Femina,* no. 262 (15 February 1911): 697.

17. Lady Duff Gordon ("Lucile"), *Discretions and Indiscretions* (New York: Frederick A. Stokes, 1932), 67ff. The quotations that follow in this paragraph are from this book.

18. Kaplan and Stowell, *Theatre and Fashion,* 119.

19. The development of this phenomenon in England is extensively studied by Kaplan and Stowell, ibid.

20. Jeffrey Weiss, *The Popular Culture of Modern Art: Picasso, Duchamp, and Avant-Gardism* (New Haven: Yale University Press, 1994), ch. 1: "'Le Journal joué': Picasso, Collage, and Music-Hall Modernism," 1–47.

21. Robert Dreyfus, *Petite histoire de la revue de fin d'année* (Paris: Charpentier et Fasquelle, 1909), 321.

22. "Mannequins on the Stage," *The Bystander* (8 October 1913): 74.

23. Jingle, "At the Queen's Theatre: 'This Way, Madam!'" *The Bystander* (8 October 1913): 77.

24. Louis Schneider, "La Mise en scène et les décors," *Comoedia* (21 September 1912): 2. Clipping in Bibliothèque de l'Arsenal, Paris, Rf 74.698 (1).

25. Vanina, "La Comédie de la mode: décentralisons . . . ," *Comoedia Illustré* 5, no. 1 (5 October 1912): 29.

26. Jean Dulac, "Vlan! . . . , Revue en 2 actes et 7 tableaux de MM Rip et Bousquet," *Comoedia Illustré* 3, no. 15 (1 May 1911): 463.

27. Jean Dulac, "Aux Capucines: 'Avec le sourire,' Revue en 3 tableaux de MM. R. Dieudonné et C. A. Carpentier," *Comoedia Illustré* 3, no. 11 (1 March 1911): 328.

28. Marcel Serano, "Au Théâtre des Capucines," *Comoedia Illustré* 6, no. 2 (20 October 1913): 62.

29. For the titles of Poiret's dresses, see the captions of Edward Steichen's photographs in Paul Cornu, "L'Art de la robe," *Art et Décoration* 29 (April 1911): 101–118. Poiret's trip through Eastern Europe and Russia is mentioned in the chronology by Guillaume Garnier in Musée de la Mode et du Costume, Palais Galliera, *Paul Poiret et Nicole Groult,* 182.

30. For an overview, see Roger Benjamin et al., in Art Gallery of New South Wales, *Orientalism: Delacroix to Klee* exh. cat. (Sydney, 1997).

31. Poiret did inscribe each dress produced by his couture house with a number, but these were used to identify individual garments (generally on the waistband or back of the house label) sold to particular clients; at the same time, as an example of a generic model, each dress went by the name of that model.

32. "They Steal Styles and Numbers," *New York Times* (20 June 1914): 11.

33. Poiret, *My First Fifty Years,* 190.

34. Ibid., 185.

35. See Ibid., 177–179, esp. 178: "Like many French artists, I was very struck by the Russian Ballet, and I should not be surprised if it had a certain influence on me. But it must be clearly stated that I already existed, and that my reputation was made, long before that of M. Bakst. Only foreign journalists could make any mistake about that and, voluntarily or involuntarily, commit the error of making my work the descendant of Bakst's. Nothing is commoner than this misunderstanding amongst the profane and the ill-informed; I have always combated it, for despite all the admiration I had for Bakst, I always refused to work after his designs [which was not true of Poiret's principal rival in the couture business, Jeanne Paquin]."

36. *Schéhérazade* is the title of a small literary journal edited by Jean Cocteau and François Bernouard, and inaugurated in November 1909 with a cover design by

Paul Iribe. Other artists close to Poiret, including Boussingault, Dunoyer de Segonzac, Laurencin, Moreau, and Süe, were also among the contributors, suggesting the currency of *The Arabian Nights* amongst Poiret's friends and associates before the Ballets Russes first performed *Schéhérazade* in Paris in June 1910.

37. See Peter Wollen's fascinating discussion of Bakst and Poiret in the context of the racial, sexual, and cultural implications of early twentieth-century French Orientalism: "Fashion/Orientalism/The Body," *New Formations* 1 (Spring 1987): 5–33.

38. Léon Bakst, quoted in Alexander Schouvaloff, *The Art of Ballets Russes: The Serge Lifar Collection of Theater Designs, Costumes, and Paintings at the Wadsworth Athenaeum, Hartford, Connecticut* (New Haven: Yale University Press in association with the Wadsworth Athenaeum, 1997), 63. Schouvaloff cites Irina Pruzhan, *Lev Samoilovitch Bakst* (Leningrad, 1975) for this quotation, but gives no page number.

39. Schouvaloff, *The Art of Ballets Russes,* 63.

40. See Ian Richard Netton, "The Mysteries of Islam," in *Exoticism in the Enlightenment,* ed. G. S. Rousseau and Roy Porter (Manchester: Manchester University Press, 1990), 39–40. I am indebted for this reference, and for information on the history of *The Arabian Nights* to a paper, "Fashionably Orientalist: The Trend of the Exotic in Early Twentieth-Century France," by Joni Haller, from my seminar on fashion and modernity at the University of Southern California in 1998.

41. Wollen, "Fashion/Orientalism/The Body," 17. Wollen cites Edward Said's now-classic text, *Orientalism* (New York: Pantheon, 1978), and Perry Anderson, *Lineages of the Absolutist State* (London: N.L.B., 1974). On the tradition of Orientalism in French theater, especially during the nineteenth century, and its relation to contemporary social and cultural history, see Angela C. Pao, *The Orient of the Boulevards: Exoticism, Empire, and Nineteenth-Century French Theater* (Philadelphia: University of Pennsylvania Press, 1998).

42. Robert Irwin, *The Arabian Nights: A Companion* (London: Allen Lane, Penguin Press, 1994).

43. Sylvette Larzul, *Les Traductions françaises des* Mille et une nuits. *Etude des versions Galland, Trébutien et Mardrus* (Paris: L'Harmattan, 1996), 33.

44. Ibid., 35.

45. Ibid., 67–68.

46. Irwin, *The Arabian Nights,* 19.

47. Ibid., 38.

48. Ibid., 38.

49. Mardrus remained loyal to Poiret despite the couturier's financial misfortune after the mid-1920s, and he later contributed an introduction to Poiret's *Art et phynance* of 1934.

50. *Nabuchodonosor.* Program, Bibliothèque de l'Arsenal, Paris, Rf 58.275 (3).

51. Al. Terego [pseud. Paul Poiret], "Les Opinions de Monsieur Pétrone," *La Grande Revue* 55 (May 1909): 147–159.

52. "Au Théâtre des Arts (Saison 1910–1911): Les Projets de M. J. Rouché," *Comoedia Illustré* 2, no. 23 (1 September 1910): 683.

53. See Zeynep Çelik, *Displaying the Orient: Architecture of Islam at Nineteenth-Century World's Fairs* (Berkeley: University of California Press, 1992), 18: The displays of non-Western peoples at the nineteenth-century world's fairs were organized around the anthropologist's concept of distance. 'Natives' were placed in 'authentic' settings, dressed in 'authentic' costumes, and made to perform 'authentic' activities, which seemed to belong to another age. They formed *tableaux vivants,* spectacles that fixed societies in history. Mixing entertainment with education, these spectacles painted the world at large in microcosm, with an emphasis on the 'strangeness' of the unfamiliar." See also Paul Greenhalgh, *Ephemeral Vistas: The* Expositions Universelles, *Great Exhibitions and World's Fairs, 1851–1939* (Manchester: Manchester University Press, 1988).

54. Maurice de Faramond, "Nabuchodonosor, Tragédie en un acte," *Vers et Prose* 26 (July–September 1911): 105–115.

55. A.-E. Marty, "Au Théâtre des Arts: 'Le Marchand de passions', trois images d'Épinal de M. Maurice Magre; 'Nabuchodonosor', un acte de M. M. de Faramond," *Comoedia Illustré* 3, no. 10 (15 February 1911): 292.

56. Grand Palais. *Salon d'Automne* exh. cat. (Paris, 1 October–8 November 1911), 221.

57. Poiret, *My First Fifty Years,* 103.

58. André Warnod, "Le Bal des Quat'Z'Arts," *La Renaissance Politique, Littéraire, Artistique* (11 June 1921): 17–20. Clipping, Bibliothèque de l'Arsenal, Paris, Ro 13007.

59. See the comment of a reviewer for *Femina*: "According to general opinion, even the Russian productions, of such rare and original beauty, have given us

nothing more sumptuous or more artistic than M. Rouché at the Théâtre des Arts for the staging of *Nabuchodonosor* by M. de Faramond. The costumes were designed by a celebrated couturier, and the slaves of the cruel king, Mlle Trouhanova, the dancer, and M. de Max as Nabuchodonosor, all splendidly attired, evoked on stage the luxurious magic of the period." "Un Eblouissement de costumes somptueux au Théâtre des Arts," *Femina* no. 243 (March 1911): 113.

60. Poiret, *My First Fifty Years,* 185.

61. Georges Lepape, quoted in Claude Lepape and Thierry Defert, *Georges Lepape ou l'élégance illustrée* (Paris: Herscher, 1983), 62. Lepape designed the printed invitation for the occasion; see the reproduction in the Lepape book, page 61.

62. Poiret, *My First Fifty Years,* 187.

63. See also the account written by Mardrus's wife, Lucie Delarue-Mardrus, "La Mille et deuxième nuit chez le grand couturier," *Femina,* no. 253 (1 August 1911): 415.

64. Poiret, *My First Fifty Years,* 188.

65. Wollen, "Fashion/Orientalism/The Body," 12.

66. *Femina,* no. 274 (15 June 1912), cover; *Femina,* no. 276 (15 July 1912): 427–430. In the same issue, see Agra, "Les Milles et quelques nuits de la saison," *Femina,* no. 276 (15 July 1912): 421. Wealthy Americans also participated in the fashion for Orientalist parties, as reported in "New York s'amuse dans la morte-saison," *Échos de l'exportation,* no. 87 (21 September 1912): 14. Mr. and Mrs. Cornelius Vanderbilt spent more than 750,000 francs on the Thousand and One Nights ball they threw in their Newport villa in summer 1912.

67. As Marjorie Garber has pointed out, the prohibition against women in trousers (and against men in women's dress) is ancient, appearing, for example in the biblical book of Deuteronomy: "The woman shall not wear that which pertaineth unto a man, neither shall a man put on a woman's garment; for all that do so are abomination unto the Lord thy God." (Deut. 22:5) Marjorie Garber, *Vested Interests: Cross-Dressing and Cultural Anxiety* (New York: Routledge, 1992), 28. See also Lydia Kamitsis, "Un Nomade dans la garde-robe féminine: le pantalon," in Musée de la Mode et du Textile, *Garde-robes: Intimités dévoilées, de Cléo de Mérode à . . . ,* exh. cat. (Paris, 1999), 36–41.

68. Georges Lepape, *Nijinski* in Schéhérazade *at the Théâtre du Châtelet,* 1910, gouache, 30.5 × 24 cm. This work, from a private collection, is reproduced in color in Lepape and Defert, *Georges Lepape ou l'élégance illustrée,* 63.

69. See the description and names of alternatives available in women's skirts designed in some cases to reveal, but in others to conceal, the existence of trousers underneath, in Sybil de Lancey, "La Mode et les modes," *Les Modes,* no. 123 (March 1911): 6–34, esp. 6–8, where the obsession with the topic is described as "the preoccupation of all the leaders of elegance concentrated on this question: should one—yes or no—wear *jupes-pantalons?* . . . it is, how shall I put it, a kind of moral revolution to be decided upon." See also Lydia Kamitsis, "Le Pantalon féminin," *Revue d'archéologie moderne et d'archéologie générale,* no. 13 (1999): 79–101.

70. Aline Raymonde, "Les propos de M. Boissonnot: la mode nouvelle," *La Mode Illustrée* 52, no. 15 (9 April 1911): n.p.

71. Garber, *Vested Interests,* ch. 12, esp. 311–316.

72. Ibid., 316.

73. "Les Essais d'une mode nouvelle," *L'Illustration* (18 February 1911): 103–104. A month after the appearance of the *Illustration* article, the *New York Times* noted that Worth and Doucet had introduced two or three models of *jupe-culotte* "and, although she has declared herself against them, Mme. Cheruit has also several models, including the garment worn by Mlle. Prévost at the Théâtre Française, which almost caused a riot in that classic house." "Paquin, Poiret, Drecoll Discuss New Fashions," *New York Times* (2 April 1911): 3.

74. "Poiret: Une Silhouette Parisienne," 243.

75. Paul Poiret, quoted in Cydalise, "La Culotte et la femme," *Madame & Monsieur* 7 année, no. 195 (10 March 1911): 1466.

76. Garber, *Vested Interests,* 32.

77. Dominique Sirop, *Paquin,* 25. See the report in *Le Matin* entitled, "A propos de la jupe-culotte" (28 February 1911), clipping in Paquin Publicity Album, Fashion Research Centre, Bath: "Mme. Paquin informe les lecteurs qu'elle n'a pas fait une seule 'jupe-culotte' et que, par conséquent, aucune robe de ce genre n'a pu être vue de chez elle ni aux courses, ni ailleurs."

78. See "Paris Gossip," *Women's Wear* (17 July 1911): 1; Edith L. Rosenbaum, "Costumes: Edith L. Rosenbaum Describes in Detail Some Interesting Features of the Poiret Collection," *Women's Wear* (8 September 1911): 1; "Mid-Winter Modes from Paris," *Vogue* 38, no. 12 (15 December 1911): 23.

79. "Paris Fashions for the Autumn," *New York Times* (1 October 1911): sec. 1, 7.

80. For information on Paquin and the Paquin firm, see the monograph by Sirop, *Paquin.* I am indebted to Albert Joire-Noulens for sharing his

reminiscences of Jeanne Paquin as well as several of the couturière's photo albums, which are in his archival collection; personal interviews with Albert Joire-Noulens, Paris, 3 and 7 May 1999.

81. "Poiret and Paquin Cling to Barbaric Colors," sec. 8, 3.

82. "Paquin," *Harper's Bazar* 49, no. 1 (January 1914): 43.

83. "Paquin, Poiret, Drecoll Discuss New Fashions," 3.

84. Jean Lefranc, "Abel Hermant et le théâtre." Undated clipping in Bibliothèque de l'Arsenal, Paris, Rf. 62.276.

85. Joseph Galtier, "Répétion générale au Vaudeville: 'Rue de la Paix'," *Excelsior* (22 January 1912): 7.

86. In his commentary on the play, Robert Dieudonné noted that several of its characters were clearly attempts to portray real people, and in this context he mentioned Poiret in particular. Robert Dieudonné, "La Soirée Parisienne: 'La Rue de la Paix.' Commentaires anodins sur une pièce d'un parisiannisme échevelé." Undated clipping in Bibliothèque de l'Arsenal, Paris, Rf. 62.276.

87. For brief but revealing descriptions of Poiret's couture house interiors, see "How Poiret Conducts an Opening," *Vogue* 39, no. 8 (15 April 1912): 36; and "Poiret: Une Silhouette Parisienne," 242.

88. "Dress on the Stage: A Disappointing Paris Play. Daring Colour Contrasts," *The Daily Mail* (23 January 1912). Clipping in Paquin Publicity Album, Fashion Research Centre, Bath.

89. Y. L., "La Mode au théâtre: 'La Rue de la Paix,'" *Femina*, no. 266 (15 February 1912): 96.

90. André Gilliard, "Actualités: La Rue de la Paix," *Bravo* (27 January 1912). Clipping in Paquin Publicity Album, Fashion Research Centre, Bath.

91. Sirop, *Paquin*, 25, 29.

92. Jeanne Paquin, quoted in Juliette Ferrant, "Les Modes de la saison: Verrons-nous celle de la 'Rue de la Paix'?" *L'Excelsior* (23 January 1912). Clipping in Bibliothèque de l'Arsenal, Paris, Rf. 62.276.

93. "Dress on the Stage" (as in n. 88).

94. Vanina, "Les Robes de 'Rue de la Paix': une 'interview' sur la conception de la robe, de M. Paul Iribe. Considérations générales," *Comoedia Illustré* 4, no. 9 (1 February 1912): 317.

95. "The Iribe Line: Fashion's Newest Eccentricity," *The Bystander* 34, no. 435 (3 April 1912): 1.

96. Intérim, "Les Premiers: Au Vaudeville: La Rue de la Paix," *La Vie Parisienne* (27 January 1912): 69.

97. This work is in a private collection in New York and is reproduced in color in Sirop, *Paquin,* 18.

98. That the revealing silhouettes and bold colors of the dresses were the source of critics' outrage is made clear in "Dame Nature Dresses," *The Sketch* 77, no. 992 (31 January 1912): X.

99. In a departure from the more common reaction, Henri Duvernois saw the three acts of the play as light and amusing, but he believed they nevertheless had substance: "In many plays, this serious and dramatic thesis is no more than a pretext for presenting models of dresses worn with a rare elegance. Here the opposite is the case." Henri Duvernois, "La Quinzaine théâtrale," *Femina,* no. 266 (15 February 1912): 88.

100. Furet, "A Paris: Nos Premières," *Dramatica* (February 1912). Clipping in Paquin Publicity Album, Fashion Research Centre, Bath.

101. Gilliard, "Actualités" (as in n. 90). For a different point of view, see Duvernois, "La Quinzaine théâtrale," 88, who suggests that the play is really about "French tradition in the face of foreign esthetes."

102. G. de Pawlowski, "Au Vaudeville: Rue de la Paix, comédie en trois actes" (22 January 1912). Clipping in Bibliothèque de l'Arsenal, Paris, Rf. 62.276.

103. "Au Théâtre: La Rue de la Paix." Undated clipping in Bibliothèque de l'Arsenal, Paris, Rf. 62.276.

104. Gilliard, "Actualités" (as in n. 90).

105. Kaplan and Stowell, *Theatre and Fashion,* 2–3.

106. "Au Théâtre: La Rue de la Paix" (as in n. 103).

107. On the effects of nationalism on cultural discourse in pre-World War I France, see David Cottington, *Cubism in the Shadow of War: The Avant-Garde and Politics in Paris 1905–1914* (New Haven: Yale University Press, 1998), esp. 25–36.

108. Kenneth E. Silver, *Esprit de Corps: The Art of the Parisian Avant-Garde and the First World War, 1914–1925* (Princeton: Princeton University Press, 1989), 167–181. For further discussion, see ch. 4 in this book.

109. For information about Paquin's donation, I am indebted to Pierre Curie, conservateur au Musée du Petit Palais, Paris, letter to me, 25 November 1991. On those in Poiret's orbit who studied at the Académie Julien, see Luc-Albert

Moreau, "Souvenir de Boussingault," in André Dunoyer de Segonzac et al., *Boussingault par ses amis* (Paris: Éditions du Vieux Colombier, 1944): 9.

110. *Exposition Internationale des Industries et du Travail de Turin, 1911. Catalogue spécial officiel de la section Française* (Paris: Comité français des expositions à l'étranger, 1911), 470.

111. Two of the wax mannequins are illustrated in V., "Le Pavillon PAQUIN à l'Exposition de Turin," *Comoedia Illustré* 3, no. 18 (15 June 1911): 584–585.

112. Ibid., 584–585.

113. "Léon Bakst," *Harper's Bazar* 49, no. 1 (January 1914): 56.

114. For the names of the dresses, see Gabriel Mourey, "Les Robes de Bakst," *Gazette du Bon Ton,* no. 6 (April 1913): 166; Vanina, "La Comédie de la mode," *Comoedia Illustré* 5, no. 12 (20 March 1913): 575.

115. Mourey, "Les Robes de Bakst," 165.

116. Schouvaloff, *The Art of Ballets Russes,* 76.

117. Robert Johnson, intro., "Bakst on Classicism: 'The Paths of Classicism in Art'," *Dance Chronicle* 13, no. 2 (1999): 170–173. See also Michelle Potter, "Designed for Dance: The Costumes of Léon Bakst and the Art of Isadora Duncan," *Dance Chronicle* 13, no. 2 (1999): 154–169.

118. "Paris Shows More Dignity in Women's Dresses," *The New York Times* (19 October 1913): sec. 7, 4.

119. Jean D'Yvelet, "La Section française à l'exposition de Bruxelles," *Le Journal* (6 June 1910): 3.

120. Ibid., 3.

121. *Le Figaro* (5 June 1910): 5. Clipping in Paquin Publicity Album, Fashion Research Centre, Bath.

122. Vanina, "La Comédie de la mode," 575.

123. See the descriptions by Poiret, *My First Fifty Years,* 183–185; White, *Poiret,* 69; and Berthail, "Bernard Naudin 1876–1946: Recherches sur sa vie et son oeuvre." Doctorat de troisième cycle (Université de Paris-Sorbonne, Institute d'Art et d'archéologie): I, 24.

124. See White, *Poiret,* 69.

125. Bagnolet, "Les Festes de Bacchus," *Revue Musicale S.I.M.* 8, no. 11 (November 1912): 41; Poiret, *My First Fifty Years,* 200.

126. Musée de la Mode et du Costume, Palais Galliera, *Paul Poiret et Nicole Groult,* text by Guillaume Garnier, 182. The program for the evening makes no mention of Isadora Duncan.

127. Ibid., 41.

128. Patricia Rae Sandback, "Isadora Duncan and Paul Poiret: The Sacred and the Profane" (Master's thesis, University of California, Irvine, 1984), 25–26, 44–45.

129. See Ann Daly, "Isadora Duncan and the Distinction of Dance," *American Studies* 35, no. 1 (1994): 5–23; the passage quoted is on page 6. This article is primarily concerned with Duncan in America, but much of the argument applies equally well to Duncan's activities in France before World War I.

130. A limited number of each fan design was created for sale. See the example in stenciled silk of *Occidental Woman* in the collection of the Los Angeles County Museum of Art. I am grateful to Sandra Rosenbaum, Associate Curator of Costumes and Textiles, for bringing this object to my attention.

131. For descriptions of the latter, see "L'Exposition internationale de Gand," *Excelsior* (7 May 1913) and "A Gand: La Section française de l'Exposition Universelle a été inaugurée officiellement hier," *L'Intransigeant* (7 May 1913). Clippings in Paquin Publicity Album, Fashion Research Centre, Bath.

   After the First World War, Poiret turned to Paquin's architect, Mallet-Stevens, commissioning him to design and construct a modernist villa in reinforced concrete outside Paris at Mézy. The project was partially completed but had to be abandoned when Poiret's finances bottomed out in the mid-1920s. After he was forced to give up his residence in Paris and sell his remaining possessions in 1929, Poiret briefly lived in the unfinished concierge's house at Mézy. Eventually the property was sold and the villa was completed for another patron, with significant changes made to the design as conceived by Mallet-Stevens. See Jean-François Pinchon, ed. *Rob. Mallet-Stevens: Architecture, mobilier, décoration* (Paris: Philippe Sers, 1986), 53–55.

132. See Mallet-Stevens's letter, April 1914, to collaborators of *Nouvelle Manière* reproduced in Hervé Paindaveine, "Lettres de Paris: Mallet-Stevens et les revues Belges d'architecture," in *Vienne-Bruxelles ou la fortune du Palais Stoclet* (Brussels: Archives d'Architecture Moderne, 1987), 75.

133. "To Display Furs in 'Persian Shop'" (c. November 1913). Unidentified newspaper clipping, in Paquin Publicity Album, Fashion Research Centre, Bath. The quotations that follow in this and the next paragraph are from this clipping.

134. Silver, *Esprit de Corps,* 171–175. See also Troy, *Modernism and the Decorative Arts in France,* esp. 63–67.

135. "La mille-et-deuxième nuit" (May 1912). Unidentified clipping, possibly from *La Vie Parisienne,* in Paquin Publicity Album, Fashion Research Centre, Bath. The Contesse Blanche de Clermont-Tonnerre was reportedly dressed for the occasion not by Paquin or Poiret but instead by Iribe.

136. Sem, *Le Vrai et le faux chic* (Paris: Succès, 1914).

137. Valerie Steele (*Paris Fashion,* 244) mistakenly identifies an outfit as one of Coco Chanel's first suits. Alice Mackrell, *Coco Chanel* (New York: Holmes & Meier, 1992), 20, follows Steele in this misattribution. Chanel at the time was barely established in the Paris fashion world. Not yet a couturière, she had opened a millinery shop only a year before the appearance of Sem's *Le Vrai et le faux chic.* The outfit in question was probably by Callot Soeurs, as Sem's text seems to suggest. Although no Chanel hats were depicted in *Le Vrai et le faux chic,* hats by other designers (Georgette and Demay) were included. Chanel and her boyfriend, Arthur (Boy) Capel, did make an appearance in another album by Sem: *Tangoville sur Mer* (Paris: Succès, 1913), n.p.

138. This and the following quotation relevant to *Tangoville sur Mer* are cited and discussed in Madeleine Bonnelle and Marie-José Meneret, *Sem* (Périgueux: Pierre Fanlac, 1979), 82–84, where the authors cite as their source a series of chronicles Sem wrote about the tango, entitled *Les Possédées,* published in April 1912.

On the popularity of the tango in prewar Paris, in addition to Sem's album, see the caption accompanying a color reproduction of Albert Guillaume's painting, *Au Cours de tango,* in *Femina,* no. 297 (1 June 1913): opp. 322; André de Fouquières, "Les Dances nouvelles: le tango," *Femina,* no. 289 (1 February 1913): 58; and Franc-Nohain, "Tangomanie," in *Femina,* no. 300 (15 July 1913): 376–378 (this article is illustrated by Poiret's friend, Bernard Boutet de Monvel). See also Lisa Tickner's discussion of English enthusiasm for the tango and related popular dances of the pre-World War I period in "The Popular Culture of *Kermesse:* Lewis, Painting, and Performance, 1912–13," *Modernism/Modernity* 4, no. 2 (April 1997): 67–120, and published in modified form in her book, *Modern Life & Modern Subjects: British Art in the Early Twentieth Century* (New Haven: Yale University Press, 2000), ch. 3: Wyndham Lewis: Dance and the Popular Culture of *Kermesse.*

139. My description of the play and the following quotations are from Paul Reboux, "Théâtre de l'Athénée: Le Tango. Pièce en quatre actes, de Madame et M. Jean Richepin," *Le Théâtre,* no. 362 (January 1914): 15–18.

140. Lise-Léon Blum, "Le Goût au théâtre," *Gazette du Bon Ton* 2, no. 3 (March 1914): 101.

141. M. P., "Le Vrai et le faux chic: la mode vue par Sem," *L'Illustration,* no. 3709 (28 March 1914): 243–248.

142. Paul Iribe, "La Seule critique que l'on puisse adresser à une mode, dit M. Paul Iribe, c'est de lui reprocher d'avoir trop duré," *Le Miroir* 4, nouvelle série, no. 35 (26 July 1914): n.p.

Chapter 3

1. Michel Melot, "The Nature and Role of the Print," in *Prints: History of an Art.* Part I trans. by Helga Harrison and Dennis Corbyn (Geneva: Skira, and New York: Rizzoli, 1981), 68.

2. Ibid., 116. See also Michel Melot, "Les Frontières de l'originalité et les problèmes de l'estampe contemporaine," *Revue de l'Art,* no. 21 (1973): 110: "[P]hotography multiplied the rival processes [of reproduction] while commerce in prints, far from accepting these novel nuances, conjured them away by opposing ever more radically the original print and the reproductive print with a Manicheism that scarcely corresponds to the complexity of the reality in which original conception and techniques of reproduction complement one another without ever totally excluding either."

3. During the nineteenth century the proliferation and the increasingly widespread museum display of plaster casts of canonical examples of Roman sculpture—many of which were themselves understood to be copies of lost Greek originals—corresponded in some respects to issues in reproductive printmaking. These examples further complicate the relationship between originality and reproduction that scholars have come to regard as fundamental to the history of western art. See n. 5, and Francis Haskell and Nicolas Penny, *Taste and the Antique: The Lure of Classical Sculpture 1500–1900* (1981; repr. New Haven: Yale University Press, 1982); and Alan Wallach, *Exhibiting Contradiction: Essays on the Art Museum in the United States* (Amherst: University of Massachusetts Press, 1998), ch. 3: "The American Cast Museum: An Episode in the History of the Institutional Definition of Art."

4. It is noteworthy that the anti-theatrical terms in which Kahnweiler criticized the public appeal of the salon cubists in 1912 (see ch. 1) were echoed by Sem when

two years later he condemned the ostentatious theatricality of certain purveyors of contemporary fashion in *Le Vrai et le faux chic* (see ch. 2).

5. Krauss makes this point in her analysis of Auguste Rodin's sculpture in "The Originality of the Avant-Garde," and "Sincerely Yours," both reprinted in *The Originality of the Avant-Garde and Other Modernist Myths,* 151–194. For more on the historical complexity and multiple dimensions of these issues, see also *Retaining the Original: Multiple Originals, Copies and Reproductions,* Studies in the History of Art, 20 (Washington, DC: National Gallery of Art, 1989); Schwartz, *The Culture of the Copy;* Richard Shiff, "Originality," in *Critical Terms for Art History,* ed. Robert S. Nelson and Richard Shiff (Chicago: University of Chicago Press, 1996), 103–115.

6. Erté, *My Life/My Art,* 30.

7. Jacques Richepin, *Le Minaret. Comédie en trois actes en vers* (Paris: Librairie Charpentier et Fasquelle, 1914).

8. Jules Delini, "Le Minaret de Jacques Richepin à la Renaissance," *Comoedia* (18 March 1913). Clipping in Bibliothèque de l'Arsenal, Paris, Rf 70.593.

9. François de Nion, "Les Répétitions générales. Théâtre de la Renaissance—Le Minaret" (20 March 1913). Clipping in Bibliothèque de l'Arsenal, Paris, Rf 70.593 (italics in original).

10. Paul Souday, "Renaissance: 'Le Minaret', comédie spectacle, en trois actes et en vers, de M. Jacques Richepin" (21 March 1913). Clipping in Bibliothèque de l'Arsenal, Paris, Rf 70.593. Souday's use of the term *munichois* refers to the style of decorative arts by designers from Munich who became well known in France in the wake of their display at the Salon d'Automne of 1910. See pp. 204–207. See the similar commentary by Edmond Sée, "Le Théâtre: Répétitions générales: A la Renaissance, Mme Cora Laparcerie" (20 March 1913). Clipping in Bibliothèque de l'Arsenal, Paris, Rf 70.593.

11. Delini, "Le Minaret de Jacques Richepin à la Renaissance."

12. Erté and Poiret reconstruct slightly different versions of the color schemes in their respective memoirs. See Erté, *My Life/My Art,* 30, and Poiret, *My First Fifty Years,* 91. For black and white as the dominant colors of the last act, see Jacques Emile Blanche, "L'Harmonie des contrastes: blanc & noir, noir & blanc," *Femina,* no. 299 (1 July 1913): 364, caption of drawing by A. E. Marty.

13. Nion, "Les Répétitions générales."

14. Louis Schneider, "Le Minaret–La mise en scène et les décors" (19 March

1913). Clipping in Bibliothèque de l'Arsenal, Paris, Rf 70.593. On *Sumurun,* see Ernst Stern, *My Life, My Stage* (London: Victor Gollancz, 1951), 85–87; J. L. Styan, *Max Reinhardt* (Cambridge: Cambridge University Press, 1982), 267.

15. Blanche, "L'Harmonie des contrastes," 364.

16. Nion, "Les Répétitions générales."

17. "Le Minaret," *La Caricature.* Undated clipping pasted into the program of *Le Minaret.* Bibliothèque de l'Arsenal, Paris, Rf 70.593: "L'Actualité balkanique donne une saveur toute particulière à cette oeuvre quit fait le plus grand honneur à leurs auteurs et a reçu la très haute approbation de M. Pierre Loti."

18. Not only did their exhibition practices set these public cubists apart from Picasso and Braque, so too did their use of bright colors differ from the grisaille paintings that Picasso and Braque produced before about 1913, when they started to exploit the larger range of color that the exploration of collage techniques led them to reintroduce in their work.

19. For an extended discussion of these issues, see Troy, *Modernism and the Decorative Arts in France,* ch. 2: "Responses to Industrialization and Competition from Germany."

20. Anonymous [Henri Lapauze?], "Juste Sévérité," *La Renaissance (politique, économique, littéraire, artistique)* 3, no. 14 (7 August 1915): 15–16, quoted in Silver, *Esprit de Corps,* 168. See chapter 4.

21. Régis Gignoux, "Avant le rideau" (19 March 1913). Clipping in Bibliothèque de l'Arsenal, Paris, Rf 70.593.

22. Cora Laparcerie-Richepin, "Aux pièces françaises il faut une mise en scène française" (19 March 1913). Clipping in Bibliothèque de l'Arsenal, Paris, Rf 70.593. The quotations that follow in the present paragraph are from this source.

23. R. D., "Le Minaret: La Soirée." Undated clipping in Bibliothèque de l'Arsenal, Paris, Rf 70.593.

24. Louis Schneider, "Le Minaret—la mise en scène et les décors."

25. Guy Launay, "Répétition générale: au théâtre de la Renaissance, 'le Minaret' de M. Jacques Richepin, est avant tout une surprenante exposition de costumes" (20 March 1913). Clipping in Bibliothèque de l'Arsenal, Paris, Rf 70.593.

26. Lise-Léon Blum, "Le Goût au théâtre," *Gazette du Bon Ton* 1, no. 6 (April 1913): 188.

27. For *8d. a Mile,* see *The Tatler,* no. 622 (28 May 1913): 270; *The Sketch Supplement* (21 and 28 May 1913); and *The Playgoer and Society Illustrated* n.s. 8,

no. 45 (June–July, 1913), which includes a column by M. E. Brooke, "In the Boudoir," in which the author remarks (p. 83), "Everyone is discussing the dresses in the '8d. a Mile' Revue." "Phèdre," described by one critic as "an orgy of costumes from Persia, Arabia [and] Assyria," was equally appealing to audiences: "The tragedy [by Racine] is nothing more than a pretext for the parade of mannequins. In the charm of the decor and the costumes, 'contemporary staging' returns again in all its satire. But at the Femina [Theatre] one neglects the satire in order to admire the originality and the taste of this tableau." Régis Gignoux, "Théâtre Femina: Très moutarde," *Le Théâtre,* no. 370 (May 1914): 12.

28. Paul Poiret, quoted in Anne Rittenhouse, "The Prophet of Simplicity," *Vogue* 42, no. 9 (1 November 1913): 142.

29. Before his departure from Paris, Poiret had shown the film to about thirty guests at a "cinematograph dinner" described by a correspondent for the *New York Times* ("Poiret, Creator of Fashions, Here" [21 September 1913]): sec. 7, 3: "It was given in the walled garden which lies between the back entrance to his house and the front entrance to his dressmaking establishment. . . . The guests sat on the marble steps that run across half the front of the house, and suddenly, into their vision, came a dramatic parade of pictured mannequins who moved in and out of the garden trees, and sauntered on the graveled garden paths, wearing the very newest clothes that had been invented by Poiret that week. . . . [I]t was difficult to believe that these visions of lovely women and costly robes moving among the trees were produced by a machine."

30. This term appeared in an ad for Gimbel Brothers in *Women's Wear* (26 September 1913): 8.

31. See "Costumes: New York—Dates of Lectures to Be Given by M. Poiret," *Women's Wear* (24 September 1913): 1; "Paul Poiret Lectures," *Women's Wear* (26 September 1913): 1; "Teachers College," *Columbia Specator* 57, no. 4 (27 September 1913): 2. I am grateful to Andrew Perchuk for locating the latter reference.

32. "Paul Poiret Talks about His Art," *Women's Wear* (23 September 1913): 1. According to the *New York Times* correspondent (as in n. 29), "He brings to America his lovely wife and one hundred gowns for her to wear: gowns which are not even distant cousins to the fashions; and he also brings one hundred cushions. The three will be grouped together—the lovely woman, wearing the gowns, seated on the cushions."

33. The photograph accompanies the article entitled "Poiret on the Philosophy of Dress," *Vogue* 42, no. 8 (15 October 1913): 41–42.

34. "Costumes: Paul Poiret Criticizes the Commercialization and Capitalization of his Visit to this Country," *Women's Wear* (22 September 1913): 1.

35. Ibid., 1, 7.

36. "Paul Poiret Here to Tell of his Art," sec. 1, 11.

37. "Costumes: New York—Dates of Lectures to Be Given by M. Poiret," 1. The same passage is quoted in "Paul Poiret Here to Tell of His Art."

38. "Paul Poiret Talks about His Art," 1, 9.

39. Ibid.

40. See Harrison C. White and Cynthia A. White, *Canvases and Careers: Institutional Change in the French Painting World* (1965; Chicago: University of Chicago Press, 1993), 8, 13, n. 6, where the authors cite L. Vitet, *L'Académie Royale* (Paris: Levy, 1861), 72.

41. For Poiret's arrangement with *Harper's Bazar*, see the beginning of an article entitled, "Exclusive Poiret Costumes," 34, in which the following announcement appeared: "Beginning with the December number Paul Poiret, the most original and daring couturier in Paris, will contribute a series of exclusive illustrated articles. Only in the BAZAR will M. Poiret give his ideas on fashions during 1914." See also Paul Poiret, "There are as Many Styles of Dress as there are Women," *Harper's Bazar* 49, no. 1 (January 1914): 47–49.

42. Benjamin & Johnes, a corset manufacturer based in Newark, New Jersey, also prominently featured Poiret's name and endorsement of their products in their ad in *Harper's Bazar* 49, no. 3 (March 1914). According to a letter from Poiret reproduced and translated in the ad, the French couturier met the owners of the company while returning to Paris aboard the Lusitania, and at that time had agreed to design several model corsets and brassieres for them.

43. Advertisement for J. M. Gidding & Co., *New York Times* (23 September 1913): 5; this text is also quoted in an advertisement for Windsor Print Works entitled "Minaret Fabrics—The Topic of the Hour," in *Women's Wear* (3 October 1913): 5.

44. "The Style Influence of 'Le Minaret'," *Women's Wear* (3 October 1913): sec. 4, 4–5: "The gown was developed in emerald green chiffon, the skirt clinging and somewhat hobbled at the foot having the lamp shade tunic trimmed with gold bullion fringe. This exhibit was one of the sensations of the Gimbel promenade a year ago and created much comment but resulted in no serious discussion. It is evident that since then, Monsieur Poiret had been working upon this style when

the Le Minaret production gave him the opportunity to use the idea which is now the most conspicuous influence felt in the world of fashion."

45. Advertisement, Gimbel Brothers (as in n. 30) and "Costumes" (as in n. 34), 7.

46. Mica Nava, "Modernity's Disavowal: Women, the City and the Department Store," in *The Shopping Experience,* ed. Pasi Falk and Colin Campbell (London: Sage Publications, 1977): 69.

47. "The Style Influence of 'Le Minaret,' " sec. 4, 5.

48. For a description of the fashion show, see Anna de Haven, "Costumes: The Wanamaker Presentation of Paris Fashions 'In a Persian Garden,' " *Women's Wear* (26 September 1913): sec. 4, 11–12. The three-story auditorium, known as Wanamaker Hall, was decorated in the Italian Renaissance style and equipped with an Austin pipe-organ. See the *Golden Book of the Wanamaker Stores. Jubilee Year: 1861–1911* (n.pl.: n.pub., 1911), 296. Wanamaker's New York store was inaugurated in 1907 but the auditorium did not open until the following year, according to Joseph H. Appel, *The Business Biography of John Wanamaker, Founder and Builder* (New York: Macmillan, 1930), 114.

49. "The Style Influence of 'Le Minaret,' " 2–3, and 1.

50. "Week of Splendid Style Displays," 1.

51. "New York—'Persian Garden' Fashion Display at Wanamaker's," *Women's Wear* (24 September 1913): 7.

52. "The Style Influence of 'Le Minaret,' " 5.

53. "Week of Splendid Style Displays," *Women's Wear* (26 September 1913): Merchandising Section, 1.

54. According to Ralph M. Hower, *History of Macy's of New York 1858–1919: Chapters in the Evolution of the Department Store*, Harvard Studies in Business History, VII (Cambridge, MA: Harvard University Press, 1943), 334, by the time Macy's moved to its Herald Square location in 1902, "The day had passed when the firm was content to have goods piled up on shelves and counters without much regard to appearances; no longer was it considered wise to fill up an entire window with a single type of merchandise. By 1909 the store was beginning to exhibit related merchandise together (e.g., shoes, stockings, and dresses, or a completely furnished room), so that customers could see total effects rather than isolated parts." On the complex issues raised by class differences in the context of the department store, see Susan Porter Benson, "Palace of Consumption and Machine for Selling: The American Department Store, 1880–1940," *Radical History Review*, no. 21 (Fall 1979): 199–221.

55. "The Store Entertainment," *The Dry Goods Economist* (18 April 1903): 33.

56. Neil Harris compares the merchandizing and display practices of the department store to those of the art museum in his *Cultural Excursions: Marketing Appetites and Cultural Tastes in Modern America* (Chicago: University of Chicago Press, 1990), ch. 3: "Museums, Merchandising, and Popular Taste: The Struggle for Influence."

57. Anonymous author quoted in *Golden Book of the Wanamaker Stores,* 247.

58. Ibid., 248, 249.

59. Ibid., 73–74.

60. Benson, "Palace of Consumption," 203.

61. Susan Porter Benson, *Counter Cultures: Saleswomen, Managers, and Consumers in American-Department Stores. 1890–1940* (Urbana: University of Illinois Press, 1986), 82.

62. William Leach*, Land of Desire: Merchants, Power and the Rise of a New American Culture* (New York: Pantheon Books, 1993), 95.

63. Rachel Bowlby, *Shopping with Freud* (New York: Routledge, 1993): 104–105.

64. Kristin Ross, "Introduction: Shopping," in Émile Zola, *The Ladies' Paradise (Au bonheur des dames)* (Berkeley: University of California Press, 1992), viii, ix. Ross draws here on Sennett, *The Fall of Public Man,* esp. 142, 144.

65. David Chaney, "The Department Store as a Cultural Form," *Theory, Culture & Society* 1, no. 3 (1983): 24.

66. Ibid., 27.

67. W. H. P. Barley, article from *The Dry Goods Economist* quoted in "Power of Store Decoration," *Store Life* 7, no. 1 (October 1904): 16.

68. William R. Leach, "Transformations in a Culture of Consumption: Women and Department Stores, 1890–1925," *The Journal of American History* 71, no. 2 (September 1984): 326.

69. Leach, *Land of Desire,* 108–111.

70. "In the World of Make-Believe," *Harper's Bazar* 50, no. 2 (February 1914): 12.

71. "The Style Influence of 'Le Minaret,'" 1.

72. "So Say the Paris Openings," *Vogue* 43, no. 17 (1 August 1914): 37.

73. "Copyrighting Clothes," *Vogue* 45, no. 3 (1 February 1915): 17.

74. Samuel Hopkins Adams, "The Dishonest Paris Label: How American Women are Being Fooled by a Country-Wide Swindle," *Ladies' Home Journal* March 1913, repr. *Dress: The Journal of the Costume Society of America* 4 (1978): 17–23.

75. Ibid., 18.

76. Ibid., 23.

77. "The Specialty Shops," *Women's Wear* (14 October 1913): 1, 6. This article reproduces a letter from Poiret to *Women's Wear* in which the couturier states that he was informed of the circulation of fraudulent Poiret labels by a New York store owner who wrote to Poiret in Paris in early September 1913, before he left for the United States. The store owner's letter is also reproduced in the article. Apparently it was only during his stay in the United States that Poiret was able to examine the offending "headpieces" and determine that they and the labels sewn into them were fakes. The identical article appeared three days later under a different title: "Poiret's Label," *Women's Wear* (17 October 1913): 3.

78. People v. William Fantel, Docket Index, Minutes of Special Sessions, County of New York, 5 August 1914–22 March 1915, 269. I am enormously indebted to Rick Richman of the law firm of O'Melveny & Myers for enabling the legal research staff of their New York office to track down this case for me. I am also grateful to Jo Cooper and her assistant, Theresa Delgado, for doing the actual work involved in locating what appears to be the only surviving legal record of this case, on the basis of a misleading mention of it in *Vogue* (see n. 73) suggesting that a case was brought by Poiret himself against William Fantell [*sic*] of the Universal Weaving Company. In addition, Andrew Perchuk tried valiantly to find evidence of this case, and although he did not ultimately locate the docket, his research has been invaluable to my understanding of related issues in American copyright law of the period that are discussed in this chapter.

79. Advertisement for R. H. Macy & Co., *New York Times* (24 September 1913): 5. So convinced was Macy's of the accuracy of its "duplicates" that it decided to display them "together with the originals, so that their effectiveness may be fully appreciated."

80. Advertisement for Gimbel Brothers, *New York Times* (19 October 1913): 16. Similarly, an ad for Bonwit Teller boasted of a model by Premet "accurately reproduced, with a fidelity to detail and finesse that Premet himself would be proud of . . ." Providing one price in French francs without clarifying that the other was in dollars made the difference seem even larger than was actually the case: "Premet Price for Original Model, 1,000 Francs. Our Price for the Reproduction, 95.00." *New York Times* (19 October 1913): 11.

81. Advertisement for J. M. Gidding & Co., *New York Times* (17 September 1913): 6.

82. Advertisement for Kurzman, *New York Times* (24 September 1913): 5.

83. Anne Rittenhouse, "Fashion under Fire," *Vogue* 44, no. 7 (1 October 1914): 41.

84. "Leading Paris Dressmakers Combine against Imitators," *New York Herald.* Undated clipping (c. mid-February 1913) in Paquin Publicity Album, Fashion Research Centre, Bath.

85. "Dressmaking Openings will Shortly be Held by Noted Paris Firms," *Philadelphia Inquirer* (18 February 1912): sec. 3, 3.

86. As a result of this illicit practice, pirated designs could be produced by copyists and even reach their purchasers before the "originals" were finished and photographed by legitimate couture houses. See "Chez nos grands couturiers," *Le Journal* (14 February 1911). Clipping in Paquin Publicity Album, Fashion Research Centre, Bath.

87. "Models Clearing House Suggested by Americans," *New York Herald* (20 February 1913): 4.

88. "Hold Back the New Styles," *New York Times* (25 February 1912): sec. 3, 1.

89. "I have no objection if my models are copied and the label indicates this, as for instance, 'copy of a Poiret Model,' and then if desired the firm's name selling the goods. But I protest against the use of false labels imitating my trade-mark with intent to deceive the wearer into believing that I made the article so labeled when I did not." Paul Poiret, "Warning Against False Labels," *Women's Wear* (14 October 1913): 3. See also the related statement by Poiret in "The Specialty Shops: Poiret Is Advised by a Friend Prominent in the Trade to Take Precautions for the Protection of his Models," *Women's Wear* (14 October 1913): 1, 6; the latter article was reprinted in "Poiret's Label," 3.

90. "Le Procès Callot Soeurs contre le 'Grand Chic'," *Echos de l'Exportation,* no. 83 (21 July 1912): 65.

91. "Il ne faut pas trop s'inspirer, pour tailler des 'patrons', des élégants modèles de nos grands couturiers," *Echos de l'Exportation,* no. 78 (7 May 1912): 17. Alexandra Palmer explains the nature of the *demi-toile* and points out its role in the counterfeiting process: "When a buyer ordered a model, a *toile* (the design made up in muslin), or a *patron à papier* (a paper pattern), included with it was a *reference.* The *reference* gave all the details and costs of the construction, yardage, and sources for textiles, trims, buttons and belts for the original. With this information, making a copy or knock-off was very easily accomplished as the template

was already purchased and the design house had no control over how it was used. The Chambre syndicale recognized that symmetrical *toiles* gave the buyer the possibility of cutting them in half [thereby producing a *demi-toile*] and generating more copies and profit while retaining the information needed in the original." Palmer, *Couture and Commerce,* pre-publication copy of book manuscript, 43.

92. "La Couture et la copie," *Echos de l'Exportation,* no. 90 (7 November 1912): 51.

93. Ibid., 51.

94. "Paris Dressmakers Withhold Models," *New York Times* (9 April 1914): 3.

95. Jules Huret, "150 Millions de frivolités: Le Rôle social d'une artiste de la mode," *La Vie Heureuse,* no. 5 (15 May 1912): 130–132.

96. Frank Morton Todd, *The Story of the Exposition, Being the Official History of the International Celebration Held at San Francisco in 1915 to Commemorate the Discovery of the Pacific Ocean and the Construction of the Panama Canal,* 5 vols. (New York: G. P. Putnam's Sons, 1921), I, 219.

97. Ibid., 220.

98. "Panama Pacific International Exposition San Francisco 1915. Résumé de principales observations du Comité Français des Expositions à l'Étranger." Brochure in Bancroft Library, University of California, Berkeley, Panama-Pacific International Exhibition Collection, Box 60, Folder "France, Jan.–Dec. 1913."

99. For the Kahn Law, see *Sixty-Third Congress* Sess. I. Chap. 14 (H.R. 7595, 18 September 1913), 112–113.

100. "French Opposition Shown to San Francisco Exhibit," *Christian Science Monitor* (28 March 1914). Clipping in the Bancroft Library, University of California, Berkeley, Panama-Pacific International Exhibition Collection, Box 60, Folder "France, Jan.–June 1914." See also "La Future Exposition Internationale dite Panama-Pacifique, à San Francisco," *L'Illustration,* no. 3707 (14 March 1914): 204–205.

101. According to the Patent Law Association of Washington,

> The law in effect grants a patent, trademark, copyright, etc., to every exhibitor who holds a foreign patent, trademark, copyright, etc., from the time his goods are dumped on the Exposition grounds to at least December 4, 1918.
>
> This protection is granted without application, without the production of his foreign patent, trademark, etc., without examination, without fee, without publication or notice of any kind to the public. . . .

> The penalty for invading the right is far more severe than for infringement of a regular United States patent . . .
>
> [The law] creates *copyright* property without reference to novelty or original authorship and may cover things long before known or used, or things which are public property or even things previously copyrighted. . . .
>
> It gives *trademark rights* to one who may have pirated the well-known mark of a domestic manufacturer.

"The Kahn Law." Brochure in Bancroft Library, University of California, Berkeley, Panama-Pacific International Exhibition Collection, Box 60, Folder "France, Jan.–Dec. 1913."

102. See the following materials in Ibid. Folder "France, Jan-Dec. 1914": "French Ambassador to Defend Alleged Fraud." Clipping, *San Francisco Chronicle* (22 February 1914); Ira E. Bennett, Telegram to Charles C. Moore (4 March 1914); Charles C. Moore, Letter to the director-in-chief (9 March 1914).

103. Todd, *The Story of the Exposition,* I, 276.

104. Ira E. Bennett, Telegram to Charles C. Moore (17 December 1913) in Bancroft Library, University of California, Berkeley, Panama-Pacific International Exhibition Collection, Box 60, Folder "France, Jan.–Dec. 1913."

105. For a vivid description of such practices by an insider, see Elizabeth Hawes, *Fashion is Spinach* (New York: Random House, 1938).

106. "La Couture et la copie," *Echos de l'Exportation,* no. 83 (21 July 1912): 65

107. Suzanne Joire was married to Jeanne Paquin's half-brother, Henri Joire; they joined the Paquin firm as partners in 1911. The tour took Suzanne Joire and the Paquin mannequins to New York, Philadelphia, Pittsburgh, Chicago, and Boston. See Suzanne Joire, "My Impressions of American Department Stores," *The Dry Goods Guide* 33, no. 6 (June 1914): 16.

108. Jeanne Paquin, quoted in Jean Laporte, "La Tournée du grand couturier," *Femina,* no. 321 (1 June 1914): 339. Subsequent citations in this paragraph are also from this article, unless otherwise noted.

109. In response to a rhetorical question about whether Paquin sent her entire spring collection to the United States as part of a sales campaign, the correspondent for *Vogue* answered facetiously, "Oh, no; for exhibition purposes only." "Paquin's Collection of Spring Models Begins its American Tour," *Vogue* 43, no. 9 (1 April 1914): 32.

110. Nevertheless, Paquin did acknowledge the commercial dimension of touring her dresses. When American clients begged her to sell them the models they had just seen parading before them, Paquin responded, "I was obliged to refuse them: I had undertaken with respect to the American commissioners not to sell anything directly. Everything had been sold in advance to one of them. This very condition structured the organization of my tour, because I did not want to do any harm whatsoever to my commissioners or to those who regularly sell my dresses." Jeanne Paquin, quoted in Laporte, "La Tournée," 342. The issue of how American buyers in Paris would be adversely affected if Paquin sold directly to customers in the United States was indeed raised before her mannequins departed; see "Paquin to Exhibit Here," *New York Times* (13 February 1914): 4; and the firm's response, "Paquin Won't Sell at Exhibit Here," *New York Times* (14 February 1914): 4.

111. Pierre Frondaie, *Aphrodite.* Program in Bibliothèque de l'Arsenal, Paris, Rf 65.199.

112. In his autobiography, Erté claimed that he himself, as Poiret's employee, had made all the costume designs for *Aphrodite.* Erté, *My Life/My Art*, 32.

113. J. G., "Théâtre de la Renaissance: Aphrodite" (19 March 1914). Unidentified clipping in Bibliothèque de l'Arsenal, Paris, Rf 65.199.

114. Ibid.

115. "Rodin chez Cora" (10 March 1914). Unidentified clipping in Bibliothèque de l'Arsenal, Paris, Rf 65.199.

116. Gaston Bellac, "L'Assistance—Mme Cora Laparcerie et R. Trebor reçoivent," Undated clipping in Bibliothèque de l'Arsenal, Paris, Rf 65.199.

117. Unidentified clipping (9 March 1914) in Bibliothèque de l'Arsenal, Paris, Rf 65.199.

118. Arsène Alexandre, "Un Vernissage au Théâtre de la Renaissance: 'L'Aphrodite de Rodin'" (11 April 1914). Unidentified clipping in Bibliothèque de l'Arsenal, Paris, Rf 65.199.

119. Walter Benjamin, "The Work of Art in the Age of Mechanical Reproduction," in *Illuminations,* trans. Harry Zohn (New York: Schocken Books, 1977), 217–251.

120. Leo Steinberg, "Rodin," in *Other Criteria: Confrontations with Twentieth-Century Art* (London: Oxford University Press, 1972), 330–331.

121. Jean Chatelain, "An Original in Sculpture," in *Rodin Rediscovered*, ed. Albert E. Elsen (Washington, DC: National Gallery of Art; Boston: New York Graphic Society, 1981), 277.

122. Steinberg, "Rodin," 361.

123. Notice on Poiret's couture house letterhead stationery reproduced in *Women's Wear* (14 October 1913): 3.

124. Herbert A. Howell, "The Print and Label Law," *University of Pennsylvania Law Review and American Law Register* 70, no. 2 (January 1922): 95.

125. The phrase is Peter Jaszi's in "Towards a Theory of Copyright: The Metamorphoses of 'Authorship,'" *Duke Law Journal*, no. 2 (1991): 455–502; see also Mark Rose, *Authors and Owners: The Invention of Copyright* (Cambridge, MA: Harvard University Press, 1993); Martha Woodmansee, *The Author, Art, and the Market: Rereading the History of Aesthetics* (New York: Columbia University Press, 1994); and Michel Foucault, "What Is an Author?" trans. Josué V. Harari (1979), repr. in *The Foucault Reader,* ed. Paul Rabinow (New York: Pantheon Books, 1984), 101–120. For my introduction to the wealth of issues that copyright law raises for understanding the visual arts, the decorative arts, and the status of the artist in the modern period, I am indebted to the work of Molly Nesbit: "What was an Author?" *Yale French Studies,* no. 73 (1988): 229–257; "Ready-Made Originals: The Duchamp Model," *October,* no. 37 (Summer 1986): 53–64; and "The Language of Industry," in *The Definitively Unfinished Marcel Duchamp,* ed. Thierry de Duve (Cambridge, MA: MIT Press, 1991), 351–384.

126. See Jaszi, "Towards a Theory of Copyright," 467.

127. Paul Goldstein, "Copyright," *Journal of the Copyright Society of the U.S.A.* 38 (1991): 1:6.

128. *Rules and Regulations for the Registration of Claims to Copyright,* Bulletin no. 15 (1910), 8, quoted in L. C. F. Oldfield, *The Law of Copyright* 2nd ed. (London: Butterworth & Co., 1912), 197.

129. Rocky Schmidt, "Designer Law: Fashioning a Remedy for Design Piracy," *UCLA Law Review* 30, no. 3 (April 1983): 867–868.

130. Paul Goldstein, *Copyright's Highway: From Gutenberg to the Celestial Jukebox* (New York: Hill & Wang, 1994), 10.

131. Russell J. DaSilva, "Droit Moral and the Amoral Copyright: A Comparison of Artists' Rights in France and the United States," *Bulletin of the Copyright Society of the U.S.A.* 28, no. 1 (October 1980): 7–12.

132. J. H. Reichman, "Design Protection in Domestic and Foreign Copyright Law: From the Berne Revision of 1948 to the Copyright Act of 1976," *Duke Law Journal* 1983, no. 6 (December 1983): 1156.

133. Ibid., 1158. Emphasis in original.

134. Claude A. Rouzaud, *Un Problème d'intérêt national: les industries de luxe.* Thèse pour le doctorat d'état, Université de Strasbourg, Faculté des Sciences politiques. (Paris: Librairie Sivey, 1946), 145.

135. "To Stop Pirating of Dress Fashions," *New York Times* (29 May 1914): 4.

Chapter 4

1. See Thomas A. P. van Leeuwen, *The Skyward Trend of Thought: Five Essays on the Metaphysics of the American Skyscraper* ('s-Gravenhage: AHA Books, 1986); and Reyner Banham, *A Concrete Atlantis: U.S. Industrial Building and European Modern Architecture 1900–1925* (Cambridge, MA: MIT Press, 1986).

2. Wanda M. Corn, *The Great American Thing: Modern Art and National Identity, 1915–1935* (Berkeley: University of California Press, 1999), 55.

3. Ibid., 66.

4. Here I take issue with Richard Martin's text in Metropolitan Museum of Art, *Cubism and Fashion* exh. cat., in which the relationship between fashion and art during the early twentieth century is largely confined to a formal comparison between changes in the design and construction of women's clothing on one hand and the innovations of cubist imagery on the other: "In short," Martin writes, "the same indeterminacy of forms that cubism fostered in painting, sculpture, and collage obtains in fashion during the same years of innovation, albeit fashion's process is more attenuated" (16). Nevertheless, Martin is alert to the possibility that the equations repeatedly drawn throughout his catalogue might be open to oversimplification. In his conclusion he condemns "the ridiculous premise that an object of clothing is the same as fashion itself" (153). He writes, "Do not, under any circumstances, use this book recklessly; do not believe in art and fashion simply on the evidences of some select relationships in one art movement. The three fundamental unities I pose—flatness and the presence of the cylinder along with the plane, denial of 'representation' in its accustomed Albertian or volumetric space, and the indeterminacy of forms—are there to be

accepted or rejected . . . nowhere wholly documented, nowhere proved other than as evidenced in the works" (155).

5. "Le Syndicat de Défense de la Grande Couture Française et des Industries s'y Rattachant," *Le Style Parisien,* no. 4 (November 1915): n.p.; Edna Woolman Chase and Ilka Chase, *Always in Vogue* (New York: Doubleday, 1954), 108–110; Caroline Seebohm, *The Man Who Was Vogue: The Life and Times of Condé Nast* (New York: Viking, 1982), 84, 88. Although basing her account on that of Edna Woolman Chase, who became editor of *Vogue* in 1914, Seebohm stresses *Vogue's* role in the formation of the Syndicat even more than does Chase. Seebohm suggests that the organization resulted from a meeting between Poiret, Chase, Condé Nast (*Vogue's* publisher after he purchased the magazine in 1909), and Ortiz. Formerly general manager of the New York branch of a French art publishing company, Ortiz was hired by Nast in 1914 and eventually became head of the Condé Nast company activities in Europe. On his role in the establishment of the Syndicat, see Chase and Chase, *Always in Vogue,* 109.

6. *The 1915 Mode as Shown by Paris, Panama Pacific International Exposition* (New York: Condé Nast, n.d. [1915]), with a slipcase and a cover drawing by Georges Lepape.

7. Seebohm, *The Man Who Was Vogue,* 133, 170–174.

8. Advertisement for Vogue Pattern Service, *Vogue* 46, no. 7 (1 October 1915).

9. "Paris Dressmakers in Protective Union," *New York Times* (24 October 1915), sec. 3, 9. As Andrew Perchuk pointed out to me in personal communication, the fact that the Syndicat planned to copyright each model demonstrates that its members had already accepted the primacy of the copy, a point to which I will return.

10. "To Protect Vogue's Originality," *Vogue* 44, no. 10 (15 November 1914): 51. See also Chase and Chase, *Always in Vogue,* 140.

11. "Projet d'organisation de la copie et de la reproduction des modèles des Grands Couturiers," *Les Élégances Parisiennes* (August 1916): 70.

12. See for example "Our Buyers Indignant," *New York Times* (12 November 1915): 4.

13. "Worth Declares America Is Right," *New York Times* (20 December 1912): 12.

14. Ibid.

15. Paul Poiret, "From the Trenches," *Harper's Bazar* 50, no. 2 (February 1915): 11. For an American perspective on the "'American styles for American women'

movement," see "Paris May See End of Style Control," *New York Times* (6 August 1914): 15.

16. "The Story of the Fashion Fête," *Vogue* 44, no. 9 (1 November 1914): 122.

17. Emily Post, "Where Fashionables and Fashion Met," *Vogue* 44, no. 11 (1 December 1914): 35–37.

18. Chase and Chase, *Always in Vogue,* 117–126. See also Seebohm, *The Man Who Was Vogue,* 91–96.

19. "New York Fashions Are Adjudged Smart," *Vogue* 44, no. 11 (14 December 1914): 38–48.

20. "The Story of the Fashion Fête," 37.

21. "Fashion Centres at War," *New York Times* (3 February 1915): 11.

22. Paul Poiret, quoted in "First News of French Fashion Syndicate's Official Plans," *New York Times* (23 January 1916): Section 6, 2.

23. For my discussion of this episode I am indebted to Kenneth E. Silver, *Esprit de Corps,* 167–185. Quotations in the present paragraph relating to what Silver refers to as the Poiret Affair are from these pages of his book, unless otherwise noted.

24. Salon d'Antin, *L'Art moderne en France* exh. cat. (Paris, n.d.). For the dates of this exhibition and much other relevant documentation, particularly about Picasso's participation, see Judith Cousins and Hélène Seckel, "Chronology of *Les Demoiselles d'Avignon,* 1907 to 1939," in William Rubin, Hélène Seckel, and Judith Cousins, *Les Demoiselles d'Avignon,* Studies in Modern Art, 3 (New York: Museum of Modern Art, 1994), 164–170. The review quoted here is by Michel Georges-Michel, "L'Art 'Montparnasse,' ou une peinture trop 'moderne,'" *L'Excelsior* (23 July 1916), quoted in translation in Cousins and Seckel, "Chronology of *Les Demoiselles d'Avignon,*" 168–169.

25. See "De l'art français et des influences qu'il ne doit pas subir," *La Renaissance Politique, Économique, Littéraire et Artistique* 5, no. 19 (15 September 1917): 11–25.

26. Silver, *Esprit de Corps,* 181.

27. "First News of French Fashion Syndicate's Official Plans," sec. 6, 2.

28. Paul Poiret, cable message, published in "Mrs. Galt's Gowns Cause Paris Row," *New York Times* (20 November 1915): 6.

29. Ibid., 6.

30. Ibid., 6.

31. "Fabrics with Broad Stripes Popular for Spring," *New York Times* (13

February 1916): Fashion sec., 3. On internal dissention within the Syndicat and its impact on the American market, see also "Predict Failure of Poiret's Plan," *New York Times* (15 January 1916): 5.

32. "Poiret About to Quit?" *New York Times* (23 January 1916): sec. 2, 3.

33. "Paris Overtures to our Importers," *New York Times* (6 February 1916): 5.

34. Seebohm, *The Man Who Was Vogue*, 99. See also Chase and Chase, *Always in Vogue,* 126–127.

35. "Paris Dressmakers in Protective Union," sec. 3, 9. Here the play is described as a one-act comedy, but in another article, "Pet Animals Figure in Winter Styles," *New York Times* (23 November 1915): 5, it was described as "a comedietta in two acts." The latter article is the more reliable as it reported on the play, *Betty's Trousseau,* after it took place.

36. "Paris Dressmakers in Protective Union," sec. 3, 9.

37. "Pet Animals Figure in Winter's Styles," 5.

38. Roger Boutet de Monvel, "Fashioning our First French Fashion Fête," *Vogue* 45, no. 12 (15 December 1915): 35.

39. Before coming to New York, Duchamp had already made several "assisted" readymades (although they had not yet been designated as such), in which he manipulated the form of mass produced objects, including *Bicycle Wheel* (1913) and *Pharmacy* (1914), which he later described as "a cheap reproduction of a winter evening landscape, which I called 'Pharmacy' after adding two small dots, one red and one yellow, in the horizon." Marcel Duchamp, "Apropos of 'Readymades,'" a talk delivered at the Museum of Modern Art, New York, in 1961 that was first published in 1966 and reprinted in Marcel Duchamp, *Salt Seller: The Writings of Marcel Duchamp (Marchand du Sel),* ed. Michel Sanouillet and Elmer Peterson (New York: Oxford University Press, 1973), 141.

40. Marcel Duchamp, Letter to Suzanne Duchamp (15 January 1916), in the original French and in English translation in *Affectionately, Marcel: The Selected Correspondence of Marcel Duchamp,* ed. Francis M. Naumann and Hector Obalk, trans. Jill Taylor (Ghent: Ludion Press, 2000), 43–44.

41. Molly Nesbit, "His Common Sense," *Artforum* 33, no. 2 (October 1994): 93. See also Molly Nesbit and Naomi Sawelson-Gorse, "Concept of Nothing: New Notes by Marcel Duchamp and Walter Arensberg," in *The Duchamp Effect,* ed. Martha Buskirk and Mignon Nixon (Cambridge, MA: MIT Press, 1995), 131–175.

42. For a discussion of this exhibition at the Bourgeois Galleries, see Thierry de Duve, *Kant after Duchamp.* (Cambridge, MA: MIT Press, 1996), 102, n. 22.

43. Duchamp, quoted by Fernand Léger, in Calvin Tomkins, *Duchamp: A Biography* (New York: Henry Holt, 1996), 137. A variation on this phrasing is found in Duchamp, *Salt Seller,* 160. See also Doïna Lemny, "Maurice et Morice: Chronique d'une amitié," in *Brancusi & Duchamp: Regards historiques.* Les carnets de l'Atelier Brancusi (Paris: Centre Pompidou, 2000), 24.

44. Pierre Cabanne, *Dialogues with Marcel Duchamp,* trans. Ron Padgett (New York: Da Capo, 1987), 47–48.

45. Francis M. Naumann, *New York Dada 1915–23* (New York: Harry N. Abrams, 1994), 22.

46. Duchamp, quoted in *Dialogues with Marcel Duchamp,* 52. For a fascinating account of Arensberg's efforts at cryptography and their impact on Duchamp, see Nesbit and Sawelson-Gorse, "Concept of Nothing."

47. Duchamp, quoted in Cabanne, *Dialogues with Marcel Duchamp,* 40.

48. Nesbit and Sawelson-Gorse, "Concept of Nothing," 137.

49. Ibid., 150.

50. On Bourdieu's comparison between the couture label and the artist's signature, see ch. 1.

51. Numerous possibilities for their acquaintance might be suggested, beginning with the fact that at the Salon d'Automne of 1912, Poiret had seen and purchased five paintings and a clock from a decorative arts ensemble known as the *Maison Cubiste* in which a painting by Duchamp was included. Poiret also owned works by Léger and Brancusi, the two artists with whom Duchamp visited the Salon de la Locomotion Aérienne in Paris that same fall. Clearly, Duchamp was at the time closely associated with vanguard artists in whom Poiret showed substantial interest. Later, during the teens and early 1920s in New York, as well as Paris, Duchamp was closely associated with Francis Picabia and Man Ray, both of whom had connections with Poiret. According to Billy Klüver and Julie Martin, Picabia "had close contacts with Poiret," who owned two of the artist's paintings. Moreover, Picabia's first wife, Gabrielle Buffet-Picabia, represented the French fashion industry in New York in 1920 and the following year, probably in July, she introduced Man Ray to Poiret in Paris. At the time Man Ray was staying in the Paris apartment of Duchamp's companion Yvonne Chastel, where Duchamp was also living. Again according to Klüver and Martin, "Chastel was now designer

Paul Poiret's agent in London and was setting up a shop for his Martine designs there." Given all these intersecting trajectories, it seems likely that Duchamp would have met Poiret at some point during the teens or early twenties. But if their social or professional milieux might have briefly intersected, it seems unlikely that they themselves would have found much common ground. On Poiret and the *Maison Cubiste,* see Troy, *Modernism and the Decorative Arts in France,* 79 ff, 116–119. On the connections of Man Ray, Picabia, and Chastel to Poiret, see Billy Klüver and Julie Martin, "Man Ray, Paris," in Foresta et al., *Perpetual Motif,* 94, 96, 132 n. 8.

52. "Duchamp appropriated the term [readymade] from its use in the clothing industry (readymade garments were those that could be purchased off the rack, as opposed to those that were custom made)." Francis M. Naumann, *Marcel Duchamp: The Art of Making Art in the Age of Mechanical Reproduction* (Ghent: Ludion Press, 1999), 299. See also André Gervais, "Note sur le terme Readymade (ou Ready-made)," *Étant Donné* 1 (1999): 118–121.

53. "The young Duchamp would have had many opportunities to witness the activities of his father, who was frequently called upon to authenticate the validity of legal documents, deeds, trusts, real estate transactions, and property settlements. After these papers have been carefully reviewed, the notary applies his signature over the surface of a small-denomination postage stamp (a practice still followed in France today), thereby diminishing the potential for forgery and elevating the status of the document to legal tender." Naumann, *Marcel Duchamp,* 20–21.

54. Molly Nesbit, "Ready-Made Originals," 62.

55. Marcel Duchamp, "Apropos of 'Readymades,'" *Art and Artists* 1, no. 4 (July 1966): 47.

56. Ibid., 47. Here Duchamp not only discounted the singularity of the readymade, he alluded to the fact that many of the objects designated as such in the late teens and early twenties had since been lost; most of those in existence at the time he made this statement were recreations or replicas, not "originals."

57. For a discussion of the possible references embedded in this name, including the manufacturer of urinals and other plumbing fixtures, J. L. Mott Iron Works, and the popular comic strip, *Mutt and Jeff,* see William A. Camfield, *Marcel Duchamp: Fountain* (Houston: The Menil Collection, 1989), esp. 21–24.

58. Molly Nesbit, "Ready-Made Originals," 63.

59. de Duve, *Kant after Duchamp,* 85. De Duve quotes Duchamp's question, which is from *The White Box,* as published in Duchamp, *Salt Seller,* 74.

60. Marcel Duchamp, quoted in Staatliches Museum Schwerin. *Marcel Duchamp Respirateur* exh. cat. (Ostfildern: Hatje Cantz Verlag, 1995), 58.

61. Nancy Ring, "New York Dada and the Crisis of Masculinity: Man Ray, Francis Picabia, and Marcel Duchamp in the United States, 1913–1921" (Ph.D. dissertation, Northwestern University, 1991), 225, 226–227.

62. Amelia Jones, *Postmodernism and the En-gendering of Marcel Duchamp* (Cambridge, MA: Cambridge University Press, 1994), 147.

63. Indeed, Rosine is itself a modified version of the name Rose and, as invocations of the flower, both of them were appropriately applied to perfumes.

64. This point is convincingly argued by Ring, "New York Dada and the Crisis of Masculinity," and Jones, *Postmodernism and the En-gendering of Marcel Duchamp.*

65. Jones, *Postmodernism and the En-gendering of Marcel Duchamp,* 172–173.

66. Paul Poiret advertisement, *Vogue* 48, no. 7 (1 October 1916): 113.

67. *Les Modèles de Paul Poiret Printemps 1917* (Paris: Poiret Inc., 1917). I am indebted to the late Alan Suddon for introducing me to this publication.

68. Cécile Amiel, "Paul Poiret: Artist and Innovator," in *Les Modèles de Paul Poiret,* n.p.

69. Advertisement for *Le* [sic] *Modeles de Paul Poiret Printemps 1917* in *Vanity Fair* 8, no. 1 (March 1917): 9.

70. Ibid.

71. "A Translation of Monsieur Poiret's Letter to the Women of America," in *Les Modèles de Paul Poiret,* n.p.

72. Swinburne Hale, Letter to William G. Hale (19 January 1917). I am grateful to Mitzi Maras and Stephen Maras for recognizing the significance of this letter for my research and for offering it to me shortly after it came into their hands. The prices given in the brochure for Poiret's "genuine reproductions" range from $7.50 for "Laveuse," a "dainty and piquant summer skirt for town or country," to $115 for "Caleche," described as "the ideal summer wrap for all sophisticated occasions." Of course Poiret Inc. would have to pay Max Grab for the costs of manufacturing and distributing Poiret's "genuine reproductions," but even so, the firm expected to make a substantial profit on sales of these authorized copies to American consumers. On the New York branch of Poiret's business, see also

"Une Succersale de Poiret à New-York," *Les Élégances Parisiennes* (March 1917): 184.

73. The Museum of the City of New York has in its collection one coat with an "authorized reproduction" label of the kind illustrated in Poiret Inc.'s 1917 brochure, as noted in Musée de la Mode et du Costume, *Paul Poiret et Nicole Groult,* 242.

74. See the description of merchandising planned for New York in the March 1917 issue of *Les Élégances Parisiennes* (84), as quoted in Musée de la Mode et du Costume, *Paul Poiret et Nicole Groult,* 84.

75. This characterization is from Alice Mackrell, *Coco Chanel,* 28. See also Victor Margueritte, *The Bachelor Girl,* trans. Hugh Barnaby (New York: A. A. Knopf, 1923).

76. Paul Poiret, remarks published in *Forum* (1922), quoted in Musée de la Mode et du Costume, *Paul Poiret et Nicole Groult,* 194.

77. Quoted in Edmonde Charles-Roux, *Chanel and Her World* (New York: Vendome Press, 1981), 156. Along these same lines, Claudia Kidwell and Margaret Christian observe, in *Suiting Everyone,* 189, "In the twenties French fashions were coveted, and although every American woman could not have a Paris gown, every woman could have a copy or an adaptation, at fairly reasonable cost, of the creations of the great French couturiers. It had been the genius of Coco Chanel to make simple, functional clothing the prevailing fashion, thus enabling American mass manufacture to bring an unprecedented equality to the dress of American women. Almost any woman in America could buy a 'Chanel' at prices ranging from $3.75 to $375."

78. Paul Poiret, quoted in Charles-Roux, *Chanel and Her World,* 157.

79. See the description in G. D., "Un Théâtre dans une maison de couture," *Le Gaulois* (4 June 1921). Clipping in Bibliothèque Historique de la Ville de Paris, 79: Mode-Couture Paul Poiret.

80. Georges Oudard, "Lettres: Le Jardin désert," *Opinion* (16 July 1921). Clipping in Bibliothèque de l'Arsenal, Paris, Rt 4278. This file also contains other clippings pertinent to the activities of L'Oasis on which I have drawn for this discussion.

81. Poiret. *My First Fifty Years,* 250.

82. Poiret, *Art et phynance,* 49–50.

83. Hôtel Drouot, *Catalogue des Tableaux Modernes* sale cat. (Paris, 18 November

1925). For an overview of the collection as a whole, see also the catalogue of its exhibition two years earlier at the Galerie Barbazanges, *La Collection particulière de Paul Poiret* exh. cat. (Paris, 26 April–12 May 1923).

84. Paul Poiret, in *L'Art et la Mode* (11 January 1927), quoted in Musée de la Mode et du Costume, *Paul Poiret et Nicole Groult,* 206.

85. On Vionnet's labels as only one aspect of her extensive efforts to prevent copying, see Betty Kirke, *Madeleine Vionnet* (San Francisco: Chronicle Books, 1991), 221–223.

Conclusion

1. Advertisement for Madeleine Vionnet, *Women's Wear* (2 August 1921): 47. This ad is reproduced in Kirke, *Madeleine Vionnet,* 222. I am indebted to Kirke's book for the following discussion of Vionnet's concerns about copying and her extraordinary efforts to protect her designs.

2. Jacqueline Demornex, *Madeleine Vionnet,* trans. Augusta Audubert (New York: Rizzoli, 1991), 61.

3. Ibid., 65.

4. Kirke, *Madeleine Vionnet,* 16.

5. "Paris Couturieres Tried on Charge of Copying Modes Made by Mlle. Vionnet," *Women's Wear* (24 December 1921): 2, 23. The department stores were Franklin Simon & Co., Bergdorf Goodman, and Saks & Company (the latter had been accused only of advertising dresses in the so-called Vionnet style).

6. "Vionnet Brings Action Against Butterick Co.," *Women's Wear* (30 January 1922): 1.

7. "Paris Anti-Copyist Society Renews its Activities," *Women's Wear* (28 February 1923): 1, 20.

8. "Sliding Price Scale for Boex Copies of Vionnet Models," *Women's Wear* (21 November 1921): 2, 21.

9. Amy de la Haye and Shelley Tobin, *Chanel: The Couturière at Work* (Woodstock, NY: Overlook Press, 1994), 57.

10. Ibid.

11. Madeleine Vionnet, quoted in Kirke, *Madeleine Vionnet,* 129.

12. Kirke, *Madeleine Vionnet,* 129.

13. Ibid., 133.

14. Recently, as appropriation itself has begun to be historicized, art historians seem to be retrospectively reinventing Sturtevant as a precursor of, if not an acknowledged inspiration for, those who introduced appropriation as an art practice and an art discourse in the 1980s. But the question remains: If appropriation did not yet exist in the 1960s, what exactly was Sturtevant doing when she made and exhibited copies of works by other artists—and what allowed her practice to qualify as art if the discursive conditions for describing it as such had not yet been created? On Sturtevant, see in particular Bess Cutler [Gallery], *Sturtevant Drawings 1988–1965* exh. cat., (New York, 1988); Württembergischer Kunstverein, *Sturtevant* exh. cat. (Stuttgart, 1992); and Francis M. Naumann, text in Curt Marcus Gallery, *Apropos of Marcel: The Art of Making Art After Duchamp in the Age of Mechanical Reproduction* exh. cat. (New York, 1999), 18–22. I am grateful to Andrew Perchuk for several stimulating discussions of Sturtevant's work and for making publications about Sturtevant available to me.

15. In addition to the readymades discussed in ch. 4, see for example Duchamp's *Tzanck Check* of 1919 and his *Monte Carlo Bond* of 1924, as well as David Joselit's discussion of these and other readymades in tandem with Duchamp's investigations of language, which Joselit reads together as a commentary on the nature of the self and representation under the conditions of capitalism. David Joselit, *Infinite Regress: Marcel Duchamp 1910–1941* (Cambridge, MA: MIT Press, 1998), ch. 2, "Between Reification and Regression: Readymades and Words."

Sources Consulted

"A Gand: La Section française de l'Exposition Universelle a été inaugurée officiellement hier." *L'Intransigeant* (7 May 1913). Clipping in Paquin Publicity Album, Fashion Research Centre, Bath.

"A propos de la jupe-culotte." *Le Matin* (28 February 1911). Clipping in Paquin Publicity Album, Fashion Research Centre, Bath.

An Act providing for the free importation of articles intended for foreign buildings and exhibits at the Panama-Pacific International Exposition, and for the protection of foreign exhibitors. U.S. House. 63rd Cong., 1st Sess., H.R. 7595, 112–113, Chap. 14 (18 September 1913).

Adams, Samuel Hopkins. "The Dishonest Paris Label: How American Women are Being Fooled by a Country-Wide Swindle." *Dress: The Journal of the Costume Society of America* 4 (1978): 17–23. Originally published in *Ladies' Home Journal* (March 1913).

Adolphus, F. *Some Memories of Paris.* New York: Henry Holt, 1895.

Agra. "Les Milles et quelques nuits de la saison." *Femina,* no. 276 (15 July 1912): 421.

Albright-Knox Art Gallery. *Sonia Delaunay: A Retrospective.* Exh. cat. Buffalo, 1980.

Alexandre, Arsène. *Les Reines de l'aiguille: modistes et couturières (étude parisienne).* Paris: Théophile Belin, 1902.

————. "Un Vernissage au Théâtre de la Renaissance: 'L'Aphrodite de Rodin'" (11 April 1914). Clipping in Bibliothèque de l'Arsenal, Paris, Rf 65.199.

Almanach des lettres et des arts. Paris: Martine, n.d. [1916].

Anderson, Perry. *Lineages of the Absolutist State.* London: N.L.B., 1974.

Appel, Joseph H. *The Business Biography of John Wanamaker, Founder and Builder.* New York: Macmillan, 1930.

Arren, Jules. *Comment il faut faire de la publicité.* Paris: Pierre Lafitte, 1912.

Assouline, Pierre. *An Artful Life: A Biography of D. H. Kahnweiler, 1884–1979.* Translated by Charles Ruas. New York: Fromm International Publishing Corporation, 1991.

"Au Théâtre des Arts (Saison 1910–1911): Les Projets de M. J. Rouché." *Comoedia Illustré* 2, no. 23 (1 September 1910): 683.

"Au Théâtre: La Rue de la Paix." Undated clipping in Bibliothèque de l'Arsenal, Paris, Rf 62.276.

Babin, Gustave. "Une Leçon d'élégance dans un parc." *L'Illustration,* no. 3515 (9 July 1910): 21.

Bachollet, Raymond, Daniel Bordet, and Anne-Claude Lelieur. *Paul Iribe.* With a preface by Edmonde Charles-Roux. Paris: Denoël, 1982.

Bagnolet. "Les Festes de Bacchus." *Revue Musicale S.I.M.* 8, no. 11 (November 1912): 41–45.

Banham, Reyner. *A Concrete Atlantis: U.S. Industrial Building and European Modern Architecture 1900–1925.* Cambridge, MA: MIT Press, 1986.

Barthes, Roland. *Système de la mode.* Paris: Editions du Seuil, 1967; *The Fashion System.* Translated by Matthew Ward and Richard Howard. New York: Hill & Wang, 1983. Reprint, Berkeley: University of California Press, 1990.

Baudelaire, Charles. "The Painter of Modern Life." In *Baudelaire: Selected Writings on Art and Literature.* Translated by P. E. Charvet. London: Penguin Books, 1972, 390–435.

"Beau Brummels of the Brush," *Vogue* 43, no. 14 (15 June 1914): 35–37, 88.

Bellac, Gaston. "L'Assistance—Mme Cora Laparcerie et R. Trebor reçoivent . . ." Undated clipping in Bibliothèque de l'Arsenal, Paris, Rf 65.199.

Benjamin and Johnes. Advertisement. *Harper's Bazar* 49, no. 3 (March 1914).

Benjamin, Roger, et al. *Orientalism: Delacroix to Klee.* Art Gallery of New South Wales. Exh. cat. Sydney, 1997.

Benjamin, Walter. "The Work of Art in the Age of Mechanical Reproduction." In *Illuminations.* Translated by Harry Zohn. New York: Schocken Books, 1977, 217–251.

Bennett, Ira E. Telegram to Charles C. Moore (17 December 1913). In the Bancroft Library, University of California, Berkeley, Panama-Pacific International Exhibition Collection, Box 60, Folder "France, Jan.–Dec. 1913."

———. Telegram to Charles C. Moore (4 March 1914). In the Bancroft Library, University of California, Berkeley, Panama-Pacific International Exhibition Collection, Box 60, Folder "France, Jan.–Dec. 1913."

Benson, Susan Porter. *Counter Cultures: Saleswomen, Managers, and Consumers in American Department Stores 1890–1940.* Urbana: University of Illinois Press, 1986.

———. "Palace of Consumption and Machine for Selling: The American Department Store, 1880–1940." *Radical History Review,* no. 21 (Fall 1979): 199–221.

Berthail, Marie. *Bernard Naudin: Catalogue raisonné de l'oeuvre gravé.* Paris: Librairie Auguste Blaizot, 1979.

———. "Bernard Naudin 1876–1946: Recherches sur sa vie et son oeuvre." 2 vols. Doctorat de troisième cycle, Université de Paris-Sorbonne, Institut d'Art et d'archéologie, 1978.

Bess Cutler [Gallery]. *Sturtevant Drawings 1988–1965.* Exh. cat. New York, 1988.

Bibliothèque Forney. *Paul Iribe: Précurseur de l'art déco.* Exh. cat. Paris, 1983.

Bidou, Henry. "Le Bon ton." *Gazette du Bon Ton* 1, no. 1 (November 1912): 1–4.

———. "Le Dîner de la Gazette du Bon Ton." *Gazette du Bon Ton* 2, no. 7 (July 1914): 225–228.

Blanche, Jacques Emile. "L'Harmonie des contrastes: blanc & noir, noir & blanc." *Femina,* no. 299 (1 July 1913): 357–364.

Blau, Eve, and Nancy J. Troy, introduction to *Cubism and Architecture.* Edited by Eve Blau and Nancy J. Troy. Montreal: Canadian Centre for Architecture; Cambridge, MA: MIT Press, 1997.

Blum, Lise-Léon. "Le Goût au théâtre." *Gazette du Bon Ton* 1, no. 6 (April 1913): 185–188.

———. "Le Goût au théâtre." *Gazette du Bon Ton* 2, no. 3 (March 1914): 101–104.

Bonnelle, Madeleine, and Marie-José Meneret. *Sem.* Périgueux: Pierre Fanlac, 1979.

Bonwit Teller. Advertisement. *New York Times* (19 October 1913): 11.

Bourdieu, Pierre, and Yvette Delsaut. "Le Couturier et sa griffe: contribution à une théorie de la magie." *Actes de la recherche en sciences sociales,* no. 1 (1975): 7–36.

Boutet de Monvel, Roger. "Fashioning Our First French Fashion Fête." *Vogue* 45, no. 12 (15 December 1915): 35.

Bowlby, Rachel. *Shopping with Freud.* New York: Routledge, 1993.

Breward, Christopher. "Femininity and Consumption: The Problem of the Late Nineteenth-Century Fashion Journal." *Journal of Design History* 7 (1994): 71–89.

Brooke, M.E. "In the Boudoir." *Playgoer and Society Illustrated.* n.s. 8, no. 45 (June–July 1913): 83.

Butler, Judith. *Bodies that Matter: On the Discursive Limits of "Sex."* New York: Routledge, 1993.

———. *Gender Trouble: Feminism and the Subversion of the Body.* New York: Routledge, 1990.

Cabanne, Pierre. *Dialogues with Marcel Duchamp.* Translated by Ron Padgett. New York: Henry N. Abrams, 1994.

Camfield, William A. *Marcel Duchamp: Fountain.* Houston: The Menil Collection, 1989.

Castle, Charles. *Model Girl.* Newton Abbot, England: David & Charles, 1977.

Celant, Germano, editor. *Looking at Fashion.* Exh. cat. Florence: Biennale di Firenze, 1996.

Çelik, Zeynep. *Displaying the Orient: Architecture of Islam at Nineteenth-Century World's Fairs.* Berkeley: University of California Press, 1992.

Chaney, David. "The Department Store as a Cultural Form." *Theory, Culture & Society* 1, no. 3 (1983): 22–31.

Chapon, François. *Mystère et splendeurs de Jacques Doucet.* Paris: Éditions J.-C. Lattès, 1984.

Charles-Roux, Edmonde. *Chanel and Her World.* New York: Vendome Press, 1981.

Chase, Edna Woolman, and Ilka Chase. *Always in Vogue.* New York: Doubleday, 1954.

Chatelain, Jean. "An Original in Sculpture." In *Rodin Rediscovered.* Edited by Albert E. Elsen. Washington, DC: National Gallery of Art; Boston: New York Graphic Society, 1981: 275–282.

"Chez nos grands couturiers." *Le Journal* (14 February 1911). Clipping in Paquin Publicity Album. Fashion Research Centre, Bath.

"Chez Spinelly." *Harper's Bazaar* 51, no. 8 (August 1916): 41.

Clayson, Hollis. *Painted Love: Prostitution in French Art of the Impressionist Era.* New Haven: Yale University Press, 1991.

Coleman, Elizabeth Ann. *The Opulent Era: Fashions of Worth, Doucet and Pingat.* Brooklyn Museum. Exh. cat. New York, 1989.

Comité français des expositions à l'étranger. *Exposition Internationale des Industries et du Travail de Turin, 1911. Catalogue spécial officiel de la section française.* Paris, 1911.

"Comment New York s'amuse dans la morte-saison." *Echos de l'Exportation,* no. 87 (21 September 1912): 14.

Cooper, Douglas, and Gary Tinterow. *The Essential Cubism: Braque, Picasso & Their Friends, 1907–1920.* Exh. cat. London: Tate Gallery, 1983.

"Copyrighting Clothes." *Vogue* 45, no. 3 (1 February 1915): 17, 100.

Corn, Wanda M. *The Great American Thing: Modern Art and National Identity, 1915–1935.* Berkeley: University of California Press, 1999.

Cornu, Paul. *Bernard Naudin: Dessinateur & graveur.* n.pl.: Les Cahiers du Centre, quatrième série, March 1912.

———. "L'Art de la robe." *Art et Décoration* 29 (April 1911): 101–118.

"Costumes: New York—Dates of lectures to be Given by M. Poiret." *Women's Wear* (24 September 1913), 1.

"Costumes: Paul Poiret Criticizes the Commercialization and Capitalization of his Visit to this Country." *Women's Wear* (22 September 1913), 1, 7.

Cottington, David. *Cubism in the Shadow of War: The Avant-Garde and Politics in Paris 1905–1914.* New Haven: Yale University Press, 1998.

"La Couture et la copie." *Echos de l'Exportation,* no. 83 (21 July 1912): 65.

"La Couture et la copie." *Echos de l'Exportation,* no. 90 (7 November 1912): 51.

Cydalise. "La Culotte et la femme." *Madame & Monsieur* 7 année, no. 195 (10 March 1911): 1463–1466.

D., G. "Un Théâtre dans une maison de couture." *Le Gaulois* (4 June 1921). Clipping in Bibliothèque Historique de la Ville de Paris, 79: Mode-Couture Paul Poiret.

D., R. "Le Minaret: La Soirée." Undated clipping in Bibliothèque de l'Arsenal, Paris, Rf 70.593.

D'Yvelet, Jean. "La Section française à l'exposition de Bruxelles." *Le Journal* (6 June 1910): 3.

Daix, Pierre, and Joan Rosselet. *Le Cubisme de Picasso: Catalogue raisonné de l'oeuvre peint, des papiers collés et des assemblages, 1907–1916.* Neuchâtel: Ides et Calendes, 1979.

Daly, Ann. "Isadora Duncan and the Distinction of Dance." *American Studies* 35, no. 1 (1994): 5–23.

"Dame Nature Dresses." *The Sketch* 77, no. 992 (31 January 1912): X.

DaSilva, Russell J. "Droit Moral and the Amoral Copyright: A Comparison of Artists' Rights in France and the United States." *Bulletin of the Copyright Society of the U.S.A.* 28, no. 1 (October 1980): 1–58.

Davis, Shane Adler. "Lucien Vogel." *Costume: The Journal of the Costume Society* 12 (1978): 74–82.

Day, Susan. *Louis Süe: Architectures*. Brussels: Pierre Mardaga, 1985.

de Duve, Thierry. *Kant after Duchamp*. Cambridge, MA: MIT Press, 1996.

de la Haye, Amy, and Shelley Tobin. *Chanel: The Couturière at Work*. Woodstock, NY: Overlook Press, 1994.

"De l'art français et des influences qu'il ne doit pas subir." *La Renaissance Politique, Economique, Littéraire et Artistique* 5, no. 9 (15 September 1917): 11–25.

Delarue-Mardrus, Lucie. "La Mille et deuxième nuit chez le grand couturier." *Femina*, no. 253 (1 August 1911): 415.

Delini, Jules. "Le Minaret de Jacques Richepin à la Renaissance." *Comoedia* (18 March 1913). Clipping in Bibliothèque de l'Arsenal, Paris, Rf 70.593.

Demournex, Jacqueline. *Madeleine Vionnet*. Translated by Augusta Audubert. New York: Rizzoli, 1991.

Derrida, Jacques. "Signature Event Context" (1977). Translated by Samuel Weber and Jeffrey Mehlman. In Jacques Derrida, *Limited Inc.* Evanston, IL: Northwestern University Press, 1988, 1–23.

Dieudonné, Robert. "La Soirée parisienne: 'La Rue de la Paix,' Commentaires anodins sur une pièce d'un parisiannisme échevelé." Undated clipping in Bibliothèque de l'Arsenal, Paris, Rf 62.276.

"Drecoll and Beer Show Conservative Styles." *New York Times* (15 October 1911): sec. 8, 4.

"Dress on the Stage: A Disappointing Paris Play. Daring Colour Contrasts." *Daily Mail* (23 January 1912). Clipping, Paquin Publicity Album, Fashion Research Centre, Bath.

Dreyfus, Robert. *Petite histoire de la revue de fin d'année*. Paris: Charpentier et Fasquelle, 1909.

Duchamp, Marcel. *Salt Seller: The Writings of Marcel Duchamp (Marchand du Sel)*. Edited by Michel Sanouillet and Elmer Peterson. New York: Oxford University Press, 1973.

———. In *Affectionately, Marcel: The Selected Correspondence of Marcel Duchamp.* Edited by Francis M. Naumann and Hector Obalk. Translated by Jill Taylor. Ghent: Ludion Press, 2000.

Duff Gordon, Lady ("Lucile"). *Discretions and Indiscretions.* New York: Frederick A. Stokes, 1932.

Dulac, Jean. "Aux Capucines: 'Avec le sourire,' Revue en 3 tableaux de MM. R. Dieudonné et C.A. Carpentier." *Comoedia Illustré* 3, no. 11 (1 March 1911): 328.

———. "Vlan! . . . , Revue en 2 actes et 7 tableaux de MM Rip et Bousquet." *Comoedia Illustré* 3, no. 15 (1 May 1911): 463.

Dunoyer de Segonzac, André et al. *Boussingault par ses amis.* Paris: La Colombe, 1944.

Duvernois, Henri. "La Quinzaine théâtrale." *Femina*, no. 266 (15 February 1912): 88.

"Un Eblouissement de costumes somptueux au Théâtre des Arts." *Femina,* no. 243 (March 1911): 113.

Eckert, Charles. "The Carole Lombard in Macy's Window." In *Fabrications: Costume and the Female Body.* Edited by Jane Gaines and Charlotte Herzog. New York: Routledge, 1990, 100–121.

"8d. a Mile." *The Tatler,* no. 622 (28 May 1913): 270.

Erté [Romain de Tirtoff]. *My Life/My Art: An Autobiography.* New York: E. P. Dutton, 1989.

"Les Essais d'une mode novelle." *L'Illustration* (18 February 1911): 103–104.

L'Eventail et la fourrure chez Paquin. Paris: Maquet, 1911.

"Exclusive Poiret Costumes." *Harper's Bazar* 48, no. 5 (November 1913): 34–36.

"L'Exposition internationale de Gand." *Excelsior* (7 May 1913). Paquin Publicity Album, Fashion Research Centre, Bath.

Exposition Internationale des Industries et du Travil de Turin, 1911. *Catalogue spécial officiel de la section Française.* Paris: Comité Français des expositions à l'étranger, 1911.

"Expositions ouvertes, Paris." *Art et Décoration* 29 (March 1911), Supplement, 9.

F., F. [Fenéon]. "Les grands collectionneurs: IX.—M. Jacques Doucet." *Bulletin de la vie artistique,* no. 11 (June 1921): 313–318.

"Fabrics with Broad Stripes Popular for Spring." *New York Times* (13 February 1916): Fashion Sec. 3.

Faramond, Maurice de. "Nabuchodonosor, Tragédie en un acte." *Vers et Prose* 26 (July–September 1911): 105–115.

"Fashion Centres at War." *New York Times* (3 February 1915): 11.

Ferrant, Juliette. "Les Modes de la saison: Verrons-nous celle de la 'Rue de la Paix'?" *L'Excelsior* (23 January 1912). Clipping in Bibliothèque de l'Arsenal, Paris, Rf 62.276.

Le Figaro (5 June 1910): 5. Clipping, Paquin Publicity Album, Fashion Research Centre, Bath.

"First News of French Fashion Syndicate's Official Plans." *New York Times* (23 January 1916): sec. 6, 2.

Foresta, Merry, et al. *Perpetual Motif: The Art of Man Ray.* New York: Abbeville, 1988.

Foucault, Michel. "What Is an Author?" (1979). Translated by Josué V. Harari. In *The Foucault Reader.* Edited by Paul Rabinow. New York: Pantheon, 1984, 101–120.

Fouquières, André de. "Les Dances nouvelles: le tango." *Femina,* no. 289 (1 February 1913): 58.

Franc-Nohain. "Tangomanie." *Femina,* no. 300 (15 July 1913): 376–378.

"French Ambassador to Defend Alleged Fraud." *San Francisco Chronicle* (22 February 1914). Clipping in Bancroft Library, University of California, Berkeley, Panama-Pacific International Exhibition Collection, Box 60, Folder "France, Jan.–June 1914."

"French Opposition Shown to San Francisco Exhibit." *Christian Science Monitor* (28 March 1914). Clipping in Bancroft Library, University of California, Berkeley,

Panama-Pacific International Exhibition Collection, Box 60, Folder "France, Jan.–June 1914."

Frondaie, Pierre. *Aphrodite.* Program, Bibliothèque de l'Arsenal, Paris, Rf 65.199.

Furet. "A Paris: Nos Premières." *Dramatica* (February 1912). Clipping in Paquin Publicity Album, Fashion Research Centre, Bath.

"La Future Exposition Internationale dite Panama-Pacifique, à San Francisco." *L'Illustration,* no. 3707 (14 March 1914), 204–205.

G., E. "Vogue Summarizes the Mode." *Vogue* 42, no. 9 (1 November 1913): 35–38, 132, 136.

G., J. "Théâtre de la Renaissance: Aphrodite . . ." (19 March 1914). Unidentified clipping in Bibliothèque de l'Arsenal, Paris, Rf 65.199.

Gachons, Jacques de. "La peinture d'après-demain (?)" *Je Sais Tout* (15 April 1912).

Galerie Barbazanges. *La Collection particulière de Paul Poiret.* Exh. cat. Paris, 26 April–12 May 1923.

Galtier, Joseph. "Répétion générale au Vaudeville: 'Rue de la Paix'." *Excelsior* (22 January 1912): 7.

Garber, Marjorie. *Vested Interests: Cross-Dressing and Cultural Anxiety.* New York: Routledge, 1992.

Garnier, Guillaume. *Paul Poiret et Nicole Groult: Maîtres de la mode Art Déco.* Exh. cat. Tokyo: Fondation de la Mode, 1985.

Garnier, Hugette. "Un Théâtre de verdure va s'ouvrir cet été au coeur même de Paris" (27 May 1921). Clipping in Bibliothèque de l'Arsenal, Paris, Rf 4278.

Garvey, Ellen Gruber. *The Adman in the Parlor: Magazines and the Gendering of Consumer Culture, 1880s to 1910s.* New York: Oxford University Press, 1996.

Gaudriault, Raymond. *La Gravure de mode feminine en France.* Paris: Editions de l'Amateur, 1983.

Gee, Malcolm. *Dealers, Critics, and Collectors of Modern Painting: Aspects of the Parisian Art Market between 1910 and 1930.* New York: Garland, 1981.

Gervais, André. "Note sur le terme Readymade (ou Ready-made)." *Étant Donné*, 1999.

Gidding, J. M. & Co. Advertisement. *New York Times* (17 September 1913): 6.

———. Advertisement. *New York Times* (23 September 1913): 5.

Gignoux, Régis. "Avant le rideau" (19 March 1913). Clipping in Bibliothèque de l'Arsenal, Paris, Rf 70.593.

———. "Théâtre Femina: Très moutarde." *Le Théâtre*, no. 370 (May 1914): 10–12.

Gilliard, André. "Actualités: La Rue de la Paix." *Bravo* (27 January 1912). Clipping in Paquin Publicity Album, Fashion Research Centre, Bath.

Gimbel Brothers. Advertisement. *Women's Wear* (26 September 1913): 8.

Gimbel Brothers. Advertisement. *New York Times* (19 October 1913): 16.

Gleizes, Albert. *Souvenirs: le cubisme 1908–1914.* Cahiers Albert Gleizes I. Audin: Association des Amis d'Albert Gleizes, 1957.

Gleizes, Albert, and Jean Metzinger. *Du "cubisme."* Paris: E. Figuière et cie, 1912.

Goldberger, Paul. "25 Years of Unabashed Elitism." *New York Times* (2 February 2000): sec. 2, 1, 34.

Golden Book of the Wanamaker Stores. Jubilee Year: 1861–1911. n.pl.: n.pub., 1911.

Goldstein, Paul. *Copyright's Highway: From Gutenberg to the Celestial Jukebox.* New York: Hill & Wang, 1994.

———. "Copyright." *Journal of the Copyright Society of the U.S.A.* 38 (1991): 109–122.

Goncourt, Edmond and Jules de. *Journal* (1892).

Gordon, Donald E. *Modern Art Exhibitions 1900–1916: Selected Catalogue Documentation.* 2 vols. Munich: Prestel, 1974.

Grand Palais. *Salon d'Automne.* Exh. cat. Paris, 1 October–8 November 1911.

Green, Nancy L. "Art and Industry: The Language of Modernization in the Production of Fashion." *French Historical Studies* 18, no. 3 (Spring 1994): 722–748.

Greenhalgh. Paul. *Ephemeral Vistas: The* Expositions Universelles, *Great Exhibitions and World's Fairs, 1851–1939.* Manchester: Manchester University Press, 1988.

Gronberg, Tag. *Designs on Modernity: Exhibiting the City in 1920s Paris.* Manchester: Manchester University Press, 1998.

Guggenheim Museum Soho. *Art/Fashion.* Exh. cat. New York, 1997.

Haller, Joni. "Fashionably Orientalist: The Trend of the Exotic in Early Twentieth-Century France." Unpublished seminar paper. University of Southern California, 1998.

Harris, Neil. "Museums, Merchandising, and Popular Taste: The Struggle for Influence." In *Cultural Excursions: Marketing Appetites and Cultural Tastes in Modern America.* Chicago: University of Chicago Press, 1990, ch. 3.

Haskell, Francis, and Nicolas Penny. *Taste and the Antique: The Lure of Classical Sculpture 1500–1900.* 1981; New Haven: Yale University Press, 1982.

Haven, Anna de. "Costumes: The Wanamaker Presentation of Paris Fashions 'In a Persian Garden.'" *Women's Wear* (26 September 1913): sec. 4, 11–12.

Hayward Gallery. *Addressing the Century: 100 Years of Art & Fashion.* Exh. cat. London, 1998.

———. *Raoul Dufy 1877–1953.* Exh. cat. London, 1983.

Hawes, Elizabeth. *Fashion Is Spinach.* New York: Random House, 1938.

"Hold Back the New Styles." *New York Times* (25 February 1912): sec. 3, 1.

Hollander, Anne. *Seeing through Clothes.* 1975; New York: Avon Books, 1980.

Holley, Brandon. "The King and I." *GQ* 71, no. 2 (February 2001): 185–186.

Hôtel Drouot. *Catalogue des Tableaux Modernes . . . de la collection de M. Paul Poiret.* Sale cat. Paris: 18 November 1925.

"How Poiret Conducts an Opening." *Vogue* 39, no. 8 (15 April 1912): 36–37, 96.

Howell, Herbert A. "The Print and Label Law." *University of Pennsylvania Law Review and American Law Register* 70, no. 2 (January 1922): 95–100.

Hower, Ralph M. *History of Macy's of New York 1858–1919: Chapters in the Evolution of the Department Store.* Harvard Studies in Business History, VII. Cambridge, MA: Harvard University Press, 1943.

Hungerford, Edward. *The Romance of a Great Store.* New York: Robert M. McBride, 1922.

Huret, Jules. "150 Millions de frivolités: Le Rôle social d'une artiste de la mode." *La Vie Heureuse,* no. 5 (15 May 1912): 130–132.

"Il ne faut pas trop s'inspirer, pour tailler des 'patrons', des élégants modèles de nos grands couturiers." *Echos de l'Exportation,* no. 78 (7 May 1912): 17.

"In the World of Make-Believe." *Harper's Bazar* 50, no. 2 (February 1914): 12.

Intérim. "Les Premiers: Au Vaudeville: La Rue de la Paix." *La Vie Parisienne* (27 January 1912): 69.

"The Iribe Line: Fashion's Newest Eccentricity." *The Bystander* 34, no. 435 (3 April 1912): 1.

Iribe, Paul. *Les Robes de Paul Poiret racontées par Paul Iribe.* Paris: Société générale d'impression, 1908.

———. "La Seule critique que l'on puisse adresser à une mode, dit M. Paul Iribe, c'est de lui reprocher d'avoir trop duré." *Le Miroir* 4, n. s. no. 35 (26 July 1914): n.p.

Irwin, Robert. *The Arabian Nights: A Companion.* London: Allen Lane, Penguin Press, 1994.

Jarvis, Anthea, ed., Special issue, *Fashion Theory* 2, no. 4 (December 1998).

Jaszi, Peter. "Towards a Theory of Copyright: The Metamorphoses of 'Authorship.'" *Duke Law Journal,* no. 2 (1991): 455–502.

Jean, René. "Bernard Naudin." *Art et Décoration* 32 (November 1912): 130–140.

Jingle. "At the Queen's Theatre: This Way, Madam!'" *The Bystander* (8 October 1913): 77.

Johnson, Robert. Introduction to "Bakst on Classicism: 'The Paths of Classicism in Art.'" *Dance Chronicle* 13, no. 2 (1999): 170–173.

Joire, Suzanne. "My Impressions of American Department Stores." *Dry Goods Guide* 33, no. 6 (June 1914): 16–17.

Jones, Amelia. *Postmodernism and the En-gendering of Marcel Duchamp.* Cambridge: Cambridge University Press, 1994.

Joselit, David. *Infinite Regress: Marcel Duchamp 1910–1941.* Cambridge, MA: MIT Press, 1998.

"The Kahn Law." Brochure in Bancroft Library, University of California, Berkeley, Panama-Pacific International Exhibition Collection, Box 60, Folder "France, Jan.–Dec. 1913."

Kahnweiler, D.-H., with Francis Crémieux. *My Galleries and Painters.* Translated by Helen Weaver. London: Thames and Hudson, 1971.

Kamitsis, Lydia. "Le Pantalon féminin." *Revue d'archéologie moderne et d'archéologie générale,* no. 13 (1999): 79–101.

———. "Un Nomade dans la garde-robe féminine: le pantalon." Musée de la Mode et du Textile. *Garde-robes: Intimités dévoilées, de Cléo de Mérode à . . .* Exh. cat. Paris, 1999, 36–41.

Kaplan, Joel H., and Sheila Stowell. *Theatre and Fashion: Oscar Wilde to the Suffragettes.* Cambridge: Cambridge University Press, 1994.

Kidwell, Claudia B., and Margaret C. Christian. *Suiting Everyone: The Democratization of Clothing in America.* Washington, DC: Smithsonian Institution Press, 1974.

Kinney, Leila. "Fashion and Figuration in Modern Life Painting." In *Architecture: In Fashion.* Edited by Deborah Fausch, Paulette Singley, Rodolphe El-Khoury, and Zvi Efrat. New York: Princeton Architectural Press, 1994, 270–313.

Klüver, Billy. *A Day with Picasso: Twenty-Four Photographs by Jean Cocteau.* Cambridge, MA: MIT Press, 1997.

Klüver, Billy, and Julie Martin. "Man Ray, Paris." In Merry Foresta et al., *Perpetual Motif: The Art of Man Ray.* New York: Abbeville, 1988, 89–135.

Krauss, Rosalind E. "The Originality of the Avant-Garde." In *The Originality of the Avant-Garde and Other Modernist Myths.* Cambridge, MA: MIT Press, 1985, 151–170. Originally published in *October* 18 (Fall 1981).

———. "Sincerely Yours." In *The Originality of the Avant-Garde and Other Modernist Myths.* Cambridge, MA: MIT Press, 1985, 175–194. Originally published in *October* 20 (Spring 1982).

Kurzman. Advertisement. *New York Times* (24 September 1913): 5.

L., Y. "La Mode au théâtre: 'La Rue de la Paix.'" *Femina,* no. 266 (15 February 1912): 96.

LaFerla, Ruth. "A Star Is Worn." *New York Times* (14 December 1999): sec. 9, 1, 4.

Lajer-Burcharth, Ewa. *Necklines: The Art of Jacques-Louis David after the Terror.* New Haven: Yale University Press, 1999.

Lancey, Sybil de. "La Mode et les modes." *Les Modes,* no. 123 (March 1911): 6–34.

Laparcerie-Richepin, Cora. "Aux pièces françaises il faut une mise en scène française" (19 March 1913). Clipping in Bibliothèque de l'Arsenal, Paris, Rf 70.593.

Laporte, Jean. "La Tournée du grand couturier." *Femina,* no. 321 (1 June 1914): 339–342.

Larzul, Sylvette. *Les Traductions françaises des Mille et une nuits. Etude des versions Galland, Trébutien et Mardrus.* Paris: L'Harmattan, 1996.

Launay, Guy. "Répétition générale: au théâtre de la Renaissance, 'le Minaret' de M. Jacques Richepin, est avant tout une surprenante exposition de costumes" (20 March 1913). Clipping in Bibliothèque de l'Arsenal, Paris, Rf 70.593.

Laver, James. "The Poiret Ball." In *Memorable Balls.* Edited by James Laver. London: Derek Verschoyle, 1954, 106–116.

———. *Taste and Fashion: From the French Revolution to the Present Day.* London: George G. Harrap, 1937; revised edition 1945.

"Leading Paris Dressmakers Combine Against Imitators." *New York Herald*. Undated clipping (c. mid-February 1913) in Paquin Publicity Album, Fashion Research Centre, Bath.

Leach, William R. *Land of Desire: Merchants, Power, and the Rise of a New American Culture.* New York: Pantheon, 1993.

———. "Transformations in a Culture of Consumption: Women and Department Stores, 1890–1925." *The Journal of American History* 71, no. 2 (September 1984): 319–342.

Leeuwen, Thomas A. P. van. *The Skyward Trend of Thought: Five Essays on the Metaphysics of the American Skyscraper.* 's–Gravenhage, The Netherlands: AHA Books, 1986.

Lefranc, Jean. "Abel Hermant et le théâtre." Undated clipping in Bibliothèque de l'Arsenal, Paris, Rf 62.276.

Lehmann, Ulrich. *Tigersprung: Fashion in Modernity.* Cambridge, MA: MIT Press, 2000.

Lemny, Doïna. "Maurice et Morice: Chronique d'une amitié." In *Brancusi & Duchamp: Regards historiques.* Les carnets de l'Atelier Brancusi. Paris: Centre Pompidou, 2000.

"Léon Bakst." *Harper's Bazar* 49, no. 1 (January 1914): 56–57.

Lepape, Claude, and Thierry Defert. *Georges Lepape ou l'élégance illustrée.* Paris: Herscher, 1983.

Lepape, Georges. *Les Choses de Paul Poiret vues par Georges Lepape.* Paris: Maquet, 1911.

Lipovetsky, Gilles. *The Empire of Fashion: Dressing Modern Democracy.* Translated by Catherine Porter. Princeton: Princeton University Press, 1994.

Mackrell, Alice. *Coco Chanel.* New York: Holmes & Meier, 1992.

Macy, R. H., & Co. Advertisement. *New York Times* (24 September 1913): 5.

"Mannequins on the Stage." *The Bystander* (8 October 1913): 74.

Margueritte, Victor. *The Bachelor Girl.* Translated by Hugh Barnaby. New York: Knopf, 1923.

Marly, Diana de. *Worth: Father of Haute Couture.* 2nd ed. New York: Holmes & Meier, 1990.

Martin, Richard. *Cubism and Fashion.* Metropolitan Museum of Art. Exh. cat. New York, 1998.

————. *Fashion and Surrealism.* Fashion Institute of Technology. Exh. cat. New York: Rizzoli, 1987.

Marty, A.-E. "Au Théâtre des Arts: 'Le Marchand de passions', trois images d'Épinal de M. Maurice Magre; 'Nabuchodonosor', un acte de M. M. de Faramond." *Comoedia Illustré* 3, no. 10 (15 February 1911): 289–292.

McLeod, Mary. "Undressing Architecture: Fashion, Gender, and Modernity." In *Architecture: In Fashion.* Edited by Deborah Fausch, Paulette Singley, Rodolphe El-Khoury, and Zvi Efrat. New York: Princeton Architectural Press, 1994, 39–147.

Melot, Michel. "Les Frontières de l'originalité et les problèmes de l'estampe contemporaine." *Revue de l'Art,* no. 21 (1973): 108–118.

Melot, Michel, et al. "The Nature and the Role of the Print." In *Prints: History of an Art.* Part I. Translated by Helga Harrison and Dennis Corbyn. Geneva: Skira; and New York: Rizzoli, 1981.

"Mid-Winter Modes from Paris." *Vogue* 38, no. 12 (15 December 1911): 23.

"La mille-et-deuxième nuit" (May 1912). Unidentified clipping, (possibly from *La Vie Parisienne*), in Paquin Publicity Album, Fashion Research Centre, Bath.

"Le Minaret." *La Caricature.* Undated clipping pasted into the program of *Le Minaret,* Bibliothèque de l'Arsenal, Paris, Rf 70.593.

"La Mode actuelle au théâtre." *Comoedia Illustré* 2, no. 13 (1 April 1910): 383–386.

Le [sic] *Modèles de Paul Poiret Printemps 1917.* Advertisement. *Vanity Fair* 8, no. 1 (March 1917): 9.

Les Modèles de Paul Poiret Printemps 1917. Paris: Poiret Inc., 1917.

"Models Clearing House Suggested by Americans." *New York Herald* (20 February 1913): 4.

Monceau, Marie. "Dressmaking Openings will Shortly be Held by Noted Paris Firms." *Philadelphia Inquirer* (8 February 1912): sec. 3, 3.

Morano, Elizabeth. *Sonia Delaunay: Art into Fashion.* New York: Braziller, 1986.

Moreau, Luc-Albert. "Souvenir de Boussingault." In André Dunoyer de Segonzac et al., *Boussingault par ses amis.* Paris: Éditions du Vieux Colombier, 1944, 9–20.

Mourey, Gabriel. "Les Robes de Bakst." *Gazette du Bon Ton* 1, no. 6 (April 1913): 165–168.

"Mrs. Galt's Gowns Cause Paris Row." *New York Times* (20 November 1915): 6.

Musée de la Mode et du Costume, Palais Galliera. *Paul Poiret et Nicole Groult: Maîtres de la mode Art Déco.* Exh. cat. Paris, 1986.

Nabuchodonosor. Program in Bibliothèque de l'Arsenal, Paris, Rf 58.275 (3).

Naumann, Francis M. *Marcel Duchamp: The Art of Making Art in the Age of Mechanical Reproduction.* Ghent: Ludion Press, 1999.

———. *New York Dada 1915–23.* New York: Abrams, 1994.

———. *Apropos of Marcel: The Art of Making Art after Duchamp in the Age of Mechanical Reproduction.* Exh. cat. New York: Curt Marcus Gallery, 1999.

Nava, Mica. "Modernity's Disavowal: Women, the City and the Department Store." In *The Shopping Experience.* Edited by Pasi Falk and Colin Campbell. London: Sage, 1977, 56–91.

Nederlands Textielmuseum. *Sonia Delaunay: Dessins.* Exh. cat. Tilburg, 1988.

Nesbit, Molly. "His Common Sense." *Artforum* 33, no. 2 (October 1994): 93.

———. "The Language of Industry." In *The Definitively Unfinished Marcel Duchamp.* Edited by Thierry de Duve. Cambridge, MA: MIT Press, 1991, 351–384.

———. "Ready-Made Originals: The Duchamp Model." *October,* no. 37 (Summer 1986): 53–64.

———. "What Was an Author?" *Yale French Studies,* no. 73 (1988): 229–257.

Nesbit, Molly, and Naomi Sawelson-Gorse. "Concept of Nothing: New Notes by Marcel Duchamp and Walter Arensberg." In *The Duchamp Effect.* Edited by Martha Buskirk and Mignon Nixon. Cambridge, MA: MIT Press, 1995.

Netton, Ian Richard. "The Mysteries of Islam." In *Exoticism in the Enlightenment.* Edited by G. S. Rousseau and Roy Porter. Manchester: Manchester University Press, 1990, 23–45.

"New Art at the New Alhambra." *The Tatler,* no. 622 (28 May 1913): 270.

"New York Fashions are Adjudged Smart," *Vogue* 44, no. 11 (1 December 1914): 38–39.

"New York—'Persian Garden' Fashion Display at Wanamaker's." *Women's Wear* (24 September 1913): 7.

"New York s'amuse dans la morte-saison." *Echos de l'Exportation,* no. 87 (21 September 1912): 14.

The 1915 Mode as Shown by Paris, Panama Pacific International Exposition. New York: Condé Nast, n.d. [1915].

Nion, François de. "Les Répétitions générales. Théâtre de la Renaissance—Le Minaret" (20 March 1913). Clipping in Bibliothèque de l'Arsenal, Paris, Rf 70.593.

Nozière [Fernand Weyl]. Preface to *Les Parfums de Rosine.* Paris: Imprimerie Robaudy, n.p.: n.d.

Oldfield, L. C. F. *The Law of Copyright,* 2nd ed. London: Butterworth, 1912.

Oudard, Georges. "Lettres: Le Jardin désert." *Opinion* (16 July 1921). Clipping in Bibliothèque de l'Arsenal, Paris, Rt 4278.

"Our Buyers Indignant." *New York Times* (12 November 1915): 4.

P., M. "Le Vrai et le faux chic: la mode vue par Sem." *L'Illustration,* no. 3709 (28 March 1914): 243–248.

Paindaveine, Hervé. "Lettres de Paris: Mallet-Stevens et les revues Belges d'architecture." In *Vienne-Bruxelles ou la fortune du Palais Stoclet.* Brussels: Archives d'Architecture Moderne, 1987, 10–75.

Palmer, Alexandra. *Couture and Commerce: The Transatlantic Fashion Trade in the 1950s.* Vancouver: UBC Press, in association with the Royal Ontario Museum, 2001.

———. "New Directions: Fashion History Studies and Research in North America and England." *Fashion Theory* 1, no. 3 (September 1997): 297–312.

"Panama Pacific International Exposition San Francisco 1915. Résumé de principales observations du Comité Français des Expositions à l'Étranger." Brochure in Bancroft Library, University of California, Berkeley, Panama-Pacific International Exhibition Collection, Box 60, Folder "France, Jan.–Dec. 1913."

Pao, Angela C. *The Orient of the Boulevards: Exoticism, Empire, and Nineteenth-Century French Theater.* Philadelphia: University of Pennsylvania Press, 1998.

"Paquin." *Harper's Bazar* 49, no. 1 (January 1914): 43.

"Paquin, Poiret, Drecoll Discuss New Fashions." *New York Times,* (2 April 1911): 3.

"Paquin to Exhibit Here." *New York Times* (13 February 1914): 4.

"Paquin Won't Sell at Exhibit Here." *New York Times* (14 February 1914): 4.

"Paquin's Collection of Spring Models Begins its American Tour." *Vogue* 43, no. 9 (1 April 1914): 32. Clipping in vertical file: Paquin, Costume Institute Library, Metropolitan Museum of Art, New York.

Les Parfums de Rosine. Cannes: Impr. Robaudy, n.d.

"Paris Anti-Copyist Society Renews Its Activities." *Women's Wear* (28 February 1923): 1, 20.

"Paris Couturières Tried on Charge of Copying Modes Made by Mlle. Vionnet." *Women's Wear* (24 December 1921): 2, 23.

"Paris Dressmakers in Protective Union." *New York Times* (24 October 1915): sec. 3, 9.

"Paris Dressmakers Withhold Models." *New York Times* (9 April 1914): 3.

"Paris Fashions for the Autumn." *New York Times* (1 October 1911): sec. 1, 7.

"Paris Gossip." *Women's Wear* (17 July 1911): 1.

"Paris May See End of Style Control." *New York Times* (6 August 1914): 15.

"Paris Overtures to Our Importers." *New York Times* (6 February 1916): 5.

"Paris Shows More Dignity in Women's Dresses." *New York Times* (19 October 1913): sec. 7, 4.

"Paul Poiret Here to Tell of his Art." *New York Times* (21 September 1913): sec. 1, 11.

"Paul Poiret Lectures." *Women's Wear* (26 September 1913): 1, 16.

"Paul Poiret Talks About his Art: He Personifies his Two Principles; Simplicity and Individuality." *Women's Wear* (23 September 1913): 1, 9.

Pawlowski, G. de. "Au Vaudeville: 'Rue de la Paix,' comédie en trois actes" (22 January 1912). Clipping in Bibliothèque de l'Arsenal, Paris, Rf 62.276.

People v. William Fantel, Docket Index, Minutes of Special Sessions. County of New York. 5 August 1914–22 March 1915, 269.

Perrot, Philippe. *Les Dessus et les dessous de la bourgeoisie: Une histoire du vêtement au XIXe siècle.* Paris: Fayard, 1981. *Fashioning the Bourgeoisie: A History of Clothing in the Nineteenth Century.* Translated by Richard Bienvenu. Princeton: Princeton University Press, 1994.

Persin, Patrick-Gilles. *Daniel-Henry Kahnweiler: L'Aventure d'un grand marchand.* Paris: Solange Thierry, 1990.

"Pet Animals Figure in Winter Style." *New York Times* (23 November 1915): 5.

Pinchon, Jean-François, ed. *Rob. Mallet-Stevens: Architecture, mobilier, décoration.* Paris: Philippe Sers, 1986.

Poiret, Paul. Advertisement. *Vogue* 48, no. 7 (1 October 1916): 113.

———. *Art et Phynance.* Paris: Lutetia, 1934.

———. "From the Trenches." *Harper's Bazar* 50, no. 2 (February 1915): 11.

———. *My First Fifty Years.* Translated by Stephen Haden Guest. London: Victor Gollancz, 1931.

———. "There Are as Many Styles of Dress as there are Women," *Harper's Bazar* 49, no. 1 (January 1914): 47–49.

———. "Warning Against False Labels." *Women's Wear* (14 October 1913): 3.

"Poiret about to Quit?" *New York Times* (23 January 1916): sec. 2, 3.

"Poiret and Paquin Cling to Barbaric Colors." *New York Times* (15 October 1911): sec. 8, 3.

"Poiret, Creator of Fashions, Here." *New York Times* (21 September 1913): sec. 7, 3.

"Poiret on the Philosophy of Dress." *Vogue* 42, no. 8 (15 October 1913): 41–42.

"Poiret: Une silhouette parisienne." *Le Miroir des Modes* 64, no. 6 (June 1912): 242–243.

"Poiret Talks about his Art," *Women's Wear* (23 September 1912): 1, 9.

"Poiret's Label." *Women's Wear* (17 October 1913): 3.

"Poiret's New Kingdom." *Vogue* 40, no. 1 (1 July 1912): 16, 56.

Post, Emily. "Where Fashionables and Fashion Met." *Vogue* 44, no. 11 (1 December 1914): 35–37.

Potter, Michelle. "Designed for Dance: The Costumes of Léon Bakst and the Art of Isadora Duncan." *Dance Chronicle* 13, no. 2 (1999): 154–169.

"Power of Store Decoration," *Store Life* 7, no. 1 (October 1904): 16.

"Predict Failure of Poiret's Plan." *New York Times* (15 January 1916): 5.

"Le Procès Callot Soeurs contre le 'Grand Chic'." *Echos de l'Exportation,* no. 83 (21 July 1912): 65.

"Projet d'organisation de la copie et de la reproduction des modèles de Grands Couturiers." *Les Elégances Parisiennes* (August 1916): 70.

Raymonde, Aline. "Les propos de M. Boissonnot: la mode nouvelle." *La Mode Illustrée* 52, no. 15 (9 April 1911): n.p.

Reboux, Paul. *La Rue de la Paix.* Paris: Pierre Lafitte, 1927.

———. "Théâtre de l'Athénée: Le Tango. Pièce en quatre actes, de Madame et M. Jean Richepin." *Le Théâtre,* no. 362 (January 1914): 15–18.

Reichman, J. H. "Design Protection in Domestic and Foreign Copyright Law: From the Berne Revision of 1948 to the Copyright Act of 1976." *Duke Law Journal,* no. 6 (December 1983): 1143–1264.

Retaining the Original: Multiple Originals, Copies and Reproductions. Studies in the History of Art, 20. Washington, DC: National Gallery of Art, 1989.

Revel, Jean-François, "Jacques Doucet couturier et collectionneur." *L'Oeil,* no. 84 (December 1961): 44–51, 81, 106.

Richepin, Jacques. *Le Minaret. Comédie en trois actes en vers.* Paris: Librairie Charpentier et Fasquelle, 1914.

Ring, Nancy. "New York Dada and the Crisis of Masculinity: Man Ray, Francis Picabia, and Marcel Duchamp in the United States, 1913–1921." Ph.D. dissertation, Northwestern University, 1991.

Rittenhouse, Anne. "Fashion under Fire." *Vogue* 44, no. 7 (1 October 1914): 40–41, 110.

———. "The Prophet of Simplicity." *Vogue* 42, no. 9 (1 November 1913): 43, 142.

Robbins, Daniel. "Abbreviated Historiography of Cubism." *Art Journal* 47 (Winter 1988): 277–283.

"Rodin chez Cora (10 March 1914)." Clipping in Bibliothèque de l'Arsenal, Paris, Rf 65.199.

Rose, Mark. *Authors and Owners: The Invention of Copyright.* Cambridge, MA: Harvard University Press, 1993.

Rosenbaum, Edith L. "Costumes: Edith L. Rosenbaum Describes in Detail Some Interesting Features of the Poiret Collection." *Women's Wear* (8 September 1911): 1.

Ross, Kristin. "Introduction: Shopping." In Émile Zola. *The Ladies' Paradise (Au bonheur des dames).* Berkeley: University of California Press, 1992, v–xxiii.

Rouzaud, Claude A. *Un Problème d'interêt national: les industries de luxe.* Thèse pour le doctorat d'état, Université de Strasbourg, Faculté des Sciences politiques. Paris: Librairie Sivey, 1946.

Rubin, William, Hélène Seckel, and Judith Cousins. *Les Demoiselles d'Avignon.* Studies in Modern Art, 3. New York: Museum of Modern Art, 1994.

Said, Edward. *Orientalism.* New York: Pantheon, 1978.

Sandback, Patricia Rae. "Isadora Duncan and Paul Poiret: The Sacred and the Profane." Master's thesis, University of California, Irvine, 1984.

Saudé, Jean. *Traité d'enluminure d'art au pochoir.* Paris: Aux Editions de l'Ibis, 1925.

Schertz, Peter J. "Constructing the Bon Ton." Unpublished Seminar Paper. University of Southern California, 1998.

Schmidt, Rocky. "Designer Law: Fashioning a Remedy for Design Piracy." *UCLA Law Review* 30, no. 3 (April 1983): 861–880.

Schneider, Louis. "Le Minaret—La mise en scène et les décors" (19 March 1913). Clipping in Bibliothèque de l'Arsenal, Paris, Rf 70.593.

———. "La Mise en scène et les décors." *Comoedia* (21 September 1912). Clipping in Bibliothèque de l'Arsenal, Paris, Rf 74.698 (1).

Schouvaloff, Alexander. *The Art of Ballets Russes: The Serge Lifar Collection of Theater Designs, Costumes, and Paintings at the Wadsworth Athenaeum, Hartford, Connecticut.* New Haven: Yale University Press, in association with the Wadsworth Athenaeum, 1997.

Schwartz, Hillel. *The Culture of the Copy: Striking Likenesses, Unreasonable Facsimiles.* New York: Zone Books, 1996.

Sée, Edmond. "Le Théâtre: Répétitions générales: A la Renaissance, Mme Cora Laparcerie . . ." (20 March 1913). Clipping in Bibliothèque de l'Arsenal, Paris, Rf 70.593.

Seebohm, Caroline. *The Man Who Was Vogue: The Life and Times of Condé Nast.* New York: Viking, 1982.

Segal, Aaron Jeffrey. "The Republic of Goods: Advertising and National Identity in France, 1875–1914." Ph.D. dissertation, University of California, Los Angeles, 1995.

Sekler, Eduard F. *Josef Hoffmann: The Architectural Work.* Princeton: Princeton University Press, 1985.

Sem. *Tangoville sur Mer.* Paris: Succès, 1913.

———. *Le Vrai et le faux chic.* Paris: Succès, 1914.

Sennett, Richard. *The Fall of Public Man.* New York: Knopf, 1977.

Serano, Marcel. "Au Théâtre des Capucines." *Comoedia Illustré* 6, no. 2 (20 October 1913): 62–63.

Shiff, Richard. "Originality." In *Critical Terms for Art History.* Edited by Robert S. Nelson and Richard Shiff. Chicago: University of Chicago Press, 1996, 103–115.

Shonfield, Zuzanna. "The Great Mr. Worth." *Costume: The Journal of the Costume Society,* no. 16 (1982): 57–59.

Silver, Kenneth E. *Esprit de Corps: The Art of the Parisian Avant-Garde and the First World War, 1914–1925.* Princeton: Princeton University Press, 1989.

Silverman, Debora L. *Art Nouveau in Fin-de-Siècle France: Politics, Psychology, and Style.* Berkeley: University of California Press, 1989.

Silverman, Kaja. "Fragments of a Fashionable Discourse." In *Studies in Entertainment: Critical Approaches to Mass Culture.* Edited by Tania Modleski. Bloomington: Indiana University Press, 1986, 139–152.

Sirop, Dominique. *Paquin.* Paris: Adam Biro, 1989.

"Sliding Price Scale for Boex Copies of Vionnet Models." *Women's Wear* (21 November 1921): 2, 21.

"So Say the Paris Openings." *Vogue* 43, no. 17 (1 August 1914): 34–37.

Souday, Paul. "Renaissance: 'Le Minaret', comédie spectacle, en trois actes et en vers, de M. Jacques Richepin" (21 March 1913). Clipping in Bibliothèque de l'Arsenal, Paris, Rf 70.593.

"The Specialty Shops: Poiret is Advised by a Friend Prominent in the Trade to Take Precautions for the Protection of his Models." *Women's Wear* (14 October 1913): 1, 6.

Spies, Werner. "Vendre des tableaux—donner à lire." Translated by Eliane Kaufholz. In Musée National d'Art Moderne. *Daniel-Henry Kahnweiler.* Exh. cat. Paris, 1984, 17–44.

Staatliches Museum Schwerin. *Marcel Duchamp Respirateur.* Exh. cat. Ostfildern, 1995.

Steele, Valerie. *Paris Fashion: A Cultural History.* New York: Oxford University Press, 1988.

Steinberg, Leo. "Rodin." In *Other Criteria: Confrontations with Twentieth-Century Art.* London: Oxford University Press, 1972, 322–403.

Stern, Ernst. *My Life, My Stage.* London: Victor Gollancz, 1951.

"The Store Entertainment." *Dry Goods Economist* (18 April 1903): 33.

"The Story of the Fashion Fête," *Vogue* 44, no. 9 (1 November 1914): 35–37, 122.

Styan, J. L. *Max Reinhardt.* Cambridge: Cambridge University Press, 1982.

"The Style Influence of 'Le Minaret.'" *Women's Wear* (3 October 1913): sec. 4, 1, 4–5, 11.

"Une Succersale de Poiret à New-York." *Les Élégances Parisiennes* (March 1917): 184.

"Le Syndicat de Défense de la Grande Couture Française et des Industries s'y Rattachant." *Le Style Parisien,* no. 4 (November 1915): n.p.

"Teachers College." *Columbia Spectator* 57, no. 4 (27 September 1913): 2.

Terego, Al. [Paul Poiret]. "Les Opinions de Monsieur Pétrone." *La Grande Revue* 55 (May 1909): 147–159.

Tétart-Vittu, Françoise. "Naissance du couturier et du modéliste." Musée de la Mode et du Costume, Palais Galliera. *Au paradis des dames: Nouveautés, modes et confections 1810–1870.* Exh. cat. Paris, 1992, 36–39.

"Le Théâtre du grand couturier." *Femina,* no. 262 (15 February 1911): 697.

"They Steal Styles and Numbers." *New York Times* (20 June 1914): 11.

Tickner, Lisa. "The Popular Culture of *Kermesse:* Lewis, Painting, and Performance, 1912–13." *Modernism/Modernity* 4, no. 2 (April 1997): 67–120. Published in modified form as "Wyndham Lewis: Dance and the Popular Culture of *Kermesse.*" In *Modern Life & Modern Subjects: British Art in the Early Twentieth Century.* New Haven: Yale University Press, 2000, 79–115.

"To Display Furs in 'Persian Shop.'" Unidentified newspaper clipping, c. November 1913, in Paquin Publicity Album, Fashion Research Centre, Bath.

"To Protect Vogue's Originality." *Vogue* 44, no. 10 (15 November 1914): 51.

"To Stop Pirating of Dress Fashions." *New York Times* (29 May 1914): 4.

Todd, Frank Morton. *The Story of the Exposition, Being the Official History of the International Celebration Held at San Francisco in 1915 to Commemorate the Discovery of the Pacific Ocean and the Construction of the Panama Canal.* 5 vols. New York: Putnam, 1921.

Tomkins, Calvin. *Duchamp: A Biography.* New York: Henry Holt, 1996.

Trachtenberg, Alan. *The Incorporation of America: Culture and Society in the Gilded Age.* New York: Hill & Wang, 1982.

Troy, Nancy J., *Modernism and the Decorative Arts in France: Art Nouveau to Le Corbusier.* New Haven: Yale University Press, 1991.

V. "Le Pavillon PAQUIN à l'Exposition de Turin." *Comoedia Illustré* 3, no. 18 (15 June 1911): 584–585.

Vanina. "La Comédie de la mode." *Comoedia Illustré* 5, no. 12 (20 March 1913): 575, 582.

———. "La Comédie de la mode: décentralisons . . . —les robes drapées—nos maîtres de la couture." *Comoedia Illustré* 5, no. 1 (5 October 1912): 29.

———. "Les Robes de 'Rue de la Paix': une 'interview' sur la conception de la robe, de M. Paul Iribe. Considérations générales." *Comoedia Illustré* 4, no. 9 (1 February 1912): 317.

"Vionnet Brings Action against Butterick Co." *Women's Wear* (30 January 1922): 1.

Vitet, L. *L'Académie Royale.* Paris: Levy, 1861.

Vogue Pattern Service. Advertisement. *Vogue* 46, no. 7 (1 October 1915).

Wallach, Alan. "The American Cast Museum: An Episode in the History of the Institutional Definition of Art." In *Exhibiting Contradiction: Essays on the Art Museum in the United States.* Amherst: University of Massachusetts Press, 1998, 38–56.

Ward, Martha. "Impressionist Installations and Private Exhibitions." *Art Bulletin* 73 (December 1991): 599–622.

Warnod, André. "Le Bal des Quat'Z'Arts." *La Renaissance Politique, Littéraire, Artistique* (11 June 1921): 17–20. Clipping in Bibliothèque de l'Arsenal, Paris, Ro 13007.

"Week of Splendid Style Displays." *Women's Wear* (26 September 1913): Merchandising Sec., 1.

Weiss, Jeffrey. "'Le Journal joué': Picasso, Collage, and Music-Hall Modernism." In *The Popular Culture of Modern Art: Picasso, Duchamp, and Avant-Gardism.* New Haven: Yale University Press, 1994, ch. 1.

White, Harrison C., and Cynthia A. White. *Canvases and Careers: Institutional Change in the French Painting World.* 1965. Chicago: University of Chicago Press, 1993.

White, Palmer. *Elsa Schiaparelli: Empress of Paris Fashion.* New York: Rizzoli, 1986.

———. *Poiret.* New York: Clarkson N. Potter, 1973.

Wigley, Mark. *White Walls, Designer Dresses: The Fashioning of Modern Architecture.* Cambridge, MA: MIT Press, 1995.

Wilson, Elizabeth. *Adorned in Dreams: Fashion and Modernity.* Berkeley: University of California Press, 1987.

Wilson, Robert Forrest. *Paris on Parade.* Indianapolis: Bobbs-Merrill, 1924.

Windsor Print Works. "Minaret Fabrics—The Topic of the Hour." Advertisement. *Women's Wear* (3 October 1913): 5.

Wollen, Peter. "Addressing the Century." In Hayward Gallery. *Addressing the Century.* Exh. cat. London, 1998.

————. "Fashion/Orientalism/The Body." *New Formations* 1 (Spring 1987): 5–33.

Woodmansee, Martha. *The Author, Art, and the Market: Rereading the History of Aesthetics.* New York: Columbia University Press, 1994.

"Worth Declares America Is Right." *New York Times* (20 December 1912): 12.

Worth, Jean-Philippe. *A Century of Fashion.* Translated by Ruth Scott Miller. Boston: Little, Brown, 1928.

Württembergischer Kunstverein. *Sturtevant.* Exh. cat. Stuttgart. 1992.

Illustrations

1.1   Charles F. Worth, princess afternoon dress, c. 1879. Ticking stripe abutted to dark brown silk satin matched with polychrome stylized floral silk brocade; machine-made lace. Museum of the City of New York, gift of Mrs. Fritz Frank, 40.74.2.

1.2   Charles F. Worth, multifunctional ensemble composed of day and evening bodices, skirt, and sash, c. 1869. Peacock blue silk faille with multicolored trimming with Chinese motifs and knotted fringe. The Metropolitan Museum of Art, gift of Mrs. Philip K. Rhinelander, 1946 (46.25.1 a–d).

1.3   Charles F. Worth, basque and full-trained trimmed skirt, 1874, from *Victorian Fashions and Costumes from Harper's Bazar 1867–1898*, ed. and intro. Stella Blum (New York: Dover Publications, 1974), 75. Photo: Brooklyn Museum of Art.

1.4   Worth label, stamped gold on white and black and woven gold on white petersham, c. 1870–1885. Brooklyn Museum of Art, label on 64.124.3. Photo: Brooklyn Museum of Art.

1.5   Fake Worth label, stamped gold on white, c. 1870s. Photo: Brooklyn Museum of Art.

1.6   Photo of Charles F. Worth, 1858, in Jean-Philippe Worth, *A Century of Fashion,* trans. Ruth Scott Miller (Boston: Little, Brown, and Co., 1928), opposite p. 87.

1.7   Félix Nadar, Charles F. Worth, 1892. Paul Nadar/© Arch. Phot. Paris/ C.M.N.

1.8   Man Ray, photo of Jacques Doucet, c. 1925. Photo: Musée de la mode et du textile, Collection Union Français des Arts du Costume, Paris. © 2002 Man Ray Trust/Artists Rights Society (ARS), New York/ADAGP, Paris.

1.9   Interior of Jacques Doucet hôtel, 19, rue Spontini, Paris, before 1912, in *L'Oeil,* no. 84 (December 1961): 46. Photo: Library, Getty Research Institute.

2.3   Louis Süe, sketch for the "Salle fraîche" in the couture house of Paul Poiret, 1909. Archives nationales/Institut français d'architecture, Archives d'architecture du XXe siècle, Paris. © 2002 Artists Rights Society (ARS), New York/ADAGP, Paris.

2.4   Josef Hoffmann, design for the music and theater room, Palais Stoclet. Pencil, pen and ink, crayon, watercolors. Museum of Modern Art Ludwig Foundation Vienna. Photo © MUMOK.

2.5   Louis Süe, sketch for a "salon de présentation," couture house of Paul Poiret, 1909. Pencil and watercolor on tracing paper glued to cardboard, 49.5 × 64.8 cm. Archives nationales/Institut français d'architecture, Archives d'architecture du XXe siècle, Paris. © 2002 Artists Rights Society (ARS), New York/ADAGP, Paris.

2.6   Pierre Brissaud, "The Theater of the Great Couturier," in *Femina,* no. 262 (15 February 1911), 697. Cliché Bibliothèque Nationale de France, Paris.

2.7   "Chez le grand couturier," in "Vlan! Revue en 2 actes et 7 tableaux de MM Rip et Bousquet," in *Comoedia Illustré* 3, no. 15 (1 May 1911), 463. Cliché Bibliothèque Nationale de France, Paris.

2.8   Jean Dulac, "The Suppliant [and] the Master," in *Comoedia Illustré* 3, no. 11 (11 March 1911): 328. Photo Michael Bonnet.

2.9   Henri Manuel, the proenade of mannequins in the French garden, in *L'Illustration,* no. 3515 (9 July 1910), 22. Photo: Library, Getty Research Institute.

2.10   Henri Manuel, mannequins modeling outfits in the garden of Paul Poiret's couture house, Paris, in *L'Illustration,* no. 3515 (9 July 1910), 21. Photo: Library, Getty Research Institute.

2.11   Henri Manuel, a group of mannequins in front of a trellis portico, in *L'Illustration,* no. 3515 (9 July 1910), 21. Photo: Library, Getty Research Institute.

2.12   Thousand and Second Night Party at the couture house of Paul Poiret, 24 June 1911, in Yvonne Deslandres with Dorothée Lalanne, *Poiret: Paul Poiret 1879–1944.* Trans. Paula Gifford (New York: Rizzoli, 1987), 49.

2.13   Thousand and Second Night Party at the couture house of Paul Poiret, 24 June 1911, in Yvonne Deslandres with Dorothée Lalanne, *Poiret: Paul Poiret 1879–1944.* Trans. Paula Gifford (New York: Rizzoli, 1987), 49.

2.26 Henri Manuel, photo of Madame Poiret dressed to attend the Thousand and Second Night Party, 24 June 1911. Cliché Bibliothèque Nationale de France, Paris.

2.27 Models wearing *jupes-sultanes* designed by Paul Poiret (top and left) and *jupes-culottes* adapted for the street by Bechoff-David (right and bottom right and left), in *L'Illustration,* no. 3547 (18 February 1911), 104. Photo: Library, Getty Research Institute. © 2002 Artists Rights Society (ARS), New York/ADAGP, Paris.

2.28 L. Sabattier, *The Races at Auteil,* in *L'Illustration,* no. 3548 (25 February 1911), cover. Photo: Library, Getty Research Institute.

2.29 Photo of Jeanne Paquin, c. 1913. Collection of the Joire-Noulens family. Photo: Jean-Loup Charmet, Paris.

2.30 *La Parisienne* atop the Porte Binet, Exposition Universelle, Paris 1900, in Debora Silverman, *Art Nouveau in Fin-de-Siècle France: Politics, Psychology, and Style* (Berkeley: University of California Press, 1989), 292.

2.31 *Rue de la Paix,* Act II, Théâtre du Vaudeville, in *Le Théâtre,* no. 316 (February 1912), 6. Document Bibliothèque Forney, Paris.

2.32 *Rue de la Paix,* Act III, Théâtre du Vaudeville, in *Le Théâtre,* no. 316 (February 1912), 9. Cliché Bibliothèque Nationale de France, Paris.

2.33 Photo of a salon in the Doucet couture house, 1910, from *L'Illustration,* no. 3534 (19 November 1910), 349. Photo: Library, Getty Research Institute.

2.34 G. Agié, A salon in the Maison Paquin, Paris, n. d., in L. Roger-Milès, *Les Créateurs de la mode* (Paris: Ch. Eggimann, n.d.), 39. Photo: Library, Getty Research Institute.

2.35 Henri Manuel, photo of Madame Poiret looking in a mirror in the Maison Poiret. Cliché Bibliothèque Nationale de France, Paris.

2.36 Paul Iribe, costume designs for *Rue de la Paix,* in *Excelsior* (22 January 1912), cover. Document Bibliothèque Forney, Paris.

2.37 Dresses from *Rue de la Paix,* in *Comoedia Illustré* (1 February 1912), 311–312. Cliché Bibliothèque Nationale de France, Paris.

2.59   Sem, images from *Le Vrai et le faux chic* (Paris: Succès, 1914), in *L'Illustration,* no. 3709 (28 March 1914), 244. Photo: Library, Getty Research Institute. © 2002 Artists Rights Society (ARS), New York/ADAGP, Paris.

2.60   Sem, fashion show, *Le Vrai et le faux chic* (Paris: Succès, 1914), n. pag. Photo: Department of Special Collections, Charles E. Young Research Library, UCLA © 2002 Artists Rights Society (ARS), New York/ADAGP, Paris.

2.61   Sem, tango scene from *Tangoville sur mer* (Paris: Succès, 1913), n. pag. The Jerome Robbins Dance Division, The New York Public Library for the Performing Arts, Astor, Lenox, and Tilden Foundations. © 2002 Artists Rights Society (ARS), New York/ADAGP, Paris.

2.62   Sem, *Le Vrai et le faux chic* (Paris: Succès, 1914), n. pag. Photo: Department of Special Collections, Charles E. Young Research Library, UCLA © 2002 Artists Rights Society (ARS), New York/ADAGP, Paris.

2.63   Sem, *Le Vrai et le faux chic* (Paris: Succès, 1914), n. pag. Photo: Department of Special Collections, Charles E. Young Research Library, UCLA © 2002 Artists Rights Society (ARS), New York/ADAGP, Paris.

2.64   Sem, *Le Vrai et le faux chic* (Paris: Succès, 1914), n. pag. Photo: Department of Special Collections, Charles E. Young Research Library, UCLA © 2002 Artists Rights Society (ARS), New York/ADAGP, Paris.

2.65   Sem, *Le Vrai et le faux chic* (Paris: Succès, 1914), n. pag. Photo: Department of Special Collections, Charles E. Young Research Library, UCLA © 2002 Artists Rights Society (ARS), New York/ADAGP, Paris.

2.66   Sem, *Le Vrai et le faux chic* (Paris: Succès, 1914), n. pag. Photo: Department of Special Collections, Charles E. Young Research Library, UCLA © 2002 Artists Rights Society (ARS), New York/ADAGP, Paris.

2.67   Sem, *Le Vrai et le faux chic* (Paris: Succès, 1914), n.p. Photo: Department of Special Collections, Charles E. Young Research Library, UCLA © 2002 Artists Rights Society (ARS), New York/ADAGP, Paris.

2.68   Sem, *Le Vrai et le faux chic* (Paris: Succès, 1914), n.p. Photo: Department of Special Collections, Charles E. Young Research Library, UCLA © 2002 Artists Rights Society (ARS), New York/ADAGP, Paris.

Index

Numbers in italics refer to illustrations.